WORKS ISSUED BY

The Hakluyt Society.

---o---

THE VOYAGES
of
CAPTAIN LUKE FOXE
and
CAPTAIN THOMAS JAMES.

VOL. II.

No. LXXXIX.

THE VOYAGES
OF
CAPTAIN LUKE FOXE
OF HULL,
AND
CAPTAIN THOMAS JAMES
OF BRISTOL,

IN SEARCH OF A NORTH-WEST PASSAGE,

IN 1631-32,

WITH NARRATIVES OF THE EARLIER NORTH-WEST VOYAGES OF
FROBISHER, DAVIS, WEYMOUTH, HALL, KNIGHT, HUDSON,
BUTTON, GIBBONS, BYLOT, BAFFIN, HAWKRIDGE,
AND OTHERS.

Edited, with Notes and an Introduction,
BY
MILLER CHRISTY, F.L.S.

IN TWO VOLUMES.—VOL. II

LONDON:
PRINTED FOR THE HAKLUYT SOCIETY,
4, LINCOLN'S INN FIELDS, W.C.

M.DCCC.XCIV.

COUNCIL
OF
THE HAKLUYT SOCIETY.

CLEMENTS R. MARKHAM, ESQ., C.B., F.R.S., *Pres. R.G.S.*, PRESIDENT.
MAJOR-GENERAL SIR HENRY RAWLINSON, K.C.B., D.C.L., LL.D., F.R.S.,
   Associé Étranger de L'Institut de France, VICE-PRESIDENT.
THE RIGHT HON. LORD ABERDARE, G.C.B., F.R.S., VICE-PRESIDENT.
VICE-ADMIRAL LINDESAY BRINE.
ROBERT BROWN, ESQ., M.A., PH.D.
MILLER CHRISTY, ESQ.
THE HON. GEORGE N. CURZON, M.P.
THE RIGHT HON. SIR MOUNTSTUART E. GRANT-DUFF, G.C.S.I., *late Pres. R.G.S.*
F. DUCANE GODMAN, ESQ., F.R.S.
ALBERT GRAY, ESQ.
C. P. LUCAS, ESQ.
A. P. MAUDSLAY, ESQ.
E. DELMAR MORGAN, ESQ.
CAPTAIN NATHAN, R.E.
ADMIRAL SIR E. OMMANNEY, C.B., F.R.S.
E. A. PETHERICK, ESQ.
S. W. SILVER, ESQ.
COUTTS TROTTER, ESQ.
PROF. E. B. TYLOR, D.C.L.
CAPTAIN W. J. L. WHARTON, R.N.

WILLIAM FOSTER, ESQ., *Honorary Secretary*.

CONTENTS OF VOLUME II.

NORTH-WEST FOX (*continued*)

	PAGE
Foxe's Preparations	261
Foxe's Own Voyage, 1631	268
Foxe's Reasons for not Wintering	407
Foxe on the Probability of finding a North-West Passage	418
Foxe's Postscript	443

JAMES'S STRANGE AND DANGEROUS VOYAGE

Facsimile Title-page	449
Letter from Thomas Nash	451
Address to the King	453
James's Preparations	455
James's Voyage, 1631-32	460
James's Letter left at Charlton Island	594
James's List of Instruments	604
James's Observations	607
Gellibrand on Longitude	612
Watts's Address to the Cambridge Divinity Students	620

APPENDICES:

Depositions relating to Hudson's Expedition, 1610-11, now preserved at the Trinity House	629
Button's Letter of Credence from King James and Instructions from Henry, Prince of Wales	635
"Motiues Inducing a Proiect for the Discouerie of the North pole Terrestriall, the Streights of Anian into the South Sea, and the Coasts thereof." [By Sir Dudley Digges?]	639
A Charter granted to the Governor and Company of Merchants of London Discoverers of the North-West Passage	642

INDEX . 665

LIST OF MAPS AND ILLUSTRATIONS.

Portrait of Captain Thomas James . . . . (*Frontispiece*)
Reduced Facsimile of Foxe's Chart . . . *To face p.* 261
Plan of Coast-line 392
Reduced Facsimile of James's Chart . . . *To face p.* 447

THE VOYAGES
OF
CAPTAIN LUKE FOXE
AND
CAPTAIN THOMAS JAMES
TO HUDSON'S BAY IN 1631.
PART II.

NORTH-WEST FOX.

May the 7th, Anno 1631.

The Voyage of Captaine LVKE FOX, in his Maiestie's *Pinnace, the* Charles, *Burthen 70 Tonnes; 20 Men and 2 Boyes, Victuals for 18 Moneths, young Sir Iohn Wolstenholme being Treasurer*

MY PREPARATIONS TO THE VOYAGE.[1]

Entlemen, our Yorkshire *Proverbe is* Plaine dealing is a Iewell. *So it is that I was neither importuned nor intreated to this vndertaking by any, eyther Noble or Gentle; but the Truth is that I had beene itching after it ever since* 1606, *when I should have gone Mate to* Iohn

---

[1] All the circumstances attending Foxe's preparations for his voyage, as set forth in the following pages, have been already described and discussed in the Introduction, where also will be found more or less extended biographical notices of all the persons mentioned.—C.

Knight, *of whom doth follow;*[1] *yet I must confesse that heere my ambition soared a pitch higher then my abilitie, as now time hath made me to know; yet his Discretion and Experience taught him to discerne of what could be in my youth; but I, presuming vpon some parts I had, as the vse of the Globes and other Mathematicke Instruments (having been Sea-bred from my Boyes-time, and had beene in the* Mediterranian, Spaine, France, Holland, Norway, Denmarke, *and the* Balticke *Sea), thought my selfe to bee fit for the best imployment,* [and] *desired to be pluckt before I was ripe; but hee durst not depend vpon me in that place for the Voyage, so as I did not proceed with him; yet I was still kept in Marine imployments along the Coast and Crossing the Sea, whereby I gained Experience, and also, at the Returnes home of all Ships from thence,*[2] *I enquired of the Masters, Mates, and others that were that way imployed, whereby I gathered, by Report and Discourse and Manuscripts, how farre they had proceeded, what they had done, and what was to doe.*[3] *To better which, I often repaired to Mr* IOHN TAPPE, *whose acquaintance was much amongst these men, he also acquainting me with Mr.* THO. STERNE, *Globe-Maker (whom I have found to have engrossed all those former Voyages by Relation, Manuscripts, and Maps); from whom I gathered much, and must needs say hee is a very well deserving Practitioner: So that I thought my selfe to be now ready for the same attempt, when occasion should present it selfe.*

Which fell out by former acquaintance I had with that famous Mathematician, Mr. HENRY BRIGGES, *who mooved*

---

[1] The narrative of Knight's voyage in 1606 (see pp 106-113) *precedes*, not follows, this. Perhaps, when Foxe wrote this account of his preparations, it was intended to place them at the beginning of his book (as might very well have been done), but that, for some reason, this intention was not carried out. hence this error.—C.

[2] "*From thence*," here, of course, means from the North-West, though there is nothing in the context to show it.—C.

[3] That is, *what was to be done*.—C

me thereto and I willingly consented, so as things could be brought to passe; the which to strengthen himselfe, hee acquainted that Hon: Knight Sir IOHN BROOKE, *whom, both to doe their King service & the Publike good, perswades with divers of their friends to come into the Adventure.*[1]

Whereupon, wee exhibited a Petition to his Maiesty for the lend of a Ship for the Voyage and countenance to the Action, who Graciously accepted and granted both; but the time of the yeare was so farre spent before we could make our provision ready, as wee were forced to desist untill the yeare following. in which processe Mr BRIGGES *deceased, and the one halfe of the Adventure fell away*

In the meane time, and before the next yeare, one Captaine IAMES, *of* Bristow, *had so wrought with the Marchants of the said Citie for to set forth one Ship for the same designe, as they were willing to adventure, so as they might share with* London *in equall honour and profit whether Ship soever found the same; and this as*[2] *was signified in a Letter from Captaine* IAMES *to Mr.* BRIGGES, *which Letter I did see, as he showed the same to Sir* IOHN BROOKE, *they both consenting to write back againe vnto him that the Request was condescended vnto; of which, and for better assurance, Capt.* IAMES *ridde from* Bristow *to* Oxford *before the death of Mr.* BRIGGES, *desiring that, seeing we were both to goe forth in one yeare, that hee might goe in the higher place; but [he] was denyed.*

In this interim, came home that Honourable Knight Sir THOMAS ROE *from his Ambassage to the King of* Sweden; *who, being made acquainted with the Designe, gave it his best furtherance; when his Maiesty, sending for this voyage's never-failing friend, Sir* IOHN WOLSTENHOLM *the elder, Knight, appointing them two to expediate forward the enterprize;*

---

[1] That is, he argued with, or used persuasion with, his friends —C.

[2] The word *as* here seems unnecessary and injurious to the sense.—C.

commanding the Master and Wardens of the Trinity-House *to be assisting hereunto; and young Sir* Iohn Wolstenholme, *that now is, was appointed Treasurer.*

The Ship of his Maiesties was (of my owne chusing, and the best for condition and quality, especially for this voyage, that the world could afford)[1] *of Burthen* 80 *Tonnes,*[2] *the number of men* 20 *and* 2 *boyes, and by all our Cares was sheathed, Cordaged, Builded, and repaired; all things being made exactly ready against an appointed time.*

My greatest care was to have my men of Godly conversation, and such as, their yeares of time not exceeding 35, *had gained good Experience, that I might thereby be the better assisted, especially by such as had been upon those Frost-biting voyages, by which they were hardned for indurance and could not so soone be dismayed at the sight of the Ice.* [As] *for beardlesse younkers, I knew* [that] *as many as could man the Boate was enough, and, for all, our dependances was vpon GOD alone, for I had neither private end, ambition, or vaine glory.*

And all these things I had contractedly done by the Master, Wardens, and Assistants of the Trinity-House. *For a Lieutenant, I had no vse ; but it grieved me much that I could not get one man that had bin on the same voyage before, by whose counsaile or discourse I might better have shunned the Ice.*

I was Victualed compleatly for 18 *Moneths, but, whether the Baker, Brewer, Butcher, and others, were Mr. of their*

---

[1] Certain facts mentioned in the Introduction tend to show that this statement as to the ship's fitness was far from correct. Probably Foxe merely made it in order to ingratiate himself with the King.—C.

[2] Elsewhere, Foxe says (p. 261) she was of "burthen 70 tonnes", while in the orders for Issuing Letters of Marque (Introduction, p. lxxiv) she is described as "of about 150 tonnes". Probably either 70 or 80 tons is correct.—C.

Arts or professions, or no, I know not[1]; *but this I am sure of: I had excellent fat Beefe, strong Beere, good wheaten Bread, good* Iseland *Ling, Butter and Cheese of the best, admirable Sacke and Aqua vitæ, Pease, Oat-meale, Wheat-meale, Oyle, Spice, Suger, Fruit, and Rice; with Chyrurgerie, as Sirrups, Iulips, condits, trechissis, antidotes, balsoms, gummes, vnguents, implaisters, oyles, potions, suppositors, and purging Pils; and, if I had wanted Instruments, my Chyrurgion had enough*

My Carpenter was fitted from the thickest bolt to the pump-nayle or tacket

The Gunner, from the Sacor[2] *to the Pistoll*

The Boatswaine, from the Cable to the Sayle-twine.

The Steward and Cooke, from the Caldron to the Spoone.

And for Bookes, if I wanted any, I was to blame, being bountifully furnisht from the Treasurer with money to provide me, especially for those of study; there would be no leisure, nor was there, for I found worke enough; and, if the matter it selfe had not been in another place when sodaine occasion was present, it had bin too late for me (like the Holland *Skipper to runne to his Chest) to looke vpon his* Waggoner *booke*[3] *But those things I feare you will say they are needlesse (yet give me leave to follow the fashion), and good for nothing but to make Courtiers and Schollers*

---

[1] This is intended as a sneer at Captain James, who, in his work, had declared that his baker and cook were Masters of their Arts —C.

[2] The sacor or saker was an ancient form of cannon, eight or nine feet in length, and of about 5 lbs. calibre. It perhaps derived its name from the French oath *sacre*, and is mentioned in *Hudibras:*—

"The cannon, blunderbuss and saker,
He was th' inventer of, and maker"—C

[3] Apparently Foxe means that, if he had not the requisite knowledge in his head, it would be useless to have it in a book.—C.

marvell at my curiositie, aud thinke strange that there should be so much adoe about making a Ship take the Sea.

Things [being] in this readinesse, I was brought to his Maiestie, where I received his Gracious favour, with a Mappe of all my Predecessors Discoveries, his Maiesties Instructions,[1] *with a Letter to the Emperour of* Iapon.

The Copies of all which Captaine IAMES had [2]

FOrasmuch as the good successe and prosperity of every Action doth consist in the due service and glorifying of God, knowing that not onely our being and preservation, but the prosperity of all our Actions and enterprizes, doe immediately depend upon his Almighty goodnesse and mercy; of which this being none of the least, eyther of nature or quality For the better governing and mannaging of this present voyage, in his Majesties ship, the *Charles*, bound for the *Northwest* Passage towards the South Sea, *May* 7, 1631, [it is ordered] as followeth :—

Orders and Articles for Civill Government, to be duly observed amongst vs in this Voyage.

1. That all the whole Company, as well Officers as others, shall duly repaire every day twice, at the Call of the Bell, to heare publike Prayers to be read (such as are authorized by the Church), and that in a godly and devout manner, as good Christians ought

2 That no man shall Sweare by the name of God, nor vse any prophane Oath, or blaspheme his holy Name, vpon paine of severe punishment

3. That no man shall speake any vile or misbeseeming word against the honour of his Maiesty (our Dread Soveraigne), his

---

[1] The text of these has not been preserved; but, from passages in Foxe's narrative, it is possible to gather a fairly clear idea of the general tenor of his instructions (see Introduction, p. xcvi).—C.

[2] The titling which Foxe here inserts has, for convenience, been removed to the commencement of his narrative.—C.

Lawes, or Ordinances, or the Religion established and authorized by him here in *England*, but as good Subjects shall duely pray for him.

4. That no man shall speake any doubtfull or despairing words against the good successe of the Voyage, or make any doubt thereof, eyther in publique or private, at his Messe or to his Watch-mate, or shall make any question of the skill and knowledge either of Superiour or inferiour Officer, or of the vndertakings, nor shall offer to combine against the authority thereof, vpon the paine of severe punishment, as well to him that shall first heare and conceale the same, as to the first beginner.

5. That no man doe offer to filch or steale any of the goods of the Ship or Company, or doe offer to breake into hould, there to take his pleasure of such provisions as are layd in generall for the whole Company of the Ship, nor that any Officer, appointed for the Charge and oversight thereof, doe otherwayes then shall be appointed him; but shall every man bee carefull for the necessary preservation of the Victuall and fuell conteyned in the hould; and that also every Officer be so carefull of his store as hee must not be found (vpon examination) to deserve punishment.

6. That, no man doe grumble at his allowance of victuall or steale any from others, nor shall give crosse language, eyther to superiour or equall, in reviling Words or daring speeches, which doe tend to the inflaming of blood or inraging of choller; remembering this also, that a stroke or a blow is the breach of his Maiesties peace, and may not want his punishment therefore, as for other reasons.

7. That, at the Boatswaine's Call, all the whole Company shall appeare above Decke, or else that his Mate fetch up presently all such sloathfull persons, eyther with Rope or cudgell, as in such cases deserve the same. The Quarter-masters shall looke into the Steer-edge while the Captaine, Master, and Mates are at Dinner or at supper.

8. That all men doe duely observe the Watch, as well at Anchor as vnder sayle, and, at the discharge thereof, the Boatswaine or his Mate shall call vp the other; all praising God together, with Psalms and Prayer, and so committing our selves, both soules and bodies, Ship and goods, to God's mercifull preservation; wee beseech him to steere, direct, and guide vs, from the beginning to the end of our Voyage; which [may] hee make prosperous vnto vs.

Amen.

May 5.[1] I Set sayle from *Deptford* and, comming by *Greenwich*, where then the Court lay,[2] I discharged my Ordnance twice, being 7 in number, and this night anchored at *Erith*.

6. This day I came to *Graves-end*, where, having bought some things needfull, I set sayle againe,[3] and anchored that night betweene the *Shooe* and *Whittaker*.[4]

7. This day, passing by *Essex* and *Suffolk*, it being in the night and calme, I anchored in *Yarmouth* Roades.[5]

8. This day I weighed and set sayle, at night I was thwart the *Shield*.[6]

---

[1] Foxe's MS commences "In the name of God, Amen. After much ado to attend the Trinity Master for our Provision, we weighed anchor in the Pool upon Thursday the 28th of this present [April], the wind presently falling calm."

[2] It appears from *The Autobiography of Phineas Pett*, fo 98 (see Introduction, p. xvii), that the king had gone to Woolwich and Gravesend to witness the launching of various ships that had been built there for the Royal Navy.—C

[3] "where, wanting some of our Principall men, we anchored, and staid there till 3 o'clock afternoon, and then, having all our men aboard, we weighed." (*Master's MS*)

[4] The Shoe and the Whittaker were both beacons situated at points on the eastern edge of the Maplin Sands, and marking the western side of the Swin Channel. The former (later known as "the Horns") was where the Maplin now stands, and near where "Shoe Hole" still exists. The Whittaker (which still exists) lies somewhat to the north of the former. Both are shown on one of the charts in Collins's *Great Britain's Coasting Pilot* (London, fo., 1693), and also on the "Chart of the English Channel, from the South Foreland to Orfordness", given in the first book of Seller's *English Pilot* (London, fo., 1671), wherein also are given (p. 4) full directions for sailing around them.—C.

[5] "The 7th we came without Gumshett [? Gunfleet Sands], and in at Bullse Shade [? Baudsey Sands], and into the Roads ... The next morning, we went on shore (where we staid near an hour and a half) to have bought more things we wanted than the town could provide us with." (*Foxe MS*)

[6] This is identical with or near Cromer, the well-known watering-

10. This day I was put into *Flambrough* 'roade, with much raine and winde at N.N.W.¹

11. I came into *Whitby* roade, where I stayed with contrary windes until the 14 day.

14. I sayled along the Coast of *Yorkshire, Durham, Northumberland*, and *Scotland*, to St. *Tab's*-head.²

15. I was thwart of *Buckhamnesse*³ in *Scotland*, where, standing to the Northwards, with sharpe winds, I broke my Maine-yard in the middest.⁴

---

place on the Norfolk coast. The name, however, seems to be quite forgotten in the district, and Mr. Walter Rye, who has written upon Cromer, knows nothing of it. It is not clear, even, to what the name was applied; but it was probably one of the sandhills on the coast between Cromer and Cley, for, in Greenville Collins' *Great Britain's Coasting Pilot* (London, fo., 1693), wherein the plate marked "V" depicts this part of the coast, two of these hills bear the names "Dagger" and "Shield" respectively. Possibly one or other of these hills is identical with Telegraph Hill, in Wabourne parish, the highest point of which is 269 feet above sea-level. "Sheld", in the Suffolk dialect, means "pied", or parti-coloured, as sheld-apple and sheldrake. Possibly the word was applied to Cromer, because of the varied colours of its sands. (Cf Moor's *Suffolk Words and Phrases*, and Delmar Morgan's *Sailing Directions*, Hakluyt Society 1889, Glossary, p. 35.)—C.

¹ "That night, steering away S.E., we were [on] the 9th, at noon, off Sister Churches; and at night, though the wind did lessen, we had fair sight of Flamboro' head. The same night, ... we plied down near Spettar Clines. The Gale, beginning to blow, put us round about the head, where we Anchored (Flamboro)... The same afternoon, the wind luffing, we went on shore, where we bought fresh Fish and Flesh meat, Fir-Deals and Sparrs, all our small allowance of that sort being spent" (*Foxe MS.*). The "Sister Churches" mentioned above are a little north of Spurn Point, perhaps those of Owthorne and Withernsea (see Greenville Collins' *Great Britain's Coasting Pilot* London, fo., 1693).—C.

² This is, of course, a misprint for St. *Abb's* Head, the well-known and prominent headland on the coast of Berwickshire.—C.

³ Buchan Ness, a headland forming the easternmost point of the county of Aberdeen. A lighthouse now stands upon it.—C.

⁴ "It being rotten half through" (*Foxe MS.*). "[It] being half rotten before, so then we got our main Topsail to our main mast, and

16. I came into *Durt-sound*,[1] a harbour in the greatest Iland of *Orkney*, but could not heere be provided of a new Maine-yard. Wind contrary.

18. At clocke 3 in the morning, I weighed and went out betweene *Pape Island* and *Sanda*.[2] At the Northend of the two heads of this Iland, there lyeth a Rocke in the midst, which doth to straiten the Flood-tyde, it bounding thereon from out the Westerne Ocean, that I was two houres overhaling ¾ of a mile, for thereabouts is the length of that straitnesse, and yet I daresay we went above 6 knots in halfe a minute.

20 I stood from hence N N W, with the N part of *Ways* or *Hays* Iland[3] in 59 degrees 8 min ; the ebbe comming forth carried us (it being calme) 9 miles to the S.W. end (which is a very steepe or perpendicular Cliffe), against a very high Sea from the West, course W N.W The rest

---

went to work to fish [see p 272] our yard" (*Master's MS.*). See note as to the unseaworthiness of Foxe's ship on p 264 —C.

[1] Perhaps Kirkwall Roads, on Mainland, but I cannot find the name on old charts More probably it is a misprint for *Deer Sound*, another good harbour in the north-east part of the island The MS. has it "We stood N N W along the Islands, within sight of the greatest Island [of] Orkney, and the next day we plied into Durtte Sound, in the north part of the same island, where we found a ship of Burmurn [?], and another was bound for Iceland, and a small catch bound for Fare [*i e*, a "ketch bound for Faroe"], and heard of a great Holland ship, [which] depted but 10 days before, bound for the North-west Passage 19th I went to Churchway [Kirkwall], the town, hoping there to find, as I was told, a mast to make a main yard upon, but could not" (*Foxe MS*) The Master's MS reads · "19th, our Captain went to a great Towne called Kerckeway, where there is building of Shipping, to see if he could get a tree to make us a main yard, but returned about 6 at night without [success]."—C.

[2] "There came off one boat with two swine, [but] we had no money to buy them" (*Foxe MS.*) Papa Westra and Sanda are two of the most northerly islands of the Orkney group.—C.

[3] I cannot identify this island. On many early maps the southern part of Hoy is marked "Waes", but Foxe cannot have been near this. —C.

as followeth in my booke of *Course, Latitudes, Variations,* and *Distances.*[1]

22. The gale increasing, I was enforced to hand both top-sayles, the Ship fell so deepe, and shipped so much water forward on, in that high Sea comming from the West.

23.[2] From this day untill the 23, I did not make above 17 leag. way W.N.W., it being faire weather with easie wind upon all points of the Compasse. I had no ground at 200 fathomes.

24. I was this noone in 59 deg. 58 min.; the weather faire and cleere; the Sunne setting and rising in our sight.

25. This morning came a great Whale by us. The last night and this day was calme; we made small way, the weather hot, as it hath been since I came from *Orkney*; latitude 59 d. 56, no ground at 335 fathomes.

26. It was faire weather, and easie wind; latitude 60 d. 0 min. at night, the Sunne went cleare to bed; the variation taken by amplitude[3] was 8 degrees.[4]

27. This day, the 28, and 29, the wind contrary, I was in traverse; had little sight of the Sunne since the 26.

30. It was easie wind and close weather, and I observed

---

[1] As the same words appear also in Foxe's MS, it is clear that they do not refer to it, but to some other record which he kept.—C.

[2] This should be the 21st. Up to this point, the dates here given are all two days ahead of those in Foxe's MS.—C.

[3] In astronomy, an arc of the horizon, intercepted between the true east or west points thereof and the centre of the sun, star, or planet, at its rising or setting. In other words, amplitude is the horizontal angular distance of a star from the east or west points. In magnetism, it is the difference between the rising and setting of the sun from the east and west points, as indicated by the compass, which, subtracted from the true amplitude, gives the error of the compass due to variation (Smyth's *Sailors' Word Book.*)—C.

[4] "The Variation was 8° 30', taken by the Semi-circle." (*Foxe MS.*)

in 58 deg. 39 m. I caused 3 peeces of Ordnance to be strooke into the hold,[1] and two of my greatest Anchors to be taken of the bowes; at night I found a drift tree, but it would not make me a maine yard.

31 It was faire, dry, calme, and close weather since the 26, and the great Westerne Sea was not downe untill this day.

June 1. This day was a faire wind, with wet foggy weather.

2. I had faire winds, but thicke close weather.

3. This fulsome ugly morning presented the foulest childe that the whole voyage brought forth, with such variety and changes of the Elements, Ayre and Water, as if all had conspired to make our destiny fatall. I lay a try in the *Mizen* course, and caused the Carpenter to make loose and strengthen the fishes and wouldings[2] of the maine-yard, which being done, I caused the *Mizen* to be strucke and the helme to be put on weather, to try if the ship would weathercoyle if I had occasion, to which she obeyed presently,[3] so as I was then put into good assurance of her quicke steerage against I was to enter into the Ice.

4. This day were many gusts of wind with small raine.

---

[1] To "strike down" is to lower casks or other goods into the hold of a ship.—C.

[2] Literally, *splicings*. "Fishes" or "fish-pieces" are pieces of hard wood, concave on one side, convex on the other, which are bound opposite one another on the opposite sides of masts or other spars to strengthen them where sprung. This is done by means of bolts and hoops or stout pieces of rope, called wooldings. Foxe's MS. has it: "Often having observed the [spliced] mainyard to give some way, I caused the Carpenter to lie on two more fishes, and the Boatswaine to new would the same."—C.

[3] "who did ill round at the weathering of the helme" (*Foxe MS.*). This is further proof that Foxe's statements as to the seaworthiness of his ship (see p. 264) were untrue.—C.

5. This day was lesse wind, and I made good way to the Westwards.

6. Faire weather. I continued my course to the Westward, and, being in 60 d. 31 m., I directed the course W. by S.

7. Faire weather, but no Amplitude; since the 26 of the last moneth, there was much driftwood.[1]

8. I proceeded with easie winds, but faire; thick fog, which ended in raine. The Seas set from S.S.E.; the wind changeable.

9. Faire weather; the Sea so smooth as [if] it had been made ready to have been bowled upon.[2]

10. Some fog, and easie wind; the ship made way to the Westward. The Sea exceeding smooth, but no amplitude of long time

11. Faire weather and easie wind; I force still to the Westward. This last was the coldest night that I felt since I came into this melancholy path,[3] and we had fewer Seafowle than before. We had no ground at 320 fathome; the wind came to the Northeast.

12. This longest day[4] came in with wet, and blew so as, since the last noone-tyde, the ship made way 44 leagues to the Westward, I am now in fore-course and bonnet, with Sprit-sayle. This evening I came by two pieces of Ice[5]; and now I reckoned my selfe not farre from sight of *Cape Farewell.*

13. The wind Veered to the Northward; I set all sayles

---

[1] "This meridian we could not see the Sun, nor have we much since the 26th of last month; and, within these two days, we have seen divers pieces of float-wood." (*Foxe MS*)

[2] "At noon, we had observation I was in 60° 49' by the forward staff, and by the backward I was in 60° 19', distance 30'" (*Foxe MS*)

[3] The MS has it *part*, which is probably correct.—C

[4] Old Style, of course.—C.

[5] "The one small, the other as big as the Eddistone." (*Foxe MS.*)

and stood to the Westward, in latitude 58 d. 30 m.[1] This evening, the Article for the watch[2] (to be diligent and to looke well foorth for Ice or other accidents) was againe read over to the Company, and a man [appointed] constantly to sit all night in the foretop. The Ayre was hazie to the landward · otherwise wee should have seene Cape *Farewell* (if I suppose not amisse[3]).

14. Close weather; the wind contrary; we in traverses. Some drisling mists, but many Grampusses[4] came in a shole, following their Leader, comming close by me, made me remember Mr. *William Browne* in his *Britaines* Pastorals,[5] where hee writes, "the *Tritons* wafted *Thetis* along the *British* shores."[6] This afternoone, the Poles altitude being 58 d 10 m, the variation by Azimuth[7] and Almi-

---

[1] "In the Evening, we espied an Island of floating Ice, like unto a Church, with a Steeple upon the one End, and as high as our main topmast head." (*Foxe MS*)

[2] He means one of the Orders and Regulations (see p 266).—C.

[3] "if it be took right off in the Plates and Journals of my Predecessors." (*Foxe MS*)

[4] The Killer, or Grampus (*Orca gladiator*) is common in the North Atlantic; but the shoal Foxe saw was probably composed of Pilot Whales (*Globicephalus melas*), which are highly gregarious, and are often called "grampusses" by sailors.—C

[5] William Browne, poet, was born at Tavistock, Devon, in 1591, and died about the year 1643 His *Britannia's Pastorals*, a lengthy work, was much admired at the time of its appearance, and still holds a high place in English poetry. It is remarkable for its admirable descriptions of simple natural scenery and objects The first book appeared in 1613, the second in 1619; and both were republished in one volume in 1625. It has, since then, been several times reprinted.—C.

[6] "so well in this sea those Fishes followed their leader. Their attendants were only Nodyes [? *Noddys*, i.e., Terns or Gulls]." (*Foxe MS.*)

[7] The complement of the amplitude (see p 271), or an arc between the meridian of a place and any given vertical line (Smyth's *Sailors' Word-Book*) An azimuth compass is used for finding the true bearing of any heavenly body.—C.

canter[1] was 18 deg. From hence, I haled up in N.W. by N. for sight of *Desolation* [2]

15. This day was faire close weather, with dispersing fogges, which I doe perceive to be incident to those Seas. *Poles* elevation was 58 d. 50 min. The Sea is here almost continually smooth, the water blacke, but not so thicke as is formerly writ of,[3] and small store of fowle to be seene.

16. This day and last night hath been thicke weather, but so as we might discerne 3 miles betwixt one Fog-drift & another. I had steered some watches W. and by N., which, for some reason of a reported Current, I altered to the N.W. by N. againe, although after the variation thwart Cape *Farewell* was found (and allowed) in my running over betwixt the same and the West Maine, or the West side of *Fretum Hudson*,[4] I found my reckoning to agree, without any interruption, furtherance, or hinderance of Current; therefore, what instruction shall as yet be laid down in this way without good judgment in the practi-

---

[1] The almicanter is, in astronomy, a small circle of the sphere, parallel to the horizon, and an almicanter staff was formerly used to take observations of the sun about the time of his rising or setting, to find the amplitude and the variations of the compass (see p. 96).—C.

[2] This was the name then given to the southern portion of Greenland, which (it must be remembered) was supposed to be a large island, separated from the mainland by Frobisher's Strait, as shown on Foxe's and other maps of the period (see p. 122).—C. "This morning I would have had a Sounding, but the Master said we should wear out all our lines too fast... At night, we argued about the course to be held more northerly, and it was thought still that the same should be N.W. b. N., for having sight of Desolation; but the ambitious Master, at his going forth, directed N.W., which I bore withall, there being more danger to the Voyage in crossing a proud fellow than could insue in that direction." (*Foxe MS.*)

[3] "The sea here is almost continually frothy; but, when the wind doth stir the same, our water hath been blackish, but not so black and thick as some doth write of." (*Foxe MS.*)

[4] Apparently he means Fretum *Davis*.—C.

tioner, and libertie withall, is but, as it were, to teach a blind man to see by demonstration.

17. This last night came by us one Whale; this day another. The water's colour is all one, and but few fowle. This Meridian I did reckon to be in 60 d. 50 m., and that I had neere two points of variation. The weather thicke, with wet fogge

18. Faire weather but foggy. This noon-tyde, I did reckon to be of the 60 parallel, 590 leagues from the place in *Orkney* of my departure. The account is but 600 from thence to *Resolution* I could not observe since the 15 day, yet I am neere in 61 d. 30 min. This day we met with overfalls and Races of Tide or Current. At clock 4, thick weather, and, reckoning to be not farre from land, I tooke in all sayles and laid to *Hull*[1] At 6, wee were no sooner risen from prayers, but we were close by a mountain of Ice, hard to Leewards of us, and wee had much to doe to cleere the same by slatting[2] the ship to the S.-wards. The most of this evening and night I spent in standing to and againe[3]

19. This day at noone I had a little cleare, and stood in to the S.W.-ward, when it fogged againe; I lay to *Hull* two times. This day we see the Sunne, but to no use, it was so hazie.

20. This last night I laid in Maine saile untill midnight, reckoning by all accounts that I must be in neere 62 d., and thought it fit to hale in W., true course, especially now it was cleare weather; but it thickned againe and blew both topsailes in, the wind veering to the W S.W., which had been betwixt E. and S., with thicke, foggy, or hazie weather, ever since the 14 day. Thereupon, with cleere weather, I stood to the N.W., close haled amongst *Islands*

---

[1] See p. 181 —C

[2] Probably a misprint for *flatting* (see p. 181).—C.

[3] "[Had] sight of a seal." (*Master's MS.*)

and peeces of Ice, for the Sea, beating continually upon them, doth undermine them, so as they fall in pieces, forced by their own waight; to the Lee of every Iland is [a number] of those little peeces, but [they] are easily to be shunned. This day, 11 clocke, I had sight of land almost buried in snow,[1] being two Islands, making a Bay betwixt them and the North maine, whereon stood two high hills, bearing North-west, covered with snow; the Bay was full of mash'd Ice, which it seemed the S.E. wind had inforced herein. By dead reckoning, I was at that instant in 62 d. 17 m., where presently, haveing a good observation, at that instant I was in 62 d. 25 m., the difference being but 8 min., & that to the W.-ward,[2] it doth not shew that there is any current continually to set out of *Fretum Davis* to the S., as is generally reported; for, from the lat. 58 d. 30 m., crossing *Fretum Davis*, 220 leag. or therabouts, to the W. side in 62 d. 27 m., and having but 8 min. difference betwixt dead reckoning and the observation, and that to the Northward, whether doth there any current appeare to come from the N. out of *Fretum Davis* or no?

Having thus met with the land, I stood to the Southward untill midnight, with the waide[3] at W., hopeing to ply up into the passage[4]

Seeing now that it hath pleased God to send me thus happily neere to the land, being the N. side of *Lumley's*

---

[1] This was undoubtedly the North Foreland (the Queen Elizabeth's Foreland of Frobisher, see p. 38), on the north side of Frobisher's Bay (the Lumley's Inlet of Davis).

[2] From the context, this is clearly a misprint for *north*-ward.—C.

[3] Undoubtedly a misprint for wind.—C.

[4] That is, into Hudson's Strait. Foxe's MS. here says: "I pray God all persons [on board] will see the good of this voyage, for I hear that some do wish themselves at home again. The Master went to his cabin, although it was his watch. I knew his proud meanings, and let him alone; for he was glad I had taken that charge off his hands, that he might go asleep, which was his meaning by trying."—C

inlet, so named after the right honourable the Lord *Lumley*,[1] an especiall furtherer to *Davis* in his voyages, as to many other Lordly designes, as that never to be forgotten act of his, in building up the peere[2] of that distressed poore fisher-towne and corporation of *Hartlepole*, in the Bishoprick of *Durham*, at his owne proper cost and charge, to the value of at least 2000 pounds. At my first comming thither, I demanded at whose charge the said Peere towne[3] was builded; an old man answered: "*Marrye at my good Lord* Lumley's, *whose Soule was in Heaven before his bones were cold.*"

Some may inquire, why I should not have incerted herein my traverse course distance,[4] with all my observa-

---

[1] John, first and last Baron Lumley (of the 1547 creation), died *s p.* on the 11th of November 1609, when the barony became extinct. He was buried at Cheam, in Surrey. According to Camden, he was "of entire virtue, integrity and innocence, and in his old age a complete patern of true nobility." He was, as Foxe says, "an especial furtherer to Davis in his voyages", and it was after him that Davis, in July 1587, named Lumley's Inlet (see p. 38).—C.

[2] According to Sir Cuthbert Sharp (*History of Hartlepool*, 2nd edition, 1851, p. 156), the earliest record relative to the pier of Hartlepool is in 1473, when Bishop Booth issued letters to all ecclesiastical and municipal officials throughout the kingdom praying their assistance for the mayor and corporation of Hartlepool in building a pier for the shelter of ships. In 1588, according to the same authority, an Act of Parliament provided for the repairs of the pier; but it was probably of little benefit, for in 1599 the corporation had to provide by statute for further repairs. Sir Cuthbert makes no reference to the munificent rebuilding of the pier by Lord Lumley, to which Foxe alludes, although it probably took place about this time; but he shows that Lord Lumley was a great benefactor of the town by his statement (p. 54) that, at his request, in 1593, Queen Elizabeth granted to the town a charter conferring upon it many advantages.—C.

[3] Perhaps a misprint for *towne peere*.—C.

[4] Traverse denotes the various courses sailed by a ship when manœuvring or under changes of the wind. The reduction of the distances run on each course constitutes the traverse-table, from which the reckoning is deduced each day up to noon.—C

tion for latit. To which I answer: first, it were needlesse, seeing that few doe looke or search after the Voyage, and many before mee have wrote thereof; besides, it lying neare upon the same parallell, there is no neede; secondly, if I had knowne any that would have taken so much paines [as] to have protracted mee, I would have prepared them satisfaction; thirdly, I feare me I should be thought to be too tedious, although I am but newly entered; yet I do purpose to bestow some time of[1] those needy ones concerning this matter.

A DISCOURSE FOR THE SAME.[2]

Setting forth and beginning my accompts from the W.-most place of *Orkney*, I made 2 observations for the variation of the compasse, evening Amplit. The one was 8 d., the other 4 d.; but I did give no certain credit thereunto; yet I do rather trust to that at 8 d., at which instant I did account I was 24 deg. or thereabout Eastward of the great Meridian,[3] and neere the paralell of 60 deg , continuing the course W.-ward, as wind would serve, untill I came into the Latit. of 58 deg. 12 min. I was then 12 deg., or thereabouts, from the place of my departure, and traversing with contrary windes, betwixt the latit. of 59 deg. 12 min. and 60 deg. 20 min., at $18\frac{1}{2}$ d. distance from my setting forth. I continued the course still Westward, with so small difference betwixt my observation and protraction or traverse as I thought I might as well trust to the one as the other. Continuing this course in the latit. of 60 deg. 19 m., W. from the first Meridian 6 deg , I found by my observation that I was to S.-ward 5 m. of my protracted course; and, though then I did perceive that the Compasse was varied Westward, yet how much, for want of Amplitude or celestiall observation, could not be knowne.

Now the wind comming freely on, and, taking Mr. *Hal's* account[4]

---

[1] Apparently this should be *on*.—C.

[2] Up to this point, both the MS. narratives (the Master's especially) supply many observations of latitude, longitude, wind, variation of the compass, etc., which are omitted from the printed narrative, but are here summarised.—C.

[3] Longitude was at that time reckoned from the meridian of Ferro, one of the Canary Islands, which was called the first or "great" meridian.—C.

[4] For Captain James Hall's account of Greenland, see pp. 89 and 99.—C.

that Cape *Farewell* in *Groyneland* (which land first I did desire to fall with, though I did not much regard) lyeth 18 d. W. from the great or first Meridian, as also, [according to] Mr. *Brigges*, is neare the same, and in latit. about 59 deg., I directed the course W. and W. and by S., thinking thereby to fall in sight of the said Cape. And, although there is no certainty of agreement amongst some of my predecessours concerning the variation there, some writing 11 d., others 14 d., confusedly, yet I did hope that course would have brought mee at least to sight thereof, report making it to be high and Mountainous land (notwithstanding Variation or current), especially having so franke a gale of wind, and but 12 d. of a small circle neere the 60 paralell, the distance being but 120 leag. at most, and in that distance holding the same course, I was 1 d. 17 m. wrekt[1] from my true course, within one point at most of my paralell; and neerer with a stiffe gale, wet and hazie, I durst not hale for engaging my selfe with an unknowne Cape, which hath both Ilands and Ice lying there off, where I might have beene endangered ([or], at the least, incumbred).[2] Now, when I had sailed 100 leag. from the said latit., I met with Ice, and, as before, in such weather, I would not deale with land, but stood away 30 leag. more to the Westward.

14. Hauing an observation in 58 d. 10 min., and by my protract or dead reckoning, I was in latit. 59 d. 27 min., contrary to expectation,[3] the same afternoone, the variation taken by *Asimuth* and *Almicanter* was 8 d. 50 m.; but, being set more to S.-ward then this allowance, I did call to minde the current which Sir *Martin Frobrisher* found upon the coast of *Groenland*, in the lat. 62, setting from N.E. to S.W., as the land doth there lye; where they doe affirme that the flood tyde did run 9 houres, and the ebbe but 3. I know no other cause for this but the large distance betwixt *Nova Zembla* on the E. and *Groenland*, in which the Ocean may take opportunity to use his naturall agitation from E. to W., being thereunto drawne by the restlesse motion and impulsion of the Heavens, and here, butting upon *Groenland*, must of necessity (the land lying somewhere neere his naturall inclination) trend along there, setting his current to the S.W., or else, as in a huge Bay, make a repercussive motion (as in the Bay of *Mexico*), by entring in at the S. side and, wheeling about by the bottome, must revert back againe along the North side by Cape *Florida*.

---

[1] Prof. Skeat writes: "'Wrekt' means *driven;* from the Icelandic *reka*, to drive. The *w* is not wrong, for the Icelandic word was *wreka* in its early life. Allied to English *wreak, wrack, rack,* and *wreck.* (See *The Concise English Dictionary.*)"—C.

[2] See Mr. *Hall, Davis,* and others.—F.

[3] Variation and current might doe this.—F.

Now this 9 houres of the floud-tyde running, may be, by this restraint of the Seas natural course (in meeting with the land), must needs enforce all the Sounds, Bayes, Rivers, and through-lets, with quantities of waters, and in through-lets especially, setting Westward, and wanting Limitation, shall continue his naturall course the longer, being assisted by that motion, untill the ebbe, being strengthened by the height of waters (or of course) from the W. Sea, shall returne againe, according to his proper retraction.

And thus much further I am of opinion [that], if Sir *Martin Frobrisher* had pursued his course Westward in his Straite, he being 60 leag. up the same, he had doubtlesse sailed into *Fretum Davis;* for he entred upon the East side, and after him *Davis* on the W., have almost met[1]; nor will be perswaded, but that, if there were a *Drogio*, as is mentioned by the *Zeni*, that that tract of land on the S, betwixt *Frobrisher's* Strait and *Cape Farewell*, is the same [2]

But, to come to my selfe, and to end this digression (although I hope what I have here incerted will not be held any way impertinent[3]); Cape *Farewell*, I holde for certaine, doth attract the Magnet more suddainly (comming from the Eastward towards it) then any knowne Cape in the world, as did appeare in all this Voyadge.

I did here reckon of 24 deg. variation, but sailed all by Meridian compasse, and have wrote this Iournall there after; therefore the allowance is to be accounted, as the places doe differ in variation.

21. This snowie morning, I stoode in againe. At clocke 7, I fell about 2 leagues more to the West off the same Ile I first discovered yesterday.[4] The Bay lay still full of Ice. This W.N.West wind bloweth hard by puffes. Standing from hence South-W., 2 leagues over *Lumley's* Inlet, wee had great store of masht Ice, and was faine to beare up for one [piece], and loose for another,[5] but the Sea

---

[1] This extraordinary delusion on the part of Foxe is, of course, accounted for by the fact (already mentioned, see p. 38, *note*) that it was then believed that Frobisher's Strait ran *through Greenland*, separating the southern portion, then known as Desolation, from the northern portion or mainland, as shown on Foxe's map.—C.

[2] See *Ortelius Univers. Mappe.*—F. See p. 29.—C.

[3] Foxe here uses this word in its old sense—*out of place.*—C.

[4] Latit. 62 d. 12 min.—F. The islands off the North Foreland (see p. 277).—C.

[5] Throughout his narrative, Foxe uses the word *Ice* as though it were a plural.—C.

was smooth; after this, for two leagues sailing, it was cleare. At night, 10, wee see land,[1] and made it upon assurance to be Cape *Warwick*[2]; and this cleere was in the Lee thereof, for, standing still the same course over, wee found more Ice in the South channell, and more comming out of *Fretum Hudson*, then I had before.[3] The wind blew here bleate and unquoth.[4]

22. This day we had boarded it up in[5] smooth water bearing a good saile betweene Cape *Chidlie*[6] and Cape *Warwicke*, and were entred *Fretum Hudson*; and now I desire a little of your patience. The Iland *Resolution*, so named by whom I know not, but sure I am *Davis* was the first of us that see it,[7] naming the East end thereof

---

[1] "The form is as appeareth in my Book of forms and shapes of Land." (*Foxe MS.*)

[2] The Earl of Warwick's Foreland was named by Davis on July 31st, 1587 (see p. 77), after his patron, Ambrose Dudley, who was created Earl of Warwick in 1561, and died *s.p.* in 1589, when his titles became extinct. The name has not been retained, the cape having long been more commonly known as Cape Resolution, after the island (see p. 165) of which it forms the easternmost part.—C.

[3] Foxe here seems to have had another difference with the Master as to the navigation, the account of which given in his MS concludes as follows: "He would have had the topsails taken in, but I would not, for I must go my voyage. Then he said, if he had known that I had been so silly, wild, a man, he would not have come in the Ship for £100."

[4] No doubt, *bleak and uncouth* is meant.—C.

[5] Query *tacked about*.—C.

[6] So named by Davis, after his friend and neighbour Mr. John Chudleigh, of Broad Clyst, near Exeter, who in 1589 promoted and commanded an expedition to the South Sea, *via* the Strait of Magellan, in which, however, he died. Foxe is wrong in saying that the Island on which Cape Chidley is should not be called Button's Isle; for Button first proved it an island by discovering and sailing through the channel which separates it from the mainland.—C.

[7] This is certainly incorrect. The island forms the southern side of the entrance to Lumley's Inlet (Frobisher's Strait), and therefore must have been seen by Frobisher in 1576-77-78. We know, however, that, through an error in longitude, Frobisher supposed his

Cape *Warwicke*, and it seemeth for good reason, for that honourable house hath (and unto this day doth) still cherish those worthy Marine enterprises (as doth appeare by *Frobisher's* 3 Voyages) to their no small charge; as also those two Honourable houses of *Darcie*, now Lord *Rivers*,[1] by whom *Davis* named certaine Ilands upon the North part of *America*,[2] wherein he found Deere; the other is *Cumberland*, to whom he dedicated other Ilands[3] in his furthest West, in a passage he entred 60 leagues, but he came backe.

Notwithstanding those Nobles, others were at great charge in his setting forth, as may be observed by the naming of Lands, as Mount *Raleigh*, Hope *Sanderson*, Cape *Chidly* (now, but not rightly, called *Buttons* Ile); for, to use his owne words, speaking by *Warwick's Forland*, this Cape as it was the Gulfe, wee passed over the 30 of this moneth, so was it the North Promontorie, or first beginning of a very great Inlet whose South lymit at this present wee see not, which Inlet or Gulfe in the night wee passed, to our great admiration, for the waters fall, and he saith that, having past the mouth of this Gulfe, he

---

strait to lie on the east coast of Greenland, where, of course, Foxe still supposed it to be when he sailed on his voyage. Davis, it is true, was the first to assign to the island its correct geographical position. Foxe says he does not know who bestowed the name "Resolution" upon the island. There is little doubt that Button did so; for, although the imperfect narrative of Button's voyage as given by Foxe nowhere says that he so named the island, Button's own ship was named the *Resolution*, her escort being the *Discovery*, while the name Resolution Island occurs several times in the narrative, and I can find no trace of its having been used by any earlier navigator (see p. 165).—C.

[1] Thomas D'Arcy, third Baron D'Arcy of Chich (succeeded 1580), was created Earl Rivers in 1626, and died in 1639.—C.

[2] Lord *Riv*. Iles.—F.

[3] *Cumberl*. Iles.—F. No doubt after George Clifford, third Earl of Cumberland, who succeeded in 1569, and died in 1605.—C.

fell [in] with the Southermost Cape thereof, which he named *Chidlies* Cape.[1]

Having made this Cape,[2] which to doe I stood over as neere as I could for ice, but was at least 6 leagues off; it appeared high, and 4 distinct Ilands.[3] (In number, I judge there is more.) Being now assured that God had sent me into the passage, I stoode over to the North with Cape *Warwick;* the middle Channell was cleare of ice, and therein I had a good observation of 61 degrees 10 min., cleare weather, and a constant gale; otherwise I durst not have stoode to the Southwards, remembring *Gibbons*[4] It blew in both topsailes, but, towards night, the wind lessened and I could perceive the ice betwixt me and the Cape to drive to Seaward, of which, neere the shoare, was great store.

The flood comming on, I caused both Topsayles to bee cast over, and wee threed it, between Ice and Ice, with a well bent flood inwards[5], so as that we had got above the Ile (that tyde) if this faire day had not ended in fogge. A motion was made before this to looke for harbour; but that I denied for those reasons [here] given: that I did not know what danger might fall me if I had put into the shore, where lay much yce (as we could see); and what yce or sunke Rocks might be in the way, I was as ignorant of; besides, not knowing whether the wind

---

[1] These words, which Foxe has previously quoted (see p. 79), are not part of Davis's narrative as it appears in Hakluyt, but are taken from his "Traverse Book" (see Hakluyt's *Voyages*, vol. III, p. 118) —C.

[2] "With the variation allowed, I marked it to lie in 61° 33' and Long. 61° 06' [from Orkney?]." (*Master's MS.*)

[3] "We had sight of the said Islands of Sir Thos. Button, being 3 and a little one. Let the arithmeticians number them. I drew them as correctly as I could." (*Foxe MS.*)

[4] *Felix quem.*—F. His altogether fruitless voyage is referred to on p. 201.—C.

[5] This doubtless means that a strong tide set into the Passage.—C.

would serve to bring me in a safe roade, and how the Tyde might set to turne or sayle in, as occasion might fall out; but the worst was (and that was [what] most I feared) the wind might Souther[ly] and then, there being such store of yce in the passage, would inforce all the harbours full, and so might cut my cable and put me on shore upon the Rockes; it flowing much water there, as *Baffin* reports. With these reasons wee were all perswaded to ply it up amongst the Ice in Sea-roome, rather then to indanger our selves in harbour or neere the shoare, where for certaine the broken Rockes, the grounded Ice, the small Ilands by restraining the Tides, must make them Reverse with Counter-sets and Eddies, as may be observed by *London* bridge, the bases of whose Arches, being set in the Tides course, doth so restraine his motion that the following streames, by heightning the waters, causeth such a Current, as it were, to ingulfe by the fall thereof, as you see the water-men cannot keepe their boates even on; the Counter tyde wheeling on her of the one side, the eddie coursing her upon the other, not joyning their separations, but goeing as it were distracted above *Cole*-harbour, before they come to themselves againe, to passe Westward. And all this hazard is to no purpose, for wee are safer at Sea. Besides, wee are not sure of any refreshing; and, if wee were, wee have no neede, being but newly come from home; and, if the wind come to South, and so Eastwards to North-East, wee, being in the Sea, may proceede night or day, but in harbour wee cannot; and therefore to take harbour were vanity, unlesse to loyter, spend away, and consume time, the thought whereof is ridiculous. The Fogge and night came both together; and, having the last 24 houres quitted abondance of Ice to Seaward, which might serve as a Baracadoe if the Wind should come from thence, and keepe us safe amongst it, as after (*blessed be God*) it proved, wee made fast to a peece of Ice, filld fresh water thereupon, and went all to our beds, save the watch. This fogge night was calme.

23. This misty morning made the Sunne clime 10 degrees in height, before he could peepe through the same, which afterwards prooved a very faire, calme, hot day, making both Ice and Pitch runne; but the ship was inclosed amongst the Ice,[1] driving with ebbe and flood about 2 leagues from the South end of *Resolution*. I had no ground at 180 fathomes. Some of my men said they saw smoake on land, and, after, it prooved true, for Captain *James* was in harbour there all that same time. My Master went with boate and killed 9 willicks, whereof he kindly bestowed upon every Messe one.[2] They make strong and good pottage.[3]

I, pressing hard for getting cleere that I might proceed, was demanded why I made such haste.[4] I answered that, as every Mountain consisted of severall peeces, so did my Voyage upon Fathomes, which must be measured here with speed, though afterward I might take leisure, which, added one to another, might in time compasse all the Mountaines of the world; and that it fared with me as with the

---

[1] "It blew very hard, so that we had many stout blows, do what we could with fenders and booms." (*Master's MS*)

[2] "It was more than I did know him afford them all the voyage, before or after" (*Foxe MS*). Foxe's MS hereabouts consists largely of uncomplimentary references to the Master —C.

[3] One would imagine that "pottage" made of willicks (see p. 107) must have been *very* strong. These birds feed chiefly on fish.—C

[4] "I called to Mr. Uring [(the Master's mate), and] asked his opinion, though I thought him unwilling to stir. And the Master, I found him always a proud fool and insolent. Uring's answer was that we could do no good, and the Master's was to the same purport, though his mate would not stir out of his cabin to look upon it.... And so I left them. Else, I had always my men willing to give their obedience." (*Foxe MS.*)

Mackarell-men at *London*, who must hasten to Market before the fish stinke.

This evening, the Sun set cleare; the Ayre breathed gently from the East; and we lay quietly all night amongst the Ice.

24. This morning the wind began to gather strength from the E S.E.; the flood came on, and the Ice began to separate; I caused one peece to be made fast unto the ship with 2 Grapnels, to the intent to towe it at the ships sterne, mooring the ship so thereunto that she might make way N.W. for the North shore; for that it hath been alwayes said that the North side was cleerest from Ice. Thus made fast, although the wind forst on the ship, yet her way was so easie as she could take no harme if she had touched upon the same, because this trayle or drag stayed her way; but, the wind blowing on, the ship broke one Grapnel off by the Arme of the flooke[1] and bended the other, so as we were loose from thence; but, meeting great store of driving Ice, I caused to make fast againe for safety, where we were presently inclosed for many miles.

25. This morning, the ship broke loose from that peece I was made fast unto; the ship and tackling, being more in the wind's power then the Ice (it being lower), caused her to drive faster.

I caused the Spritsaile to be loosed to binde the ship's Stem to the Ice, which gave alwayes way with the flood which set Westward; so the East wind forcing it backe made it cloze with the ebbe, returning Eastwards, which put mee in good hope that, further within the straight, I should finde all cleare, or at least the Ice so thinne as

---

[1] Flukes (pronounced *flues*), or palms, are the broad, triangular plates of iron on each arm of the anchor, which, entering the ground, hold the ship.—C.

I might passe betweene one and another[1]; and, with this perswasion, I drew on the Company: that the S.E. winds which had blown for 6 or 7 dayes before we came into this Freet,[2] had kept in this Ice, and those West winds, which had blowne 3 dayes before and at our entry, comming (from about 140 leagues) from the bottome here, in some places 20, in some places 30, and in some 40 leagues more or lesse broad, had packt all from thence, unto this straitened place betwixt Cape *Chidley* and the body of *Resolution*, and so choaked this entrance, [it] being not above 14 leagues broad. The wind E.N.E.; we drive all this time inwards with the ice.[3]

Now this prodigious thing we call Ice is of two sorts[4]; as mountainous ice, wch is a huge peece, compact, of a great

---

[1] See note about Ice on p. 281.—C.

[2] Fret, a narrow strait or arm of the sea; contracted from the Latin *fretum*.—C.

[3] "This evening the Company presented a letter to the Master and me for the increasing of their allowance. The same and answer shall follow in due place." (*Foxe MS.*)

[4] Foxe's discourse on the two kinds of ice is correct in every particular, and his distinction between them at the period is interesting. His first sort, of course, consisted of icebergs, which are formed by the breaking off of masses from the advancing front of an Arctic glacier as it reaches the shore and becomes undermined by the action of the waves; these masses, which are often of enormous size, afterwards float far to the southward under the influence of the Polar currents. They are, of course, composed of fresh water. Foxe's second sort of ice includes all pack-ice, floe-ice, and ice-fields, which, of course, owe their origin to the freezing of salt water. Captain Markham (who passed through Hudson's Strait on the *Alert* in 1886), in commenting on these remarks of Foxe's, says (*Proc. Roy. Geog. Soc.*, 1888, p. 553).—"It would not be possible to give a more accurate account of the conditions of the ice in Hudson's Strait at the present day than is furnished by this description, written by Captain Luke Foxe more than 250 years ago. It exactly describes the peculiar nature of the ice that is usually met with during the navigable season in this channel, and which I have not observed in any other part of the northern regions."—C.

quantity, some of more, some of lesse [size]; but, in this Freet, you seldome have any bigger then a great Church, and the most therof lesse, being of severall formes, as some 20, some 30, some 40 yards above the superficies of the water, but farre more under; of these, you may tell sometimes 7 or eight in sight, so that they are no hindrance to us.

The other [sort] is smaller, and that we call masht or fleackt ice.[1] Of this you shall [there] have numbers infinite, some of the quantity of a Rood, some a Pearch, ¼ an acre, some 2 acres, but the most is small and about a foot or 2 or more, above the water, and 8 or 10 or more under the water; and those are they which doe inclose you, so as, in much wind, from the topmast head, you shall hardly see any water for them; but, whilst you lie amongst them, it is so smooth as you shall not feele the ship stirre. Onely, if it be much wind, make the ship snogge[2]; and, at returne of the Tydes, when the ice doth loozen, have all care to the Rudder. At shift of wind, the ice will make way one from another[3]; in the meane time, have patience; and, in trailing of ice on sterne, if the ship doe touch but against it with the stemme, so that the stroke sodainely stay her way, then have care to keep the helme in midships, for your traile, with its way, will come presently at the backe of the Rudder, and it, lying on either side, is in danger to breake or set it on wry.

There is another way, which is to muzzell the ship with a peece of ice close to his stem and bowes; the ice being so swifted, the ship is to drive it with head saile; but this I doe not comend, for that the ship, not having fresh way, shall not have her steering beside the edy water the forst

---

[1] See p. 293, *note*.—C.

[2] Possibly this means *snug*, but Hallıwell gives "to snog, to *shake* or *shiver*". The term *to shake a ship* is explained elsewhere.—C.

[3] That is, *will separate*.—C.

ice shall make; not comming quicke to the Rudder, it shall not command her, so as, if any wind be, shee shall cast athwart, with head to the wind, and drive sternewayes, to the great danger of her Rudder, if ice be in the way.

25. This day hath been wet fog unto evening, 6; then it cleered. At 10, we see land to the N.; not certaine whether *Resolution* or no, for there was no remarkeable thing thereon. This Evening Sun kist *Thetis* in our sight[1]; the same greeting was 5 d. W. from the N.; and, at the same instant, the Rainbowe was in appearance, I thinke to Canopy them a bed.

At the beginning of flood here is wheeling streames, like edie tides, [which] I take to be caused by the ice themselves, one drawing more water then another; and [it] continueth all the time of their moving, untill they be setled, so as it may be conjectured that it doth runne $\frac{1}{2}$ tyde under other, as in most places elsewhere. All this time, since the wind came E.-ward, it hath not blowne above course and bonnet Gale.[2]

26. This morning the Sun rose cleare, and so continued all this cold Virgin day, for I have not seene one cloud to interpose, yet he went peeping through a cloud to bed. And now the frost takes care that there shall no more pitch runne from off the Sun side of the ship; and the land towards Sun-set doth so alter by the exhalation of vapours that it shewes now firme land, then a Bay, now high, then low, that we cannot say whether we make

---

[1] This means that the sunset was clear and free from fog, so that they could see the sun "go to bed" below the horizon. Thetis was a sea-nymph or goddess, and the mother of Achilles.—C.

[2] Captain Wharton, R.N., writes: "The bonnet was an extra piece that was laced on to the courses, or principal sails [see p. 55]. I should imagine this term implies that the wind was such that they were able to carry the bonnet as well as the full course."—C.

maine land, Bayes, or through-lets[1]; the ice, with the uncertain reflex of the Sun, made such unconstant shapes.[2]

27. This morning the Sun shewed himselfe through Fly-land,[3] and the South wind drave away the vapours, which fully satisfied our mistaking of land the last evening; yet we were not mistaken, but that we drive into the passage all this while. This wind with tyde helpes to separate the ice (a little). It being advantageous for the N. Main, I caused to make loose, whence we furtherd ¼ a mile. The wind comming W., with fog, caused us to make fast againe.[4] God thinke upon our imprisonment with a *supercedias*. This evening Sun dog,[5] I hope may bring some change to our good.[6]

28. This overcast day proved faire, and a pretty W.N.W. gale, untill towards night. My Carpenter made straight a peece above the backe of our Rudder, which was set awry with the ice.[7] I caused the lead to be cast in 220

---

[1] "Yet they serve us to contend about." (*Foxe MS.*)

[2] "We lay still fast among the Ice, and no speeches but of discoveries of new Islands and strange sets of Tides betwixt the Master and his Mate, [who are] the most discontented men in the world. I would with all my heart they were changed, and others in their places. I have no incouragement from them." (*Foxe MS.*)

[3] One of Foxe's side-notes says "Vapour Land".—C.

[4] "which making fast I always found the Master willing, and the Company as willing on the other side to prefer the Voyage; for the often sounding of the pumps could not dishearten them; for they were always as willing as I could desire, either to bear the ice from the ship, or to shift the fenders from place to place to save the ship's sides." (*Foxe MS.*)

[5] Captain Wharton, R.N., writes that the sun-dog is "a fragmentary bit of rainbow".—C.

[6] "Variation 29^d 5^m." (*Master's MS.*)

[7] "which being a little piece put about the lower back in Taler's Dock. This Taler hath mainly abused us in the sheathing and working the Carpenter's work of the ship." (*Foxe MS.*)

fathomes, but the under-ebbe-tide did carry it so far to the E. as wee could not thinke wee had lesse stray then 30 fathomes.[1] The ground was small blacke sand, with long crooked things the length of a needle, and the small body of two shell fishes, like Lobsters, but no bigger then Maggots.[2]

29. This faire hot day is now almost neere at end. We lye amongst the [blocks of] Ice, and I doe not know what wind to pray for to quit us of them, they lie so thicke every way[3]; but I thinke we feare more danger then wee are in.[4] God, for his mercies' sake, set us at libertie. I can perceive we drive to the N.W.-ward, and have 210 fathomes of water under vs The Sunne set cleere this Evening.

30. This hot day is also at an end. I have had an Ayre of wind, with all sayle on board, and, threading betwixt the Ice, got about 4 miles N.W.-wards, and stucke fast againe. By the way, I came by one peece of Ice something higher then the rest, whereupon a stone was, of the Contents of 5 or 6 Tonne weight, with divers other smaller stones and mudde thereon. It seemeth to condescend with reason that these peeces of ice are ingendred upon the Winter's snow, which, falling in drifts by the forcing & wheeling of the wind, condensing and compacting a great quantity together over the steepe brow of some high mountaine, cleaving thereto untill [the] dis-

---

[1] Presumably Foxe means that the current carried his lead-line so far out of the perpendicular as to add at least thirty fathoms to the real depth.—C.

[2] Foxe's observations on natural objects are often ludicrously vague and unscientific, as in the above instance. The creatures were probably small crustaceans of some kind. "Fine pepery sand with the feet and horns of small crawfish" (*Master's MS.*).—C.

[3] "When it is wind, we do not sail [in order] to save the ship; when it is calm, we cannot." (*Foxe MS.*)

[4] "We lie here in greater danger than I dare make shew of." (*Foxe MS.*)

solving time of the yeare, when the earth receives her naturall warmnesse, [are] then inforced by their weight to tumble into the Sea, carrying with them all such trees or stones as they have formerly inclosed.[1] God be thanked, the [blocks of] Ice begun to thinne and separate; this hot weather doth fast dissolve them.

This night, clocke 2, came a small Iland of Ice, brought up with the latter flood, and, by his draught being deeper in the Tydes' way then the flact or masht Ice,[2] had a greater motion continued by the undertyde then that which had inclosed us, of which we were fast unto one of the biggest content[s], to wit 3 Acres. This Iland did drive right with us, and, but that some few masht Ice interposed, thereby diverting the course thereof some 2 or 3 ship's lengths, it had drove directly upon us, and had crusht us, mainely, if not to peeces, it being 9 or 10 fathomes above water.[3] And, if it had boarded us, being undermined by the waters continuall working, the outside thereof, by that shake, might have fallen into the ship and have sunke her. This was the greatest danger we were in since I came into *Fretum Hudson*, the fault being in the watch, who did not call, that we might have set the ship the one way or the other about the peece we were fast unto, before we were so ingaged as I could doe neither. About one houre after, the said Iland tooke his

---

[1] Foxe's description of a glacier and theory of the formation of icebergs (see also p. 288) was highly ingenious for the period, though it is observable that he had no conception of the gradual forward motion now known to take place in glaciers. Foxe hereafter repeats his views on these subjects (see p. 295).—C.

[2] Query, *flaked* or small floe-ice, as distinguished from icebergs (p. 288).—C.

[3] "It forced other Ice upon us so that it endangered our ship very much; for it sore bruised us between two great pieces of ice, [so] that to a man's judgment it was impossible for a ship to swim...." (*Master's MS.*)

recourse backe againe to the East with the ebbe, faster then the other ice could doe.

July 1. This morning, 8, the Sunne was up before we saw it. The day was warm and close, but calme, so as I could not stirre for want of wind. The straight doth cleere, and this N. land that hath continued with us since we departed with *Resolution*, it now bearing from E. and by S. to N. & by E. If *Baffin* writ truely that *Resolution* is an Iland, separate from this, then is this another (though formerly taken for the N. Maine), and longer, as shall be showne at my returne homeward.[1] The tyde doth set as the land doth lie, South-East and North-west.

This night, 7, it was an Ayre, farre better than a younger brother.[2] The ice [being] well thinn'd, I caused the ship to be loosed,[3] and by that time the Master with the boat was come from killing of Fowle; I stood to the N., about foure miles. This fayre day being at an end, I made fast, set the watch, and went to Cabbin.

2. This morning, 2, an easie gale breathed from the E. by South, which caused mee to send to the boatswaine to call up the Company, when a chiefe one amongst us, being too suddenly awaked, speaking something peevishly, I told the rest that the matter was not great, for the children did so when they were awaked out of their sleep. I began now to find the want of a Shallop, which at home

---

[1] As nearly as one can understand this confused sentence, Foxe was under a wrong impression. There is no island in the position indicated. Foxe's MS has it "There doth show, as it were, a parting of Land, of a mile at most in breadth. . . . The Master and Mate doth make the E. for Resolution, and that parting for the North Channel, and the other Northward for the North Main; but my opinion is that it is all Resolution, and the opening the Harbour Baffin was in" [see p. 206].—C.

[2] This is a pun!—C.   [3] See p. 180.—C.

I did so earnestly desire,[1] for my Cocke-boat[2] would nor Rowe nor Sayle to any purpose, so as I durst hardly send her from me; for, when it was any billow, she was not to be rowed, and with saile to windward shee would doe nothing, although I had caused a large Lee-board to be made to helpe her.

This Meridianall observation, the wind came West, and I was in 61 d. 57 m.,[3] and stood in close to this inremarkeable shore, & so all the land within this straight may be called, for it is all shoring or descending from the highest mountaine to the Sea. Whereon the Snow, falling by degrees, doth presse and burthen itselfe, making the masse more solid, which, at the Spring time, when it looseneth from the earth, its own weight doth force downward into the Sea; being all composed of fresh water, it may be conceived that the most Ice we meete in this passage is thus ingendered.[4] In the Vallies betwixt the Mountaines is some Snow undesolved. We are now cleere of chattered Ice, yet (in sight) are some Islands [of ice], about which wee can compasse as we please. Here lyeth many small Ilands close by the Mayne,[5] and there doth appear to be fayre sounds into the land. Upon the Sea, this calme time that hath beene, doth swimme a kind of corrupt

---

[1] "But it is not this alone that is wanting, but many other things, all which I gave in to Sr John Westonholme in a Particular. He urged for me, but to no purpose. The Trinity Master to whom I was referred would not allow of [them]. The want of a Shallop was indeed the Master's fault, for there be some men that doth think they should not be thought wise if they do not alter or add to other men's devices when they see them; but yet I hope all these wants notwithstanding will not be wanting" (*Foxe MS*) It seems, however, that Foxe took out a pinnace with him in pieces, for he tells (p. 340) how he fitted her together in Port Nelson, but afterwards had to abandon her.—C

[2] A cock-boat is a small boat used in rivers or near the shore.—C.

[3] "Andrew Hume was but in 61° 35′." (*Foxe MS.*)

[4] See *ante*, p. 288.—C.

[5] The Isles of God's Mercy, so named by Hudson.—C.

slime; one may thinke it may come by generation of great fishes, for it feeles soft and unctious, but put it into the fire it will not burne.[1]

I doe thinke that, all this time of our imprisonment, this North shore hath beene free, as I could espie it at *Hiperion's* going downe, valed with a blacke Skreene of moyst Fogge, which wet through our Coates before we see it againe. This fayre daye's West wind blew cold and uncouth from out the passage. Wee are all upon kinde tearmes, drinking one to another. God hold it.

3. This morning the Sunne lickt up the Fogge's dew as soone as hee began to rise and made a shining day of it. I cannot say hot, it being counter-checkt by a coole Topsayle Gale[2] from West-North-West, which made our Noses runne. The cleare day emboldened me to stand within two leagues of land, to the deepe of 32 fathomes. The ground white sand and gray, with shels; the water was falling.[3] The houre 11 before noone, the Sunne and Moone in opposition, a good Tyde set along the shoare to the Northwards. The Sunne set cleare. It was faire weather and calme. The ship drove along the shore this night to the Westward.

4. This morning at clocke one, I called to lanche the Boate, to send to shore to try the Tyde, and, against that time that I could send to land, I had drawne those instructions following, and giving them to *Iohn Coatesworth*,[4]

---

[1] "A kind of corrupt slime, stinking, but doth not burn [on] being put into the fire." (*Foxe MS.*)

[2] Captain Wharton writes:—"I can only guess this to mean a force of wind in which topsails could be carried."—C.

[3] "Lat. 62° 10'." (*Foxe MS.*)

[4] This man is several times mentioned, but the post he held is not stated. Foxe evidently had considerable faith in him, and afterwards made him boatswain. The printed narrative here differs from Foxe's MS., which contains a long account of the sending on shore of the boat. From this it appears that it was, not Coatsworth, but

whom I appointed alway to goe in the boate, at whose returne I expected an account.

THESE ARE THE INSTRUCTIONS.

First, You shall take with you into the boate one halfe-houre glasse, one halfe-minute glasse, one logge and line,[1] cleane Paper, one Pensill of blacke Leade, and one Compasse, with some peeces of Iron.

Secondly, One quarter Saw, two Axes, three Carbine Guns, with Powder and Shot, two or three Lances, two Swords, two Pikeaxes, and every man his one day bread.

Thirdly, At your departure from the ship, turne the halfe-houre, and when it is neere out, set your Logge to goe by the halfe minute, that thereby you may estimate the distance betweene the ship and land, as also what the boate can rowe an houre.

Fourthly, When you shall approch neere the shore in the Tyde's way (I meane cleare of Bay-point or Rocke), Anchor the Boat, sound the deepe, and marke the Tyde how it doth set, and by your Logge what it doth passe in the halfe minute. Having rode there for halfe a Glasse, weigh your Anchor and goe to land, and duely observe what quantity of water it doth flow or fall perpendiculer in one Glasse, whether the heightening or lessening be equall in every Glasse while yee stay, or noe

Fifthly, Being thus on land with your Compasse, set all Lands or Islands in sight, draw the forme with your paper and Pensill, and estimate their distance.

Sixtly, Remember I give you no libertie to goe within the land. Yet, if [you land] for recreation, goe no further then the full Seamarke, and armed, leaving two to keepe the Glasse and Boat. Looke

---

Urin, the Master's Mate, who went in charge of her. It seems that, on his return, he complained that it was not a suitable hour to send the boat on shore, and grumbled about other matters, giving an account to the Master, but not to Foxe. The Master, it seems, supported him in his complaints and was very impertinent, which leads Foxe to say. "I fear a Mutiny or Hindrance to the Voyage, yet I have good hopes of all the men . but Sir John Westonholme was much to blame in thinking to cross me (and thus I doubt to cross the Voyage) when there are many noble and gentle engaged as well as he ; and, if it please God I do live to come home, I will make it appear that the Trinity Masters are as much to blame and more to put off a Voyage of this consequence so inconsiderably."—C.

[1] See note on Foxe's use of the log on p. 371.—C.

for stones of Orient colour[1] or of weight, Seamors teeth,[2] Vnicornes' horne,[3] or Whale Finne,[4] Plants, Herbes, or anything Spungy [that may] fleet out of the Sea. If you finde Scurvie grasse, Orpin[5] or Sorrill, bring them all on board to me.

Seventhly, If you will goe above the full Sea-marke, looke for footing of wilde Beasts, by that or their dung, you may imagine what thay are ; if Deere, do not chase them into the land for feare of being betrayed, for the people in those parts are all treacherous, how faire soever they intreat you. Remember also that the losse of you or the boate is the utter overthrow of the whole Voyage.

Eightly, If you finde of their Tents, and they fled, doe noe harme to any of their buildings, but bring with you the most things of marke, leaving in the same place a peece of Iron, bigger or lesser, as you estimate the same to be of worth unto us And, so neare as you can, chuse a beach or sandy Bay to land in, for there you shall espie most liklihood of Inhabitants

Ninthly, Leave one Carbine, one Lance, and one short Sword to defend the boat, with whose (two) keepers you shall give charge that, if either they shall espie any token from the ship, as striking the maine Topsaile, Mison, and Spritsaile, Gunshot, or Firesmoke, or be assaulted by any of the Inhabitants, that then they shall discharge the said Carbine To the first intent that you repaire with speed on board ; to the second, for their rescue and your owne saftie When you come cleere in the tyde's way, try it as before [directed] in the 4 article. The rest is referred to your own discretion, & so I pray God for your safe returne.

4. This morning at clocke 6, the wind came faire, the weather like to be thicke and raine. I beckoned them to come on board, but they saw me not. At their departing, the dawning being cleare, the Ayre calme, and it was within an houre of Sun-rising, the Sea smooth, the ship nearer the shoare then at any time before since we came into the passage, and the whole day towards,[6] I would not loose this opportunity to send to land the boat. After

---

[1] That is, bright, shining, or glittering, as the rays of the rising sun.—C.

[2] See p. 189.—C.   [3] See p. 45.—C.
[4] See p. 208.—C.   [5] See p. 232.—C.

[6] This clearly means that the whole day *was before them*, but I do not find the word used in just this sense in any Dictionary.—C.

5 houres, they returned and gave account that it was flood-tide about clocke 5, and that they thinke it flowed halfe an houre. The land lay N.N.W. In this time, with the ship, we drive by an Iland of Ice aground in 50 fathome. They found where people had been of old; their Tent walls[1] were of stones, laid one upon another, & square built; found one knife haft[2]; three severall sorts of herbes, but my Chirurgion knew not what they were; [and] one peece of drift wood. They [also] found the dung and footing of Deere (lately made); and, if they may be beleeved, they affirme that, in ¼ of an houre, it did flow above 4 foot water, and that it had above 5 fathomes upright to flow to the full Sea marke, which they could easily perceive by the beach, they being forced to rowe and saile 4 miles before they could come to a place to land at. This E.S.E. wind blew on, with stiffe gale and durt.[3] At noone it fell thicke raine, and continued untill 4 next day morning, in which time wee made way neare 30 leagues in cleare Sea, and then had like to have beene imbayed, which Ices lyeth thick off *Prince Henries* Foreland,[4] the South land bearing round from W.N.W. ½ Westerly to 108 degrees Southwards; to cleere which wee were glad to put tackes a board, and turne it forth to the Northwards, where it was cleare of Ice.

5. This morning the Sun was vailed with drisling raine. I stood over for the N. shoare; the Master would have perswaded me to stand over for the S., saying the Capes on the S. which wee had seene were *Savage* Ilands,

---

[1] In more than one other place (see pp. 298 and 311), Foxe uses the word *tent* in a way that would make it include buildings of stone, but I cannot find that the word ever had that meaning generally.—C.

[2] "I hear they found a knife-haft, but Urin hath it." (*Foxe MS.*).

[3] Presumably *dirty weather* is meant.—C.

[4] So named by Hudson after Henry Prince of Wales (see Introduction, p. xvii); but now known as Cape Hope's Advance.—C.

so named by *Bylot*.¹ This, being after wee had an observation of 62 deg. 40 min,² we had some circumstance about it, but he went away well satisfied,³ and it proved as I tolde him, for at night wee had *Savage* Ilands N, but noe land Northward in sight.⁴ This evening the Sunne set with a weather gall opposite,⁵ and *Zephyrus* blewe on a pretty gale. At the same instant, the lead was wet in 150 fathomes, the line having 20 fath straie to the E, and I thought the Tyde set W. The most of this day, I stood away N.W., but was glad sometime to alter course to the N. for Ice, for the S land lay all full [of ice].

6. This day hath bin very hot. Before this S. wind came, I did thinke the wind had blowne either right up or right downe the passage, viz. E. or W., as for the most part it doth. The W. is cleare, fair and hot Sun-shine,

---

¹ "so named by Baffin" (*Foxe MS.*)

² Variat 29 d --F "Variation 24ᵈ" (*Foxe MS*). If, as appears to be the case, Foxe was at this time some way to the south of the Savage Islands, which are in Lat 62° 35′ N., this observation must be wrong.—C.

³ This is the first piece of evidence the book affords of the differences and ill-feeling which existed between Foxe and his lazy sailing-master, but there are many passages in Foxe's MS. which show how badly they got on together (see Introduction, p lxxxvii) Many of these I have already quoted in the preceding pages It may be explained here that, in the Royal Navy of those days, the "Master" was the officer charged with the sailing of the ship, under the general orders of the Captain, who held supreme command This officer is now known as the "navigating lieutenant" In merchant ships, the terms "master" and "captain" have come to be all but synonymous.—C.

⁴ "All this time, I would have borne to the S -ward of the Islands, but the Captain would not." (*Master's MS*)

⁵ A weather-gall, or wind-gall, is "à luminous halo on the edge of a distant cloud, where there is rain, usually seen in the wind's eye, and looked upon as a sure precursor of stormy weather" (Smyth's *Sailors' Word-Book*, p. 733).—C.

but the aire is cold when it veereth about, as once in 3 dayes, and by the S. it is either thick raine, soft sleet, or warme fog, the wind E. or thereabout; these done, he changeth to the W. againe, bringing the weather faire as before.[1] I did thinke that this day the Tide set forth; this morning we saw Cape *Charles*[2] 12 leag off, S.S East.[3]

7. The Sunne did rise cleare At clocke 8 came on a Fogge, and continued unto one. Wee had store of Ice to the S. off us; then it cleared, and we were come to the Westward, amongst much ice,[4] and had sight of a high Iland bearing W, about 6 or 7 leag. off.[5] Wee saw also

---

[1] From Foxe's MS, it would appear this means that the West winds brought clear fair weather; the East, rain and fog.—C.

[2] Probably the cape on Charles Island. Hudson mistook the Island for part of the mainland, but he named Mount Charles, which is on it.—C

[3] *Hudson* named all on the S. in his Straite.—F. "I did hasten to put through [the Ice], which the fearful Master observing came forwards and told me we should run ourselves among the Ice, we knew not whither I answered that we came to run and go, and that we must do both, and therefore [I] wished he would be contented, which he seldom is, except he be in the boat shooting at Willocks or asleep. The men take notice of this fearful alteration, and doth but laugh behind his back, and they may well Seeing God hath done so much for us, blessed be his name . He doth but show us danger; and no men ever before entered this passage with so good weather, and of such long continuance; for it is as hot on [some] days as in Scotland. The west wind only is sharp, making our noses run like limbecks [*i.e.*, alembics or stills], for certain, the air is far more sufferable than report makes it . . . This day in 63° 10'." (*Foxe MS.*)

[4] "At 12, the Master coming to his watch . . . [said] we must about. . . . Well, I would not trust him, and therefore staied up to conduct the Ship 2 Glasses. . . . Going into my Cabin to ease myself, being weary with watching and wet, I fell asleep, and he bore to the leeward 4 Glasses, just as at our entering [into the Strait] he had [done] before, and also would have done the like again, but I would not suffer [it]." (*Foxe MS.*)

[5] Probably Salisbury Island.—C.

the high land of the N. maine 12 leag. off.[1] The Sun set valed, and we had no ground at 150 fath. It fell to raine and I tooke in both topsailes, and stood to and againe among the Ice.

8.[2] This morning was cold, with some snow, and the W. wind blew hard. We made the ship fast to a great peece of yce, which she plowed through the rest, by force of the Gale, although we had made her as snug as we could. At Noone, we were in 63 deg. 31 min.[3] Now the wind calmed, and I made loose, and stood to the N., and at Sun setting I had sight of the N. maine again.[4] The Sun set cleare this evening.

10. This morning's Sun raise cleare, and I stood to the N., close to an Iland nere the Maine, which Iland at my returne I named Ile *Nicholas*.[5] From which, with a S.W. wind, I stood over to the Southward, and stood with the Iland I saw the 7th day before I hoped it would prove *Salisbury*. This day ended, wee made fast againe,[6] for all this North Channell was thick with ice, upon which we filled 2 hoggsheads with fresh water. I loosed againe, and with a small gale came within 4 miles of *Salisburies* Iland, for it can be no other; it is high land but not cliffed. I caused to make fast againe, for that nere the land and the middle Channell was all full of ice, and no ground at 120

---

[1] Probably the high land near Cape Dorset.—C.

[2] This should be 9th (see Foxe MS).—C.

[3] Both the MS. and one of Foxe's marginal notes say 63° 40'.—C.

[4] Probably it was again about Cape Dorset.—C.

[5] Foxe afterwards says —"I named it in remembrance of Master Edward Nicholas, secretary to the said Lords [of the Admiralty, after whom he also named capes or islands], whom I have often troubled."—C

[6] "as both the Master and Mait are always willing to do, but never once wished me to move from them again, he so long as I will. Nothing grieves them both but that they came upon this voyage." (*Foxe MS.*)

fath., and untill 6 the tide set Westward, and then it returned. What tide it was I could not discerne, although I came so nere the land for that purpose. I made loose againe presently, because the Master's mate was of opinion that it was cleare to the W., or at least that was the clearest way.[1] For my parte, I had no more purpose to have tryed betweene *Salisbury* and the N. maine or *Mill* Ile (so named by *Bylot*), for *Mill* Ile, being a great Iland lying in the middle of the N. Channell, must needs straiten all the ice that fleets from the N.W. Yet, for the good of the Voyage, it was fit to try all conclusions; but, thus striving to the W, we were presently inclosed againe, where we lay vntill the next morning, all too nere the Iland if I could have got further off.

[11.] This night had a stiffe gale at West with one showre of raine. The Sunne was obscured 2 howres before night, and wee slept safe in our old Innes.[2]

12 I cald at clocke 3, and by 6, with haleing, saleing toweing, and pulling, wee were got cleere, and thought to have gone about the East end of the Iland, but the flood faceing of the winde had choaked all the East end, so, their being one glade or cleere [space] betweene the shoare and the Channell ice, we plied it up therein for 2 or 3 miles, but, comming nere the W. end, it was all choaked there, so, shutting betweene one and another for the N. Mayne, I stood to see what better comfort; but at halfe straite ouer I was forced back againe for ice and Fogge.[3]

---

[1] "The Master's Mate, Urin, hath, by his growling, caused me to stand along the land to the West; yet I doubt, without some accident happens, this is our wrong way." (*Foxe MS*)

[2] This is one of Foxe's figurative phrases. It appears simply to mean that they slept in their berths, as usual. Foxe's MS. here says: "Mr. Urin hath had his pleasure of the ship's going W.-ward and, finding it all choked up with ice, hath made the ship fast."—C.

[3] "The Master, being come forth of his cabin in my absence, was treating of the small hopes of the voyage and using disheartening

Well, wee stand againe for *Salisburies* Ile, of which I was now assured, and so named by my predecessour *Hudson* after the right honourable and not to be forgot *Robert Cicell*, Earle of *Salisbury*, then Lord High Treasurer of *England*, an honourable furtherer and Adventurer in this designe, as well as in others, as appeareth by Sir *Walter Raleigh* in his *Guianian* discoveries.[1] In my standing over, I espied a glade, wherein I hoped, if I did returne, I might recover the N. Maine, wherefore I called to tackle about[2] the ship.

The Master, not seeing what was on the weather Bowe, bid the helme man put on Lee. The ship, obeying her helme, presently answered, so as in her winding, her way being not fully ended, she checkt upon a peece of ice and twined off her cut-water which was before the stemme[3]; thus constrained, I bore up the helme and went along to the East end of the Ile; and, makeing fast to a peece of Ice, the Carpenter made good againe the hurt wee had

---

speeches. . I fear [for] the voyage when the master doth begin to meddle and his mate also." (*Foxe MS*)

[1] Robert Cecil, 1st Viscount Cranborne, was created Earl of Salisbury in 1605, and died in 1612. He was Lord High Treasurer of England, and one of Hudson's Adventurers, but, as he died just before the granting of the Charter to the North-West Passage Company in July 1612, the credit for the latter is given in the Charter to his son and heir, William, second Earl, who was one of those incorporated.—C.

[2] Probably a misprint for *tack about*.—C.

[3] The first harme & all I received.—F. This may be taken to refer to the whole voyage, and it was a great deal for one of the early north-west explorers to be able to say. The cutwater is the sharp part of a vessel's prow. It projects forward and cuts the water, dividing it before the vessel's bows. The Master, who throws the blame on the Captain, says in his MS "This day, having much wind and thick [weather], I desired the Captain that we might hand our sails and not to come so much among the Ice, being thick and foggy, but he would not; but, within half an hour we ran against a piece of ice and broke away a piece of our stern, with our Cutwater, but we knew not what hurt we had done under water."—C.

received. In the meane time, our men went to supper. The afternoone was more then seven houres old before this was done; then I called againe to make loose; for I thought that the ice was now, with wind and ebbe, well cleared from the East end of the Iland, as it proved; but many discontented and doubtfull speeches past[1]; but to no purpose; for I must runne to discover this losse time[2]; when motion was made to make fast againe, which I denyed for these reasons:—that wee could see the Sea to be reasonable free and cleere at the East end from the Iland, and the South Channell would be to be dealt withall, or, if not, the passage was forbidden untill the ice were dissolved. And, to fasten nere the land, I would upon no condition listen unto, for the winde comming to blow to land, I must upon necessity bee put thereon, the Shippe alwayes pulling the ice she was fast unto faster then the other could drive. And for anckoring there was none, if the land had not beene steepe to; for the Eddie Tides, which every Rocke, Bay, or poynt made, would have wheeled the Shippe about in the ice, so as it had not beene possible to have kept my rudder from breakeing, and amongst ice there was no loosing of any saile to have beaten it off shoare.[3] It seemeth these reasons had

---

[1] "We had all supped and I called to make loose the Ship from the Ice, which the willing men did. The Master said to me, in mocking, I must launch the boat to fetch the men on board." (*Foxe MS.*)

[2] No doubt he means, to *recover lost time*, as in his MS.—C.

[3] A passage Foxe here introduces into his MS. is worth quoting, as it shows his conscientious resolve to do his duty. He says "I would not lose one minute that God would give me to employ for the good of the Voyage, if it were but set forth by Private Merchants. For it is a Voyage of the greatest consequence; the King [being] our Adventurer (who could well spare the Ship), together with the Nobility and Gentry of the Realm, all which expected more from us than [from] any of our Predecessors; and what a shame it would be for us to go home and pass [along] the streets to be pointed at, as we were worthy to be. For my part, the Adventurers should see us home (if it was the Ship's

the force of perswasion, for wee willingly past about the Ile to the South, as well where we found all over-laid with ice, so that wee must make fast; having toyled thus all day untill night, I thought it fit to repose.

13 This morning, clock 4, I called to make loose. We had much to doe to get cleere, being all fast immured. It was easie wind. I could perceive by the bearing of the land that we had drove above 2 miles S.-wards; now wee thred-needles[1] to the East, hopeing, at further distance from the Ile, to get cleare into the South channell. At clocke 10, the West winde brought on thick Fogges, so as we could not see one hole to peepe through. The ice inclosed us and there we lay; it blew hard untill clocke 7, then it both calmed and cleared. I loosed and, plying 2 leagues to the Southwards, had the South Maine in sight from the South-East to the S West

14. All this day, untill night 7, we kept our colde lodging,[2] and then, looseing with an easie breath from N.E., we

---

fortune to come home, which I did not make any doubt of) and with the best voyage that ever any people made, all things considered; that I had not taken their money and eat up their provision like a Slave to cousin them and so go home, but, while life lasted, I would have the voyage proceeded Nor did I care for their growling or grumbling; for, if they did but know how little I cared for it, they would never vex themselves to make a laugh" (*Foxe MS.*). Much more in the same strain follows Foxe tells the Master that the want of a shallop was his fault, for the Master had altered the list of requisites that he himself had drawn up, "thinking you should not be thought wise if you could not in one instance better and alter the devices of another that had been hammering and enquiring 20 years about the same [*i e*, the voyage]; besides 20 Iron bonne Poyes [?] and 12 ship howers [? oars], all which you are now come without, although I put you oft in mind of them; but, because you did not devise them, they were needless, and now you see the want of them."—C·

[1] This is one of Foxe's figurative phrases, and may be taken to mean that he threaded his way to the eastward through narrow lanes of water between the masses of ice.—C.

[2] "God, for thy Mercy's sake, send what thou knowest we stand

minnemd¹ betwixt ice and ice S.Westward untill we got cleare. In which time came under the sheeting of our head (easie to have been strooke, if our provisions² had beene ready) a Sea *Vnicorne*. He was of length about 9 foot; back ridged, with a small fin thereon; his taile stoode [a]crosse his ridge, and indented between the pickends, as it were, on either side with 2 Scallop shels; his side dapled purely with white and blacke³; his belly all milke-white; his shape, from his gils to his taile, was fully like a Makarell; his head like to a Lobster, whereout the fore-part grewe forth his twined horne, above 6 foote long, all blacke save the tip. This evening I had sight of 20 more. The Sun set cleare, and this easie gale continued from the E.N E. All night, wee stood S.W., having the straite cleare to the S.

15. This delicate morning, the ice seemed to trent from *Salisburies* Ile into the middle channell. I caused the

---

in need of, for, if it thus hold, it will break my heart. I have no comfort of one or the other nor doth any man bear a part of [the] care with me We lie fast here; he eats and drinks and is well pleased to sleep two ☉. That this noble voyage should be lost for want of fitting associates!" After stating that the Master and his Mate were both East Indiamen, Foxe continues. "Too late do I remember Mr Briggs, who, in his letter, gave me warning not to carry an East Indiaman, a man of war, or one out of the king's ships; but I could not do [so] withall I write truth, compelled by grief, for these fellows think to spin out time, and have wages due, come home and take it, never meaning to come here again, as they have vowed.... Now are they well pleased, while I grieve; for they are never pleased without, every night at least, the ship be tied to ice.... Well; tobacco, strong water, and the warm cabin are their only companions; yet they complain of Mr. Giles, who hath not made the Aqua Vita strong enough." (*Foxe MS*)

¹ I can trace no such word. In Foxe's MS journal the word is *passed*—C.

² This word (now generally used in a more restricted sense) had once a wider meaning, and implied anything provided beforehand. —C.

³ "All spotted as a Panther" (*Foxe MS.*)

sailes to be clewed up, and lie untill *Sol's* beautifull appearance, and, at that fit opportunity, wet the lead in 60 fath., the E. end of *Salisbury* lying N. by E. from me about 4 leag., the W end (which is *Salisburies* plain) N W. about 4 leag. of[f], *Nottingham* at that instant peeping out from beyond it, about 7 leag. off; I stood to the S., into ⅓ of the channell, shooting shuttles in the old loome[1]; and heare the lead fell downe 160 fath. before ground made it stay. It brought from thence such stones as lye upon the most of the ice here in this part of the passage, especially brought from the Mayne, cleaving to the Ice by winter's frost (more broad then thicke), at whose dissolving they fall to the bottome, and the yeerely Ice, since the generall Deluge, bringing in such quantity cannot chuse but have covered all the upper part of the Sea's bottome there.[2] All this ice is but chattered[3] No great Ilands since we came by the Ile of *God's Mercy*, so that here may be a plaine argument remonstrated, that the Tide, setting more strongly into *Fretum Hudson* then the ebbe doth set forth, doth haile in those mountaine's bred in the W. side

---

[1] This metaphorical expression seems to mean that they were perpetually tacking, passing backwards and forwards, like the shuttle of a loom.—C

[2] This observation of Foxe's is of great interest for the period at which it was made. Had he known enough to apply it properly, he would have hit upon an important geological fact at least two centuries in advance of the time when it first became recognised; for it is only within the last thirty years or so that geologists have come to recognise that the "boulder clay", which covers so large an area in Central and Eastern England, and consists of an unstratified clay, full of ice-worn stones and boulders, owes its origin to the melting of icebergs, as they floated southwards on a sea which, during the glacial period, covered the southern part of our island, dropping, as they melted, the stones and dirt which they had brought from their more northerly home, just as those which Foxe observed in Hudson's Strait were doing, and are still doing to this day.—C.

[3] That is, *shattered*. Probably it is a misprint.—C.

of *Fretum Davis*, into *Fretum Hudson*, as they are passing by to the South.[1]

As also this may be noted: that here, and especially nere within the mouth of this strait, the Compasse doth almost loose his sensitive part, not regarding his magneticall *Azimuth*, without much stirring. The smooth water may be some cause, the Ship wanting her active motion; but I should [think it] strange that the cold should benum it, as it doth us. Nay, I should rather think that the sharpenesse of the ayre, interposed betwixt the needle and his attractive point, may dull the power of his determination; or here may be some mountaines, of the one side or the other, whose Minerals may detaine the nimblenesse of the needles mooving to his respective poynt; but this I leave to Phylosophie.[2]

By this time, the kind E.N.E breese hath brought me nere the Iland of *Nottingham*, and I am making ready to send the boate on land (within 2 miles) to try the tyde, having cast the lead amongst shels and stones 35 fathomes

---

[1] This is nonsense. In Foxe's MS it reads "No great Islands [i e, Icebergs] since we came from Resolution, [which] makes me conceive that the Mountain Islands at the Passage mouth and thereabouts is Ice bred in Fretum Davis and the bottom of Baffin's Bay [that], in their setting S.-wards, drove into the mouth of this Straight by the Tides."—C.

[2] Foxe's speculations as to the properties of the needle are amusing, and wide of the mark. It need hardly be said that the sluggishness of the needle is in no way due to the temperature or the proximity of mountains, but that what Foxe observed was due to electrical disturbance, and to the proximity of the magnetic pole. A very extraordinary idea as to the properties of the needle occurs at this point in Foxe's MS., wherein a portion of the above paragraph reads: "the ship wanting her action, but I should seeing that she could shake, if here in the land there be no Unicorns." This is obviously nonsense, due to some clerical error; but it appears to mean that Foxe thought there might be unicorns inhabiting the adjacent lands, whose presence affected the compass! Extraordinary as were the properties ascribed to the horn of the unicorn (see p. 45), I cannot find that the compass was ever supposed to be affected by it.—C.

deepe.¹ Sir *Dudly Diggs* his Iland bare from mee W.S.W.; the E. part of *Nottingham*, E.S.E.,² the Pole elevated 63 d. 12 min.; and, comming betwixt Cape *Wolstenholme* and the E. end of *Nottingham*, at noon I met the ebbe comming from the N.W., as I could perceive by the over falls. I towed my boate into 19 fathomes, and sent her on land, driving along the Iland untill her returne.

16. These Iles, as *Resolution*, *Salisbury*, and *Nottingham*, are high at the East end and low at the West; this Iland was also named by Master *Hudson*, in due bequest to that most honourable Lord *Charles Howard*, Earle of *Nottingham*, then Lord high Admirall of *England*, a small remembrance for the charge, countenance and instruction given to the Search of the enterprise, and, though smaller,³ yet, being by his Lordship accepted, neither time nor fame ought to suffer oblivion to burie, for, whensoever it shall please God to ripen those seedes, and make them readie for his sickle whom he hath appoynted to be the happie reaper of this crop, must remember to acknowledge that those honourable and worthy personages were the first Advancers.⁴

The boate went at clocke 5 in the afternoone; they were away 5 glasses. It was flood, and in one houre it flowed 10 inches; they said that it had 2 houres to flow, and had about 2 foot to high.⁵ They brought a little fire-wood and

---

¹ Latit. 63 d. 20 m.; Variat. 29.—F.

² It seems to me that this should be E.N.E.—C.

³ Query *small*.—C.

⁴ Charles Howard, second Baron Howard of Effingham, was created Earl of Nottingham in 1596, and died in 1624. He was one of those who sent out Hudson, and was also a member of the North-West Passage Company.—C.

⁵ "[Tide] setting to the N.W., but not so strong as Sir Thos. Button reports." (*Master's MS.*)

3 stint birds.[1] They found the foundation of an old Tent.[2] At their comming on board, the W. end of the land bore N. and by E.; the S.E. end, S. by E. I edged off untill I brought the N.W. end N.E., the E. end E. by S. There I caused the boate to anckor in 60 fathomes; the tide came from S.E., 2 leag. a watch. We see great store of Sea Mors playing by the Iland's side. From thence I directed the course S.W., with carrying away with stiffe gale from S.E., with both top sailes a trip all the night, being twi-light, cleare. Some few Ice was in the way, but, by the help of the same[3] (thankes be to God), wee shunned them.

17 This morning, clocke 8, I had sight of *Mansil's* Ile,[4] for I fell right with the North end thereof. It is lowe land, but the highest is to the East. At that instant, I had also sight of Sir *Dudly Diggs* his Iland, and I was not certaine whether I saw the East Mayne or no, for a fogge came on presently. Master *Hudson* also named this Iland of Sir *Dudlie Diggs*, a gentleman who hath planted many of the best Vines in this Vineyard, succeeding his father and Grandfather in the Mathematiks, whose learned knowledge, together with his purse, added no small proportion to this building, to whom my selfe and many others of my quality shall be still beholden while time's age continues.[5]

This afternoone was 3 fogges [and] 2 cleares; the 3 was wet fog. At clocke 7, I thought I see Cape *Pembrooke*

---

[1] These were probably the American Stint (*Tringa minutilla*), which breeds abundantly throughout the region Foxe was now in.—C.

[2] See p. 299.—C. "They saw the foundations of an old Tent, a place the Savages do stack up their Food in." (*Foxe MS*)

[3] By this, he clearly means the twilight.—C.

[4] Foxe here rightly spells the name. It is usually spelled *Mansfield*, which is wrong (see p. 188). Even Foxe spells it so in his MS.—C.

[5] For a brief notice of Sir Dudley Diggs, see p 118.—C.

upon [the] N. Mayne. At clocke 4, I had 90 fath. This afternoone, wee see many Sea-Mors, and had store of Ice W. from this Iland of Sir *Robert Mansils* (I thinke so named by Sir *Thomas Button*, as also Cape *Pembrooke*, *Southampton*, and *Carie Swans'* nest, the last most eminent of the 3).[1] I stood, as Ice would give leave, S W. and to the Westward. At clocke 8, wee clewd up all sailes and drive 2 leag. in 18 houres. The next morning 4, wee had 120 fath, owsie ground; at 7 before, the deepe was but 96. Here wee see Sea-Mors; had one sight of the Sunne in the afternoone; and all this day we heard the Sea beate upon the ice to windward of us.

18. Wee stood 2 glasses to the North with wind at East, to get cleare off the ice wee drive in all this last night, and had those depths at 55, 55, 54; the lead brought up a little white Corrall.[2]

I set saile this day at clocke 4, and thought then that I see land at N. It was hazie, and at clocke 12 I thought I had got as much as I lost the day before. I pusled all this day amongst the ice, and at night was glad to make fast to a peece, whereon was a white Beare. The ice here is not so dirty as it hath been, and I iudge my selfe now not farre from *Carie Swans'* nest.

19 Was foggie and calme; the wind all over. The afternoone began to cleare. The Beare came again, and wee pursued him from ice to ice, he swimming and diving At length the Master kild him with a lance, and wee made about 12 gallons of oyle of him, although he was but young.[3] Some of it wee eate boyld; without any [? bad]

---

[1] The origin of this name has already been discussed (p. 165) I cannot explain the reference to the person after which the place was named, as the "most eminent of the three" persons named above —C.   [2] Latit. 62 d. 20 min.—F.

[3] "Our men going on [the Ice], he ran away; our dogs overtook and pinched him; he turned again to the dogs, but would not abide

taste at all, but like beefe; but, being roasted, it tasted oylie and rammish.¹

This night was cleare above head, but [with] fog bankes about the *Horizon*. At clocke 12, there was Pettiedancers or henbanes² (as some write them) North in the firmament, betokening a storme to follow within 24 houres. There was many Starres also in appearance,³ as those of note, *Charles-Wayne*, *Auriga*, *Botes*, and *Antonius*.⁴ I could have no observation, for ice and fogge dimmed the horizon. I thought I see land againe at clocke 8, and had deepe 70 fathomes.⁵

20. The Master cald to make loose this morning,⁶ and all those 3 or 4 dayes wee have beene fast, I could not observe any thing of the tyde's set, yet I doe account wee are not far from *Carie Swans' Nest*. Wee steered as ice would suffer, betweene W.N.W. and W S.W., and did iudge

---

the men, he took the water and could dive . . He was but a young one, but wondrous fat" (*Foxe's MS*) "We made about six gallons of bear's oil" (*Master's MS*.).

¹ That is, strong, rank, and ram-like.— C

² Undoubtedly the Aurora Borealis, or some particular form of it. Admiral Markham, in speaking (*Good Words*, 1888, p. 118) of a brilliant display of aurora seen by him in Hudson's Strait, when on board the *Alert* in 1886, says · "No streamers were visible, but vivid luminous patches would suddenly appear in the heavens near the zenith, and then fade gradually away These luminous patches, occasionally seen with aurorae, are, I think, the same so frequently alluded to by the old navigators as the 'pettie-dancers'" There is a form of the aurora, seen in beautiful perfection in Scotland, where it is known as the "Merry-dancers". Foxe has previously spoken of Auroras as *Harbours* (see p. 193). His MS has it. "At 12, saw (as Sir Thos. Button wishes to be called) Hexbones [?], a sign of a storm to follow within 24 hours"—C

³ The first sight of Starres.—F.

⁴ Perhaps Antinous, part of the Constellation Aquila.—C

⁵ "I stand in doubt we shall be sore troubled with ice and much fog in this *Mare Nigros*, for so may it well be called." (*Foxe MS.*)

⁶ "Which I am very glad of. I hope God will bless our proceedings." (*Foxe MS.*)

wee made way about 4 leagues and one mile; easie winde and reasonable cleare. At clocke 9 wee make fast to the ice, a reasonable distance from a low Iland, as it seemed, for I thought I could see both ends.

Vpon sight hereof, I caused the Boate to be anchored betweene the ship and Iland in 30 fathomes. The tyde went E. 2 knots.[1] The land lay E. and West, but I could not fully say it was an Iland, for it lay like a Ridge, or, to simily it, like to the Retyres, in the mouth of the River of *Saine* in *Normandie*.[2]

I do hold that all those peeces of ice here are ingendered about those low Capes and Bayes, as *Mansils* also is, where easie tides goe; they are soone frose over; the Snow falling thereon thickneth them, so that by degrees they increases. The Pettiedancers, [seen yesterday, neither] brought nor sent us any storme.[3] This night ended in raine, and it was easie wind from the E.N.E.

21. Wee made from the Ice this morning to stand to the land we see last night. It was ebbe tyde, and set to the E., and I plide alongst it to find a fit place for the boate to land in. It was iust at low water, for they were glad to stay the setting of their glasse untill the tyde began to flowe. And after that time, clock 10, they staied untill it began to fall, viz. 4 houres; and so I accounted on ship-board, riding upon 6 fath. nere shoare, the water so transparent as you might easily see the bottome. The ice comming upon us, we weyed Anchor; the wind came

---

[1] 2 miles 1 houre.—F.

[2] No doubt the long, narrow sand-bank, forked at one end, and dry at every tide, which lies in the mouth of the Seine. It is shown on recent Admiralty charts as the "Ratier Bank". There are also two smaller banks, named the "Ratchets", near one end of the larger bank.—C.

[3] "I bless God this assured storm of Sir Thos. Button's Atexbones [?] came but was favourable" (*Foxe MS*)

gently from the N.; we stood it upon the tyde to and againe along the land, loosing and wareing from ice, which came driving with the flood.

At their comming on board, their accompt was this: that the tyde did flowe but 4 howres, and that it heightned but 6 foote; and this was 2 dayes after the Coniunction of the Sunne and Moone, so that the flood began at ½ past 10 and ended at ½ past 2. By this, a South and by W. Moon makes a full Sea; and the tydes motion ends with the flowing. Assuredly this was *Carie Swans'* nest, for both from East and West ends, it stretcheth to the North. Our men chast *Swans* on shoare, but got none. They say there is earth, strange mosse,[1] Quag-myres, and water plashes.[2] At clocke 4, I took leave and stood along from 6 fathomes into 30, loosing sight thereof, and from thence I stood to the Westwards, with North-West wind, close haled, leaving both the Cape and the Ice behinde mee for the Sea-Mors to sleepe upon, there being good store [of them] thereabout.

22. From the Cape or Swannes Nest, this noon-tyde I was 16 leagues and one mile; no ground at 70 fathomes, for I was loth to stay the ship at any time. Me thought sayling had been uncouth, but at 4 this morning I had 90 fathoms, owzy ground. Thicke weather, the wind easie, and shifting betwixt N. and N W. My way was to Southward of West.

23. This Meridian I was in 61 deg. 37 min. At 8 the last day, I tooke the ship about, and made way, untill this day 12, 11 leagues 2 miles N.W. ½ W. It hath beene a faire, cleare day, easie winds, the ayre warm, and no Ice

---

[1] No doubt the lichen known as Iceland Moss (*Cetraria islandica*). —C

[2] *Plash*—a shallow pool or collection of water (see p. 124).—C.

since I came into this Sea (I did but thinke I saw land at N.E. by E.¹

This smooth Sea hath a small set from the West, with lippering,² rising and falling, as other Shallow Seas use to have; the deepe last night was 115 fathomes; I made way to this [day at] 12 N W. by W. ½ W, 13 leagues.

24. This close morning hid the Sunne untill noone, we being in 120 fathomes; the afternoone was cleare, and gently breathed from W.N.W. I have not tryed for fish in this Sea, as I did in *Fretum Hudson*, where I got none. I thanke God here we have not the like leisure³ Here are some Seales, but few Fowles. The latitude of noone was 62 deg. 20 min. Here appeares to be more Riplins of Tyde.⁴ The variation by Azimuth and Almicanter was 26 deg. 31 min. at most. The Sunne went cleare to bed, and at midnight we had 60 fathomes deepe.⁵

25. This morning, Amplitude was 5 deg. The Refraction is great here, and the Horizons thicke, which begets uncertainties, besides the Needle yet is very slow in comming to his respective point.⁶ I now hope for warmer weather, and clearer Sea than heretofore. At noone I had 55 fathomes, in latitude 62 deg. 36 min; since last day, I made way N. by E. 18 leagues. Faire weather; the

---

¹ No doubt Cape Southampton —C

² According to Smyth (*Sailor's Word-Book*), a *lipper* is a sea which washes over the weather side of a ship, or spray from the small waves breaking against her bows. Foxe's MS. reads "The smooth sea hath a set from the W S.W, but not much, and the leaping and falling, as other seas used to have."—C.

³ He means he was not now detained by ice, as he had been in Hudson's Strait, where he fished.—C

⁴ "I hope from the west." (*Foxe MS*)

⁵ "This night the firmament was full of henbeams." (*Foxe MS.*)

⁶ "In smooth water not willing quickly to obey his determinate points" (*Foxe MS*) See note on p. 309.—C.

Sunne went downe cleare.¹ (Ioy to our *Antipodes*). The *Henban* flashing all night.²

26. [This] was a hot day as in *England*. In the mornıng, I had 58 fathomes and white Corrall. The latitude 63 deg. 20 min³ The way since last day was N. 4 deg East, 18 leagues. Since clocke 4, wee lay Larbord Tack N.W. It was a few drops of raine this Evening, yet the Sunne set cleare, and wee had deepe 65 fathomes at midnight, and there was in the Ayre many *Pettie-dancers*.⁴

27 The last night was so hot as it dryed up 15 fathomes water, for this morning we had but 50. The wind was betweene W. and N.N.W.⁵ Here was great store of Rockeweed and Tangle.⁶ In the Ripline of a Tide,⁷ I caused the boat to be lanched in 31 fathomes; the Tyde came from N by W, ½ a mile in an houre.

---

¹ "We have setts of Tyde, but how as yet I know not. I hope from the West" (*Foxe MS.*). "We have had a hummıng sea from the N W. It came not very long, as the sea ın Bıscay Bay, but something shorter This day we found a leak ın our bread-room, which spoılt us much bread, so that we took up all our bread ın the after bread-room, and took up some 300 lbs of wet bread" (*Master's MS*).

² "The Sky was very full of henbeams or pettiedancers I hope token of fair weather" (*Foxe MS*). The connection between the needle's loss of power and the appearance of the Aurora may here be noted.—C.

³ From the MS, ıt appears that the 27th day should commence here.—C

⁴ "The sky had many petty flashıngs red, yet the ☉ arose and set clear" (*Foxe MS*) "The sky flashed and opened much ... Sıght of strange comets ın the aır Variation 28° 40'" (*Master's MS.*). See p 327 for note on the Aurora.—C

⁵ "In 63° 55' Lat. by my three ınstruments, vızt ——— [?] Staff, the Seaman's Rıng, and the Forward Staff." (*Foxe MS.*)

⁶ "We have lost sıght of our falls and stream sets. Thıs nıght we had sıght of Strange Comets in the aır, bloody and gem yellow." (*Master's MS*)

⁷ Presumably *rıpplıng* ıs meant. It was probably a current settıng down Sır Thomas Roe's Welcome.—C.

All this day the fog banks[1] hath deceived mee, but now I am sure I see land, both the maine and Ilands,[2] of which there are many lying about 2 leagues into the Sea, all ragged and broken rocks within. This land bore from N.E. by E. to W by S Here are great store of fish leaping, and fairer weather cannot be I have sent the boat to land, and, to my comfort, three things I could espie by the shore: that it was flood Tyde; and that it came from the Southward; and that it doth flow and fall very much water. Before we came neere the Iland, wee came over a banke of 8 fathomes, and neerer the Iland we fell into 15, there seeming upon the land to be Poles erected, and buildings of stone, and other hillocks like Haycocks.[3]

The boat went on land at clocke 6, and stayed 3 glasses, or one houre and ½, in which time it flowed neere sixe foot. It was flood before they went; for, while they were rowing to shore, I did observe it had flowed at least 3 foot, by certain rocks that were dry at our first approach. They say that it had about 9 foot to flow At clocke 8, the tide returned, and set to S.W.-ward, which sheweth that it runs halfe-tide, or else the Main beyond it is an Iland about which the tyde may have an uncontrary course, as in some of the Sounds of the Iland of *Selly*, at *England's* W. end. This Iland doth lie in 64 d 10 m. of latitude[4]; and I took this place to be the N.E. side of Sir *Thomas Button's ut*

---

[1] It seems, from the narrative, that Foxe must have passed near Tom Island. As he makes no mention of having seen it, the fog-banks probably prevented him —C

[2] Undoubtedly this was Cape Fullerton and the broken land and islands lying off it.—C

[3] "There seemeth upon this Island some Stand of Timber erected right up, and other things like haycockes." (*Foxe MS.*)

[4] There is no island exactly in this latitude Probably the observation is somewhat out, and that one of the islands off Cape Fullerton is the island in question.—C.

ultra.[1] I could see to the N.E.-ward of this at least 10 leagues, but no land at E. or S.E., it being as cleare an evening as could be imagined. The land to be seene was from the N.N.E. to the West Southward.

The newes from land was that this Iland was a Sepulchre, for that the Salvages had laid their dead (I cannot say interred), for it is all stone, as they cannot dig therein, but lay the Corpes upon the stones, and wall them about with the same, coffining them also by laying the sides of old sleddes above, which have been artificially made. The boards are some 9 or 10 foot long, 4 inches thicke. In what manner the tree they have bin made out of was cloven or sawen, it was so smooth as we could not discerne, the burials had been so old. And, as in other places of those countries, they bury all their Vtensels, as bowes, arrowes, strings, darts, lances, and other implements carved in bone. The longest Corpes was not above 4 foot long,[2] with their heads laid to the West. It may be that they travell, as the *Tartars* and the *Samoides;* for, if they had remained here, there would have been some newer burials. There was one place walled 4 square, and seated within with earth; each side was 4 or five yards in length; in the middle was 3 stones, laid one above another, man's height. We tooke this to be some place of Ceremony at the buriall of the dead.[3] Neare the same place was one

---

[1] Such it undoubtedly was (see p. 179).—C. It flowed here above 23 foot.—F.

[2] "They seem to be people of small stature. God send me better for my adventures than these." (*Foxe MS*)

[3] Crantz (*History of Greenland*, vol. 1, p. 237) describes the ceremony as follows "They prefer an elevated and remote situation for the tomb, which they build of stone, and line with moss and skins The nearest of kin brings the dead, swathed and sewed up in his best pelts. . . . . He lays him in the grave, covering him with a skin or sods, and places over these large heavy stones, as a protection against foxes and birds of prey. The kajak (a species of boat, six yards long

station laid, stone upon stone, as though they would have something remarkeable. There was fowle, but so skadle¹ as they would not abide them² to come neere them; and Ravens bigger than ours. We rob'd their graves to build our fires, and brought a whole boate's loading of fire-wood on board. Their Corpes were wrapped in Deare skinnes Their Darts were many of them headed with Iron (and nailes), the heads beaten broad wayes. In one of their Darts was a head of Copper, artificially made, wch I tooke to be the work of some Christian, and that they have come by it by the way of *Canada*, from those that Trade with the *English* and *French*³

---

and shaped like a weaver's shuttle) and the weapons of the departed are deposited near the grave, as are also the knives and sewing implements of the women, that the survivors may contract no defilement from them, nor, by the constant beholding of them, be led to indulge too deep a sorrow, which may injure the departed soul" The idea largely prevails that the same weapons will be necessary for subsistence in the other world, and it is a frequent custom to lay a dog's head on the grave of a child, that the soul of the dog, who always knows the road home, may guide the child of no understanding to the land of souls Over the grave a woman waves a lighted chip, saying, " Here thou hast nothing more to hope for "—C

¹ Prof Skeat writes "'Skadle' or 'skeddle'=*shy* It is in my edition of Ray's *Glossary* published by the English Dialect Society, but only in the sense of *mischievous* But, in Yorkshire [where Foxe was born], it means *timid, shy* The modern English form is *skathel*, and it is from the verb *scathe*, to harm "—C

² That is, the men that went on shore in the boat.—C.

³ "They brought on board all the wood from the graves, being a boatfull. The Dead was wrapped with Deer Skins for winding-sheets They came with their bows, arrows, and fishing implements, headed with copper, iron, and stone (for want of the two former), which seemeth they have traded with some civil People, or with those that doth trade with them; for one copper head I have is near of the thickness of ¼ of an inch in the middest, shagged like the head of a lance" (*Foxe MS*). " There had been buried some 500 Savages. Our men opened their tombes where they found them to lie with their deer-skins, as they used to wear about them when they were living, and by them their darts, with arrow-heads—some of bone, some of stone, some of iron, some of

LUKE FOXE'S VOYAGE, 1631.

Our men found stinking oyle in a fish gut, and some small Whale Finnes. This Iland I named Sir *Thomas Rowe's Welcome*.[1] I stood off into 33 fathomes that night, until clocke 2, the wind West; for I was directed by the letter of my instruction to set the course from *Carie Swannes Nest* N.W. by N., so as I might fall with the West side in 63 d., and from thence, Southward, to search

---

copper. There was a skin full of train oil, for they had killed a small whale. Through the midst of their graves, they put certain pieces of sledes and fir poles, to keep the stones from falling upon them. These wooden instruments we laded our boat with and brought them aboard" (*Master's MS*). The source whence the iron and nails were derived forms an interesting speculation. It is just possible, though not probable, that they had been obtained from some of the earlier explorers of the Bay, but Button, who was the only one who had been in this part of it, makes no mention of having traded with the natives there. Possibly, as hereafter suggested (p. 333), they obtained the nails from the wreck of Button's ship at Port Nelson. On the whole, it seems more probable that they had been passed on to the inhabitants of this remote spot by those more southerly tribes who had come into contact with the early French fur-traders from Canada. That the trader's wares should have been spread so far over the country at so remote a period is, however, very interesting; for the first white men who are known to have attempted to reach the southernmost part of Hudson's Bay by travelling overland from Canada were two French-Canadian traders, Peter Esprit Radisson and Sieur des Groseilliers, who made the attempt between 1660 and 1665. The account of this and their other journeys has been published by the Prince Society of Albany, N.Y. (Boston, 4to, 1885). It is much easier to account for the copper dart-head, for the vast region between Lake Superior and Hudson's Bay is rich in copper, and the Indians are known to have made use of it from a remote period. The Rev. E. F. Slafter of Boston has published, in the *New England Historical and Genealogical Register* for January 1879, an interesting article on *Pre-Historic Copper Implements*, especially those of Wisconsin.—C.

[1] It is difficult to identify the particular island upon which Foxe bestowed this name, as there are several small islands thereabout. Whichever it was, the name is not now retained, but the bay or strait is known as Sir Thomas Roe's Welcome. This was the first point Foxe speaks of his having named. In his MS. Foxe says nothing of his having bestowed the name on the island.—C.

the passage diligently, all the Bay about, untill I came to *Hudson's* Bay.[1]

28. I was in latitude 63 d. 37 m., plying up with S.W. winds; very faire and cleare weather. I saw, as it were, a headland to the South, and petty Islands, and broken ground of the Maine[2] Here was great store of fish leaping, and many Seales. I saw one Whale. This day the land lyeth S.W. and by S. along.[3]

29. I stood W. about the headland the last day shewed me, in 7 and 8 fathomes, untill I raised another white Iland[4] bearing S W., and betwixt that Iland [and] the Maine, which I had now brought N W on me, there was as it had been a Cawsee or ridge of stone[5]; but, bearing with

---

[1] As elsewhere explained (see p. 168), this should be understood to mean *James's Bay*, which then bore the name of Hudson's Bay exclusively —C.

[2] This must have been Baker Foreland, and the islands those in the entrance to Chesterfield Inlet —C

[3] "This day we had sight of another island, full of Graves, with Pyramids like the other." (*Master's MS.*)

[4] This "white island" Foxe named Brooke Cobham Island, after his patron Sir John Brooke, afterwards Lord Cobham, who is mentioned in the Introduction (p. lxiii) His name has not been retained, but there is no doubt that the island is that since known as Marble Island, from the white marble of which it is formed Prof Robert Bell, of the Geological Survey of Canada, who visited the island in 1884, says (*Report of Progress*, 1882-84, p. 35, DD) —" The whole of the western part of the island consists of white and light coloured quartzite, bearing a strong resemblance to white and veined marble, from which circumstance it has no doubt received its name Viewed from sea, the shores have a very white appearance, the rocks being free from lichens, etc., and the hills in the interior, which are rounded, are also pure white, and contrast strongly with the dark brown of the peaty flats and hollows Even the boulders and coarse shingle forming the raised beaches remain quite white, and these beaches appear as conspicuous horizontal lines against the dark vegetable matter The beds of quartzite are usually very massive."—C.

[5] This causeway is shown on the Admiralty Chart as being " dry at half ebb".—C.

the E. thereof, I fell into 35 and 40 fathomes. The tide runne W. by S., one mile ¾ in one houre.

After this, it fell to be easie wind. I sent the boate to the land, and plyed with the ship thereunto,[1] for that wind which was blew from thence; and, comming neere it after Sunne-set, we could see 2 or three huge Whales playing close by the land side in shoale water; for we, without them in the ship, had but 12 fathomes. I stood to the S W. end of the Island, and there stayed for my boat, which came at clocke 11 in the night. She had been 14 Glasses from the ship, which [time] was thus imployed: *Item:* in Rowing to the land, 4; one in chasing of Duckes; in the next, the water fell 9 Inches; and for 3 more in the one it fell 3 Inches, in the other, it flowed 3 Inches, and in the 2 last it flowed 2 foot ½, so as it flowed about 10 foot, but I doe [not] trust to this.

In their comming on board, they Anchored in 8 fathomes at the Iland point, and that was 2 Glasses after those formerly accounted. The Tide came from N E. and by E. at 3 miles ½ one houre This point of the Iland made the Tyde goe sharpe; by this it may be gathered that it was full Sea at ½ past 12. It cannot be otherwise computated but that it floweth here S W, it being 3 dayes before the full Moone. But I am not fully ascertained of this Tyde as yet; for those Ilands have their severall indrafts and sets betwixt one another; for, at clock 1, it set W by S., and now it hath neere the same set, continuing from 1 unto 10 of clocke, more then 9 houres; it seemeth strange unto me, being a Tyde and no Current. To be better satisfied, I cannot; for the best will runne at their pleasure when they are on land, to seeke for such things

---

[1] "From the top-mast head, we see no land S or W. from us. I take this to be Hopes Advance" (*Foxe MS.*). Such it certainly was not (see note on p. 178) —C

as the shoare may afford them; the worst, & worst able to give account, must keep the boat; therefore this account cannot hold with truth, nor doth it.[1] I named this Iland *Brooke Cobham*,[2] thinking then of the many furtherances this Voyage received from that Honourable Knight, Sir *Iohn Brooke*, whom, together with Master *Henry Brigges*, that famous Mathematicall Professor, were the first that countenanc'd me in this undertaking. This Noble Knight graced me in the delivering of my Petition to his Majestie, and afterwards brought me to his Royal Presence, there to shew the hopefull possibility of the attempt. And, after this, persisting in his kindnesse, invited mee to his owne Table, where I had my dyet, continually assisting me with monies towards my expence, as also paying for the charge of the Privie Seale, and for the ship's bringing about from *Chatham* to *London*, and in some with Master *Brigges* was at all the charge hereof, while the Voyage was put off untill the next yeere, when that young Sir *John Wolstenholme* was appointed Treasurer.

Now, for this Iland, it is all of a white Marble,[3] of in-

---

[1] "I cannot be better satisfied than by my own observation and the examination of some of the company who doth understand it best, for my Instructions are not to adventure the boat on land but armed, and the Master or his Mait must be in her, so as, if he [the mate] will go, or the Master send him, I dare not deny him, as they know well, having by Sir John Worstenholme the copy of my Lesson, and now, for divers times, I have made trial that he doth but go to see what he can find and hunt; and he being a man of command in the ship, the rest of the boat's crew doth follow him and thereby take liberty, so as no one stays with the boat but one or two, such as the rest can make fools of, and by these I am glad to gather all I write concerning the land" (*Foxe MS*)

[2] For a reference to this name, see the Introduction, p. lxiv As usual, Foxe's MS. contains no mention of his having given the island this name, but it is therein spoken of as "White Island" —C

[3] "like Alabaster, but I take it to be such as they pave their houses with in Holland—they say brought out of the Mediterranean" (*Foxe MS*). "A firm alabaster stone" (*Master's MS*).

different height, with many water Ponds therein, and great store of Fowle, especially water-fowle.[1] They brought on board two goodly Swannes, and a young Tall Fowle alive; it was long-headed, long-neckt, and a body almost answerable. I could not discerne whether it was an Estridge or no, for it was but pen-feathered. Within 3 or 4 dayes, the legges by mischance were broken and it dyed.[2]

Our dog, being on land, hounded himselfe at a Stagge or Reine Deere, and brought him to obey.[3] *Peter Neshfield*, one of the Quarter-Masters, followed the chase, and having neither Gun nor Lance, let him goe. (It may be, he tooke compassion when he saw the Deere shed teares.) The dog, having hurt his feet very sore upon the hard stones, was not able to pursue him, and so they parted with blood-shed, but it came from the Deere and Dog's feet They did imagine that there was store of Deere in that Iland I tooke it to be 6 or 7 miles long; but they thought it to be parted in two.[4] It is all shelves and ridges betwixt the shore and it, making, as it were, a Bay betweene the North land, which is high, and the South;

---

[1] "but skadle" (*Foxe MS.*) See p 320.—C.

[2] Foxe's idea of an ostrich (or "estridge", as he calls it) in the Arctic regions is very comic. The bird was, no doubt, a young Whooping Crane (*Grus americana*), or perhaps a Sandhill Crane (*Grus canadensis*) The Master calls it "a young Stork".—C.

[3] Query, *to bay* The word does not appear in the MS.—C

[4] Probably this erroneous idea was due to the fact that the boat's crew had observed the entrance to the small harbour in the south-west part of the island. A plan of this is given in the Admiralty chart (No. 1221) of the Harbours and Anchorages in Hudson's Bay and Strait, and descriptions of it will be found in Lieut. A. R. Gordon's *Reports of the Hudson's Bay Expeditions of* 1884 *and* 1886. The harbour is a resort of the New England whaling vessels, several of which have wintered there in recent years. It seems not to be the "Cove or Harbour" mentioned below, which is stated to have been at the *East* end of the island.—C.

for all the land to South of this is all low land, except 3 or 4 places neere unto the West part of *Hudson's* West Bay, where Captaine *Iames* wintered[1] They say, in comming on board, hard by the Iland, they did espie 40 Whales, some say lesse; but it seemeth there were many lying there to sleepe, so as they tooke them for Rocks. They say there is a *Cove* or *Harbour*, made by small Ilands, that a ship may ride in safety for all weathers, and have two fathomes at low water; it is on the East side[2] The Master's mate told me he wisht the ship therein, because there was a bolt in the Stemme which stucke out since the Cut-water was twined off,[3] and that it was dangerous to hurt a Cable if wee should Anchor. I said wee might Anchor 100 times and yet have kept the Cable cleare from the bolt by letting fall an Anchor of the weather bowe; but, to conclude, the time was too farre spent to neglect the opportunity of Discovering to put into harbour for such a trifle[4]

30. When I had stood W S W away from this Iland twelve leagues, I hal'd in againe, W by N, as I see the Ridges and broken lands stretch, and, keeping the West Maine alwayes in sight, many Ridges did appeare, which, to goe to Seaward off, I stood S W. and by W; for here is dangerous sayling in the clearest weather Yet I must not part from sight of the Maine, for making my discovery

---

[1] Foxe should have said *afterwards* wintered —C

[2] "This Island, with the S W. part of the Main, maketh a great bay, with broken ground I take it to be Hope Advance [It certainly was not —C] All this bay is very full of Whales. We saw some 20 playing" (*Master's MS*) The Master, elsewhere in his MS, speaks of the Island as "the Alabaster Island", and says "Upon the S E end of the Island, I saw 14 stones reared, where they use to bury "—C

[3] This accident had happened near Salisbury Island on July 12th (see p. 304) —C.

[4] "Well, let speeches pass So long as I am sailing, I bless God and care not." (*Foxe MS.*)

exactly Our Deepes from *Brooke Cobham* have beene 37, 40, 35, 30 fathomes Thanks be given to God, it is, and hath been long time, faire weather, and now faire windes (from land), which makes the better discovering. We have still of those *Henbans*, or *Pettie-dancers*,¹ but no storme I anchored athwart a little Iland, twelve leagues from *Brooke Cobham*. The Master, with the boat, went on land, where it was low water about ¼ an houre before 8 at night. Within this Iland, he sees other Ilands and Ledges at low water, so as he thought he could have gone on foote to the Maine From hence wee see other Ilands, bearing W S W At this Iland the Salvages had been, and there was great store of Sea-Pigeons thereon. He brought alive a dunne Foxe on board, and had encountred two Seamors, whereof hee launc'd one, but, for want of helpe, they both got away.² They brought on board good store of Scurvie-grasse,³ wch I caused to be pounded, and the juyce to be prest forth, and put into a Hogshead of strong Beare, with command that every one that would should have a pint to his morning's draught; but none would taste it untill it was past time, and themselves almost past meanes.

The Master told me he had named this Island *Dunne*

---

[1] The number of names under which Foxe speaks of the Aurora is curious. In Button's narrative (p 193), he speaks of "strange Harbours", meaning perhaps *Harbingers* In his MS., he refers to "Sir Thos. Button's Alexbones", or (?) "Atexbones" Here and in many other places, he calls it "Henbans" and "Pettie-dancers", while, in his MS, the former word is always written *Henbeams* (probably in error) The master, too, in his MS, writes of "strange Comets", evidently meaning the Aurora.

[2] "we saw two Sea horses Having lances in the boat, I, with another of our men, went to kill them, but, we not knowing the manner, they got from us. I thrust my lance up to the socket in them, and many times it was bent double and would not enter, so they got in the sea and went away" (*Master's MS*)

[3] See p. 127.—G.

Foxe Island, after his owne name and the Foxe's colour, which I liked well[1]

The Tyde came from Northeast, and it flowed about twelve foote water. Now I began to know that I went from the Tyde, for, sayling from this Tyde, I lost the passage, but I must still follow instruction and hope[2]

I wayed at the Master's comming aboord, clocke 9 in the Evening, standing away with those Ilands the day light had shewed me; the Direction was West South West, as they bore; the deepe 7, 8, 10, 15, 12 fathomes; I altered the course more Southerly, for deeper water; and, going South-West, had 12, 15, 12, 10, and so to 25 fathome From 9 to 4 a Clocke, I stood still away, with flood South West, ebbe West, untill 8 a clocke, in 35, 30, 20 All to Starreboard was Ridges and broken lands, even close to the Maine. This night was something darke The Sunne declines fast Southward, and wee, sayling as fast the same way, must needes darken the nights a pace, especially those that are thicke and clouded, as this was.[3]

31. All this morning watch, from foure to eight, it rained, but was faire weather all day after, untill towards night. It was halfe an houres fogge betweene three and foure in the afternoone. After that came North windes, raine, and wet fogge all night. The steering was foure leagues West South West, the deepes from 30, 36, to 6 fathomes.[4]

With this wind from land, I bore in among the Ilands,

---

[1] This passage is not very clear Probably Foxe meant to write that the Master named the island after *my* (Foxe's) own name and the fox's colour. Foxe's MS, as usual, contains no reference to the giving of the name, which has not been retained The Master, in his MS, says he "caught a live fox", but does not mention naming the place There can be little doubt the island was that now known as Sentry Island —C

[2] This reflection does not appear in Foxe's MS —C

[3] "Lat 62° 20'. Lo. 42° 26'" (*Master's MS.*)

[4] Latitude 62^d 05^m —F.

fearing to loose the Maine at any time[1]; standing in betwixt West and West North West, as the wind veered or haled, my depth was sixteene fathomes, but amongst those Ilands wee came in sundry Over-falls of sixe fathomes, and had brought them to beare severally from me, North-East by North, North by West, West South West, South West by West. At night, clocke tenne, I came to anchor in seven fathomes; it fell three foote water after that anchoring; the weather was wette fogge, the flood put in fourteene foote water, it did not fall any water from clocke eleven untill foureteene Glasses were out; the flood was so small (being inclosed with Ilands) as it did not make the ship port, yet, blowing but to Course and Bonnet, it kept the Tide in seven houres.[2] I durst not hazzard any further within these Ilands untill I sent the boate to make tryall, who sounded from seven fathomes to tenne foot. I named those Ilands *Brigges his Mathematickes*.[3]

August 1 This morning, the Master and I in the Maine top might see two ridges dry, which last evening wee came hard by. I doe thinke that in Winter the windy stormes puts in some flowings of water incredible to be beleeved in respect of other places; for it may be perceived that the water hath been upon the land and Ilands higher by five or six fathome then the usuall Spring-Tydes, as also our men did perceive the same at *Carie Swannes Nest*[4]

---

[1] "It clearing up, I desired the Captain to stand in, that we might perfectly discover in this latitude, according to our Instructions, the which he was very loth to do, so at last consented." (*Master's MS.*)

[2] *Note* North wind kept up tyde —F.

[3] This very quaint name has not been retained on modern charts. Foxe, of course, bestowed it upon the group of islands in honour of his friend and patron, Henry Briggs (see Introduction, p lx). Foxe's MS does not contain the name.—C.

[4] These marks were probably not due to winter storms They were no doubt the ancient "raised beaches" (as geologists call them) which occur on the Western Coast of Hudson's Bay.—C.

Being satisfied for what concerned this place, I weyed and stood to Sea in sixe fathomes the least water, fearing to deale any more within the Ilands. When I was cleare, I went to the old course againe, S W by S ; but, the land flying me, I hal'd in West, and had water from 14 to 6 fathome, uneven ground The land met me againe, stretching more to S , and had many humlocks[1] therein I stood toward it, W and W S W., so neere as I durst for shoale water, at which time I dare presume it was seven miles from me, and yet I had but 6, 7, or 10 fathome I runne off a long time before I came into 20 fathome, and, in this wearing off, I came by two dry ridges that had been farre without me I anchored at night in 25 fathomes, 10 leagues S S W from the land and Ilands which I roade amongst last night , the Tyde came S S W.[2]

2 This faire morning I weighed at clocke 6, and stood along West South West, having 25, 25, 25 fathomes At the distance of 7 leagues from my last night's anchoring place, I met another Iland, & three or foure more within it, all lying almost without sight of the Maine. I stood within them to seven fathomes, and tooke about to make a perfect discovery of the Maine, which done, I Veered away, the wind still about North North West I went to Seaward off the said Iland, at whose North-east end there lay a reefe, which, with the ebbe that fell over it, made a great Ripling or Race, so as I could discerne thereby when I might edge up againe Here in this Over-fall was a

---

[1] Query *hummocks*, or low conical hills near the sea-coast   Prof Skeat writes "*Humlock* for *hummock* is a great find   It's all right   Both are derivatives of *hump*, with different suffixes   Only lately, I read a paper arguing that there was a verb *hummle* in Middle English, meaning 'to be humpy', and now we get its derivative *hum-l-ock* = *hummle-ock*   Both -*l*- and -*ock* are diminutives " In Foxe's MS it is "low land full of humlakes" —C

[2] Lat 61° 00' Lo 42° 49' " (*Master's MS*)

Sea-Morse. I tooke this to be the Checkes, [we being in] latitude 61 degrees 10 minutes[1] I went over in nine fathomes, and then, standing Southwest, came presently into twentie. I hoped now for a sight of *Hubbert's comfortable Hope*.[2] The land lay along Southwest and Northeast[3] It hath blowen all this day to Course and Bonnet; at night, I anchored at twenty fathomes, two or three leagues from shore.[4] The land is low, but within are many water ponds, and small growne wood[5]

---

[1] The island was probably Sentry Island, off Cape Esquimaux, which is about in the latitude named The "Checks", or "Hopes Check" of Button, is referred to in notes on pp. 165 and 172 —C

[2] We are largely in the dark as to what "Hubbert's Hope' was. Josias Hubart, it will be remembered, was a companion of Sir Thomas Button, but what his "Hope" consisted in we are not told in the narrative of Button's voyage given by Foxe However, from a note on a map by Mr Briggs in *Purchas* (see *ante*, p. 178), it appears that his "Hope", whatever it was, lay in Churchill Bay, although one would have thought that Sir Thomas Button's explorations would have dispelled any hope of a passage westward from thence At all events, Foxe sought it there, and from what he elsewhere says, he considered the "chiefest hope" of a passage to lie there. As he sailed into Churchill Bay, he says, "Hubbert makes me hope", but, as he reached the bottom, he says, " I could see the bottome of *Vainely Hoapt Hubbert*, for so I call it" The letter which Captain James left at Charlton Island affords further evidence of the expectations which were at the time centred in Churchill Bay As he entered this Bay, he says (see James' *Voyage*, p 114) "We entered that inlet which heretofore was called Hubbart's Hope, which was the very place where the Passage should be, as it was thought by the understandingest and learnedest intelligencer of this Business in England [probably either Sir Thomas Button, Mr Henry Briggs, or Sir John Wolstenholme]. We sailed to the very bottom of it, into three Fathom water, and found it to be a Bay of some 18 or 19 Leagues deep."—C.

[3] "We had the one end of the land which lieth between the Checks and Hobards' Hope We adventured the nearer to try Hoberd's Hope We had our Boat ahead all this day" (*Master's MS.*)

[4] "Lat 61° 19' Lo 42° 56'" (*Master's MS*)

[5] If Foxe was now about in lat. 61° N, as seems to be the case, the northern limit of tree-growth at this point used to lie more to the

3. I stood along all those supposed Checkes from my last nights Roade into 3 fathomes upon the shoare; the land lowe, but now and then a Sandie knowle or downe would appeare, much like the coast of *Holland* and *Flanders*, wee made way S.W. and by W. 10 leag, and divers times see dry shelves betweene us and the shoare. The Latit. was 60 d. 22 m. This afternoone was small wind from S.W., and I sent the boat to the land, being about 3 miles off; my selfe with ship anchored in 7 fathomes. I gave a token that if the water should shoale sodainely they in the boate should shoote off a Musket, which before they came to shoare they did. Here were many Musketoes.[1]

The Master was in the boate, and had but 2 fathomes when they shot. All the water within us was shoald, so that then we were glad to wade forth, although the tyde was flood, it flowing 14 inches in two glasses, but in further examining I found no good account; onely this doth suffice: that, as I range along the coast, I do goe from the tide, and that it keepeth course with the Moone, and that, the further I speed from Sir *Thomas Roe's Welcome*, it still floweth lesse water, and the tides' current is the easier. Here on land the Mr. found the reliques of a birch Cannowe, the footings and hornes of Deere, both small and greate, and of fowle, an Arrowe headed with a nayle, the head beaten broad and put into a shaft of

---

north in 1631 than it does now; for reference to Dr. Bell's map, already alluded to (p. 192), shows that no trees now exist on the western shore of Hudson's Bay to the north of Port Churchill.—C

[1] "This afternoon, since it hath blown easy wind, we have had great store of midges or musketous come off Land, [which] maketh me think, together with the spars we found at the first island we landed at in this Bay [see p. 319], that there is wood further up into the main. The Fir, it is the best that I have seen, and I do think the best in the world; for I never saw finer, or any so fine as this is." (*Foxe MS*)

18 inches long.¹ He thought it flowed about 7 foote; the floode began about clocke 8. I am sure it was slacke tyde at ship then; and I will be slacke to write any more hereof, for I cannot season the reckoning taken on shoare²

After the boates comming on board, I stood off 3 glasses to anchor in 13 fathome water (*Hubbert* makes me hope), for now I draw nere.³ Here the tyde did set S.W. and by W., the ebbe E. and by South.

4 From the last day to this, I made way S.S.W. 5 leag., and am now in 59 d. 53 m. of Latit,⁴ standing along betweene 10 and 20 fath S.S.W. At night, 10, I came to a land lying about 2 leag. from the Maine,⁵ but so dry at low water that you may goe to the firme land, betwixt the one and the other; this lyeth from my last night's roade 10 leag. S. and by W.

---

¹ "They found a piece of a rib of a Canoe, such as in Canada, for it hath been boarded with birch-rind, a piece of a bow, an arrow headed with a nail, the head flat beaten, the point into the body of the arrow and about 16 inches long" (*Foxe MS*) "Here I saw the footing of Elks, as I take them, for they were as big as the footings of our Oxen in England, with many Geese, but so shy that I could not come near them I saw a Covey of Partridges, bigger than ours in England far, and the fire where the savages had been. Here I found an arrow, the head being made of a nail. I suppose it came from Port Nelson. . It was very good land, and full of grass like our hay, with Daisies, and some small shrubs of Birch" (*Master's MS*). The interest of this discovery has already been discussed (see p. 321). —C

² "they had not well observed the time of the Tyde..... I do see they go [ashore] more for pleasure of hunting and fowling than that any of them hath duly observed the service they do owe the Adventurers." (*Foxe MS*)

³ "I do yet hope well, or else I say Hubbard was an ass. I could otherwise explain myself, but it is needful only to say the doubt." (*Foxe MS*)

⁴ "Lat. 60° 03'. Lo 43° 17'. Variation 18° 46'." (*Master's MS*)

⁵ Doubtless Egg Island.—C.

5 At the dayes appearance, I went to this Iland It is all stones as the other The Sea hath bin smooth of long time, the Sunne rose cleare[1], and, at the 4 glasse after lowe water, it did flowe 21 inches; this was when the half tyde came to take his first set, and came with a shuft[2], I did account that it would not flow lesse then 18 foote; but, after this shuft, it flowed lesse and lesse untill full Sea, that tyde, the 3 first glasses did not flow above 2 foote.[3] Upon this Iland were many corpses, laid in the same manner as at Sir *Thomas Roe's Welcome* The *Salv* inhabitants had lately bin there, & left the skaddles[4] of their fire, they had also sunk a well & ston'd it about, for there was fresh water therein There was here some store of the ruined fragments of Cannowes, and other firre wood, with which we laded the boat on board, there was also carved toyes in their graves.[5]

---

[1] "Praised be Almighty God! This fair weather and heat doth still continue, with abundance of Musketous" (*Foxe MS*)

[2] Presumably a flow of water or rushing wave of the nature of a bore Nares gives, "to shuff to contend?" and quotes Vicars's *Virgil*, 1632

"Like adverse winds burst out with fierce cross-puffs,
Eastern with west, west winds with southern *shuffs*"—C

[3] It flowed 12 foote —F

[4] Perhaps *ashes* are meant, but Nares does not give the word, nor does it appear in the MS (See note on p 347)—C

[5] "We got only firewood for 14 days on this Island, it being some drift, other pieces [were] laid over the graves of the dead, of which many here had been buried" (*Foxe MS*) "At 2 in the morning, the Captain went ashore and found many graves of Savages, with Sledes and pieces of Cane, and a Copper Chisell, with a Drill, so he brought the boat loaded with wood The Indians had burnt the grass not long before It is close to the Main In this Island, they had dug a well of fresh water I think they come down to the waterside but at the time they take the young birds" (*Master's MS*) This is the first time we hear of Foxe himself having left his ship in order to go ashore — C.

I did Anchor at clocke 8 (now these nights begin to be long), lest I might slip by some Inlet unseene. This day was very hot, and a small gale from S.S W, we had all this time very hot dayes, euer since we came from *Carie Swan's* nest, if that the cold N W. wind had not delayed them. This Meridian I was in 59 d 05 m. I stood off into 20 fath, and went in againe to 15, the broken Iland in sight, since noone untill this midnight, I made way S 3 leag, and then I discerned the land to meete upon my weather bough[1] and ahead, so I caused to tack about, and lay N W by N., in wind W. by S, 5 glasses, 2 leag. It seemed to be higher land then I had lately seen, from 15 fath deepe. Yesterday I came S, as before, upon 18 and 20 fathoms. I stood thus to the Northwards untill day light, and then I see my land I was upon yesterday morning, and the land within it, which I see yesternight, stretching into *Hubbert's Hope*. I stood about to the Southwards,[2] and the day light being come on, I could see the bottome of Vainely *Hoapt Hubbert* (for so I cald it), and the South land meeting E and W, the length of it at least 15 leagues. I anchored the boate in 20 fathomes, the Tyde came N W, and this is that supposed Tide that set E and W, which was no more but the same Tyde I brought along with mee from Sir *Tho Roe's Welcome*, comming all along the coast S.W by S, [and] falling into this Vaine *Hope* is enforced to alter his course by opposition

---

[1] Prof Skeat writes:—"*Weather-bough* is all one with *weather-bow*, and, strange to say, it is not wrong. *Bough* is the 'arm' of a tree, and *bow* is the shoulder of a vessel. They are the same word, etymologically that's why everyone pronounces them the same. The spelling differs only because *bough* is English (A.-S *bōh*), and *bow* is Norse (Icel *bōgr*)"—C.

[2] "the land looking more pleasant than before, and bolder shore, heigher and full of wood." (*Foxe MS*).

of the S. side of this large Bay, and there to set E. and W. (as the land doth lye), 1 mile ¼ in one houre.

6. The Iland I was upon yesterday was doubtlesse the Checks,[1] named by Sir *Thomas Button*, for what reason I know not, except for that here his hope was crost; he tooke it as a checke.

This land bore from me to the S E. by E , and was gentle descending down to the Seaside, the greenest & best like I have seene since I came out of the river of *Thames*, and as it were inclosed with thick rowes of Trees betweene one meadowe and another, distinct as it were *Barne Elmes*,[2] nere *London*, and at sight hereof I did thinke of them, and if there be any keeping of tame Deere or other beasts, or tillage, in all that countrey, I should think it to be there; for certainly there must, by those burials, be great store of people, for it is not to be thought that they will bring or carry their dead farre to buriall, and it cannot be thought also but that we were seene by them, although they were not seene by any of us, for we stayed not but in the night; all day wee made as much way as sailes would drive forward, so as, if they would have come to us, wee were gone before they could make ready; and, although they might see us, whether they durst come or no, I know not, having, as I suppose, never seene ship in their lives before; as *Hudson* who sought after them in his Bay (though far

---

[1] There is unquestionably some error in this paragraph On August 2nd, Foxe had reached what he also says he took for Sir Thomas Button's "Checks" (see p 331), and in this he was, so far as I can see, quite correct The MS contains nothing about the Checks at this point.—C.

[2] A hamlet in the parish of Barnes, which is pleasantly situated on the banks of the Thames, five miles south-west from London The hamlet consists mainly of two fine mansions, and takes its name from its many majestic elm-trees —C

distant from hence), they set their woods on fire hard by him, and yet would not come to him, although he was but in his Shallop.[1]

But to proceed: I stood along the land, and had deep from 20 to 30 fath This morning was gray overcast; the Sun rose thinly valed, but visible; there was a Rainebow in the firmament, and some drops of raine fell. Standing along, whiles this land trented E. and W., wee see the entrance of a large river,[2] but all full of scaupes, shelves, and shoale water, w^{ch}, comming forth, changeth the Sea to be more white. At the S. entrance of this River was a Cliffe, like unto *Balsea* cliffe, nere *Harwich*,[3] and on the S. again, another great Bay, whose bottome was esie to be seen. I was nere the entrance thereof, and found it was all full of shoales and ridges; at this [point] was Capt. *James* on ground, as I found by his speeches afterwards. The S. part of this Bay lyeth E. and W., and at the E. end thereof lyeth an Iland S. and N., about 3 miles long[4] I stood from the mouth of this River

---

[1] See p. 137.—C.

[2] This was, of course, the Churchill River, which, in spite of the rocky and forbidding entrance which Foxe describes, forms a very fine harbour within, for ships of the largest size By "scaupes", Foxe probably means *scarps*, or rocky precipitous cliffs. Lieut. Gordon, who, in 1886, spent several days in surveying the harbour, gives a good description of it (*Report of the Hudson's Bay Expedition of 1886*, p 8) He says that, "though the tide runs very rapidly, this harbour is an eminently safe one The approaches .... are well marked, and in clear weather the land stands out bold and high . Nature seems to have left little to be done in order to make this a capacious port, fit for doing a business of great magnitude."—C.

[3] No doubt Foxe here alludes to the cliffs at Bawdsey, on the Suffolk coast, some miles north of Harwich, which are of considerable height.—C

[4] There is now no island in the position indicated. Probably the island Foxe describes was little more than a sand-bank, which in the course of the last 260 years has disappeared through tidal action The sea is still very shallow in the place referred to by Foxe.—C.

and Bay to go to the N of the said Iland, and came into 7, 6, 5 fath., easie winde. The ebbe came 2 miles an houre along the E. side of the Iland, & I stood along in 3 fath, the ground to be seen under water At night, the flood tyde came, & we were got above the S. end of the Iland & went along in 7 fath, well harrowed and even ground[1]

At clocke 10 we anchored, and could not perceive by our lead that tyde did flowe and fall above 12 foote, the tyde set S. and by N, and here we see white Whales. This afternoone was one of the hottest that ever I have felt. (At noone I was in 58 deg 46 min[2])

7 This beautifull day was promised at Sun rising, it hath blown to course and bonnet all day, the wind going downe with *Sol*, and in the night up againe, we have run along the land all day with W N.W. wind, sometimes loosing too, sometimes wareing off, as the water did deepe or shoale from 7 fath into $2\frac{1}{2}$ upon the shoare, the land lyes S We think we saw some peeces of ice in the offine, we runne this day 16 leagues untill clocke 8, when we anchored; the land faire in sight, but lowe, with aboundance of wood growing thereon At this anchoring, we can make no certainty of the tydes, but that it still commeth N, running easilier, and flowing lesse water.[3]

8 This faire day we blesse God for, and have plide it up for *Port Nelson*, the wind veering to S S E ; Latit. 57 d 48 m.[4], the shoalding wee plide in was betweene 7 and $2\frac{1}{2}$, and we could see many shelves and high stones lye upon

---

[1] Foxe evidently means that they could see the sea bottom to be smooth, like a well-harrowed field.—C

[2] "Lat 58° 46' Lo 43° 06' Variation 17^d 42'—17^d 25' Sight of Ice" (*Master's MS*)

[3] "The Passage is to be feared when the Tide doth abate" (*Foxe MS*)

[4] "Lat 57° 37'. Lo. 43° 11'." (*Master's MS.*)

the N. side of the River's mouth,[1] appearing as it were trees on land, 3 times bigger then they be, and that is through the vapours which the Sun exhaleth Haveing plide all day in shoale water, at night we anchored in 6 fathomes

In the mouth of *Port Nelson*, at first comming of the tyde, it came with a Shuft or Boare[2] at clocke 10, for one houre, and flowed upon the Ship's Bowe, and it flowed 9 foote water, the tyde runne not above 5 houres; and 2 knots was the speede it made, yet I could perceive the under-tyde to Roome an houre before the ship came up[3], the land faire to see, both on S and N side Here were many white Whales, the running of the tyde was caused by the out-set of the River upon the Coast-tyde, there was a ledge dry at lowe water hard by me when I anchored

9 This day we consulted, and consented to goe into *Port Nelson*,[4] for these reasons following:

> 1 *Considering what hazzard wee had vndergone for want of our Pinnace, she being made ready for setting vp, yet for the losse of time we were content to hazard*

---

[1] Nelson Shoal, doubtless —C

[2] A tidal wave (see p 334)—C.

[3] "I could perceive the other tide set an hour before the Ship came up" (*Foxe MS*)

[4] Discovered and named by Button in 1612 (see p 166) Lieut Gordon, in 1886, spent some time in making a careful survey, and gives a full description and a chart of it (*Report of the Hudson's Bay Expedition of* 1886, p 9). Notwithstanding the fact that during the last two centuries the vessels of the Hudson's Bay Company and others have annually sailed to and from Port Nelson, Lieut Gordon describes it as "one of the most dangerous places in the world for shipping to go to" He also says that it is "no port, nor would the expenditure of any amount of money make it a desirable place for shipping" He is incorrect in saying that Button must have wintered above Flamborough Head.—C.

it, having bin so faire weather as I was loath but to make good vse thereof.[1]

2 The wind was contrary to go Southwards, and like to be bad weather

3 The Pinnace could not be set up in the Ship as I desired.[2]

4 I hoped to have some intelligence by the Salvages, and to search the head of the River, of which I did know nothing from Sir Tho. Button [3]

5. I was in great hope to get a Maine yard amongst so many trees, as also some refreshing, fresh water, and fire-wood, and to rummidge the Ship, and to see her on ground, and to make her cleane, or to repaire what else she wanted, as Ballast, or else what.

Thinking now it was good to provide for winter, for what is formerly done is so exact as no discovery was more painefully followed, nor with greater hazard and lesse helpe, but God alone, besides the knowledge of this harbour, might more embolden my men in staying the longer forth to follow the Search [4]

---

[1] Foxe probably means that his explorations, up to the present, had been dangerous, because of the want of a pinnace for the crew to escape in, in the event of any accident befalling their ship —C.

[2] "Thirdly When [? while] I did desire the Pinnace might be so made as she might be set up in the Ship [when] amongst ice or at anchor, it is otherwise; for the ship's deck will not contrive her, except the mainmast was out" (*Foxe MS*) It seems, therefore, that Foxe had taken out with him a pinnace in pieces, although he has not previously mentioned the fact —C

[3] " Fourthly I hope for some intelligence from some of the Inhabitants, if any can be found, which may something further our design, especially because I do not hear that the head or bottom of this river was searched, and I think [it] could not [be] for ice in the Spring, because I perceive by the answers to some demands of Hawkridge that the head had not been sought before the last frost came on when Sir Thos Button did winter [see p. 170] " (*Foxe MS*)

[4] In his MS., Foxe speaks of these as "concealed reasons", and

Now betweene *Port Nelson* and *Hudson's* W. Bay (all yet for a great distance not looked upon by any Christian), wee were to discover[1], which, having done, the perfect knowledge of this River might cause us to repaire hither for refuge when the winter tooke us from our other labours, if in the meanetime wee should not discover a better [refuge], or [a] passage.

This Raynie morning, with S. wind, I stood in lowe sailes with bonnets along the S. side, which I take to be the plainer and evener ground of the two. And, bearing in upon 3 fath. ½, I espied an overfall on head; it was flood tyde, and I caused to beare up. It blew much wind, and more then at any time since I came into this Sea. In the channel's edge of this overfall, I fell into 10 fath., being now come within the lippes hereof; the wind shrinking, I anchored at about ½ flood[2]; for that, if it had beene a channell well knowne unto me, yet I could not have handled my sayles to have turned in Wee thought wee saw tokens on land of Inhabitants. At 3 houres flood in the night, with much adoe I wayed anchor, and, making 2 or 3 boards, I got up a leag. farther before day (for I was loath to loose any time[3]), but with fearefull sounding,

---

says. the men "shall not know these reasons, nor that I do hope to dispatch all this search, together with Cape Comfort, this year, [if God be pleased, and so come home the winter. . . . Therefore now it is high time to have the Pinnace ready, for by the nights now growing long, they may do [in her] that which I dare not in the Ship."—C.

[1] It will be remembered that Button's discoveries along the southern shore of Hudson's Bay, in 1612-13, extended no further east than Port Nelson, while Hudson's and Prickett's, in 1610-11, had extended no further west, at the furthest, than Cape Henrietta Maria (see p. 131). It was this intervening portion of the coast-line, therefore, which still remained for Fox to discover.—C.

[2] "Lat. (the mouth of the River) 57° 4'. It is some five miles farther up where we rode. Variation, 24° 5'." (*Master's MS.*)

[3] "The Master and his mait said they thought I was weary of the

as 5 fathomes at most, and it would shoalden 2 fathome at once; and, as I found afterwards, that channell was full of high Rockes in the best of it. This night I had many gusts of Winde, with showres of Raine.

10. I plide up a mile with flood, and thought to have gone beyond a point about 2 miles higher, where I might have ridde land lockt[1]; but, the river being full of stones, I grounded in the tide's way, there being deepe now 5 fathomes, then 6 foote, anon 7 fathomes[2]; so that, espying a Wally[3] in the clay cliffe on the North side, I sought and found a place of 5 fathomes to Anchor the Ship safely in, and intended in the Vallie to set up my Pinnace. This river is on both sides full of small woods. The North side is a clay cliffe, like of that to the Nase in *Essex*,[4] but not so high. The ship being moored, I went on land and found the Vallie very convenient to set up a Tent and to build the Pinnace in; and here wee found

---

ship and men. I persisted to the contrary, knowing it was for ease only, and to prolong time. I have always found my men very willing to obey me in plying the voyage." (*Foxe MS*)

[1] Doubtless Flamborough Head.—C

[2] " In some places, 3 fathom; in some, one; in others, 7; and [in others], 3 or 4." (*Foxe MS*)

[3] No doubt a misprint for *valley*. Reference to a note on p. 166 will show that the valley in question was that of the stream now known as Heart Creek. This is further shown by a passage in the Master's MS, which reads "We set in. It is very dangerous, and full of sholds, especially the S side. The least of the depth is 5 fathom, and no certain channel, but full of great stones. Upon the flood, we tacked aground, but staid not; and anchored against a creek a mile above Sir Thos Button's wintering-place, where we got ashore, our Shallop to set up."—C

[4] The prominent headland forming the south side of the entrance to Harwich Harbour and Hamford Water, in Essex. Hence *Walton-on-the-Naze*, a thriving sea-side resort. Like the Beacon Hill or Cliff, near Harwich, on the opposite side of the entrance to Hamford Water, the Naze was unquestionably a very much more prominent headland than it now is; for it has long been decaying very rapidly, through the sea's action.—C.

some store of Hogsheads and Pipestanes[1] which had beene yron-bound, one Maine top, a top-gallant Mast, diverse blocks, and the sides of staved chests, with divers reliques of some *English* Vessell, which I tooke to have perished, or beene left, not farre from hence. And indeed I did assure my selfe it must be that of Sir *Thomas Button*[2], but as yet I have not found a tree will make a Mayne yard.

11. This morning earely, I cald to rommage for the percels of the Pinnace to be had on land; which being put into the boate, on land wee goe. The Carpenter at Sea had provided himself of things necessarie against this occasion, haveing all materials in readinesse, which to further, with his mate, I caused *Peter Nesfeild*, quarter Master, the Cooper, the Gunner, *Exposer Russell*, and my selfe to assist him; and this day wee set up the keele, and made a false keele to it, thinking thereby to make her hold a better wind; brought on all the ground timbers, and 3 strokes on each side, while the Mr. and others went to looke for refreshing.[3]

The wind being come about to the N.W, I sent the Master word that it was fit to bring the ship to ground while it blew from land (as he determined before our comming in), and for that I would not have any thing to doe that might stay mee after the Pinnace was set up, that such things as was needfull should be taken in hand and brought to passe with all expedition.

12 This morning I was glad to bring the ship to land

---

[1] Probably a misprint for *pipe-staves*, a *pipe* being a wine-cask, usually containing two hogsheads, or 125 gallons. *Staves* are, of course, the strips of board of which such casks are made. The MS. has it *pipes* merely.—C.

[2] They were, of course, relics of Button's expedition, which had wintered near the spot in 1612-13.—C.

[3] "This day the Master and Company went to [hunt] fowl or deer, and did nought else" (*Foxe MS*)

myselfe upon a fine smooth sand,[1] against the Valley, where wee strengthened on the Cutwater, and tooke away the bolt which stucke out,[2] and made smooth the shipside; for any harme else, our Anchors had done more to the sheathing then the yce; in this river, we had set on side a peece of our false keele, which we helped [3]

And now I sent *Samuel Blades* and the Chirurgion to the E., to search the shoare and to looke for a Mayne yard; who, returning, told me that for a Mayne yard there was not a tree to be had of that squarenesse, but that by a little creeke about a mile off, they had found on shoare certaine broken Anchors and cable rope, with other small ropes, also one broken Gun, with many round and crossebarre shot of lead and yron, one Grapnel, and store of firewood pilde up, with one Tent covered with old sailes, and a Crosse, which had beene set up, but was puld or fallen downe, with the inscription raced out [4] This night was

---

[1] "least the Master and Mait (for any excuse will serve) should say, the shallop being ready, that now we must have the ship on ground (and so hinder time), which this I meant to prevent." (*Foxe MS*)

[2] See p. 326.—C.

[3] This is nonsense. In Foxe's MS the passage runs "We mended the fore-gripe, which was knocked off with the ice, [and] found the false keel, for want of bolting, fled away in the midships, and had started the sheathing 20 foot off, so we set it away [?]. One shock we have received upon the false sternpost, but when and where I cannot know." In the Master's MS. we read. "We hauled our Ship ashore in a very good place, where we could go round about her adry. There was gone some 5 foot of the Stern, with two bolts." Foxe's MS. shows that, at this point, he and his lazy Master again fell out Foxe repeats his contempt for the latter, saying he cares only for the good of the voyage, and concludes as follows. "If I do harbour this winter here, I hope in God it shall not be yet, for such weather and [so] hot no man needs better. I bless God's name."—C.

[4] That is, *erased*. Foxe's MS. here reads "the relics of a decayed ship, as anchors, cables, a tent covered with old sail-cloth, a gun, an iron crow, [and] great store of shot of lead and iron; and that they do think that some have wintered there, for there is great store of fir-

very hot, with much lightning, and some drops of raine. Here are, comming in with the floode and goeing out with the ebbe, innumerable company of white Whales, a fish as big as Porke fishes with us, and much alike in shape.[1]

13. I went with the Chirurgion to the creeke, and found the same, as they had told mee, leaveing the Carpenters and others at worke, and thinkeing to send for those things at the next leisure, after the Shippe was Rummadgt. This Tyde did flowe nine foote, to floate the Shippe off ground.[2]

14. This being the Lord's day, wee rested and served God, the afternoone, our men walked abroad to recreate themselves, and looke out for fresh releife.[3] This night did the Ship fleete off, and wee moored her againe in 3 fathomes at lowe water.

15. This fayre hot day, some wrought at the Shallop,

---

wood piled up, and a place where they think some ship hath lain." These, of course, were further relics of Button's wintering.—C

[1] In Foxe's MS. this passage reads. "we saw here more White Whales than we can count at once, continually coming in with the flood and going forth with the ebb." The White Whale or Beluga (*Delphinapterus leucas*), which Foxe has several times before mentioned having seen, is common throughout the Polar Seas, and sometimes wanders to our own shores. It especially frequents the estuaries of large rivers, like that in which Foxe now was. The whalers from New England and the servants of the Hudson's Bay Company still pursue this whale in Hudson's Bay, where it is apparently as numerous as ever; for Lieut. Gordon, who gives much interesting information as to the whale-fishery of the Bay (*Report of the Hudson's Bay Expedition of 1886*, pp. 60-63), says that, when in Port Nelson, he was "much struck .... by the almost incredible number of these animals which were passing up and down the estuary." Under the name of "Pork-fish", Foxe doubtless alludes to the porpoise (*Phocæna communis*), which is often called by that and similar names; but this animal cannot be said to be as big as the White Whale, as it seldom exceeds six feet in length, while the latter often exceeds fifteen —C.

[2] "we made an end, but could not get off, the tide being at least." (*Master's MS.*)

[3] "The Master, Mait, and his Man, are gone a-hunting for venison without a dog, for Urin's is good for nothing, as himself saith; but here is no fowl or venison." (*Foxe MS.*)

others fetcht ballast, others romisht,[1] others fild water, and strooke downe the Gunnes.[2] It joyed mee thus to see all hands at worke.[3] The Pinnace was almost finished, but wee were hindered by one houre of as much rayne (in the time) as ever I was in, with thunder, from the South-East.

16. In this day, the most of our labours were brought to end concerning the ships readinesse.

17. The wind blowing E.S.E , stiffe Gale, so as I could not come forth of this River to follow my discovery, the Master and I went with the ship's boate up the river, where, about the turne of a point 6 miles above the ship, lay 2 Ilands in the middle[4] The tide did not runne above 5 miles from the ship, nor flow above eight miles. The river strucke W N W.; up so farre, and above the Ilands, as we could see, it was Clay clift on both sides, and of reasonable height[5]; but the fresh[6] came down with great force, or else you might wade it over. It is also thicke as can stand of Firre and Spruce-trees, but small ones, for there is no ground for the wood to take roote upon, for the thicknesse of Mosse, so they cannot roote in the earth, but grow up, and fall downe and rot. I landed on both sides, and *Peter Nesfield* (who I had set out of the boat, with the Master and others, for lightning her, that I might have sayled up the higher, but could not, the water was so shallow and came

---

[1] *Rummaged*. Custom-house officers are said to rummage a ship when they search her for smuggled goods (see p. 113). Foxe spells the word in a curious variety of ways.—C.

[2] That is, stowed them away in the hold (see p. 272) —C.

[3] "We fetched three broken anchors and other things we found upon the shore for ballast" (*Foxe MS.*). "We got 3 pieces of anchors and 2 grapnells, with a broken fowler, and some 200 round shot, with half a score lengths of her cable, being very good" (*Master's MS.*)

[4] Seal Islands, just above Flamborough Head.—C.

[5] "about the height of the Ness Land, near Harwich." (*Foxe MS.*) He refers to the Naze (see p 342) —C.

[6] The stream of a river as it flows into the sea.—C.

downe so fiercely) told me hee had seene the footing of a man, but he could not bring me to it again, so I stood over to the S. side, the boat still grounding as I went (where wee landed). Me thought the vallies was good grasse, store of wood; and here we gathered black-berries, as we found in other places, with straw-berries, goose-berries, and Vetches, with several sorts of small shrubs and trees; and upon the shore we found the broad footing of Deere, and hard by them, the frame of a Tent standing, which had lately been made, with the studdle[1] of a fire, the haire of Deere, and bones of fowle, left heere.[2] I tooke leave of the S side, and named the farthest and head thereof *Ramsdens Hall*, after an Alderman of that Corporation[3]; but the Master and his man travelled by land to thwart of the ship. We have seene no Salvage since I came, although I caused fires to burne night and day; but the woods are so thicke as cannot be seen 12 score yards, so that none could come

---

[1] This is a perplexing word etymologically. On p. 334, we read of "the *skaddles* of their fire", which I believe to be, like *studdle*, a misprint for *staddle* It seems possible that the compositor, having previously set up the provincial word *skaddle* (see p. 320), without understanding it, confused it with *staddle* (which he probably also did not understand). Prof. Skeat writes. "I don't believe it means 'ashes' ... I believe he means the *scar*, the *mark*, the *burnt patch*, or whatever you like to call it. One sense of *staddle* is a mark or stain left on metal after the rust has been cleaned off; also the mark left on a place where something has been lying.... I connect staddle with stead, sted-fast, station, stand. Stad-dle = a small place where a thing has stood." Webster says that Tusser and Bacon used the word in the sense of a young tree, and that it still retains this meaning in America. If so, studdles might be the half-charred logs.—C.

[2] "we found many Savages' Tents, but [they] had been longer [?long time] made, with part of an arrow." (*Master's MS*)

[3] On the map, it is *Ramsden's Hull*. I am unable to explain the significance of the name, unless it commemorates an Alderman Ramsden, who was a member of the Corporation of the town of Hull. Neither of the MSS. contain anything about it.—C.

to us but by water. This day the Pinnace was brought on boord; God grant that with her helpe my hopes may be accomplished, which heretofore had been dangerous[1]

18. From a boord, wee see a Stag trotting from *Port Nelson* along the sand. We mand our boat presently, but, before they got to shore, he tooke up over a Valley into the woods, where they mist him.[2] I caused the Crosse which we found[3] to be newly raised, and this inscription of lead nailed thereon[4]:—

I suppose this Crosse was first erected by Sir Thomas Button, 1613. *It was againe raised by* Luke Foxe, *Capt. of the* Charles, *in the right and possession of my dread Soveraigne* Charles *the first, King of Great* Brittaine, France *and* Ireland, Defender of the Faith, *the* 15 *of* August, 1631.

This land is called New Wales.

19. The wind being E.S.E., I could not yet come to Sea, wherefore I sent the Carpenter upon the S. side to fell the likeliest of 5 trees the Master had made choyse off, to serve us for a Mayne yard, and [there was] not one of them but was rotten within.[5] The wind doth begin to come about. The Mrs. mate and I fetcht one boate lading of firewood this afternoone, the Whales have now left to come in,[6] but my chiefest [aim in] going on land was to see where the

---

[1] "We have not, as yet, found a tree for a main yard; but, God sending the wind fair, [I] must, I doubt, go without one; for, God willing, I will not stay here" (*Foxe MS.*)

[2] "They . . . came aboard with some fire-wood; about a fortnight's spending." (*Foxe MS.*)

[3] "where the wrecked ship had been [see p. 344]." (*Foxe MS*)

[4] The wording given in the MS contains some unimportant differences.—C

[5] "They all proved adle." (*Foxe MS.*)

[6] "Within this 7 days, the White Whales have not come in. I think the tides do go too hard this spring" (*Foxe MS*)

highest tyde this spring had left his marke; and [I] found it to have flowen 14 foote; but the tydes at height of this spring were inforcd in with E.S.East and E.N.East windes, or else they would not have flowed above 12 foote

This night, 10, were many Pettiedancers.[1] I hope faire weather to come, yet have wee had such as I pray our neighbours in *England* have no worse, and then they cannot have better harvest weather to have in their crop; and, though this may be thought nothing pertinent to the History of a Sea Iournall, yet, having been disswaded from this voyage in respect of the ice, I may thus much write for the incouragement of others that may happen to navigate this way, God giving good successe to this enterprise, that a Sea voyage of discovery (to a place unknowne, and farre remote, and in the like clime) cannot be taken in hand with more health, ease, and pleasure. I am sure it hath beene warme ever since we came from the yce.[2]

20. The wind came about. I sent the Pinnace on land to ballast and to bring one broad stone to make a fire upon in her, which I had formerly marked for that purpose at Port *Nelson*. They found a board broken in two, the one halfe quite gone, whereon had beene the King's Armes, and inscription of the time of Sir *Thomas Button*, his owne name, when and why he tooke Harbour, with other expressions.[3]

---

[1] See p 327 —C.

[2] "I doubt they in England hath had worse." (*Foxe MS.*)

[3] "We found a part of the Inscription of Sr. Thos. Button, in the right and on behalf of our late King James, with his arms, and Prince Henry's" (*Master's MS*) "which board being broken, and no more to be found, take what I have and imagine the rest" (*Foxe MS*). For the wording of that portion of the inscription that remained, see the Introduction, where an effort has been made to restore the missing words. Although, in his book, Foxe does not give the

This peice of board I brought away, for I was under saile when the Pinnace came on board, so as I could not goe on shore againe: otherwise I would have endeavoured to have renued the same, as the act of my noble predecessor.

This ebbe I came to Seawards; but, for feare of shoalewater, I Anchored in 4 fathome, having little wind to chase the ship, and a strong ebbe.[1] Feare called what I had observed at my in-comming into my remembrance, so as I durst hazzard no farther whiles flood came[2] And now I must adde one word or two to what is before concerning this dangerous river, which I would be loath to seek in thick weather[3] Of either side, the S. is best, but is flat a great way off, and Rockie ground; the best of the deepe is ⅔ Channell to S.; there is 12 fathomes in the entrance. In one place, wee chafed our Cables sore against the stones, of wch you might see 4 or 5 drie in the river at once. The last quarter ebbe come swiftest, and in spring-tydes it flowed 3 foot before the tyde set up. The tyde returned to the Sea at a full Sea on shore. The Sun and Moone did both set cleare this night In this River wee got no reliefe[4] but one Duck. Heere a N W. Moone maketh a full Sea.

I wayed againe about halfe flood, and stood to Sea from 6 fathomes to 10, and Anchored in high water in 9 fathomes, cleare ground, making ready to ply or sayle the

---

wording he found on the board, this is given in the MS, together with a portion of the Royal Arms, and the monogram, "I R."; also the Prince's Feathers and the monogram, "H.P."—C.

[1] "Lat. observed 57° 13'." Lo. 0° 28' E [from Port Nelson]. Variation 24° 5'." (*Master's MS.*)

[2] Dangerous rocks were observed by him on entering (see p. 342).—C.

[3] For other observations on the dangers to navigation in Port Nelson, see p. 339.—C.

[4] By this Foxe no doubt means fresh meat, game, or edible herbs of any kind.—C.

next flood; for now I am to discover to the East, betweene this and Master *Hudson* his West Bay, of which I must onely, making a journall, there being nothing else of note[1]

21. In the morning, I tooke the Cocke-boat into the ship. With the flood, I stood to the S.E., and went into the Pinnace at the ship sterne to see her fitted to sayle. Wee came to 7 and 5 fathomes, the land full of woods, but lowe, and stretched here E. and by N. from the River's mouth. Here is good smooth and even ground, if any occasion were hereafter to use it; the land is faire to be seene (at 10 fathomes deepe) upon the hatches; the wind easie from S.S.W.; and we stood 2 or 3 leagues in 7 fathomes. We were at noon in 57 d. 10 m.[2] All this night, I could well discerne the land as I stood under sayle; standing S.E., the land met us.

22. This hot Meridian, I was not in observation.[3] After dinner (with easie wind), I tooke the Pinnace to sayle to shore, but it fell to be calme, and wee rowed all the way, and therein found a white Beare, which we kild coming to shore; it was flat, and many great stones lay at the low water mark.[4] We were no sooner landed but we spied a blacke cloud at N. by W., when presently we see the ship had handed both top-sayles, so as I was constrained to leave this uninhabited shore without erecting any thing thereon, and stand to the ship, which we recovered, but our coats were wet through first, and yet the ship was come to

---

[1] There is an obvious omission of some words in this incomprehensible sentence, but the MS. throws no light upon the matter. Foxe, it may be again remarked, was now beginning actual discovery (see note on p. 341).—C.

[2] "Magnetical amplitude was 2 S. of E." (*Foxe MS.*)

[3] Presumably Foxe means that it was not his watch, but the Master's.—C.

[4] "Lat. observed, 57° 13'. Lo. 0° 38'. Variation, 16° 4'. 16° 50'; 15° 59'." (*Master's MS.*)

us within 5 fathomes upon the Maine. We stood along with land in sight, where there appeared to be a Cape,[1] the land trenting more S. from our bowe. (We stood off and on all night, from 7 to 20 fathomes.)[2]

23. I packt[3] away along the land, as neere as can be thought to lie S E. by E.; the morning was faire, yet the Sunne was valed.[4] This calme afternoone we see 3 Beares in the Sea, five miles from land, the Mr. kild them in the Pinnace. This day we tryed the tyde 4 times, and it set alwayes from the E.-wards; we are now so far from his *primum mobile*, as I think it not worthy the looking after; yet account must be taken.[5] This night the Sunne set cleare as could be, and it was easie wind. I have seene all the land hither from *Port Nelson*, as I did before I came

---

[1] This was, no doubt, Cape Tatnam It is surprising that Foxe did not name so prominent a headland —C

[2] About this point, Foxe's map displays the words, "Wenforth wood huse", but I am utterly unable to explain their meaning. Neither in the printed narrative nor in the MS is there anything to explain them. There can be little doubt that Foxe named the place after the princely seat of the present Earls Fitzwilliam, Wentworth Woodhouse, near Sheffield, in Yorkshire, but why he did so is not stated. Wentworth Woodhouse was then in the possession of Sir Thomas Wentworth, Bart., who was created Baron (and Viscount) Wentworth of Wentworth Woodhouse in 1628, and afterwards Earl of Strafford He was beheaded in 1641. Foxe nowhere says that this man was among his patrons, though he very likely was —C.

[3] Probably *tackt away* is meant. I can find no such word as *packed*.—C

[4] "This beautiful morning the Magnetical Amplitude not worth noting, but some 30' North of East" (*Foxe MS.*)

[5] I fail quite to understand what Foxe means by "his *primum mobile*". Does he mean Sir Thomas Button's or the tide's? Apparently the latter is meant; for, in some copies, I find the words "The Del Zur" (meaning The Mare Del Zur, or South Sea) have been inserted as a marginal note, as though, while the work was still in the press, the expression was found to require explanation. In any case, the expression may be taken as showing clearly that Foxe recognised the uselessness of further search in that direction.—C.

there, but I cannot see any high land, nor find any deepe water; I would gladly see that comfort, and then I would say that the M. were in the increase[1]; howsoever, I thanke God it doth make the nights grow the lighter. The ship is anchored, the watch is set, a marke set on the lead-line, and sleep, like a theefe, doth slily steale upon me.[2] At 12 this night the tide did slacke.[3]

24. I call'd to lift the anchor from the ground & bring the ship to saile.[4] The other daye's N.N.W. wind doth make the Sea's swelling still continue; now the wind S.E. by S. I must stop the ebbes and ply the floods. The distance were too tedious, and to [too] small purpose to insert here.[5]

25. Prayers being ended, I called to heave up anchor; at clock 8 we anchored again; this day we made good way to the E.S.E., and in one Ripling had 40 fathomes; land faire in sight upon the hatches; but this great comfort was not a furlong long, for the water shoaled to the

---

[1] I cannot explain this passage, unless it should read "I would say that the *matter* [*i.e*, the discovery] were on the increase." Foxe's MS. has it. "If God send high land and deep water, I do hope the passage may be won."—C.

[2] In the MS. (fo. 62) this passage reads:—"The watch is set; the ship anchored; a mark set on the lead-line. I hope for flowing tides I sleep like a theef doth, expecting some to steal upon me. My wife is now upon her second sleep, being in bed, as I suppose, about 5 hours. Good night."—C.

[3] "Lat. observed 57° 16'. Lo. 1° 8'." (*Master's MS.*)

[4] This order, given by Foxe, was at once vexatiously countermanded by the Master, who ordered the men to dinner. This led to another wordy conflict between the two, which Foxe's MS. narrates at some length. His remarks end quaintly · "All being done, to dinner we go. Not one word passed betwixt him and me; nor have we drunk one to the other since he told me he cared not for me. It spareth drink well, for now the allowance holdeth out, which formerly was spent in needless pledges."- C.

[5] "Lat. 57° 10'. Lo. 1° 28'." (*Master's MS.*)

old rate againe presently. This night was calme, with much raine.¹

26. I had up my anchor clocke 5, and stood along to the East, sometimes E.S.E., sometimes S.E., as the land lay, or met mee. At noone it came fog, and I anchored for 1 houre. It clearing up again after dinner, I see the land trent to the S.-wards, wherefore I tooke the Pinnace and went within 2 miles of a point² that lay upon our Bowe as we were at anchor, nere wch point all the land was belaid with round Rocks, and all along the shore were ledges of the same, and halfe a mile without us, towards the ship.³ I stood off to give the ship warning thereof, who had espied the same before I came to them; so I stood into the shore, which lay S. along. The ship came along in sixe fathomes, and I had 4, hard within the ridges.

This day a N N.W. wind hath conveid away abundance of wilde Geese by us; they breed here towards the N in those wildernesses. There are infinite numbers, and, when their yong be fledge, they flye S.-wards to winter in a warmer countrey. I hoped, by their taking flight, the wind would have continued.

This low land thus trenting makes me doubt it will bring us still with this shallow water to joyne with *Hudson*, and then leave us and fall away S., and there also

---

¹ "Easy winds; fair and dry. I do remember my friends at Whitby and at Eyton last day, wishing them as fair hot dry weather this hayling as we have. We have seen half a dozen Sea Pigeons, which shows me we are not far from some place of better relief [? for] them than Wild Bears and Seals" (*Foxe MS.*). "Lat. pr. judgment 57° 3'. Lo. 1° 47'" (*Master's MS.*)

² Probably the headland near the mouth of the Severne River.—C.

³ "Upon the shore, being bare stones, there lay a rock or something like Dungeness Lighthouse. The Shallop went within us this day [for the safety of the Ship]." (*Master's MS.*)

must I leave it.[1] I could not perceive that it did flow above five foot water yesterday, and the flood set S.E. The water's side is so flat and Rocky that we cannot land with the Pinnace. We can discerne the going in of many small Rivers, and there out-sets by the change of waters, whose colour is more dunne then the Sea it selfe.[2]

27. Was thicke close weather. At night, 7, it wet. The night proved close. The wind changed from N.W. to S.E. The land lay S.E., and we had a great clumpe of wood on shore like an Iland. I stood twice into 4 fathomes of land, and once into 3 and a halfe, but could not see the trees on hatches. The land stretching, the tydes running and flowing, the expected high land, and all hopefull things are now at an end. This night, casting up my Cards, I did account I was from *Port Nelson*, true course, E S.E., 60 leagues, and that I must be in 55 degr. 50 min. latitude.[3]

28. This, [the] coldest day I felt since I came from *Nottingham's Ile*, was but the Harbinger of Winter. I Anchored in 7 fathomes, and 3 leagues offine I had but 4 fathomes. I stood off into 25 fathomes, and in againe into 11, and Anchored.[4] It blew to top-sailes halfe Mast high. The land low, full of trees; the night was thicke, with reasonable wind at East.

29. I road still all night, for I could get nothing by plying against wind; the wind now doth Souther. About clock 7, we espied a saile standing right with us. It was Captaine *James* of *Bristoll*. Hee came close in at our sterne, and wee saluted each other, he standing in towards

---

[1] This is another sign that Foxe had recognised the uselessness of searching further for a passage in this direction.—C

[2] "Lat. pr. judgment 56° 37'. Lo. 2° 07'." (*Master's MS.*)

[3] "Lat. pr. judgment 56° 07'. Lo. 2° 42'." (*Master's MS.*)

[4] "Lat. pr. judgment 56° 04'. Lo. 2° 49'." (*Master's MS.*)

the shoare, which was in sight, but standing off againe. Hee could not fetch vs, for it was ebbe, the streame and wind setting him to lee-ward; whereupon hee stood into Sea and out of sight, which greeued mee much, fearing I should not see him againe, nor know what discouerie he had made; but he tackt about inward againe, and, the wind Estering at night, hee fetch't me and sent his Shallop on board, inuiting mee to dinner the next day, with my Master and his mate.

There came on board of mee his Lieutenant, his Coxen, and three more. I gaue order to my Officers to take downe the 4 rowers betweene the Decks, and to entertaine them at severall messes, and to enquire of them with what land they fell first after their comming from our owne Coasts; what lands they had beene at, or in what harbours; when they entered *Fretum Hudson;* how long they had beene amongst the Ice; and at seuerall times what Islands they had seene, or Capes formerly discouered; what was the most Northerliest latitude they had beene in; and what day they see first this side or bottome; and in what latitude they came ouer this bay in. I enquired also the like of his Lieutenant, whom I entertained in my Cabin; so that, before they went away, I heard that they first met with Ice at Cape *Farwell,* and that they entered *Fretum Hudson* the 20 day of *Iune;* they had beene distrest in harbour, and had like to haue lost their shippe , the fire-smoake my men see on land the 23 day of *Iune*[1] was theirs. They had seene the Iles *Nottingham* and *Salisbury*, and was on land on Sir *Robert Mansfell's* Isle, hauing before beene sore pestured with Ice The greatest latitude North was 64 deg., and that in this bay of Sir *Thomas Button's* they had beene troubled with Ice, talking thereof as though they tooke pleasure to runne against it;

---

[1] See p. 286.—C.

nay, they said they had runne into the Ice as far as the maine mast, and that they came ouer in 59 deg. of this their Northmost latitude ; of their suffering at *Resolution ;* their grounding in this Bay; the harme of their men throwne at *Capsten ;* and what else I desired to haue, I had ; and that they had been on shoare here but two dayes before, and kill'd two Partridges.[1] They said also that there was no offering to goe home if they found no passeage ; for that the Ice could not bee disolued this yeere, but they must stay vntill the next yeere to haue light nights to shift themselues amongst them. And this I did for that I did not know how wee might be separated beefore I talked with Cap. *Iames* himselfe ; and I gaue order to acquaint them with what also they demanded of vs, telling them that I had beene in Port *Nelson*, and that I had seene [signs of Sir Thomas Button there[2]], and came along this coast, neuer without sight of land, from the latitude of 64 deg. 2 quar., and that in Port *Nelson* I had beene on the S. side and on the land also, before they came, and had named it New *Yorkshiere*[3] ; but, being a barren waste Wildernesse of Birds and wild beasts of

---

[1] No doubt the Willow Ptarmigan (*Lagopus lagopus*), on which Hudson's and Button's crews so largely subsisted during winter (see pp. 134 and 167).—C.

[2] Some words are evidently omitted here from the printed narrative, and neither of the MSS assist in supplying them ; but we may assume they were to the same effect as those I have inserted.—C.

[3] Foxe undoubtedly named the place after his native county, just as Sir Thomas Button, before him, had named the country on the other side of Port Nelson New Wales, after his native country. In both cases, too, the name has been discarded. Foxe's name for the country has no connection with that of York Factory, the important post of the Hudson's Bay Company, in Port Nelson, which was not built until long after, and was named after the Duke of York of that day Although Foxe told James he had so named the land, no previous mention of his having done so occurs either in Foxe's printed narrative or in his MS. journal.—C.

A A

prey; and (chiefely for that it is out of the roade of trading and the passage, where none hereafter will desire to come), I conceiue that I can haue no great honour thereby (although I haue giuen it a name), and therefore doe leaue it to those that are disposed to intitle themselues therein

30. Last night I made loose, and stood along in small sailes vntill this day, 10, moosling[1] my ship with the foresaile. I then stood for Captaine *Iames*, who was a great way on sterne. At his comming vp, hee sent his shallop on board of mee, who, at much perswasion of my Master (although much against my will), I tooke them in, they rowing mee on board (to bee better confirmed). I did begin to reiterate the last euening's discourse they had aboard of mee, to the end I might vnderstand the difference of severall reports (for euery man will report the best of his owne Actions); but the conclusion was that they came ouer and fell in land with this bay in 59 deg. I was well entertained and feasted by Captaine *Iames*, with varietie of such cheere as his sea prouisions could aford, with some Partridges; wee dined betwixt decks, for the great cabin was not bigg enough to receiue our selues and followers; during which time the ship, but in 2 courses and maine bonnet, threw in so much water as wee could not haue wanted sause if wee had had roast Mutton.

Whereat I began to ponder whether it were better for his company to bee impounded amongst Ice, where they might be kept from putrifaction by the piercing ayre; or in open Sea, to be kept sweete by being thus daily pickled. Howeuer, they were to be pittied; the ship taking her liquor as kindly as our selues, for her nose was no sooner out of the pitcher, but her nebe,[2] like the Ducks, was in't againe.

---

[1] Halliwell gives "moosling" as a west-country form of "muzzling". —C

[2] *Neb:* the bill of a bird. *Nib* (meaning the point of a pen or other instrument) is the same word.—C.

The Gentleman could discourse of Arte (as obseruations, calculations, and the like), and [he] shewed me many Instruments, so that I did perceiue him to bee a practitioner in the Mathematicks; but, when I found that hee was no Seaman, I did blame those very much who had councelled him to make choyce of that shippe for a voyage of such importance, for to indure two winters in (as hee must haue done, if hee had any such intent) before hee could come about by *Bonn Sperance*[1] home. Our discourse had beene to small purpose, if wee had not pried into the errours of our predecessors And (being demanded), I did not thinke much for his keeping out his flagg; for my ambition was more[2] Aetheriall, and my thoughts not so ayerie, so to set my sight towards the skie, but when I either call'd to God or made Celestiall obseruation. To this was replide, that hee was going to the Emperour of *Iapon*, with letters from his Maiestie, and that, if it were a ship of his Maiesties of 40 Peeces of Ordnance, hee could not strike his flag. "Keepe it vp then", quoth I, "but you are out of the way to *Iapon*, for this is not it." Hee would haue perswaded mee to take harbour to winter in, telling mee that Sir *Thomas Button* tooke harbour the 14 of this instant.[3] Quoth I, " hee is no precedent for mee. I must paralell my pouerty with poore *Hudson's*, who tooke no harbour before the first of *Nouember;* and that then I durst not take harbour vntill the midst of the same"; besides, I was not come to do so much as another man, but more then any, as I had already done.[4] And if I did forbeare him in this, or any other

---

[1] The Cape of Good Hope.—C.

[2] The context leads one to think that the word here printed "more" should be *not so* —C.

[3] Prickett (p. 166) says the 13th Hawkridge (p. 169), the 15th; but Button's inscribed board, which Foxe found (see p. 349, and Introduction, p. ci), says the 27th.—C.

[4] This was a vain boast, if by it Foxe intended to claim that he had

thing, it was because I was on board of him, and had made some former obseruation, of which I acquainted my Master with, that thereby wee might the better brooke what might bee offered, as boasting of our selues or the like; for it was enough for vs that wee had so great odds in the discouery. Hee said I was to winter I told him hee had a copy of my Commission, as also of all my letters, that I was limmited; but, so as hauing sought all this bay from 64 2 quar. to 60 leag. E S.E. from Port *Nelson* (both my selfe & men hauing visibly beheld all the land along) and that I must [next] see the N.W. from *Nottingham*, as both hee and I were instructed,[1] and [this] I would performe, after I had ioyned *Hudson's* W. Bay with this land now thwart of mee To which words my Master before him preferred mee his hand, to bee willing to the same, which I gladly excepted,[2] although, within three dayes after, he caponed.[3] Wee parted not vntill the next morning's dawning, and this 17 houres was the worst spent of any time of my discouery.[4]

---

already effected more original discovery than any of his predecessors. It cannot be denied that he had, up to this time, carried out an admirable piece of exploration, and he afterwards accomplished much more; but both Hudson and Button before him, to mention no others, had done far more in the way of original discovery Foxe afterwards (pp. 412 and 415) repeats this unjustifiable boast, or makes a very similar one; but his claim (p. 417) that Capt. James had "not performed so much as I by very much" was perfectly justifiable.—C.

[1] See Introduction, p xcvi —C

[2] Of course, *accepted* is meant —C

[3] By this, presumably, Foxe means that he went back on his promise. The word is, perhaps, from the French *caponner*, to dissimulate or play false.—C.

[4] Whether justifiable or not (and they probably were so), nothing could show worse taste on Foxe's part than these contemptuous remarks of his in print concerning Captain James, who, from Foxe's own account, clearly desired to show him all possible courtesy. Some passages in Foxe's MS. are even worse. For instance "About 7 o'clock we espied a sail ... It proved to be a merchant ship of Bristol, wherein one Captain James was." By alluding to Capt. James's ship as

My men told me his men gaue them some Tobacco, a thing good for nothing.[1]

Whilest wee were on board of Captaine *Iames*, wee stood off into the Sea; the Mary[2] in two courses and one bonnet, and the Charles but in maine course and Bonnet; yet went faster then the Mary.[3]

31. I came on board with[4] the Mary early this morning; wee made fast our pinnes,[5] and set saile. I called to take

---

"a merchant ship", Foxe, of course, wished to emphasise the fact that his was (or had been) one of the King's ships; but the tone of the passage betrays the man's great want of good taste. Again Foxe says "I have been 140 leagues to the N of him..... He is minded to do I know not what..... He hath bid me take notice of some lands he hath named; and to small purpose spent we our day and night." We meet with no contemptuous remarks about Foxe in Capt James's narrative, although Foxe elsewhere says (p. 416) James had abused his name and character. The narrative in Foxe's MS. of his meeting with Capt James is very much shorter than that here given, and many of the statements made above are not mentioned in the MS. In the Master's MS we read "This 30th, we came aboard of Capt. James. I had much ado, for all his [*i.e.*, Foxe's] promise, to get him aboard. And when we were there, we staid most part of the night, when we understood that he had made no discovery to the N. of Sea Horse Point, nor had been to the N-wards of 59^d 30', but had been in danger of losing his ship twice. He would that we should agree upon wintering near together, when we had made end of the Summer, but our Captain would not hear [of it] upon no terms, for he was minded to go home; and, before Capt. James, I propounded to the Captain that, when he had done with the S. discovery, that I would go to the N-wards, and if anything should befal us, he [*i.e*, Capt. James] might give information after [his return home]."

[1] See the Introduction, p xcv.—C.

[2] This is a short name for Captain James's ship, the *Henrietta Maria*, so named after the Queen.—C.

[3] "Lat. pr judgment 55° 55'. Lo. 3° 17'." (*Master's MS.*)

[4] This is clearly a misprint. Foxe evidently meant that he came on board his ship *from* the *Mary*.—C.

[5] As Mr Delmar Morgan has suggested to me, this no doubt means *pinnace*, though the word is not so spelled elsewhere in Foxe's book. —C.

my leaue as I came by him (for I could ouer-hale him, as the winding of a Clew), but his men told me that he was in his Cabbin. I gave him 10 Musquets, one Falconet, and presently I hailed in to the land, for we were 8 leagues off by account, and in 36 fathoms deepe. It was morning, 6, when wee parted. At 10, I had the land faire by. I stood S.W. in, for that I knew I could see so farr to the W.-ward as I was when wee both stood off; I bore as much saile (vntill I had the land bould) as the Ship and masts was able to stand vnder; and all the time I had the Maria in sight, I did obserue that shee went away S. or S S E. I made way 10 leagues that day, and anchored at Clocke 8 in 8 fathoms, thwart of a Riuer[1]; low land, and wooded It was faire weather, and easie wind all night

September 1. This day morning, I stood E South-ward, as the land did beare, it being sometimes higher, sometimes lower; one knoale bearing S.W. was higher than all the rest.. Here seemeth to bee riuers and bayes Our deepe this day hath beene betweene 7 and 11 fathomes; I ankored at night, 8, in 7 fathomes, hauing come from shoare two houres in shoale-water, stonie ground. The wind continuing N.W. doth driue a great Sea before it into this bay The *Meridian* latitude was 55 deg. 14 min.[2] I did account [myself to be] 95 leagues from Port *Nelson;* and, if this strong ground doe not deceiue mee, it flowed 12 foote; the flood ranne but 4 houres.[3] Here, a good way to the E., seemeth to bee the opening of some great riuer, or the land doth wind S.-wards.[4] Here is in sight two ledges of great stones that lie almost as farre off as wee ride, about 6

---

[1] No doubt the Wainusk River.—C.

[2] "Lat observed 55° 23' Lo. 3° 51'." (*Master's MS*)

[3] "It hath flowed about 12 foote, if this rocky ground doe not deceive us. The N.W. wind brings the tide along; it runneth 4 hours flood." (*Foxe MS.*)

[4] He afterwards found it to be Cape Henrietta Maria.—C.

miles of the mayne, bearing S.E.[1] This night was faire weather, and cleere Moonelight.

2. This morning earlie, was the ankor vpon the bow, and I stood into 3 fathomes of the shoare, still trenting to the E. Heere was thicke Riuer-water, and small drift wood, such as vsually driue out of Riuers, without whose mouthes lie alwayes shelues, barres, or ridges; I did now account I was about 105 leagues E.S.E. on this side Port *Nelson*.[2]

This day, being thwart the land I sawe yesterday (when I supposed it the W. point of some River, or else the winding of the land to S.-wards, and could see no land to the E. of the same), I made motion at dinner for the N.W. (to the Master and his mate), declaring that now all this vndiscovered land, betwixt Mr. *Hudson's* and Sir *Thomas Button's* [discoveries] was now perfectly finished by vs; for that the land now trenting from this Cape S.-ward must assuredly bee the cheeke of Mr. *Hudson* his West-bay, as may appeare by those Maps brought whome by *Bylot*,[3] after

---

[1] "I perceive that by reason of these Shoals that Hudson never made any perfect discovery here, for, by his draft of Land, it should lie S. and N, but we find it lie rather E. and W And by our lead the water rose 14 foote, but that upon the sheering of the Ship and our rise of the ground, there is no truth for the rising of the water. I desired that we might search from whence this strong tide came, he then being of the mind to go East over for the other side, and so go home. He said it was a Bay, and by reason of the Shoals made the tide so quick, we being some six leagues off So he said 'Well, so you will have it searched, I will stand in near enough', thinking to see So we weighed at 7 in the morning and stood in S.W, passing by 2 or 3 shoals; and, coming within some 12 miles of the Shore, we tacked off again E." (*Master's MS*)

[2] "Lat. pr judgment 55° 33'. Lo 4° 28'." (*Master's MS.*)

[3] This, of course, means maps he brought home when he sailed with Hudson in 1610-11, and not when he sailed with Baffin in 1615 or 1616. The originals of these maps, which would have been of the greatest interest, have not been preserved; but there can be little or no doubt that they included Hudson's own "Card", from which was drawn Hessel Gerritz's Map of 1612 (see note on pp. 130-132).

he[1] was exposed; and now the further search of a passage this way was hopelesse, and there needed no more search in all the side of this Bay, from 64 deg. 30 m. circularly to 55 deg. 10 m ; and, seeing that we could not attempt the N.W. from *Notinghams* Ile (as I was instructed), for the heavie quantitys of Ice which had choaked all the 3 channels at our entering in the midle of *Iuly*, now I did hope were disolved, or els never, and it was best to make tryall thereof whilest this good wind lasted[2]; and withall [I] charged them with their promise made at my parting from *Notinghams*, which was to haue seene a tryall before their going home, at what danger soever (though then there was no attempting), if no passage proves[3] else-weere, and to this same purpose did wish mee to write what I would, and they would set their hands therevnto, which for some concealed reason I did manifest, showing them also that we had long time to spend, for Mr. *Hudson* did not harbour vntill the first of *November*, and, [as] for S *Thomas Button*, hee was constrained [to take harbour earlier]; and that I was not

---

Doubtless Foxe had been shown these maps personally by Bylot, whom we know he knew (see p. 370) Foxe's opinion corroborates the statement already made (p. 131) that the most northerly land Hudson reached on the western side of his bay was identical with Cape Henrietta Maria.—C.

[1] That is, Hudson, not Bylot.—C.

[2] Foxe, in his MS., inserts the following argument—

"*The Reasons and Answers to some as were answered.*

"The north-west search beyond [Cape] Comfort was the first given in charge [for us to do], therefore, now we must do it."

"The Ice did hinder; besides, at Nottingham Island, in 60 fath., we (contrary to Sr Thos. Button's [experience]) found the tide to come from S.E , both on Land and Sea ; nor could we, for ice, have done it, without we had staied from doing this."—C.

[3] Apparently this is a misprint for *proved*.—C.

to obserue any precedent of that nature, for I was not come to see what my predecessors had done, but to doe more; either [to] finde the *Passage* or bring home a good account, which I could not do if I did not speed my Commission with what haste I could ; and, [as] for harbouring, there was none vntill the midest of *November*.

Now how I shall spend all this time and bee able to giue that account his Majestie doth expect, I know not, if I do not goe to the N.W. For, besides it, I am not instructed to search ; which, being put into practice, if it proue not to be had there, but that the land doth stretch to the E., as *Baffine* reports, in 65 deg. 25 m.,[1] then the account will be satisfied, and we may retourne in short time; for this is not aboue sixe dayes worke, if God please this S. winde shall stand; and we may come downe betwixt *Sr. Dudlie Diggs Ile* and Cape *Wolstenholme* into the bottome of Mr. *Hudson's* E. *Bay*, and there winter.[2] Which, if we doe, we must stay vntill *August*, as experience had shewne vs (which was neere a whole 11 months), and therefore now would be the best ; but, to write truth, the Mr. would giue no consent, but [*i.e.*, except] to keepe all safe by seeking for harbour; but his mate's answere was : "Captaine, if there bee any thing more to be done, let vs fall to it whilest the wind is good."[3]

---

[1] See p. 216.—C.

[2] The reference to Hudson's *East* Bay, as distinguished from his *West* Bay, will be found explained on p. 131 —C.

[3] The preceding paragraph is by no means lucid. It may, so far as I can understand it, be read as follows —" If I go home so early in the year, his Majesty will blame me ; but I cannot fill out any more time, unless I search to the north-west of Nottingham Island, as instructed , for I have no instructions to search elsewhere, and I have finished my search in the southern part of the Bay. I could not search in that direction on my outward voyage in July last, because of the ice ; but, if that is not now dissolved, it never will be. If I find the land in that part lies as Baffin reports, then I can return home at once ; for it is not more than about six days' work, if this south wind lasts.

So, grace being said, I came forth and, weering out the maine sheate, commaunded him at helme to goe away N.E. by E.[1]; when, comming more open *Hudson's* Bay (the winde at S. blowing, but to both top-sailes on taut) there

---

But, if not, and if further search is required, then I can go down in to the bottom of Hudson's [*i.e*, James's] Bay, and there winter, ready to search next year, but Hudson's experience has shown that, if we do this, we shall have to wait there till August next (or about eleven months) before we shall be free to recommence exploration, therefore it is best to explore the part now, if possible, and return home; but the Master, as usual, desired to do nothing but remain in harbour." In Foxe's MS, the argument is set out at greater length and more clearly. His concluding words are "I hold it as fit to go home and bring word of what we have done as to go again into Hudson's Bay to seek an unknown harbour, whereby (if we should have perished) my country might have wanted the knowledge of this my expedition Besides, those .. [who go home may begin again in the middle of May] and be as ready with fresh men and victual to perform the hopes as the winterer who hath spent his provision and withered his men, and then shall not be able to proceed (if there were such a passage to be found), having no more victual than will bring him home." This, and Foxe's other conclusions, show the sound common-sense which governed his actions The Master's version of the affair does not altogether agree with Foxe's. It reads as follows —"This afternoon he demanded what was best to be done I answered 'Let us see whether this be a river or indraught' He answered that he would not try amongst these shallows, but he would go home, and, if the Adventurers would set out [another ship], there would be provision for the discovery, and he would go the next year I made answer that, being we came out, and our Instructions lead us to two principal places, that we would never leave the one behind us, for then we should do worse than Hackridge. Then again he was in the mind of wintering, saying (to have the men come to his will) that he would not put up the ship till the 10th of November, as Hudson had done, so as I used still. I went from him and gave him no answer, but went to my Cabin; for he would follow his own will. So he still would say that he would believe no one that had been there before, nor any man's writings but his own Neither, from the first to this present, that he would follow any part of his Majesty's Instructions. .. Lat. pr. judgment 55° 33'. Lo. 4° 28'."—C.

[1] "After dinner, I weighed the Ship, seeing he [*i.e* the Master] would not consent." (*Foxe MS*)

came so high a Sea from S.E. as if it had come from land 200 leagues distance, it came so naturally hoaming; and therefore I doe belieue that the E. side of those Bayes lyeth farther E.-wards towards the River of *Cannada*, and the Longitude thereof is more Easterly then is placed in the Marine Maps.[1]

Standing hence, as before, we fell into 20 and 30 fathomes, making way 7 or 8 leagues the watch. This day was faire weather; in the night was much lightning.

I named the Cape I last parted from *Wolstenholmes Vltimum Vale*,[2] for that I do beleeue Sr. *Iohn Wolstenholme* will not lay out any more monies in search of this Bay. And yet thus much: if he had beene wanting heerein, I am of opinion that the most of those discoueries had never beene attempted. For my owne part, I can say (for so I find) that he hath been for 8 Voyages the principall adventurer in stocke (and Treasuror), supplying the slacke adventure when the stocke came slowly in; and I dare affirme, concerning this Voyage of mine, that he was at least 400 l. out at my home comming, although I did retourne in 6 compleate monethes, [thus] saving 12 monthes vituall and pay; and, besides, am confident that hee cannot bee lesse out then 1,100 l. about this discovery.

Yet I am perswaded that, vpon good grounds (of which I doe knowe him to bee very able to judge), that no subject

---

[1] The "River of Canada" was, of course, the St. Lawrence. The "Marine Maps" Foxe here alludes to were Hudson's Chart (see p. 130) and those which were drawn from it, as Baffin's Chart of his voyage in 1615 (see Markham's *Voyages of Baffin*, facing p. 103), for no one except Hudson had visited the east coast of Hudson's Bay up to this time. Hudson's map shows the east coast of the Bay as lying 303° E (? from Ferro). Foxe (probably on account of the belief he above expresses) places it in 305° E —C.

[2] This is the Cape Henrietta Maria (still so called) of Capt. James, who so named it on the same day. Foxe's cumbrous name (which does not appear in his MS) has not been retained.—C.

in this kingdome parrallelling his degree, would sooner advance to the furtherance of this, or any other designe of such worth, which hee thinkes may redownd to his Majesties honour and his countries good.

[3.] This morninges W. winde brought in a Sea so high and grimme as though it had in fury overthrowne all lands and shoales enterposing the passage betwixt vs and *Iapon*. It swelled so Mountanous high from the N.W. as who of sea-men had seene the same would haue said that there could bee noe land from whence the same came, not of 6, or 700 leagues, and my selfe also, if experience had not shewne me the contrary.[1] I was in latitude 57 deg 28 min., and, from my setting from *Vltimum Vale*, 48 leagues; the winde came from N.N.W. and stript mee into a lease of cources, or 3 lowest sailes[2]; almost as much wind as at any time since I came from home, and more behalfe then I found since I entered *Fretum Hudson*, or 300 leagues beyond. Towards night, I layed to the West in maine course, for feare I might hazard my selfe in the night amongst those Ilands which Mr. *Hudson* (for good reason) calls by the name of *Lancaster's Iles*.[3] All this night I had deepe 47, 44, 40, 54, 50 fathomes.

4. This day morning I tackt to N.-wards; at noone I was in 52 fathomes: lati. 57 de. 55 m.; both top-sayles cast

---

[1] "rain and lightning with a very great westerly sea, so if a man should come in between Mansfield Island and the East Main, and bound for the west, he would say that such a sea, both long and huming, there could be no land so long as we know full well." (*Master's MS.*)

[2] Captain Wharton, R.N., writes "I imagine this term means that the wind freshened so that he could only carry his courses—no upper sails." Captain James also mentions this great storm.—C.

[3] I cannot, either in Hudson's or Prickett's narratives, trace any record of Hudson having named these islands; nor do they appear on Hudson's Chart. They were, of course, named after Sir James Lancaster, one of those who sent out Hudson, and seem to have been either King George Islands or one of the groups of the Sleepers.—C.

over the low-sayles, or courses now goeth on *Bonnets*.[1] I made way in Try 6 lea. S.W & 12.2 m. N.E.[2] This night came the wind S.E., a pretty gale; it was over-cast with darknes.[3] Wee came by a small Iland at clocke one, the highest I haue seene since I came from *Brooke Cobham*[4]; the deepe 70 fathome. I named the Ile *Sleepe*.[5]

5. I made way from last noone to this, 30 leagues N.,[6] and this morning was some slight [fog].[7] I was constrained to breake vp the Pinnas (now growne leakey), although I did soare doubt the want of her, what ever might befall me[8]; but she, being[9] a dragge at sterne, and it was too could

---

[1] "We have had both topsails abroad all day. Over the courses, now goeth the bonnets." (*Foxe MS*)

[2] "To try, or lie-to, in a gale is, by a judicious balance of canvas, to keep a ship's bow to the sea, and, with as much as she can safely show, prevent her rolling to windward in the trough of a sea" (Smythe's *Sailor's Word-Book*) No doubt Foxe means that he made way, in this manner, 6 leagues S.W. and 12 leagues 2 miles N E. This distance he no doubt measured by the log, of which he was one of the first to make use Speaking of the Master and his Mate, Foxe here says in his MS.—"All their former delays have been but to procure £7 per month and then come home and take it; but I hope in God. . . The Master came not to prayers nor dinner this day. The one is a greater miracal than the other."—C.

[3] "We have been forced to keep our tackels upon our pumpes this 48 hours, for our pumpes hath been stocked and the Ship leaks with labouring." (*Master's MS*)

[4] Foxe's MS. here has it "Brooke's Island".—C.

[5] It is not at all clear why Foxe bestowed this name upon the Island, or rather Islands, for there is no doubt that it was one of the groups now known as the "Sleepers". No mention of his naming the islands occurs in his MS.—C.

[6] "From 12 [o'clock on] the 4th to 12 [on] the 5th, [we] sailed N. 10° 50' W. Leagues 31⅔. Lat. pr. judgment 59° 36'. Lo. 5° 15'." (*Master's MS.*)

[7] "some slight thick and overcast." (*Foxe MS.*)

[8] "Though the setting her up did hinder me 14 days [in Port Nelson], yet I pray God we do not stand in need of her" (*Foxe MS.*). "Hail and snow. And now the Capt. caused the shallop to be turned off this afternoon" (*Master's MS.*).

[9] *Was*, instead of *being*, would make better sense.—C.

and wet to keepe men in her, to haue kept her at sale, and as much hindrance to shake the shippe in the winde[1] vntill shee were made dry; besides, my men were pittifully wet. I cutte out the t[h]oughts and nayles, and saved as much as I could, and sent the rest to hazard, though against my will; for I did thinke, if shee had stoode tyght, she might haue afforded mee some helpe in the N.W., whither now I am going; and, if it proue a Bay, or trent E.-wards, then, God willing, I will hazard to winter in Port *Nelson*, to the intent I may the next yeare search *Ut Ultra*,[2] where the passage I hope doth lye. For, if it bee not in that vndiscovered [region] betwixt Sr *Thomas Button's* ankoring last vpon the W. side and *Cary Swanns-Nest*, nor at this hoped N.W., then it is not to be looked for to the W. of *Groynland*.[3] And, though as yet I haue not tryed the N.W.; yet, by what I heard from *Bilot* and *Baffin* in their life time[4] (which was that, if there had bin hopes, they would haue persisted; but, quoth *Baffin*, there I will neuer goe to seeke it), my selfe haue farre greater confidence that it should lye neerer Sr. *Thomas Rowe's Welcome*,

---

[1] That is, "to bring the vessel's head so near the wind, when close hauled, as to shiver the sails" (Smythe's *Sailor's Word-Book*).—C.

[2] He means Button's *Ne Ultra* (see p 179) —C.

[3] "God willing, my intent is to prove the bottom of the North-West, if I can, this year (for which we are now going), and then to look for harbour, which I think may be [found] in the River where Sir Thos. Button did winter, to the intent [that next year] I may see if the Passage do not lie in that undiscovered [region] betwixt *ut ultra* and Cary's Swan's Nest, for I suppose that there it doth lie, or else for certain not in this Bay" (*Foxe MS*) This paragraph confirms the reading I have suggested for the confused paragraph on p. 365 Foxe was, however, as we know now, quite wrong in saying that if a passage was not found in the two directions he names, none existed to the west of Greenland —C

[4] As already pointed out (Introduction, p. lviii), Foxe had personally met these and many other of the earlier navigators. Baffin had lost his life on January 23rd, 1622. The date of Bylot's death is unknown; but the above passage shows that it took place before 1631 —C.

being moved by the high flowing of the Tyde and the *Whales*; for all the tydes that floweth [in] that Bay commeth (neere) from thence.

6. The Master is not in health.[1] The Boateswaine hath not been vpon the vpper decke these 2 or 3 dayes. All els are in health,[2] thankes be vnto God. This morning, the hoary frost hung in our Roapes.

This coole after-noone, the wind veered N.N.E. It blew at most but to course and bonnet. Our ship begins to make water, when shee comes to bee wrunge with lowe sayles.[3] Wee were much troubled with stockadge of Coales before we came into the passage, and heere, again; which Coales wee brought for fiering, if need should stand.[4] The windes are variable here.[5] This night was calme. This easie gale S.E. brought vs since last day 13 leagues N.W. 2 parts N.[6]

7. Wee made way from last day 12 to this 12, 34 leagues[7] by the logge-board,[8] and at noone I was in 61 15

---

[1] "for which I am very sorry" (*Foxe MS*)

[2] "except sore legs and sore fingers." (*Foxe MS.*)

[3] "Our ship now, when she cometh to be wrong in the Sea with sail, is sometimes waterish. God keep her safe for us" (*Foxe MS.*)

[4] "We have been much troubled with packages of Coals we brought for firing." (*Foxe MS.*)

[5] "The wind doth not continue 24 hours without changing in these parts. We steered to the W.-wards, in hope of wind from thence." (*Foxe MS.*)

[6] "From 12 the 5th to 12 the 6th, sailed N W. Leagues 13¼. Lat. pr judgment 61° 48'. Lo. 4° 47'." (*Master's MS.*)

[7] "From 12 the 6th to 12 the 7th, sailed N Leagues 34⅜. Lat. pr judgment 61° 48'. Lo 4° 47'." (*Master's MS.*)

[8] Foxe was perhaps the earliest navigator to make a systematic use of the log This useful invention seems to have been first foreshadowed in Bourne's *Regiment of the Sea* (London, 4to, 1573); but very few references to it occur in the narratives of navigators before 1620, while many passages show that they were not familiar with its use. Foxe, however, in 1631, several times speaks of it, and seems to have made use of it almost as a matter of course.—C.

m.[1]; the deepe was 90 fathomes. All this day, with E.S.E. winde, I stoode N.E. by N., close hailed, 13 leagues. This night I see the land, by my account about *Carie Swann's-Nest*, from whence I departed the 21 of *Iuly*. The morning was sleete; the day after[wards] was faire, and frost. Now the Master and three men more are downe; God better it. I thinke, if I had not come foorth vpon the Decke as I did, we had runne a shoare vpon this low land. I caused presently to tacke about, and we stoode off againe into 70 fathomes. Wee had but 14 presently after wee were tackt.

8. Wee were in 62 deg. 21 m.[2] The land true North 6 myles off. I found it to be Cape *Pembrooke*, 2 or 3 leagues distance N.E. from *Carie Swan's-Nest*.[3] With this S.E. winde, I was faine to plye it up for *Sea-horse point*, hoping, as before, for change of Winds; untill then, wee must bite upon the Bowline.[4] This land is stonie, and a good bold shoare. I stood off into 90 and in againe into 13 fathomes, and sometimes lesse, as I had sight. There goeth but small Tydes, for here are neither Riplings nor over-falls This morning's *Amplitude* was 21 deg; the Land doth

---

[1] Foxe's MS. has it "60^d 15^m", which is probably an error of the copyist.—C.

[2] "From 12 the 7th to 12 the 8th, sailed N 4° 25' W. Leagues 12¾ Lat. observed 62° 26'. Lo 4° 44'." (*Master's MS*)

[3] Some error is obvious here. Cape Pembroke is much more than "2 or 3 leagues distance north-east from Cary's Swan's Nest" Foxe in his MS. says: "I take it to be Cape Pembroke, and not Swan's Nest." He also says that it lay in lat. 62° 18'. Probably the Point he calls Cape Pembroke was the nameless headland lying to the north-east of Cary's Swan's Nest. "This day we had sight of land. [It] was not unlike the piece of land we saw outwards [bound]; low and smooth and whiteish by the waterside" (*Master's MS*) Here, for the first time, it becomes difficult to follow Foxe's course on a chart. —C.

[4] Captain Wharton, R.N., explains this to mean that, until the change came, he would have to sail close to the wind.—C.

make *Bayes* and *Capes*, lying one from another about N E. It is still faire weather, and wee have carried both Top-sayles out since the 4,[1] both day and night.

9 By this, we have plyde up another Cape, the deepe of whose *Bay*, betwixt the same and Cape *Pembroke,* maketh the E. side thereof lye neare S and by E I was in 7 fathom in the *Bay* After this cleare Sunne-rising fell a short fogge, the blowing away thereof blew in both our Top-sayles[2] When I doubled this Cape, the Land stretcht to the N In dutifull remembrance, I named it *Cape Linsey*[3] At some boords wee gate but little,[4] as I could perceive by the Land, and yet I cannot discerne any Tyde to come against us. The Land lyeth now N E Last night were many *Petty-dancers* We had in both Top-sayles, and stood off and on betweene 20 and

---

[1] "the 4th day" (*Foxe MS*)

[2] Apparently he means that the wind blew so strongly that it made him take them in, but, in his MS, he adds "at 12, they went out again"—C

[3] It is very difficult to identify this cape, or to follow Foxe's course hereabouts If, as seems probable, Foxe had mistaken Cape Pembroke, this may have been it. It appears more likely, however, from the description given, that it was the nameless headland lying in about lat 62° 36′ N, long 81° 55′ W, on the east side of Coats Island This is to some extent supported by the Master's MS, which gives the position at noon as lat 62° 28′ N, long 4° 48′ [? 5° 45′] E. (from Port Nelson) No mention of the cape occurs at this point in Foxe's MS. Foxe's chart only confuses the matter further, and some error seems clear; for no Cape Linsey is marked anywhere on the east coast of Southampton Islands, but a cape of that name is shown on the east side of Foxe Channel, near his most northerly point, which he did not reach until some weeks later. In any case, Foxe named the cape "in dutiful remembrance" of Lord Lindsey, one of the Lords Commissioners of the Navy. This would be Robert Bertie, tenth Baron Willoughby de Eresby, who was created first Earl of Lindsey 1626, and died in 1642. He was Lord Great Chamberlain and a Knight of the Garter —C

[4] Probably a misprint for *got* or *gained*. The MS. does not contain the expression —C.

80 fathomes. The Sea came high, and we purchast nothing.[1]

10. This faire morning's cleare ayre blew hard. I cannot conjecture of the Tydes; for if, as Sir *Thomas Button* doth write, that the Floud doth come from N.W. at Isle *Nottingham*,[2] I am sure there is another comes from S E. at the same Ile. Those two, meeting, should both set into the *Bay* of *Hudson* and *Button*, and especially upon this W side, passing from *Sea-horse Poynt*, by those Capes to *Cary Swannes-Nest*, should strongly be forced here, being backt by those Winds; but I find no such thing; for, notwithstanding the Sea comming *Comptor* from *Hudson's Straights* and about *Mansil's Ile* (from the E. Mayne), yet I gain'd, yea and in low sayles, when much Winde compells in my Top-sayles, which doth show that, of the two, the Tyde doth set with me. These cold mists, thicks, and drops, doth make many men droope, and those who formerly complained are not willing to come above-decke.[3]

11. This morning's fresh breese shakt both my Bonnets off, and stript us into over-lowest sayles[4], for all this, in 48

---

[1] Probably by this also he means they could not advance.—C.

[2] See p. 198 —C.

[3] "God, for his Mercy's sake, turn all things to the best for us Our men, with this cold, doth begin to hurkle [i e., *to shrug*], and those that complained are not willing to come above the Deck." (*Foxe MS*)

[4] "Both Bonnetts were on, with a press gale, but, having made our ship leak, we took them off ... The night was as yesterday, clear, with Pettiedancers and much wind. These winds have continued the longest here that we have had any in one place since we first saw Resolution Of all the Ice we met here, betwixt this and Mansfield Island [on our outward voyage], we saw not any now. Blessed be God, whom we beseech, of his mercy, to alter this wind with fair weather" (*Foxe MS.*) "In the morning, we broke two chain plates on our starboard side of the foremast, having but one shroud left, with a backstay" (*Master's MS.*).

houres by the Land, we had gained about 6 leagues, by which it may be discerned what Tyde goeth here.¹

12 I stood off 19 leagues S.; no ground at 80.² I made way 20 leagues, in againe N.N.E. Every night here are *Pettie-dancers*, and red fire flashes in the Ayre, most fearefull to behold. I have plyed 8 watches in but 3 Courses, by reason of much wind betweene S.E. and by E. I had sight of a headland, with a knowell thereon, descending to the Sea³; the Deepe 50. I take it to bee the same Sir *Thomas Button's* Boate was at, where the small Island lyeth there off.⁴ All this day, I was in three courses; the Ship beate sore in this Counter Sea, and no ground at 80 fathomes

This night was all Raine, as the day before in part was sleet At clocke 2, the Raine became Victor, which before was food to the Wind, that in his Calming came S ; and then I directed the Course N.N W., thinking to have sight of my last headland, and from thence to have gone along to *Sea-horse Point* in sight of land, as I might have done if the S W. wind had continued. This cleare Sunne-shining *Meridian*, I was in 62 deg,⁵ but the *Horizon* was not cleare.

---

¹ Sea to N E – F

² "Many times heaved the lead, but could get no ground in 200 fath" (*Master's MS*)

³ So far as one can judge, both from the printed narrative and Foxe's MS, this must have been Cape Pembroke of the Admiralty Chart. "We had, this two nights [past], infinitude of pettiedancers. We have borne but three courses this 8 watches, for much wind, being all the time upon lee shore This afternoon [at] 4, we had sight of it. . . . The N part formed a headland with a knot upon the top, falling a declivity to the sea. The depth was 58 fathoms" (*Foxe MS*). The Master's MS gives the position at noon as lat. 62° 28' N, long 5° 17' E, which must be wrong —C

⁴ See p. 193. This seems to point to Cape Pembroke, though the island has now disappeared —C.

⁵ This must be an error of observation or a misprint. Foxe seems at the time to have been nearer 63° N. His MS. says that they were

This sight of the warme Sunne did marvellously cheare up our men, yet the weather is now very Cold.[1]

13 From Noone I stood away N.E. by E., with flowne Sheat. The Wind veered againe to S.E. open of the *Bay* betwixt *Point Peregrine*, for so I call the last Head-land having the *Knowle* thereon.[2] I had from 70 to 100, 120, 80,

---

in 62° 44′, and on the day after 63° 41′, none of which statements can I reconcile with his apparent position.—C.

[1] "At noon in 62° 44′. God be thanked, this little ☉ shine of change hath made us all more cheerful. The weather here is not [? now] very cold." (*Foxe MS.*)

[2] This affords additional ground for believing that the Point Peregrine of Foxe is identical with Cape Pembroke of the Admiralty Chart. The position of Point Peregrine on Foxe's map, and the description he gives of it as high land, all go to identify it with what is known as Cape Pembroke. At the same time, as he says that there was a "knowell" [? knoll or hillock] upon the cape, one cannot help thinking that he may have reached Terror Point, and that the knoll was Mount Minto (1,050 ft.). If this latter supposition be correct, the headland which he next arrived at, and which he says he "tooke to be the S.W. side of Sea-horse Point", was probably McMurdo Point, which has deep water very close to it, as Foxe says, and the bay between it and his Point Peregrine (which he says may be a throughlet "for anything yet known") would be the northern end of Fisher Strait. Other writers have evidently found great difficulty in locating the Point Peregrine of Foxe (although it appears on his map), for, on a chart of the "Land discovered by Luke Foxe, A.D. 1631, laid down from the Journals of Foxe and Yourin", which accompanies Sir W. E. Parry's *Journal of a Second Voyage for the Discovery of a North-West Passage* (London, 4to, 1824-25), Point Peregrine is shown in lat. 66° 35′ N. as the "northernmost land seen by Foxe". The latest Admiralty Charts show it in the same position, although, according to Foxe's published narrative and chart, the cape so named by Foxe was several degrees further south. Rundall says (*Voyages North-West*, p. 182, *note*):—"Between Lord Weston's Portland, and Fox's Farthest, the charts introduce a Point Peregrine. This name is not to be traced in Fox's [printed] journal or chart in this place. It may have been inserted on the authority of Hurin's journal, of which a manuscript exists, but to which I have not obtained access [see Introduction, p. cix]." As will be seen hereafter, Foxe did name a cape thereabouts Point Peregrine, according to his MS. journal, in which

and to 30 fathomes. This equally arbitrated day and night with wet hazie.[1] I stood in, two Top-sayles over my Courses, N.E. by E., 24 leagues.

14. This day morning, I met with Land I tooke to be S W. side of *Sea-horse Point*, and this 120 fathomes was open upon the *Bay* betwixt point *Peregrine* and this Land, where, for anything yet knowne, there may be a through-let.[2] This land is of an indifferent height, descending by degrees to the Sea.[3] This night was thicke wet fogge. Here was yce put into this *Bay*, as might be suspected by the S.E. Winds, which had blowne so long before untill now.[4] I stood [in] neare to see if anything of note were upon the Land, but, comming neare Yce, we Tacked to Sea againe.[5]

---

several other capes and bays on the east side of Foxe's Channel bear names different from those they bear in the printed narrative and on the chart. The great and inexplicable confusion thus occasioned is discussed hereafter It is not at all clear after whom Point Peregrine was named. Foxe, in his MS. journal, says he named it " in remembrance of that honourable Lord, Principal Secretarye to his Majesty", but I cannot discover that anyone ever bore the title —C.

[1] "The weather is wet, haze ; this day and night hath equal length." (*Foxe MS.*)

[2] There *was* a "through-let", now known as Evans Inlet, near his present position, but he failed to observe it.—C

[3] "The land above was higher than heretofore." (*Foxe MS.*)

[4] "It is only the thick ice that doth the longest remain undissolved" (*Foxe MS.*) "Along the land lay much ice, by reason of the E. winds continuing so long and it being fronting upon the opening, for I take it to be Sea Horse Point (we being close upon the South side) by our Latitude and Distance. . . . Lat. observed 63° 16'; Lo. 6° 07'" (*Master's MS.*)

[5] "This morning, sleet and rain. I do hear that our people be grumbling, saying that all Fretum Hudson is full of ice, and we shall not get home this year. Also the Master (being this morning come out of his cabin once in seven days) doth tell them the same ; and the rogue, the Boatswaine, doth fearfully terrify them, because he hath been in Greenland, and says the Ice will never be melted ; and this is

This morning was sleight, fogge, and raine, but after prayers the Sunne shone, and thawed our men,[1] and made them more limber[2] I was in 63 deg. 41, the *Horizon* was thicke, but I think I was not farre amisse[3] At ½ past 12, it fell calme; the weather beganne to thicke I Anchored in 55 fathomes, the Tyde came from the W., for so lay the Land, and I have boulted it upon a Bowlin,[4] with more or lesse Wind, ever since the 6 day I rid at

---

also the first of him in seven days he hath laid in, yet, as soon as he s by the fireside, this is his talk of despair he said the adventurers may be ashamed to send us to seek a needle in a Bottle of Hay, where many hath been before There is none that withstands but the Gunner . At my coming forth [from my Cabin, the Master being in charge], we were so near as, if the ship had not stayed, we must have been amongst the Ice which lay betwixt us and land, whereupon I found great fault, and he answered (coming forth out of his cabin) that I would not tack when he would I told him I came to discover the land along, and not to run from it as soon as I saw it Upon my soul, he is the most unpleasant fellow that ever kist his Majesty's hand; nor had he been sick [*i e*, he would not have been], but for this going to the Northward; nor is he, but only doth hold off his hand to see what the company will do I must, in this case, speak well of Mr Urin, who doth as yet boldly stand to it God willing, I will prosecute [my voyage] until I am able that I may, by his means, bring good satisfaction, which I hope in him I shall" (*Foxe MS*) The proverb about "seeking a needle in a bottle of hay", above introduced, is very old Most dictionaries give the word *bottle* (meaning a "bundle") as now obsolete, but it is still in use in the hay and straw trade, at least in Essex —C

[1] Prayers are good —F "This morning, after Prayers, it cleared up, having [had] loose snow and sleet all the morning before, and you will not believe how much a little clear [weather] and ☉ shine did stir up the Spirits of our men" (*Foxe MS*)

[2] Skeat (*Etymological Dictionary*) gives Limber = flexible, pliant, supple —C.

[3] "After observation (of which we all despaired), I found I was in 63° 40′, Mr Urin in 64° 01′; but the Horizon was thick I think I was not far amiss." (*Foxe MS.*)

[4] The meaning of this expression is not clear, but Captain Wharton says it may be taken to indicate that he was sailing close to the wind. —C.

Anchor this night, and at past 11 the ebbe Tyde did not leave his course, but onely slacke from 7 to that houre; the Wind at N. blew off the Land, and the Ship came not to Wind-road.[1] I had duly marked the Lead-line, and tryed divers times how the Tyde did flow; and at slacke water I found it to have flowed 20 foot, and this was 24 houres before the Conjunction[2]; and, as I doe remember, Mr. *Baffin* saith that on the other side of this Poynt it doth flow a S. and by E. Moone[3]; this night, I did sit up on purpose to be satisfied herein[4]

Henceforth I doe write true course, variation and wreke[5]

---

[1] "A ship is wind-rode when the wind overcomes an opposing tidal force and she rides head to wind." (Smythe's *Sailor's Word-Book*)—C

[2] "Riding 12 hours at anchor, we found the tide to come from the W b S the first four hours, and after[wards] from the West, and so from the W b N and W N.W.... Yet would the Capt. cast this tide to fall with our tide that we had outwards [bound] at Kary's Swan's Nest, and [he] caused the lead to be hove to try the rising of the tide. The lead would be astern before it came to the ground, the tide going quick and [the depth being] 54 fath" (*Master's MS*)

[3] See p. 217.—C.

[4] "At 11, I (having duly, at 6, marked the line, to know the quantity of water flowing) examined it. It had flown 20 foote. The tide, in this place and time (being 24 hours before conjunction), doth flow (as I remember Mr. Baffin doth register [it] as flowing not far from hence) about S b. E." (*Foxe MS.*). "The rapidity and irregularity of the tides in this neighbourhood were particularly remarked by our early navigators, and indeed gave the name to Mill Islands, 'by reason of grinding the ice.' There can be little doubt that this irregularity is principally occasioned by a meeting of the tides hereabouts, for there is tolerable evidence of the flood coming from the northward down the great opening leading to Foxe's Farthest, and which I have called Foxe's Channel. Baffin particularly insists on this being the case, both near Trinity Islands and off Southampton Island; and, I think, notwithstanding a contrary opinion held by Foxe and Yourin, our observations on the tides in this neighbourhood, and subsequently at Winter Island, serve to confirm those of Baffin" (Sir W. E. Parry's *Second Voyage*, vol. 1, p. 30).

[5] See p. 280.—C.

allowed. The Compasse hath neare 26 deg [variation] heare[1] This night, clocke one, I was under Sayle and Runne 4 Leagues E N E., when I met with yce (but small as chaffe), and, at the dawning of day, I did by this yce assure my selfe that I was the length of *Sea-horse Point* to the E[2] For that this North wind had blowne the mash't yce from above the North side of the Poynt; and so it proved. This yce was both small (and small of it) and thinne. We Runne through it without stay or abatement of Sayle.

15 I stood away from hence, close hal'd, E N.E, 25 leagues 2 miles, then, being towards night, I had sight of *Mill's Isle*, so named by *Bilot* (because of the Ice grinding against him like the grinding of a Mill)[3] and also of *Salisburie*, bearing S E., and *Mill Ile* from N E. to N.N.E. This day and night were hazie The lands had much snow on them. Our Sailes, with wet fogge and frost, were stiffe as Vellome Standing this *Milner's Ile* along, in the night came off either small mash't Ice, or else the shadow of the Moone deceived me, to trie whether I durst not but cast about to the West againe along the Isle, thinking here in this milde[4] Channell to try the Tyde that, all obstacles being removed, the difference betweene *Baffine* and Sir *Thomas Button* might now be reconciled,[5] before I put to the N.W from *Nottingham* (in practice), as I was in-

---

[1] "This night I took the middle course out of Charles' Wain, and place him 30° 40' above the horizon, from Palle [?] 32° 55' Altitude 63° 35'." (*Foxe MS.*)

[2] The observations for latitude given above show he was now near Sea-Horse Point —C

[3] See p. 213 The statement by Captain Coats (*Geography of Hudson's Bay*, p. 72, London, Hakluyt Society, 1852) that Foxe so named them, is an error —C

[4] Probably this is a misprint for *middle* —C.

[5] "I am, by trial, always on Baffin's side" (*Foxe MS*)

structed.[1] All night I stood to and againe, and found a good flood Tyde set to N.W. The Mr. was up this night but was not able to continue.[2]

16. This morning I plyde it up to the West end of the Island, and, when the Tyde was done, I put into a through-let I named *Hurin's Through-let*, for that hee, upon the fore-yard, conducted in the Ship.[3] In the entrance of this Harbour, lyeth a Rocke in the middle, which is covered at ½ Tyde; we bore close upon the W. side, in 10 fathomes, and Anchored in 13; the sound [was] about 3 flight shot[4] over; the Tyde did flow about 4 fathomes; the flood doth set through it to the N., it lyeth N E. in; a S.S E. Moone maketh full Sea.

This Iland lieth along E. ½ S.; *Nottingham's Ile* lieth from this S. ½ E., *Salisbury*, S.S ½ E.; the North Mayne N. ½ W.; all in sight at once, and yet it was none of the cleerest dayes. There is 6 goings out and in to this sound: 5 to the N and but one to the South.[5]

---

[1] See remarks on Foxe's Instructions in the Introduction, p. xcvi. —C

[2] "This cold doth make our men hurckle [see p. 374], yet all [are] willing. The Master was up and is down again. I hear he will come no more to my mess, nor (were I as he) I would not, so long as I could be suffered to spend the ship's store of flower, rye, and spices. However, when we go to Prayers, he will take occasion to go away and walk or read in his Cabin, which example hath made our men very slack that way." (*Foxe MS*)

[3] No doubt the narrow passage between Mill Island and the small island lying close to its western side. Foxe afterwards says there were five entrances on the north, but only one on the south. The chart does not show this, but it is possible that the details of the coast-line have changed since 1631. Hurin, it will be remembered, was the master's mate. Foxe's journal abounds in allusions to Hurin. —C.

[4] See p. 207.—C.

[5] "This afternoon, we harboured amongst certain Islands lying at the W. end of Mill, where, to sea, there were 6 or 7 goings out and in, we went in one the S. side, where doth lie a rock almost in the middle

17. I went on land this morning to hasten our men to fill water in a Coue, where there is a good landing for Sea-Mors, of which wee see here good plentie; and, going on land, one amongst the rest, with her young, being in our way, strucke her yong diuers times, to make it diue downe, which, when shee see it would not, shee encountered our boate, and, with her teeth, strucke at her. *Iohn Coatesworth* strucke her through the necke with a Lance, that all the water about the boate was bloodie; the young and damme went downe, and once againe mounted, but after wee see them not. I haue heard the Mors killers say that their skinnes are so tough as no Lance will enter, it doth yeeld so; and, therefore, to kill them, they must bee before them, to pricke them vpon the nose, that shee, by casting vp her head, may stretch her skinne tought at her breast, wherein the launce will enter with more facilitie (but this proued otherwise).

After wee had watered and come aboard, the flood bending with easie winde N.N W, wee could not ouer haile to get forth the same way wee came in, but turned it to the N. Westward with tide, and came out at the W-most sound, where in the N Channell I found it to come more then 3 houres Tide, after full Sea on shoare, and that very sharpely. The next night's flood, I plied vp to the N. mayne.[1]

18. This morning flood I plied vp by the N. mayne, and stopt [during] the ebbe in 60 fathomes, neere shoáre; the winde N.N W., with sometimes showers of small snow and

---

entrance" (*Foxe MS*) "The Lat. of these Islands (for they are many, to the number of 6, great and small), as [near as] I could tell they lie in the Lat. of 64°, and Long to the E. of Port Nelson 7° 37'" (*Master's MS*)

[1] "The weather . . . very cold and freezeth hard, and our men get up and go down God help us. Some complain one time . some another." (*Foxe MS.*)

hard frost, so as all our tackling and shippe-bowes where the water came were all jce-sickles¹; but it was easie winde and smooth Sea. Here I was 5 miles to N. of a faire headland, so made by the land trenting E. and N. from the same. I named it *King Charles his Promontorie*,² with another Cape to the N. (the land being there N and S. 4 deg W) which I named Cape *Maria*,³ in a most bounden and dutifull remembrance of my King and Queene (because, if this proue a passage, these [capes] are the most remarkeable and of greatest note and most eminencie) drinking their health, with the young Prince's. I had no obseruation since the 14, but doe account the *King's Promontorie* to lie in 64 deg 46 min., the *Queene's* about 8 leagues distant N. from thence. There lieth to the N W of the *King's* Cape 3 Islands, passeable round about, standing like an Equilaterall triangle, which I named *Trinitie Isles*, in the remembrance of the house of *Deepeford Strand*.⁴ A 4ᵗʰ, and out-most, I named *Isle Cooke*, thinking of my good friend and countenancer, Mr. *Walter Cooke*, an assistant in that Corporation.⁵

This little recreation wee had at this Celebration hath

---

¹ "This morning snow [fell], and our ship tubs doth freeze, as all the ship's sides, fore and aft, where water comes." (*Foxe MS*)

² This name is still retained. In his MS, Foxe speaks of it as "the western cape [which] I have not, as yet, named." The latitude given by Foxe is a little too far to the north.—C

³ This is still marked on modern Admiralty Charts as the *Queen's Cape*, a name Foxe also uses for it.—C

⁴ These islands are still so called. They were visited by Sir W E Parry in 1821, when on his second voyage for the discovery of a North-West Passage (*Second Voyage, etc.*, vol. 1, p. 24). Foxe, it should be remembered, was an official of the Trinity House. —C

⁵ He was, perhaps, a personal friend of Foxe's. The MS. has it Coke. Possibly he was a relative of Sir John Coke (see p. 396). —C.

much comforted our men that were aboue, and something cheered those that were downe, as the Master, the Boateswaine, & his mate, the Gunner, Carpenter, Exposer *Russell*[1]; yet they seeme to bee the worse, since this certaine triall of the tide to come from S E, with his constant flowing and ebbing, doth make them conceiue that this hard labour is in vaine.[2] Yet they say nothing to mee but that the N.W. tide was mistaken[3], for the Masters of the *Trinity House* were very carefull that I should bee well man'd, so that I had not aboue 5 but were capable of an accompt, and therefore the easier to bee gouerned and more helpefull to the designe. Thus wee ended the euening in feasting, and reposed vntill clocke 12 in the night, and then wee weighed ankor againe, Mr. *Hurine* and my selfe hoping by this faire meanes to jndure our sufferings, thereby to see the hopes of the supposed passage

---

[1] Previous mention of this celebration seems to have been omitted by accident from the published narrative, but the following appears in the MS. "There are 4 islands lying to the N W of the King's Cape, which I take to be lying about 64° 46' odd minutes I have named three to be Trinity Isles, in remembrance of that house, the 4th and outmost Isle Coke, in the like of my good Friend, Mr. Coke, a master of that Corporation. In remembrance of this, I have caused our men to have pancakes made, what Beer they will, with our health to the King; another the Queen's, in Aqua Vitæ, and so to bed, to be ready against I call" The MS also says that the day was Sunday.—C

[2] "We have now sick the Master (if he do it not on purpose for keeping warm and eating fresh meat), the Gunner, the Cook, the Boatswain's Mate, [and] the Boatswaine. Russell is up again Tom Brown and all the rest complain of cold pains. This working in cold, without hope of passage, doth quite discourage them; nor, indeed, can we long hold out; therefore I thank God for my own health, being enforced to look to both watches; and I pray God I may carry home (if it be my fortune to come there) such satisfaction as may please and satisfy his Majesty, my dread Sovereign,". (*Foxe MS.*)

[3] They no doubt meant the tide observed by Hudson, Button, and Baffin.—C

this way.[1] This ebbe wee held it vp vnder saile (and ankored not).[2]

19. This day wee plide about the *Queene's* Cape. The S side thereof is all Rocks, small Islands, shelues, and ouer-falls, from 45 fathoms into 20. The land to the N. of the *Queene's* Cape doth lie N.E.; this Cape doth lie in abouc[3] 65 deg. 13 min. of latitude.[4] It hath beene showers of snow all day. I ankored at Clocke 5 in 30 fathomes, blew oaze.[5] The ebbe was come on, and therefore wee came to a sharpe bitter before our ship staid.[6] This Tide run from the N E., as the land wended, 3 miles an houre.

The night Tide, I plide vp N.E. 6 leagues, and stopt in 23 fathomes, clammy oaze, 4 leagues from land.[7] At [the]

---

[1] "Our people had made themselves merry, as Mr. Urin and I did also I hope, by this means, to procure them to abide their larger hindrance; for so I may well call it I would do anything to have a perfect discovery here, which I much doubt of, yet, for certain, those great tydes cominge through Fretum Hudson must have recourse to another Ocean, in respect of their constant ebbing and flowing" (*Foxe MS.*)

[2] "This close weather, we have had no observation since I came from [Sea] Horse Point, but I do imagine we cannot be in less this noon than $64\frac{1}{2}°$." (*Foxe MS.*)

[3] Probably this is a misprint for *about*.—C

[4] "This morning we were plied up about five Leagues, as the land lies, towards the Queen's Cape The shore is full of Islands and Bays. We had (one league from ledges of islands, lying off shore) 40 fath.; shells and stones. Three leagues off N W. from the Cape [was] all full of overfalls and great races, and 45, 36, 36, 23, 35 [fathoms] deep. Standing along N E, the land doth lie so, and still more to the E I do reckon the Queen's Cape to be in 65° 13' Lat." (*Foxe MS.*)

[5] He means that, when he sounded and found it 30 fathoms, the lead brought up *blue mud* (ooze).—C.

[6] This expression (which is explained on p. 390) means that the ship had to be brought up sharply by letting down the anchor.—C.

[7] Foxe was now again commencing what was practically original discovery; for (although Baffin and Bylot had, in 1615, reached what

first comming of the flood tide, it came W., and in 3 glasses it set round about by the S to the N, still running without any stop. Heere doth appeare to bee Islands and throughlets that doth alter the Tide's course, when hee beginneth not to take his Currant, vntill the ½ flood bee past, and then hee retaineth his constant course.[1] It is now and then snowing.[2]

20. I rid now in latitude about 65 50 min.[3] The day came on, and I see the land lie along N E. by E, with 2 Islands neere,[4] the one a league off the other, bearing S.E. and S E. by E Cloase weather, some snowie. The low water slacke was this day at Clocke 11.

I made way from 11 (that I weighed anchor) to 5, 12 leagues N.E. by N, when I raised a point or head-land of good height, descending to the Sea, or W.-wards. The *Throughlet* or Bay on the *Starbord* (as I did coast the E.

Foxe named the King's Cape) to Foxe belongs the honour of having thoroughly explored the coast-line beyond, and of having named its more prominent features. The land along which Foxe was sailing is now known as Foxe Land, while the large channel up which he was sailing is known as Foxe Channel, both names having been bestowed by Sir W. E Parry on his second voyage in 1821. It is, I believe, true that this coast has never been visited since Foxe discovered it, and it seems quite likely that it is by no means correctly laid down upon our charts.—C

[1] "The flood come W, and in 3 glasses set round about to the N, and so to the E.N.E, within my sleep [?], running easy still, which I much marvelled at, and do think that the land doth lie S.-ward, or else we should be near some Islands, or Bays, or Rivers, or Indraught Being come up, the Ship rode the whole Ebb." (*Foxe MS*)

[2] "The 18th, at 11 o'clock, we weighed Till ½ past 4 [on] the 19th, we found the land stretch away N.E. b. E This two tides, we plied it up some 28 leagues. Depth 60, 45, 50." (*Master's MS*)

[3] "Where now we rode, I take to be in 65° 50', odd min" (*Foxe MS*)

[4] These two islands are mentioned in the MS, but a side-note says "The round hill and great island proved mainland and high." If, however, he was, as he says, in 65° 50' N, the islands would be those marked on the charts as lying along the coast between Capes Weston and Dorchester of the Admiralty Chart.—C.

side) I could not see the bottome, not of 7 or 8 leagues deepe. I had 43 fathomes oazie ground. From this Cape the land doth trent to the S.-ward of E. The further I came to the N.-wards, I haue still darker nights. The Moone is waineing, and it's could weather.

Comming neere vnto this Cape, I see many ouer-falls and races in the Tide's face, being deeper, & with more breacke[1] then heretofore, so as I caused an ankor to bee made ready, hauing then 20 fathomes; but, before I came to the first ouer-fall, I had but 7, 8, 10, differing as fast as the lead went down. I anchored in 8. The Cape bore S S W. 2 leagues off At the full Sea slacke, I could see betwixt vs and the Cape all broken grounds, and the ebbe came on so swiftlie, as it was bent before wee could get vp our anchor, thinking to fall from those ouer-falls, and wee were iust at the S. end of those broken grounds. The land stretcht away S E. from hence. It runs about ½ Tides, for the broken grounds were drie within vs before the Tides returne.[2]

To conclude, I doe account this Cape to lie some mi. within the *Artick Cirkle*.[3] It stretcheth E.-wards as before, which, in hazie weather, as in the night, is easie to discerne in those parts, for the land lying hid in snow, doth cause a white reflexe in the Ayre all night, as though it were

---

[1] Presumably *more broken water* is meant Drayton uses *brack* for salt water. The MS. simply says that coming near the Cape, they had "shoald water... with many overfalls".—C.

[2] "From 10 o'clock the 19th at night till four in the morning the 20th, the land stretcheth away pr. compass N E. b E, E.N.E., [and] E. b. N Upon this flood, we plied it up some eight leagues, still keeping some 3, 4, 5 leagues off the shore. Depth 60, 45 fathoms. Wind, N W.W., and, heaving the log, the ebb run some three knots and ⅓, having one part East some five leagues distant, the other S by some 8 leagues. Very fair weather and smooth water." (*Master's MS*)

[3] "We do account with our Compass some 65^d 50^m odd, and that we are about the Artic Circle—that is in $66\frac{1}{2}$. (*Foxe MS*)

dawning or twi-light, before and after sun-set. This Cape I named my Lord *Weston's Portland*.[1]

Hauing weighed ankor, I stood off N by E. and N.N.E.[2]

---

[1] Foxe named this cape after Richard Weston, first Baron Weston, who was created Earl of Portland in February 1633 He was Lord High Treasurer and a Lord Commissioner of the Navy, and died in 1634. A Cape Weston still appears on our charts, but there is, I think, some error as to its position On the latest Admiralty Chart (which appears to be based on the chart drawn by Parry from Foxe's and the Master's MS. journals; see p. 376), it lies in lat. 65° 35' N , but this is almost certainly not the position of the cape to which Foxe applied the name He has just informed us that he rode in lat 65° 50', or 15' to the *north* of the cape now called Cape Weston, and had sighted some islands which lie in that latitude Further than that, he says (p 387) he accounted his Cape Weston "to lie some min within the Artick Circle" (which is in lat 66° 32' N) Elsewhere, moreover (p 411), he repeats that his Cape Weston lay "in the latitude 66 d 47 m.", or about 15' within the Arctic Circle It seems probable, therefore, that the Cape Weston of Foxe is that to which our modern charts assign the name of Cape Willoughby, and which lies in lat 66° 37' N , or thereabouts. This complication is only the first of a series, for several names which, according to his MS, Foxe bestowed on certain geographical features on this coast, do not appear at all in the printed narrative, where these capes appear to bear different names Thus, in the MS, Foxe speaks of having given the following names in the following order —

Cape Dorchester,	Lord Dorchester's Inlet,
Cape Weston,	Browe Carleton,
Cape Willoby,	and
Cape Peregrine,	Wolstenholme Vale

In the printed narrative, he mentions —

Cape Weston,	Point Barte,
Cape Dorchester,	and
Foxe's Furthest,	Point Carleton

The inevitable result of this confusion is that it is impossible now to tell to which points Foxe applied these names. The muddle thus caused seems to me inexplicable, and is increased by the fact that none of these names appear on Foxe's map, the scale of which is too small to show them I have, therefore, appended portions of the MS. Journal for comparison with the printed narrative

[2] Probably this is a misprint for "N. by *W*. and N N.*W*." See p. 411.—C.

10 leagues (thinking to stand with the W. side), that thereby, if I had found the land to stretch to the E. and S.-ward, as this did, the flood going accordingly, would haue giuen good satisfaction to his Majestie; but I was not able (the reasons you shall find after the sequill of this journall, amongst the reasons for my home-comming this yeere[1]), and ankored, some while before the ebbe had done runnning, in 28 fathomes.[2] I commanded the watch to trie the streame of the Flood-tide by the log[3] (when it was bent) In the fourth glasse of the watch, my selfe, comming foorth of my cabbin and looking ouer-board, see the Tide did not goe aboue 2 knots. The watch answered that it did not runne so fast as at first comming on; then it went $3\frac{1}{2}$, but was now abated. I was no sooner laid downe in my cabbin but that I heard the Cable run forth, and wee had

---

[1] See p. 411.—C

[2] It should be mentioned that, about this spot, Foxe's map shows "Cape Linsey", though, according to the narrative, he applied the name to a cape on the east side of Southampton Island (see p. 373). The MS contains no mention of another Cape Lindsey in this region, and on the whole it seems most likely that its appearance here is due to an error of the draughtsman who prepared Foxe's map. The confusion seems inexplicable on any other supposition.—C "[We] are past a point of high land, falling low towards the sea as from the Island at which we weighed. It hath been a bay with 4 Islands and broken land within . The land hath laid along N.E by N., 5 leagues off, all the way we have come, only the cape is come off to the Northward and met us within $1\frac{1}{2}$ almost I can as yet see none to the E of this Cape Coming near this Cape, we had shold water with many overfalls. . . . We do account with our compass some 65 50 odd, and that we are about the Artic Circle; that is in $66\frac{1}{2}$. At 6 o'clock, we were constrained to anchor in 8 fathoms, thereat the Cape, which I call Cape Dorchester. . . And blessed be God we did; for, before we weighed (which, with first of the Ebb, we did), many of these overfalls proved to be upon rocks, dried With the Ebb, we stood off N. b. E , N , N. b. E , and N.N E., as the wind \aried." (*Foxe MS*)

[3] See p. 371.—C.

all much adoe to bring the shippe to a bitter[1] before it was out, end for end.[2]

Now you shall vnderstand that the ankor had Cadged a great while, when comming to take (a sudaine) hold, broke the two Lashers of our stoppers,[3] and hal'd the Cable about the bitts, the tide taking the ship away 4 knots ½, shee hauing driuen an houre or more before. In the morning, the land beare S. by W from vs, so that wee though[4] wee had run through it the last night's ebbe, when it prooued the former, as Lord *Weston's Portland*, for in that bearing it seemed like an Isleland. The deepnesse of the Bay to the S E tooke away the sight of any other land, for, making account that the ebbe set W, standing as before 10 leagues from the Cape, it should haue beene so; but, finding it otherwayes, as wee stood with ebbe S.W., wee were drawne into the Bay on the S side of the Cape, where we espied the land to stretch as it did the day before, with the same forme which I drew, then I knew that for certaine it was the same *Portland* Wee stood along S S W. this ebbe, and got not so much, with both ebbs and wind, by 2 leagues, as wee lost the flood betwixt them.

[21?] This day wee see the Sun, but to no use   I drive

---

[1] The *bitter-end* of a cable is that end which remains on board the ship and is made fast to the "bitts" when the ship is at anchor. The "bitts" are pieces of strong oak timber, fixed upright in the fore part of a ship, and bolted strongly to the beams, for the purpose of making fast the ship's cable when she rides at anchor   Thus, when the cable is let out to the bitter end, no more remains to be let go   Hence the now-common expression, "to the bitter end —C.

[2] "We anchored off 28 [fathoms] somewhat before Ebb was spent, it coming from the E and E. b. S, as it did upon the last shoalds; the flood from W" (*Foxe MS*)

[3] The lashers are pieces of stout rope, made fast to a ring-bolt on deck and to the "bitter end" of the cable, as an additional security in the event of its parting from the bitts   In this case, however, both gave way, and apparently Foxe lost his anchor and cable.—C

[4] Query, *thought*.—C.

along the coast with an easie breath from N.[1] (Some snow fell.)[2]

The tydes do abate, to-morrow being quarter day. The last night was some lightning

But, for the Sea-man's better vnderstanding (of this), I conceiue it may bee made appeare[3] by a familliar example nearer our owne doores, and especially by both example and demonstration; here, as followeth, may better satisfie then the historie it selfe can jllustcrate

The Example.[4]

ADmit a ship to be nere the shore to the N.W. of the point of *Portland*, in *Dorset-shiere*, with easie S S.W. gale, standing W., close hal'd; the Flood-tide, being comming in from about the *Berry*, into the Bay of *Lyme*, falling S.E. into the *Race*, shall take the said ship vpon the Lee-bowe, and, in despight, carrie her into the *Race* at the S. point of *Portland*, it setting E., where then shee shall

---

[1] Apparently Foxe was now returning southwards, though he does not distinctly say so, either in the printed narrative or the MS. In the former, a marginal note (which was probably added because the omission was observed) simply says "I returned".—C.

[2] "From 12 in the morning the 20th till 5 in the afternoon, we found the land to trent away to the E ; E. b S. pr compass. This tide (by the setting of two headlands, by distance and bearing) we got about 8 leagues, finding the land to fall away E., E. b. S., lower land than any between Mill Island and this place, and our depth from 35, 20, 15, 12, 8, 7, 8. And, anchored and riding upon the Ebb some hour, we saw a large rock adry; so, seeing the water shoalding, the land low and with the N.N.W. wind, our Captain being fully resolved and we still carrying our flood with us, we weighed about 6 o'clock and stood it over N , N N.E , N b. W the whole Ebb. Depth from 8, 12, 20, 30, 40, 30, 20 fath., and anchored with the flood and found it to run by the log 4 knots 5 fathom. Smooth water and fair weather" (*Master's MS.*) With these words, the copy of the Master's Journal, preserved in the British Museum, ends abruptly. – C.

[3] Probably *apparent* is meant.—C   [4] Note, Seamen —F.

stemme the same, whose greater force (she not being able to ouer-hale) shall tacke her about the said Point, and then, setting E.N.E. and N.E. vpon her wether bow, shall carry her into the grasse.[1] Now, with same wind, same tide, and same winding, shee shall bringe the same land W.S.W. or S.W. vpon her. This same happened to me at this new head-land, which, being in the night, did not a little stumble mee to find out, vntill my remembrance questioned with my experience to find the cause, which otherwise we must haue thought that we raised a new land, for which similie, as other jnducements to the furtherance of this enterance, I haue named the same fore-land my Lord *Weston's Portland*.

Here followeth the Demonstration.[2]

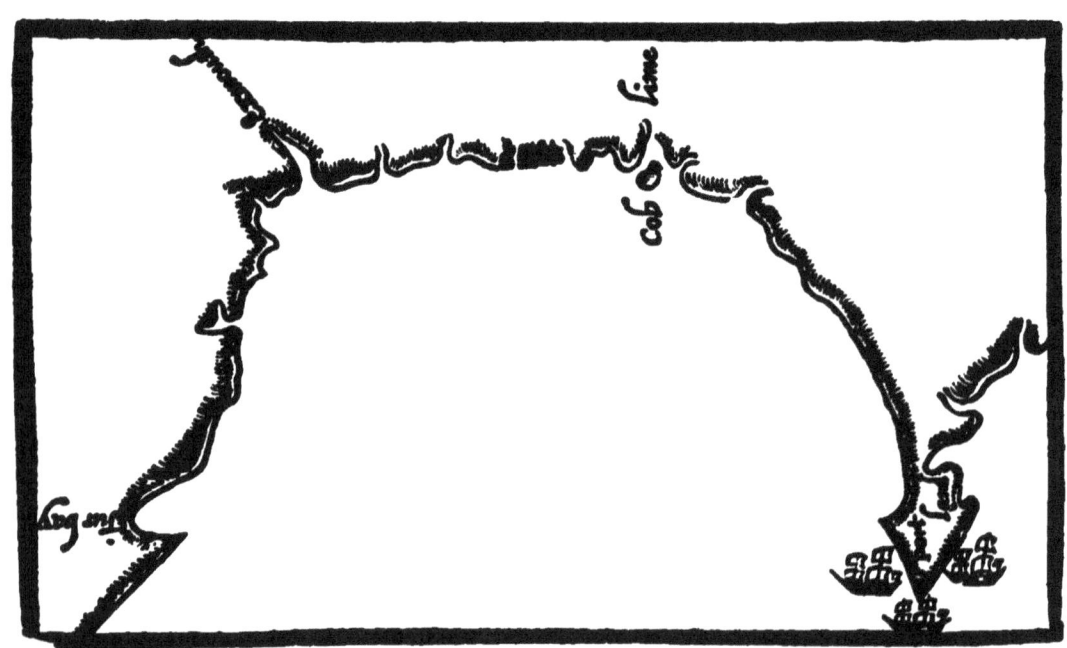

22. Standing along this coast, betwixt the Queene's Cape and L. *Weston's Portland*, I named another headland Cape

---

[1] Query *race* —C.

[2] This "demonstration" is a fairly-correct map of the coast-line of Dorsetshire and Devonshire from a little east of Portland Bill to a little west of Berry Head, Brixham —C

Dorchester,[1] remembring Captaine *Davis*, writeing of *Secretarie Walsingham*, who saith that, at his death, this Voyage was left freindlesse, though I am sure this Noble Successour revived it againe with his best furtherance and my incouragement. I came to this Cape at 6 this morning. I had along the land 20 fathomes. There are store of Sea-Mors in this Sea. The land doth lye full of Snow. It freezeth the very Ship side and steepe tubbes.[2] The Capes, as L. *Weston's Portland*, and Cape *Dorchester*, are distant about 20 leagues The land stretching to the S.E., to the North of L *Weston's Portland*, I named *Foxe his farthest*.[3]

---

[1] This name still stands on our charts. Foxe, as he tells us see p. 397), named this cape in honour of Sir Dudley Carleton, first Baron Carleton, one of the most skilful diplomatists of his time, a great patron of the fine arts, and a friend of Rubens. He was born in 1573, created Baron Carleton in 1626, and Viscount Dorchester in 1628 He died in 1631-2, when his honours became extinct. It is, however, by no means certain that the cape marked as Cape Dorchester on our charts is the one Foxe so named   Certainly it is not, if Cape Weston is rightly placed on the charts, for Foxe says his Cape Dorchester was "betwixt the Queene's Cape and L. Weston's Portland". As Foxe says, " I was in 65 deg. 30 min. Cape Dorchester bore S E. by E. four leagues [off]", it seems more likely that Foxe's Cape Dorchester is the cape called Cape Weston on our charts, or else the nameless cape a little to the south of it ; but the confusion is so great, that it is impossible to speak with any certainty.—C.

[2] The tubs of brine containing the ship's salt provisions.—C.

[3] It is not clear from the narrative whether he applied this name to a cape, or a bay, or only to a geographical position. He seems, however, to have correctly calculated its latitude as 66° 47' N. In his printed narrative, Foxe says absolutely nothing as to his reasons for thus turning back, just when it might have been supposed he would have been most anxious to press forward , for he had been sailing for some days more or less in the direction in which he hoped to find a passage, and through an open unobstructed sea. In his MS. journal also, he gives no explanation, while the Master's journal ends on the 21st, or the day previous. In the Postscript to his narrative, however (p. 441), Foxe most clearly states his reasons, which are conclusive. The continuation of the coast-line northwards from the point where Foxe turned back, remains to this day as unknown as

The deep Bay or Inlet to the S., betwixt the same and Cape *Dorchester*, I named the North side Poynt *Barte*[1]; that on the South [side] Browe *Carleton*.[2]

This Meridian, I was in 56 d 30 min Cape *Dorchester* bore S E. by E. 4 leagues. I have come backe againe from L̃ *Weston's Portland* 26 leag. S.E. by S , which is about 1 deg 5 min., and I was to the W.[3] of it 12 min., [which,] added, maketh 1 deg 17 min, to 65 deg 30 min maketh 66 d 47 min., my furthest N [4] This day, the wind was all over at

---

when Foxe left it , but it must be admitted that this is because it lies out of the main lines of Arctic Discovery —C.

[1] This is one of those names which appear neither on the map nor in the MS. journal It is impossible to be sure which Cape was so named, or in whose honour it was named I cannot learn that there was at that time any peer or person of eminence after whom Foxe is likely to have named it.—C

[2] This, again, is a name which does not appear either on the map or in the MS., and it is also impossible to locate it Clearly, however, it was intended further to honour Sir Dudley Carleton, first Lord Dorchester —C.

[3] Doubtless a misprint for *N* —C

[4] "At six in the morning, we weighed ; small winds , we came across a Cape to the N of the Queen's Cape I called this Cape Weston, in remembrance of the Lord Treasurer . Store of Sea Mors are in these seas We hurried up faster in 2 floods than back in three Ebbs. It is still close weather The land full of snow, and it freezeth the ship's sides. The Cape furthest to the N E of this part discovered, I have named Cape Willoby; the low land Eastwards, Peregrine, in remembrance of that honorable Lord, Principal Secretary to his Majesty , the Bay between it and Cape Weston is the Lord Viscount Dorchester's Bay or Inlet ; the North side thereof (being three of the steepest cliffs hereabout) Browe Carleton. The land E.S E 3 leagues from Peregrine, I have named Worstenholme Vale, and the furthest in this discovery The Capes of Willowby [and] of Worstenholme are distant about 23 leagues N E. b. N Carleton Browe or Dorchester Inlet the midway betwixt them the furthest N. We were here 4 leagues from Point Peregrine This meridian we had observation, and I was in 65° 33', the Cape Weston S.E by E. 4ᵈ E. It doth begin to be wet fog God turn all to the best for us. We have come back from Point Peregrine 26 leagues S E. by S., which is about 1° 5', and we were to the N. of it 12'—in all 1° 17', added to 65° 23' is 66° 40',

clocke 4. It came to the North, and having stopt the flood tyde going 2 knots & ½, I wayed and came along S.S.W. and S.W. by S., as the land did cost,[1] and fell into 40, 60, 78 fathomes; and then, it being night, I did recount[2] I was past the overfals to S. [of] the Queene's *Forland.* Then I directed the course to be S.[3]

23 This morning *Aurora* blusht, as though shee had ushered her Master from some unchast lodging, and the ayre so silent as though all those handmaides had promised secrecy. The Eastermost of *Mill* Ile bore S.E. by E, the North Mayne from the King's *Promontory*, stretching E away; Prince *Charles* his Forland, so named by *Bilot*, bearing E.N.E.[4]; and, at the East side of the said Forland, goeth in a very fayre sound. I named it the *Prince his Cradle*[5] An Iland on the West, I named his *Nurse.*[6] Off this Cape 1 league, I had 120 fathomes.[7] The

---

my furthest being N" (*Foxe MS.*) Apparently, on further consideration, Foxe decided to cancel the name "Wolstenholme's Vale", which he here says he gave to a cape in Foxe Channel; and, in his printed narrative (p. 367), he bestowed it upon the cape now known as Cape Henrietta Maria. He seems to have acted similarly in several other cases —C

[1] No doubt a misprint for *coast*, meaning *trend*.—C.

[2] No doubt he means *account* —C.

[3] "Then were we past the overfalls of the Queen's Foreland, so we come S.-Westerly" (*Foxe MS*)

[4] This name does not appear on our latest charts. It was presumably named by Bylot in 1615, but there is no mention of it in his narrative. It seems to have been one of the headlands to the east of the King's Cape of Foxe.—C.

[5] This curious name has not been retained —C. "We have come to Prince Charles Cape, so named by Mr Baffin I have only named a rock at the one the part to E goeth in a dirty sound hard by it I call the Cradle It lieth about 5 leagues N.W. and S.E. from King Charles' Cape, and N from the E. end of Mill Island. The Coast to the E-ward lying E S.E, all high land descending to the Sea without any Cliffs, as I see none in all this country" (*Foxe MS.*)

[6] This name also has been dropped —C.

[7] Variat. 29d. by Amplitude.—F.

Prince his Forland doth lye 5 leagues S E. from the King's *Promontory*.[1] Yesterday the Carpenter laid downe, haveing not beene well for diverse dayes before.[2] It was little wind, with great store of *Henbans* and *Pettidancers*, a common incident to these parts in cleare nights[3]

24. This fayre day, wee came along the North Mayne E.S.E, with N.W. wind 10 leag distant from the Princes Cape E. South-East, lyeth a fayre Cape I named Cape *Dorcet*[4], and 3 leagues to the East of that is another I named Cape *Cooke*,[5] in due respect to Sir *Iohn Cooke*, Secre-

---

[1] "In this calm morning, we had the furthest land of Mill Island S E b. E and the furthest of the N main E, having passed the King's Foreland but in sight, and were S S W in Charles Foreland in 120 fath" (*Foxe MS*)

[2] "It still continues close weather; last night some snow, but now it freezeth not" (*Foxe MS*)

[3] "A Comet incident to these parts in clear nights (but no storm followed)" (*Foxe MS*)

[4] Cape Dorset still appears on our charts, but it does not seem to me very certain that it is now applied to the exact point so named by Foxe. Foxe named the Cape after Edward Sackville, Earl of Dorset, who succeeded to that title in 1624, and died in 1652.—C

[5] It seems to me probable that this is the cape to which the name of Cape Dorset is applied on the latest Admiralty charts, but this is by no means certain. Foxe named it, as he says, in memory of Sir John Coke (not Cooke, as he spells it), one of the foremost statesmen of his day. He was born near Derby in 1563, and, though starting life on very narrow means, raised himself to a position of eminence. In 1618, he was appointed one of the first Commissioners of the Navy, and in 1625 it was said of him that, "the rest of the Commissioners were but cyphers unto him" In 1624, he received the honour of knighthood. He was first appointed one of the principal Secretaries of State in 1625, and he afterwards held many of the highest offices of State. During the whole of his tenure of public offices, he was active and intelligent, bestowing laborious attention on all the business that passed through his hands. It has been written of him that, "as an official, he was honest and capable, and his private character was blameless. The servility which stains his public career was inseparable from the theory of absolutism which he professed" He died in 1644. Cape Cooke is not mentioned in the MS.—C.

tary of State, with a deepe Bay betwixt them, as it were halfe incircleing an Iland remote from the Mayne. I named it Ile *Nicholas*¹ The former names given (as Cape *Linsey*, Cape *Portland*, Cape *Dorcet*, Cape *Dorchester*, Cape *Cooke*), I gave in dutifull remembrance of those Lords Commissioners for the Admiraltie, whose furtherance and countenances, in my dispatch for his Maiesties Pinnace the *Charles* I had towards the accomplishment of this designe Ile *Nicholas* I named in remembrance of Master *Edward Nicholas*, Secretary to the said Lords, whom I have often troubled I named those Capes as the occasion in my discoverie offered itselfe.

The land to the East from Ile *Nicholas* along the North Mayne lyeth in sight North-East by East, and the same Mayne from Cape *Dorcet*, by Cape *Cooke*, lyeth East by North about the former distance. At the end thereof, there is no land to be seene to the N. I directed the course from Ile *Nicholas* E.S.E.

This evening, clocke 8, I was distant as before from the Ile, 8 leagues, and *Salisbury* was from mee West by South one halfe Southerly, 12 leagues. I lancht away from hence (true Course, as all is set downe) East South East.

25 This noone I had steered this course 4 watches, 25 leag, to bring mee betweene the *Salvage* Iles and Prince *Charles* his Cape, upon the South Mayne² At this time, the

---

¹ Although this name has not been retained, it is not difficult to identify the island, which must be that a little to the south of Cape Dorset on the Admiralty chart (see also p. 302). Mr Edward Nicholas, secretary to the Commissioners for the Navy, was born in 1592. In 1636, on relinquishing his post as Secretary to the Admiralty, he became Secretary of State, was knighted in 1641, and died in 1669. His voluminous private correspondence with the King has been recently published by the Camden Society.—C

² Perhaps one of the Capes on Charles Island, though the name is not now retained for any of them It must not be confounded with the Prince Charles Cape of Bylot, upon the north main.—C.

body of the Northermost Ile bore from mee N.N.E. one halfe N., about 6 leagues. The night was close, but faire weather; this night and last day wee came by many small Ilands of Ice, all the small chattered, which this strait laid so full of, being desolved and gone, for we see none since we came from Sea-*Horse Poynt*.[1] This day was some Snowe. God continue this W.N.W. wind, for wee have many that already have made a Scurvie Voyage of it. The Mr. is up againe.[2] Running, as before, 5 leagues, at clocke 4, Cape *Charles* bore S.W. by S. ½ S., about 12 leagues off. These Ilands, called *Salvage* Iles, lye N.W. from one greater Iland[3] I cannot say it to be the North Mayne, because it

---

[1] "many great pieces of mountain ice All the small shattered [ice] which we were so long fast amongst, I hope is dissolved," etc (*Foxe MS*) He means that the large quantities of ice they saw when they were passing through the Strait westward earlier in the year, had disappeared (see also p. 401) In this respect, Foxe's experience coincides with that of nearly all those who have navigated Hudson's Strait since his time. They have almost all found the Strait very much obstructed at the time of their entering (generally in July), but comparatively clear at the time of their going out (generally in September). I have discussed this point in my work, *Manitoba Described* (London, 8vo, 1885, p. 192) Foxe himself, it will be observed, occupied about 25 days in passing westward through the Strait, while he only occupied about 10 days in returning, and this is the usual experience With reference to the ice in Foxe's Channel, and at the western end of Hudson's Strait, Sir W E Parry says (*Second Voyage*, 1824-25) —

"Now on the eastern side of Foxe Channel, there is reason to believe, as well from the account of that navigator in 1631, and that of Baffin in 1615, as from our own observation, that there is little or no ice during the summer season. In the course of Foxe's progress along the shore, from the Trinity Islands to his farthest north, no mention is made in his Journal of any obstruction from ice, which would hardly have been the case had he met with any; and, in our own passage, as well as that of Baffin, from Trinity Islands towards the middle of Southampton Island, little or no obstruction was met with from it until well within sight of the latter coast."—C

[2] "The old proverb is 'The Hackney will drive best homewards.'" (*Foxe MS*)

[3] Probably Big Island.—C.

doth bend to the Northwards, both from the W. and E.; and, therefore, the W. end I take to be that named the *Queene's Cape*.[1] At the E. end, doe lye 2 Ilands, the one bigger, the other lesse. I named the one *Sackfield*, the other *Crowe*, after Sir *Sackfield Crowe*, late Treasurer to his Majesties Navie.[2] From the W. to the E. of this land or Iland is many showes of Sounds or Bayes, ragged and high, the land being barren to sight.[3]

26 From the last noone to this, I made way 32 leagues nere the S.E. by East; the land of this North side meeting us bore from the E. by N to the N.N.West, and is the Mayne or Iland betwixt the Iles of *God's Mercy* and *Salvage* Iles, all upon the North side of *Fretum Hudson;* and nere those bearings of land, my Latitude was 62 degrees 40 minutes.[4]

27 From the last Meridian unto this, I made way 13 leagues E by S, and had Ile *Sackfield* N E. by E. ½ E., 7

---

[1] I know not by whom —C.

[2] These names have not been retained. The former name Foxe spells wrongly; for he named the Islands after Sir *Sackville* Crowe, knight and baronet, of Lanherne, in the county of Caermarthen, son of William Crowe, Esq., of Socketts, Kent, by Anne his wife, daughter of John Sackville, Esq., of Sussex. He was created a baronet in July 1627, and who married a sister of the eighth Earl of Rutland. He was active in public business, and Treasurer of the Navy, having received a grant of that office for life on March 20th, 1627. However, in 1635, Foxe speaks of him as *late* Treasurer, and in 1638 he was appointed Ambassador at Constantinople, but whilst there he was accused of various frauds and corrupt practices in connection with the Levant Company, and on his return home in 1648 was arrested and committed to the Tower. He was probably convicted at his trial, as he died in the Fleet Prison in 1683, when he was succeeded by his son, Sir Sackville Crowe, who dying *s p* soon after, the baronetcy became extinct.—C.

[3] "All this northland is full of Islands, Bayes, and Sounds, and high I pray you put in barren also." (*Foxe MS.*)

[4] "At noon, the Lat. was 62° 41'. The Master was 62° 30'." (*Foxe MS.*)

leagues off.[1] At this present, I had sight of the land from *Resolution*, and it bore from me from the N N.E to the E, about 9 or more leag. This day and night was fayre weather, the one by sight of the Sun, the other by the Moone, although the wind came against our wils to the S.E. by S., with a frostie fog Turning up to the North land, it was cleare, but at Sea it was thicke; and thus, plying up to the Eastward, [we] came within 4 leagues of this land, which lay from East to N N.E., and was the same wee drived along, immured amongst the Ice, at our entrance inwards Wee got little by plying with contrary winds, and yet I durst not put into a Sound for harbour, or which wee might perceive some, as also Roade-steeds made by Ilands, lying nere the Mayne Our weather side was froze, as also all our ropes were a quarter of an inch thicke about.

28 The wind continued contrary, and I stood off into the Channell, and on againe, with frostie fogge, and very cold, but the wind blew not to above Course and Bonnet This day, I appointed 4 beefe dayes in the weeke[2]

---

[1] This must be an error —C

[2] Probably before this they had had less; but, now that they were fairly on the way home, Foxe evidently thought he might use his stores more freely. As to this, Foxe's MS says (fo 75) —"The Master hath, I hear, appointed four beef days a week, and Saturday shall not be one; and, to please the Company, whom now going home he doth extremely flatter, promising them that some waters shall be again broached, which I caused to be knocked up, for, [on] that same evening [when] I named the King's and Queen's Capes, some of our people had broke into the hold and let forth a matter of at least 12 Gallons of Aqua Vita, it being known amongst them [that] I [had] said they should have no more until I knew the parties offending They said they would rather have none by half, than have any man punished for what was done. He hath also promised them sack; indeed he had made some to lie it upon; for (when the Aqua Vita question was) there was some that said they would tell of some that had by night divers times filled bottles of Sack that I did not know

30.[1] With wind contrary, I plyed it to the Eastwards. The Aire was both thicke and cleare, as I was neere or farre off the North Mayne. Sometime it blew to both topsailes, and sometime was easie winde. The evening, 8, I stood to the S.-ward, being S.W. from the E. point of the N land stretching toward *Resolution*, 4 leagues.

[30][2] I stood over untill this day clocke one, S.S.E., wreck and variation allowed,[3] 28 leag., at what time we thought we had sight of the S Maine, about S.W. by S., 5 leagues off, very high land. This night was hazie, and blew to Course and Bonnet. Comming betweene 2 Ilands of Ice, the Sea had beate much from off the weathermost, which lay floting betwixt it and that to Leeward; so as I loosed for one and bore up for another for the space of the 60th part of one houre, and this was all the trouble the ice put me unto homeward bound.[4]

October 1. This first day, it blew lesse wind, but all the morning was Snow. The Lord for his mercy sake looke upon us, for we are all in weake case, dispairing more since this last frost and contrary winds that hath bin within these 5 dayes (although the frost hath not beene uncouth to us) then for the same weather we had for 3 weekes before, and yet our allowance is enlarged to so

---

of Because I have denied the Sack. he says I do not know what belongs to men, thereby to bring me in hatred with them, as it hath been his purpose" Much more in the same strain appears in the MS. (fo. 78) on October 18th.—C

[1] Both Foxe's MS and the context show that this should be the 29th, not the 30th.—C

[2] The MS. and the context both show that the 30th should commence here, though it does not do so in Foxe's book.—C

[3] See p. 280.—C

[4] See p. 398. "We were troubled more with pieces of Ice which the Sea beat from the great Islands [*i e*, Icebergs], than we were with the Islands themselves, which [*i.e*, the pieces] fleete to leeward thereof" (*Foxe MS*.).—C.

much as we cannot eate, with Sacke, *Aqua-vitæ*, Beere, as well Oatemeale, Meale, Rice, Pease, and Beefe, for salt fish our men can eate none, nor doe I hold it fit they should.[1]

2, 3. These 2 dayes were spent in plying to the E., sometimes in the sight of the N. land, or Maine, whereof lay 2 small Ilands,[2] which we drive by as I drive inwards, being then fast amongst the ice. At 12 this day, I tacked to the S.-wards; and at this instant the said land bore from N.W. by W. to the E. The Iland at the N. end, by estimation, was one league distant from the Maine; that at the E. was 2 off. This day hath been faire and cleere,[3] and it cleereth with bright Horizons at N E God send the wind from thence to take us out of those dilatory sufferings, which we have more through lingering doubt of what wee shall feele then as yet we doe feele, and expecting our freedome, if wee were freed out of *Fretum Hudson*, which, upon a sodaine change, wee may happely expect.

4. From last day noone unto this day 12, I stood upon a bowling,[4] making a S.E. way, 31 leagues. The wind veering more Northerly, I stood E.S.E., so neare as I could lie, 20 leagues more, and at midnight I had the Cape *Chidley*[5] (since called *Button's Ilands*) E, 4 leagues from me; whereupon I stood to the North, because I could not carry it about the Cape untill this day 5 in the morning,

---

[1] "It has been snowing all this morning since 4 o'clock, and now it bloweth something less. God, for His mercy's sake, think upon us; or we are all with ship low and very weak, though our people hath the allowance enlarged to so much as they can well spend, both of Sack, Aqua Vita and Beer, as well as Meal, Rice, Peas, Oatmeal and Beaf; for Fish they cannot [eat] now, neither do I hold it fit they should." (*Foxe MS*)

[2] Undoubtedly the Lower Savage Islands.—C

[3] "Much snow, but freezeth not and is fog" (*Foxe MS*)

[4] See p. 372, *note*.—C   [5] See p. 283.—C.

and then tackt to the E., the wind larging about to the Northward.

5 I doubled the Cape at clocke 12, weathering the same about 2 leagues, having, as at all headlands (with Sea winds and cold weather), a great Sea with an inset into *Fretum Hudson* against me, that the shippe strucke in the Spritsaile-yard and bowlspright[1] under water. I, much fearing that[2] the springing of our yards or Masts, setled the topsailes so to ease them, that I thought I did but double the Cape with much adoe.[3] It was high land, consisting of divers ilands, seeming as they were to bee sayled betwixt. These were covered with Snow, as also *Resolution*, whose Cape *Warwicke* I see bearing N. and by W. At that instant, after I had brought this Cape or Iles of *Chidly* W.S.W., either the Tyde or Current did set me fast to the S.-ward. This day, it froze so sore, with the ship's dipping in the Sea, that our head and wet tackling were Canded over with Ice-sicles, and many Snowie showres in earnest were sent from *Boreas* his frozen forge. And, for the haire of our faces to be of his hoary colour, had been no noveltie to us these 4 weekes.[4]

6. I stood from the Cape, bearing S.E. ½ Southerly, variation and wreake allowed, 51 leagues and 2 mile, untill this noone time.

---

[1] This curious spelling of the word does not appear in the MS.

[2] The word "that" seems to be unnecessary, and injurious to the sense.—C.

[3] "This strong tide did so bind us upon them [the Islands], with a high sea setting right in from the E., as is usual in cold weather or at headlands, that we had much to do to clear them, and I think should not if, at need (God be blessed), the wind had not come to N., and (as was at this time) stiff gale." (*Foxe MS.*)

[4] "Many snow showers were sent from Boreas's frozen forge, which searcheth our very beards; and, indeed, for this three weeks, [this] hath been no novelty." (*Foxe MS.*)

7. From thence, untill this 12, E. by S., 54 leagues, at what time motion was made to come home in lesse sayle,[1] but answer was that I was not discharged as yet, and therefore I would runne the ship out of victuall and pay, for as yet I never durst carry sayle (to see how fast I could drive *Charles* his Waine to the best advantage[2]), fearing that if I had sprung any of my Masts, yards, or tackling (or wrong the ship[3]), it might have beene supposed I had done it upon purpose, that then, if I had stood need of excuse, for feare or neglect, I might have used that false colour Blessed be the Almighty, who never faileth those that depend on him truly, this warmth we find in the open Ocean doth much revive us; for truly, if this extremity of the frost and snow had continued on with the Easterne winds we had within *Fretum Hudson*, wee had beene constrained backe to have wintered in *Hudson's Bay* or elsewhere, for the most of us were ready to fall downe with the rest that were downe already[4]

After I was got cleere, I had, for some reasons, thought to have come home by the N., but the weaknes of our persons, the long nights, the cold dark weather, with the decayed Moone, altered my purpose, although the N by *Orkny* was the shortest cut, and so nearer some refreshing

---

[1] The remarks thereupon which Foxe entered in his journal are quoted in the Introduction, p. xcii —C

[2] This is, of course, a sample of Foxe's figurative language He means that he had never tried to discover how fast he could sail his ship, the *Charles* —C

[3] No doubt he means, if he had *wrung* his ship—made her leak See also p. 371.—C.

[4] "It may be thought his [the Master's] Mate, Urin, hath got a great drink, for he is all wamble, and, seeing the Sack hath been let loose our folk are pretty pleasant, which this extreme cold had made hurkle [see p. 374], for the Cook is down; and I think, if God had not sent us forth at the first coming of the North wind and snow, we had the most of us fallen down" (*Foxe MS.*)

Yet this being the warmer, and, in darke nights, the more comfortable, I directed the course to fall with the Iland of *Silly*, having yet great care day and night specially to looke out for the Ice, which I supposed might be set from off *Groenland*, or out of *Fretum Davis;* but, God be thanked, we see none after we came from the Cape.

The daily courses and distances homewards were as followeth; the wind as in the Margent.[1]

8. Our sicke men are as yet able to doe nothing. The Master is laid downe againe.[2] We had last night, and especially this morning, a whole storme. The afternoon it faired, and the wind came about with Sunne to the West. Wee carried both topsailes a trip. [S E.]

9. This day, considering the great want I found of the Boatswaine, our sayles and tackling being sore torne (in this time he came not above Decke), I placed *John Coatesworth* in his roome, for his diligence. This day was reasonable weather. We made way the 8 day and this, 56 leagues 2 miles, E S E. ½ Southerly.

10. This day was topsayle Gale. Last night, the wind Southering made us hand them both. We made from last 12 to this, 49 leagues E.S.E. ½ S. The wind veered S.-ward, but staid not. [S.W]

11. The wind was fickle, but we made way E.S.E. 34 leagues, and were in 57 d. 35 latitude. [S.W.]

12. The wind variable; our way S.E. by E. 27 leagues.

13. After midnight, the wind came to S.E., with much raine. I tooke in topsayles and clued up the foresaile,

---

[1] For convenience, these wind-directions have been inserted in the text, within brackets.—C.

[2] Our sick are all able to do nothing. The Gunner is sometimes on Deck. The Master is laid down, and Mr. Urin [also]." (*Foxe MS.*)

sorting the yard Arme's thigh.[1] After clocke 4, the wind favouring, came to S.W., and I made way by account as before, 33 leagues South-East. [S.E., S W.]

14. This day the Master came abroad againe, and not since the 7 day before The wind was all day about S W, thicke and wet. The true way, traverse excepted, of the last day and this was 47 leag S E. by East [S.W]

15. Thicke fog; and the way from last day to this 47 leagues S.E by E.; and at clocke 8 we were in 59 degrees 15 minutes latitude. [W.]

16 The way was S E 8 d. E.-wards, 36 leagues ⅔.

17 The way 30 leagues E S.E [Betwixt S.W. and W]

18. The way Veering, 37 S.E. 4 d. E -wards[2]

19.[3] The way 57 S E 5 d E

20. The way 17½ E. by N

---

[1] I cannot explain this expression, which does not occur in the MS.—C.

[2] "This day the Master came to me again for consent for another tierce of Sack to be opened for the men, [because] the last did them so much good. I told him it could not be so, for that they had not above half-pint the morning for 7 or 8 mornings before I heard it was out, nor did I hear any desire of their's thereto; for, when there was none, they were able to eat their allowance of Meale, Pease and Beef, Butter and Cheese, and refused to have any fish, and, .. at the last stealing into the hold, when the Aqua Vita was stole or let forth (12 gallons [see p. 400]), and the cook's gimlet had done the deed, they answered that they had rather be without wine or water than any man should be punished, which showed they had no need. Well, yet he urged, saying that, if I would not consent, he would do it of himself. I told him I had no quarrel to a drop of Sack, though it were ever so sweet, and for the men's good needs I would nor I hope needed not please them with the expense of the adventurer's provision needlessly wasted; yet he persevered. I called to put on bonnets to hasten home, for this drone, I do undertake, if he might have had his will, would never have loosed above two courses all this time. Well, he saith he will look well to the Sack, and I believe him." (*Foxe MS.*)

[3] The 19th, 20th, 21st, and 22nd, are all blank in the British Museum copy of Foxe's MS.—C.

21. The way, true course, 26 E.
22. The way 28¼ E. 4 d. N.
23 The way 33 E S.E.; latitude 51 d. 16 m.[1]
24. The way 42 E.
25. The way 35 E. 4 d N.
26. The way 14 E. 4 N.; latitude 50 d. 9 min.[2]

These courses were all true, variation allowed.

27. The way 08[3] E. [The wind veering from S.W. to S S E. and S.E. by —.]

28 This day, in the morning, I had sight of *Sillie*, distant foure leagues off.

The 31, blessed be Almighty God, I came into the *Downes* with all my men recovered and sound, not having lost one Man, nor Boy, nor any manner of Tackling, having beene forth neere 6 moneths, all glory be to GOD.[4]

To whom this may concerne.

Answere to uncertaine rumors, or aspersions, given forth against me, concerning my returne home from the Northwest this yeare (Given at my home-comming).

AS, wherefore I had not found the passage? and why come I home and did not Winter? hath he fulfilled

---

[1] "This evening, after prayers, stood a sail from the W.S.W. in with us. Being night, we spoke not." (*Foxe MS.*)

[2] On this date, Foxe's Journal terminates.—C.

[3] Probably a misprint for 38 or 48.—C.

[4] This was a great thing for Foxe to have been able to say. Very few, if any, of his predecessors could have said as much, and the fact affords good evidence of the masterly way in which Foxe had carried out the work entrusted to him.—C.

his Commission? how farre hath he beene? And those that had more insight inquired, Whether I had been North-West from Ile *Nottingham* or no? with, Why did hee not bring letters from Captaine *Iames?* some concluding that I have done nothing.[1]

I did attempt the Discovery towards the Northwest from the Iles of *Nottingham* and *Salisbury* about the midst of *Julie*, and had at that time proceeded according to the letter of my Instruction, if I had not beene prevented by these following meanes,[2] viz. :

1. *I had been immured with Ice from the first day of my entering* Fretum Hudson, *being the 23 day of Iune, vntill the 4 of Iuly following, after which time I got cleere, and, comming unto* Salisbury Isle, *I lay fast againe betweene the South and the North Maine, about 7 dayes, amongst ice, where, being neere the said Isle, I could easily discerne the Tyde come from the East, through* Fretum Hudson, *and not from the Northwest*

2. *Getting cleere of the ice, I went about the said Isle to the South, as also* Nottingham's, *where, sending the Boat on land, [they] brought word that it had flowed so much water as in my Iournall is mentioned of,[3] and that the water had more to flowe; and, after that, running off into 60 fathomes and anchoring the Boat, I found the Tyde come from the South-East, or through* Fretum Hudson

3. *Standing along the said Isle to W-ward, vntill I brought the same (I meane the W. end) N.E, it began to be*

---

[1] We may regard the following as a sort of manifesto, inserted by Foxe in reply to the aspersions cast at him by his detractors, probably, in some cases, on account of jealousy, and, in others, of disappointment that he had not found a passage.—C.

[2] Foxe here again gives his reasons for disregarding his Instructions (see Introduction, p. xcvi), which he had previously stated (see p. 364). What he says, both there and here, shows that he had the best of reasons for acting as he did

[3] See p. 310.—C

full of ice in the W. Channell, betwixt Nottingham *and* Shark Point,[1] *as before betwixt the North Maine and Salisbury, so as the Master, his Mate, and my selfe conclude that there was no entring the said Northwest as yet, or untill the ice was dissolved, and to that point the Master and Mate wished me to write what I would concerning that impossibility of passage untill the ice were gone, and they would signe the same, promising that they would bee willing to see the same before their going home, if no passage proved elsewhere to be found.*

Whereupon, considering that that Tyde came not from the North-West for certaine, which is the absolute ground of my instructions, but from South-East, disproved also by Master *Bylot* (who was in the same Voyage and ship with Sir *Thomas Button*[2]), saying that both he and all his Company did plainely see the Tyde come from S.E. at Cape *Comfort*,[3] and also the Ile *Nottingham*, averring that they which tooke that account were mistaken in the time, taking 8 a clocke for 10.

Now, as it was not possible as yet to enter for ice, the wind being liberall, I directed the course towards *Carie Swannes Nest*, hoping to follow the instructions, in the search of *Button's* and *Hudson's* Bay[4] (of which there was

---

[1] This name does not appear on Foxe's map, nor has it been previously mentioned, either in the printed narrative or the MS. So far as one can gather from the context, it appears to have been identical with Cape Pembroke, but I have failed to discover who bestowed this name upon it. It can only have been Button, Baffin, or Hawkridge. The name appears on Thornton's Chart of the North-West part of America (1705?).—C.

[2] See p. 164.—C.

[3] So named by Bylot and Baffin on July 12th, 1615 (see p. 216). Foxe does not mention it in his printed narrative, though it appears on his map as "C. Comforth". It lies on the north shore of Southampton Islands.—C.

[4] See Introduction, p. xcvi.—C.

as great hopes as at the Northwest, and there were as many, and as strongly, of that opinion, as of the other), and come backe again thither by that time the ice was dissolved (which I hoped would be about the fine of *August*,[1] or not at all), if no passage proved in the said Bay to be had; but, finding none, I proceeded from that search, having first finished the search of the foresaid Bay, as followeth in briefe.

Being come out of *Hudson's* Bay, and Anchoring at *Sharke Point*, I found the Ebbe to goe with good Current from the West; but the South-East flood-tyde did slacke the same when it came; but how it did flow and what water, I cannot report for want of my journall, it being now out off my hands; but I did finde the same flood-tide to answere the report of Master *Bylot's* journall writ by *Baffin*[2]; and I found some quantity of ice betweene Cape *Pembroke* and *Sharkes Point* undesolved at that time, being the foureteenth of *September*.

Having made those observations, I stood over (with North-winds) for *Mill Iland*, mentioned in my instructions, but for no intent to coast the East-side; for I had with that winde much adoe to fetch the same, with bording and turning under the South side of it, two Tides before I got into a Throughlet at the West end thereof, whereinto I put, and there found it to flow at least foure fathomes. The Tide running halfe Tyde, and comming from South-East, as well upon the North and Southside, as upon the South of *Nottingham* at my departure from thence, whereupon I plied up with North-West windes every Tyde, being forced to stoppe the Ebbe (nor could I recover the West side with those winds), untill I attained the Cape I

---

[1] Foxe means by this the *end* of August. Compare the Latin and French.—C.

[2] See Baffin's narrative of Bylot's voyages, *ante*, p. 217.—C.

have called *Lord Weston's Portland*, in the latitude about 66 d. 47 m,[1] where I found the Tyde of flood to come still along as the coast did lie, which was to coast from Northwest to North, to Northeast and to East, and to Southeast; the deepest water not above 30 fathoms (as I remember) five leagues from land; the Sea slight and smooth with these winds, so as it is easie to conjecture thereof either ice or land was not farre off; for wee found good store of undesolved ice at *Sharke Poynt*. Whereupon I stood 10 leagues from hence (as I supposed) for the Westside, which I could not attaine; and, if I had continued this course for the West side with this winde, I must have stopt the Ebbes; and *Baffin* writing of 130 fathomes deepe there (the just length of my small cable-shoat), I must have bid the ship to have stoopt for the rest; and, to have done the same by my biggest, I had not strength enough to have wayed the same from ground againe. Likewise, I had no reason to follow the East, finding it to Trent away South-East from that Headland which, for resemblance and simile to this of ours, I named *L. Weston's Portland;* from whence I do perswade my selfe the Ebbe doth take his halfe course through those Ilands of *Cumberland's* into *Fretum Davis*.[2] The flood cannot bee great (which conjecture may say should come through that straight, and meet ours at *Portland*), being hindred by these foresaid Iles, where *Davis* saith hee met a strange Tyde from the South-West may be the cause, which, by that straightnesse, may retort the floods way.

But, to the purpose. The winds were North-west, nor could I stay the change thereof, for the most of my best

---

[1] For remarks on the position of Foxe's Cape Weston, see p. 388, *note*.—C.

[2] Foxe's surmise that there was a channel leading from his most northerly point, through Cumberland Island into Davis Strait, was erroneous.—C.

men (as Master, Gunner, Carpenter, Boatswaine, his Mate, and one or two of the common men) were downe, the rest complaining of cold paines; and no marvell, they having beene over-toyled in the bottome of Sir *Thomas Button's* Bay (and [in] that [previously] undiscovered [part] betwixt him and *Hudson*), with watching and warding day and night, manning both Shippe, Boate, and Pinnace, both in Anchoring and Sayling, but especially at Leade, when in all the time of my Sayling the said Bay there was never one from keeping the same.[1]

The weather had beene, for about 3 weekes before, nothing but Snow, Frost, and sleet at best; our selves, ropes, and sayles froaze, the Sunne seldome to be seene, or once in five dayes; the nights 13 houres long; the Moone wayning; and, in conclusion, I was enforced either to seeke for Harbour, or freeze to death in the Sea[2]

Whereupon I sent Master *Vrine* to aske the Master's opinion, who brought [word] unto me that he thought the Tydes setting from S.E almost round about to E. would give good satisfaction (for this N.W. search [was] begun by a wrong report of the Tydes comming from thence) to the Adventurers, and that hee helde it fittest to returne. Yea, and the best also, as I thought; and homewards [we went], and for good cause, as hereafter followeth:—

First, I referre it to the judgment of indifferent[3] men whether, having proceeded in these Discoveries further then any other my Predecessors, in lesse time and at lesse

---

[1] He means, of course, that the continuous soundings he had had to take in the Bay had been specially trying to his men.—C.

[2] The preceding paragraphs give Foxe's reasons for turning back from his most northerly point, as to which he gives no explanation in his narrative. Mention of the fact that he stood westwards 10 leagues from his "Farthest", across Foxe's Channel, is also omitted from his narrative, though probably by a printer's error (see p. 388).—C.

[3] This is used in its old sense, *impartial*. This use of the word still lingers in America.—C.

charge, I have closed up all the expected hopes upon the W. side of *Button's* Bay, from 64½ circularly to 55, and on the Point from *Swan's Nest* to *Sharke Point* (not [before] perfectly discovered, but now by me), and carried a Tyde, comming from South-East, through *Fretum Hudson*, all along that East side to 66 degrees 30 minutes, or thereabouts (things not knowne heretofore), that I should hazzard the losse thereof to my Countrey, if I should have perished in seeking an unknowen Harbour, in long nights and cold weather, with so many men sicke, who could not have recovered in the wintering; howsoever, their helpes would have beene wanting in lying [up] or Barracadoing[1] the ship from ice (for, wheresoever I had wintered, I must have haled the ship high on shore, and Barracadoe), as also in making my provisions of fresh victuals and fuell. The necessitie of this, Sir *Thomas Button* is able to approve, to his dear bought experiment.

Well, if I had wintered, it must have beene with intent to make search to the North of Sir *Tho. Roe's Welcome;* for, in all the hopefull places else, I was denyed; and there, and not far from thence, as about *Vt Ultra*, it is[2]; for, to give a wise Gentleman his right (who, perusing Sir *Tho. Button's* journall about that place, quoteth in the Margent these words[3]), "I doe not find *it is proved a Bay*".[4] This was suspected by him before I came to that knowledge thereof which I have now. But, to proceed: how should I be able to doe this service, when the winter would have consumed

---

[1] See p. 167.—C.

[2] Foxe has previously stated his belief that the passage would be found near Ut Ultra, if at all (see p. 370).—C.

[3] From the fact that Foxe received parts, at least, of Button's journal from Sir Thomas Roe (see p. 163), he was probably the "wise gentleman" Foxe here alludes to.—C.

[4] It *was* not proved a Bay, and is now proved *not* to be. It was explored by Captain Middleton in 1741-42, and by Captains Moor and Smith in 1748.—C.

all the best of my comfortable stores (as strong Beere, strong waters, sacke, spice, fruite, Rice, Wheat-meale) and of my Chirurgery; and, if no reliefe had beene otherwise got from land, to have lengthened the most of the provision, as Beefe, Beere, and Fish?

Yet had I had no more then would have brought home the Ship, if my men had stood; and if, by their death, or reliefe of birds or Deere, I had store remaining, yet I doubt the remayning stomacks would have beene too weake (before the long winter there had left them) to have endured salt meate in the Summer, so as the more victuall the fewer hands for labour; and there would be no sparing, as I conceived, by short allowance.

All these, and many other sufferings endured, is but all for the next yeares Search, about which I have shewed I had no reason to stay to put so much to hazzard, knowing what I had inquired from some, both of Sir *Thomas Button* and Mr. *Hudson's* men, of their sufferings, and yet it was *July* before they could get well to sea to returne home. And it doth appeare by Sir *Thomas Button's* owne words,[1] that he would have proceeded the next yeare if he had not been disabled.

For when, after my home comming, I told him hee could not be certaine if the Tyde he tooke at *Nottingham* was true, for that his boate was never on land, his answere was· "*God a mercy for nothing, for I had not above 8 sound men.*" So this doth appear, as I did cōceive before my returne. I cōclude that these things, in part knowne to me, in part imagined, that if I should not have made good use thereof, having discovered so much as I had done, if I would thus have suffered I had bin well served to have come home unpittied.

---

[1] No words to this effect appear in Button's narrative as given by Foxe. From the following paragraph, it appears they were spoken in conversation with Foxe.

The benefit ensuing by my comming home this yeare.[1]

IMprimis, my sicke men are (God be glorified) all recovered.

The account of my service, by my selfe and others, [is] brought home, I hope to the satisfying of my King and Country, and more then ever was formerly done by any of my predecessours by much, and at farre lesse charge.[2]

The ship and tackling all safe, and without any losse of either, which was not done without great hazzard, going from the Latit. of 55 in *Hudson's Bay* into the Articke circle towards the end of *September*.

There is also 6 months pay and victuals saved, at above 75 pounds per month, amounting to the some of nere 450 poū.; and, if they doe not set forth the next yeare, then there is 11 months pay and victuals saved. There is one Sommer's time gained; for, if this be distrusted or more required (I meane in discovery), who is so pleased may set forth the beginning of *May*, and satisfie their desire this nexte yeare, with ship newly repaired, newly manned with fresh men, and untainted with skurvie, crampe, or cold paines, but more and better able to performe the enterprize then the Winterer can be.

To conclude: I referre it to the judgement of reasonable discretion, whether it may be held fit that I should suffer, either by want of liberty, good reward, or imputation (as hath been wished), untill the returne of Capt. *James*, who had no intent, as by his answer doth appeare, who, when I inquired of him why he, being so late, had not attempted

---

[1] It will be at once allowed by any competent critic that Foxe's reasons for not wintering in the north-west are very forcibly stated by him, and prove conclusively the wisdom of his decision. The hardships endured by Captain James and his crew, who wintered in the Bay, are further proof of this.—C.

[2] See p. 359.—C.

the N.W., as we both were instructed, answered that *Baffine* satisfied in his Iournall that the Tyde came from S E, and that himselfe had beene no more N. then 64, the latit of Mill Ile, and then, having come over to the W. side of Sir *Thomas Button's* Bay but in 59, and discovered but from thence to 61 leag. E S S. from Port *Nelson*, where wee met, having this yeare neither bin at N.W., as before said, nor made any discovery betwixt the south side of *Hubbert's Hope* to 64 ½, where the chiefest hope was[1] (as I had done), nor ioyned *Hudson* and Sir *Thomas Button*. It may bee thought he, being a Gentleman of quality, will not come untill he have done as much as I, being a man of meaner Ranke in his conceite (for I have heard since that his ambition hath abused my worth and name[2]) I told him my further intent, which was to attempt the N W this yeare, all which to do he must stay the next yeare, as my selfe would if he had left me in the like case Nor can no unkindnesse be laid to my charge for not bringing of letters from him [when] taking a fayre farwell of him, for he had time enough in two dayes to have writ, nor was I certaine as then of my returne, which now I doe thanke God for If this will satisfie to stop the mouth of Rumor, which hath already touched too much vpon my deserts, I shall bee glad. Otherwise, I wish they would suffer themselves to be judged by performing the like labour.

These rumours, like ill Newes, ridde poast, for they came to Court, insomuch as, comming by Boate with a Gentleman from *Oatlands*[3] to *London*, where I had beene to deliver my Accompts to his Majesty, it pleased the

---

[1] See p. 331 —C.   [2] See p 361.—C

[3] Oatlands Park is in Surrey, and on the banks of the Thames, three miles from Chertsey. Henry VIII made it his favourite seat, and it continued to be a royal residence for about a century. It is now broken up into building plots. —C.

Gentleman to say that now is Captaine *James* in the *Mare del Zur*, and will come home by Cape *Bon Sperance*.[1]

I was so confident that he could doe no more for that yeare I did leave him, and for the yeare to come, that I replyed with three wishes or desires to my good or ill.

The first was that, if Captaine Iames *did passe through and come home that way, that I might be severely punished, according as I did acknowledge I did deserve.*

The next was that if, at his home-comming (for which I prayed vnto Almighty God), *that it did appeare vpon examination* (equally ballanced) *that hee had done as much as I, and no more, I might have reasonable Reward, for so I had deserved.*

The third [was] *that, if hee had not done so much, that I might be rewarded with what I had saved, to wit: Eleven moneths victuall and pay, at 75 pounds* per *Moneth, and according to the wearing and tearing of Cordage and Tackling that I had saved, which hee would spend.*

Now, since hee is returned home, and hath neyther beene through nor performed so well as I by very much,[2] I desire to be rewarded as before; and for that this was rehearst before his home-comming and when I did not know where hee was.[3]

---

[1] The Cape of Good Hope.—C.

[2] Foxe was amply justified in saying this much.—C.

[3] As Foxe says (p. 407) that the foregoing statement was "given at my home-comming" (which is clear also from internal evidence), it follows that he added this concluding paragraph at the time of publishing his book in 1635.—C.

That there is a Passage, hath beene proffered to be proued very Learnedly by S^r. *Humphrey Gilbert*, Knight, foure severall wayes, as followeth[1].

The first by Authority, alledging America *to bee that Iland called by* Plato *and others* Atlantes, *sayled vnto by the* Carthagineans, *and that it is bound on the East by the* Atlanticke *sea, from which it is named, on the South by* Magelan *straights; on the West by* Mar del Zur; *on the North it is severed from* Groenland *by the Sea, through which the Passage doth lye. And, to confirme the former Discovery, he brings in Money found by the* Spaniards *in the Gold mines of* America, *having the stampe of* Augustus Cæsar; *and since that time the discontinuance hath beene, for that it hath beene swallowed vp and overflowen with water through a mighty Earthquake, so as the Navigation thereunto was, since that time, lost, vntill the yeare* 1492. *That* Columbus *did after discover the same* (although *Malga*, Prince of Wales, was before him), *pretending that since its appearance againe, the Seas about it are made deeper, and the Northwest made more easie to be sayled, confirming the Conclusion by the Cosmographers of those modern times, especially* Ortelius, *who maketh ooth* Groenland *and* America *both Ilands, disjoyned by a great Sea from any part of* Asia.

The second is by Reason; for, sayling from Iseland *to where this Freet should be, it is thought to bee more deeper water; and that, if* America *were not an Iland, it and* Asia *should participate of each other's animals, or things of like*

---

[1] Sir Humfrey Gilbert's *Discourse of a Discouerie for a New Passage to Cataia* (of which the following paragraphs are merely a summary) was printed in London, in black-letter, in 1576. It was reprinted by Hakluyt in the third volume of his great work.—C.

shape or condition, as Men, Beasts and others, of which there hath bin found in eyther; also hee alledgeth the Seas naturall and circular running from the East to West, following the diurnall motion of Primum Mobile,[1] *it carrying all inferiour and moveable bodyes; so as the Current from the East, comming about Cape* Bona Spei, *cannot be digested by the narrow straite of* Maggellane, [*and*] *must needs be spent about the North by some passage through this Freet, as also the Current setting from forth the* Scythian *Sea doth spend itselfe in this Strait; and also that these Currents could not have beene maintained vntill this day had it not beene for this same passage, that, by its circular motion, it might meete againe to maintaine it selfe. Hee concludes that this current was found in the* Mare del Zur *by* Barnard de la Torre, *sent to the* Mollucas *by the Vice Roy of New* Spayne, *who sayled* 750 *leag. on the N. side of equator, and met with a current from N.E., which drove him back againe to* Tidore; *so, by this motion thus continued, it doth passe by the* Mollucas, *and thence againe by Cape de* Spei.

The third is by experience: Paulus Venetus *saith he dwelt many yeares in* Cataia, *affirmeth that he sailed* 1,500 *miles upon the coast of* Mangia *and* Anian, *towards the N.E., the Sea alwayes open before him, both as farre as he went and as farre as he could discerne*

Also Francisco Vasques, *in his Voyage to* Sierra Nevada, *found a great Sea, wherein were certaine ships laden with marchandise; on their prowes were pictures of certaine birds cald* Acatrazy, *made of Gold and silver. They made signes that they were* 30 *dayes in comming thither. Those must come from* Asia, *for that in all the discovered* America *there hath not bin found any ships.*[2]

---

[1] "Primum Mobile" was the name given by the early astronomers to the tenth imaginary sphere, by the revolution of which, every 24 hours, diurnal motion was supposed to be given to the heavens —C.

[2] A good reason —F

He proveth, also, that the Cosmographers of China have extended their Sea coast N.E. to 50 deg. Latit., being the furthest that the Portingale *had knowledge of, and that they know no other[wise] but they might continue it further* [1]

The 4th by circumstance: He offereth to prove by 3 brethren which sailed through from Europe, *as also by certaine* Indians *driven by tempest upon the coast of Germany; and out of* Plinie, *through the abundance of moysture to the North, those and other* Indians *must come to the North-west, and here is as much as is to any purpose in this [place].*

Mr. *Willes* tryeth also to prove this,[2] first by the 3 brethren out of *Gemma Friscius*, then by a *Portingale* from Sir *Martin Frobisher; Andreus Vrdaneta*, a Frier of *Mexico*, which he preferreth also who came out of the [*Mare*] *Del-zur* into *Germany* this way. This Fryer (saith he) was a great discoverer, and his Carde was showne to many Gentlemen

Againe, from *Sebastian Cabotta*, that the entrance hereof doth lye nere the 318 Meridian, betwixt 61 and 64 d of Lat., and that it doth continue that breadth 10 d. W., where it openeth S.-erly more and more untill it come under the tropick of *Cancer*, & so runneth into *Mare del Zur*, avouching this Strait to be at least 100 *English* miles wider then *Magelans;* perswading still upon this circuiler motion, he demands from whence, I pray you, came that tyde Sir *Martin Frobisher* met when hee had sailed no small way in his straite, if there were an *Ismus* of land, *which, since that time, we finde to be the 3 howers ebbe which came through the Ilands of his straite out of* Fretum Davis *far di-[? —] to the East of* Anian.

And here is, in effect, what is alleadged to prove this

---

[1] This makes our passage the shorter.—F.

[2] A treatise, entitled "Certain other Reasons or Arguments to prooue a passage by the North-west", by Richard Willes, also formed part of Hakluyt's third volume —C.

passage both by Sir *Humphrey Gilbert* and Mr. *Willes*, which, though they make little for our purpose, yet they give us to know what they knew in former time; for all these arguments, as I conceive, are but Phylosophiall conjectures; and, seing Sir *Martin Frobrisher* is the last spoke on, as whence, I pray you, came that tide Sir *Martin Frobrisher* found and as Mr. *Willes* requireth,

Heare his owne opinion:

That the current setting forth of that Bay of Mexico, *saith hee, doth wash upon the S W. part of* Iseland, *as he found in his 3 voyage a current carrying him one poynt to the N-ward of his course, which current he thought to be continued towards* Norway *and other the N.E. parts of* Europe *to the* Scythian *Sea; and, by the strengthening helpe of the* Mare Glaciale *from the E., rebounds againe from thence Westward by his naturall reverboration, which will not be resisted, but must strike upon his object,* Groneland; *nor, saith he, it is unpossible that so great course of floods, currents, and so high swelling Tides can be disgested here, without unburthening themselves in some open Sea beyond this place*

And here Sir Martin Frobisher *was not amisse; for we finde that, on the W. side of this* Meta incognita (*or, as we call it,* Groneland¹), *Mr.* Iames Hall *found the tyde to flow 3 and a halfe fadoms, which tyde* Bylot *and* Baffine *found to flow lesse and lesse, as hee past vp to the bottome of his Bay; so as, if he found not a new tyde from the West, there was no hope of a Passage to* Cataia. *And so it proved; for, at the bottome thereof, it flowed but about two foote, and proved a Bay.*

The like of Mr. Hudson, *who found the tide at the* Ile of God's Mercy *to flow* 3½ *fath; and, following of this Tide into this Bay, it flowed but 2 foote; so that it doth appeare here evidently that those great quantity of waters*

---

[1] Meta Incognita and Greenland are not identical, as Foxe supposed (see p. 38).—C.

are, in part, consumed with flowing and reflowing into 2 Bayes.[1]

The remainder may be spent along the coast of America, *from Cape* Chidley *Southward, for Mr* Iohn Knight, *before his death, writes that the Tide came from the* N.; *and* Oliver Browne, *after his death, writes, the Current came from N Capt* Waymouth *also saith the Ice drive from the North, and by this it is probable that here is the period of this irregular Current*

And, to conclude, with these 10 Fathoms it flowed up and downe, can be by no other meanes then some such Receptacle there, to restraine this great Ocean's flood; as at *Garnsey* in *Normandy*, and in *Severne* betwixt *England* and *Wales*, the Tyde comming out of the Ocean about *Ireland* into the one, and from thence betweene *Silly* and *Vshant* into the other, for want of issue, being thus affronted, must perforce elivate his waters to those great heights, vntill the Floods retract.

Wee have now made visibly appeare the best Arguments thes times did affoord; for, beleeve mee, if I could have pickt out any better, I would not have left them forth, they being pertinent to the purpose I have in taxe, yet hereby wee doe not finde any certainty thereof, as that the 3 Brethren came through our Freet; or that any *Indians* were cast vpon the coast of *Germany*, or that a *Portingall* who for his paines was banisht into *Africa*, or that, if we will take such commodity vpon credit, you may have more of *Andreas Vrdanatus;* and I thinke we may have also of a *Spaniard* that past it of late in King *Iames* his time, and, to binde up this rabble, put to *Iohannes de fuco*, the Greeke Pylot.

Your Phylosopher *Plato*, nor *Plinie*, your Cosmographers

---

[1] He may mean either Hudson's "East and West Bays" (see p. 131), or the Bays of Hudson and Button (see p 168).—C.

of these moderne times, *Ortelius* and *Mercator*, doth not all give us any thing that we can make reasonable assurance, or that we dare adventer upon; yet see how apt wee are to take those neighbouring fables into beleife, whereby we may deprive our selves of our honour before we obtaine it; for it may credibly be affirmed that this Virgin is yet pure and untoucht, either by Christian, Indian, or other nation, although many great dowries have beene spent about her, and some brave Knights have bid faire for her; yet it is not to be doubted but that the *English* have imbrac't her about the middle. Onely these make for our purpose, that the *Chinois* extend their coast to the N.E. into 50 d., and know no other[wise] but that they may continue it further

The other is *Paulus Venetus*, who sailed along the coast of *Mangia*, from *Cataia* towards the N.E., 1,500 miles. This doth argue that we have not straits or passage to saile from so far W. as we have bin to the end of our Discovery into *Mare del Zur*. Resting my weary invention upon the staffe of this opinion for a while, to bee better satisfied concerning this Current (which the most Authors insist so strongly vpon, as makes me doubt, if I were to follow thereby, to find the end of this *Dedalus* his Laborinth), I should very hardly have any hopes of returning againe the same way, because they urge so vehemently upon this naturall motion of the Orbes (so as, in *Magellan's* Strait, men are violently driven backe), inferring thereby that all things included shall by consequence follow the same; so that I should fight against the streame to Returne the same way. But, while I am thus pondering out this doubt, its prompt into my minde that, if all things included must follow, then should also the Earth walke in the same Revolution with his neighbour the Sea, as also my selfe, and yet keepe at the same distance so as I am never the nearer nor further for my purpose (by those Circular motions) But now my Iudgement wishes me to stay nearer home, and let these wandering travels of the thoughts past, for that my owne experience is better able to satisfie me then all those Elimentary cogitations; and thus, in few words, as thou didst carry a flood tide along with thee through *Fretum Hudson* to *Swan's Nest* from the E out of the Hyperborian, so hast thou found another on the W. side thereof, comming from the W., out of the *Mare del Zur*, which shall bring thee home again with the like expedition whereby thou wert carryed forth.

The Probability[1]

WEe have observed in the former Iurnals of Sir *Martin Frobrisher, Davis, Waymouth, Hall, Knight*, and Mr. *Hudson*, that the current doth set from the E. side of *Groneland* over to the S.W. and W., and that, nere the coast, it sets W in, wherein we have floated all this time, and thereby are brought to harbour in *Resolution*, where it flowes 5 fathomes right up and downe; and, if the account brought unto me by my men may be beleeved, that the flowing doth farre surmount this, and that a ESE. Moone maketh full Sea, it doth also appeare by Mr. *Bylot* that, farther within the straits (as at *Salvage* Ile), a S.E. Moone brings high water, and that it flowed equall water with *Resolution*, as also at the Iles of *God's Mercy*, by Mr *Hudson* it flowed above 4 fath., they being almost in the halfe way, the distances being nere 85 leag, the course

---

[1] The following tedious and far-from-lucid discourse seems to be from Foxe's pen. The diction is, in many parts, very vague; and, although the arguments are ingenious, the deductions drawn from the directions of the flow of the tides in different places are (as we now know) so unsound, that the treatise cannot be said to have ever had a high geographical value. It has, however, some historic value, and is interesting as showing the minute care Foxe bestowed upon any matter he took in hand.—C

W N.W. 31 deg., and differing in Latit. nere about 1 d. From *Salvage's* to *Mill* Ile is 59 leag. W. by N., where it floweth nere 4 fath. and a S S.E. Moone; and, in all those three channels in which I have beene (viz., betwixt Sir *Dudly Digs* his Ile and *Notingham's* Ile; betwixt that and *Mill* Ile, as also betwixt *Mill* Ile and the *King's* Promontory), in all these 3, I say (for I have had sure triall, and so had no man before mee) that the tide of the flood doth come from the S.E., running halfe tide, and with as swift a current as goeth in the River of *Thames.* From Mill Ile to the S. side of Sea Horse Poynt, they being distant 25 leag, I found the tyde to flow, as nere as I could take it by the lead-line, 20 foote, and a S by E. Moone full Sea, the tide of ebbe there holding his course doth but onely slacke for the time of floud about 4 howres, which strong tide in the two N.-most channels betwixt *Nottingham* and the King's *Promontory*, by all likelyhood doth continue his passage beteene Cape *Comfort* on the West and my Lord *Weston's Portland* on the East, returning their waters into *Fretum Davis* by the Iles of *Cumberland.*

For the tyde that commeth on the South Channell, between Cape *Wolstenholme* and *Salisbury* Ile, are consumed in strength and flowing, setting into *Hudson's* Bay, beteene *Swan's nest*, Sir *Robert Mansil's* Ile, and Sir *Dudley Digges'*, the most part of the latter flood falling into *Hudson's* bay.

From *Sea-horse Point* on the West to *Carie's Swan's-nest*, the distance is about 58 leagues; there it doth flow but 6 foote in height, and but 4 houres in time (for *Hudson's* Bay hath devoured the latter flood), so as heere wanteth both tyde and time, to wit, from neere 5 fathomes to 4 to neere 4 to 20 foot, but now to 6 foot; yet this flowing is continued according to the Moone's course, to wit, from E.S.E. to S.E. to S.S.E. to S. by E. to S by W.; which is an evident and assured token that this Tyde was fed and continued from the Easterne Ocean, comming in betwixt Cape *Farwell* in *Groynland* and the North maine of *America*, but now ended heere into this great Bay, and ebly returned backe againe at the recourse of the tyde. For, in Mr. *Hudson's* Voyage, the tyde of flood (the Ship setting on ground upon a Rocke[1]) was found to come from the E, the ebbe from the W, which was no other then the Tyde that came in and set forth betwixt Cape *Wolstenholme* and Cape *Digges*.

It is now probable that this Tyde of the S. Channell, comming from the East, is not an end, and that Tyde on the North is turned away, as I have found by experience at *Carie Swanne's Nest*.

Standing from hence 72 leagues, into the latitude of 64 10 m., which is to the North of that high land called *Hopes Advanc'd*,[2] I found a Tyde setting from the North, as the land did their[3] coast, which Tyde did flood above 20 foote water in the dead neepe (as it was at my being there), and that it did runne halfe tide, being full Sea about clocke 11, so as about a W.S W Moon maketh full Sea. I was commanded by the letter of my instruction[4] to make a perfect Discovery, either by Ship or Boat, of all that undiscovered betwixt this latitude and *Port Nelson*, and also that betwixt *Port Nelson* and *Hudson's* West Bay, in which discovery I now came to finde that I was out of my way, for, sayling from this land where I found this new Tyde (wch land I have named Sir *Tho. Rowe's Welcome*), it being on the Northmost known part upon the West side of *Button's Bay*,[5] whereas there it flowed so much water as before, and a W.S.W. Moone; now, coasting

---

[1] See p. 150.—C.

[2] Probably either Baker Foreland or Cape Fullerton (see p. 177).—C.

[3] A misprint for *there*.—C.

[4] See Introduction, p. xcvi — C.

[5] See p. 168.—C.

along this West side upon a S.W. by S. true course, as the land did lie, about 18 leagues, to an Iland I named *Brooke Cobham*. There, the best observation that I could make, I found that it flowed a West by South Moone, and but 10 foot the neepe Tide; but indeed I doe distrust this account, as in my journall doth appeare.[1] Coasting from hence to *Port Nelson*, 130 leagues, I found it there to flow a N W Moone, and in the neepe Tide but 9 foot water; and the best Spring Tyde, assisted by the wind, brought in but 14 foot water; and after, from thence towards *Hudson's* West Bay, it flowed lesse water, yet runne with course; for the time of full Sea went with Sunne, so as it was easie to conjecture that I went from the Tyde, which is especially to be incerted to make this Treatise to be better understood, and how this tide doth waste it selfe. Now it cannot be denyed but that this Tyde that is moved according to the course of Tydes, with his constant ebbing and flowing so great a distance as about the West side of this Bay, cercuting neere betwixt *Hudson's* Bay and Sir *Thomas Roe's Welcome* (the distance of it neere 253 leagues), having many rubbes and checkes by the way amongst the ilands and shoals, should be able to repaire and recall againe this huge quantity of waters every 12 houres, if it were not fed and supplyed from some great and waste Ocean; nor, if there prove to be a passage (as is most likely, as hereafter shall follow), it cannot be conceived but that it must be so spatious as cannot be visable betweene land and land. And why may it not be that there is no straight, but that the Sea lies open to the North (as at C. *Finmarke*)? after that the land doth trent Westward, as may be suspected by the want of ice, that the land, being farre remote to the North or West, the Sea doth keepe it selfe from frigitating by its continuall chafing and adjectating, as we see by the iles of

---

[1] See p. 323.—C.

Farre, Shotland, and *Orkney*, standing in and neere the same parallell with our frozen *Fretum Hudson*, where no Snow will lie for any time in Winter. The cause may be by the Seas moving about them, their circuits being so small, as the Seas breathing through the Tydes and winds continuall chafing about them, doth evaporate some part of his waremesse into the Ayre, whereby the frost is restrained from the exercise of his power; for the Sea hath a kinde of temperature betwixt too hot and too colde in the hot and cold *Zones*. It is much to bee hoped, by this want of ice, that, as at the North Cape of *Finmarke* (although I doe assure mee that this passage lyeth Southwards off that parallell, and about the Articke Circle), that this Continent of the Septentrionall part of *America* may incline to the West Southward about this latitude, as that of *Europe's* doth to the East; for, by this flowing of water in 60 d. 10 m. neere 4 fathomes (as at *Resolution* in the East), it cannot be farre to the winding of the land Westwards

The next is to inquire from whence this Tyde should come, for that is the way to the passage; for it cannot be said to come from the East, through *Fretum Hudson;* for there need no more to disprove that then what went before, when that Tyde did end at *Carie Swan's Nest*, in flowing but 6 foote and 4 houres, as it doth at the height of all Rivers being farre from the Sea.

Should it come from the North, then it should as well Current that land on the East side of this Bay to *Carie Swan's Nest*, along that small distance of 40 leagues, if such a thing be at all or no, as upon the West side. For 250 leagues of now knowne discovery setting from the North, it should divide equall waters betwixt them, which is found to the contrary; and, if such land doth lie 40 leagues along from *Swannes Nest* Westward, then is there not aboue 30 more for the bredth of the passage frŏ through whence this tide doth come, which I should thinke were to narrow to let in and out so much water in the time mentioned, to bring any flood on this side, now in handling, for at *Swannes Nest* the flood set West and the Ebbe East; and, if this Tyde, going West, were met with more water from thence, it must flow extraordinarily high at the Nest (as in great Rivers in time of land-waters, the Sea flood meeting, puts up the waters to such heights as doth inforce all their bounds) and rejected the Tyde's course, which I found to be constant, for that I was there two floods one ebbe and a halfe.

How can it now be imagined but that the tide doth come from the West, and so coasteth along the same side, as wee may observe upon all Tydes, from what sea soever they come; looke upon what side they enter, they Current the same, and so doth this, for that called *Vt ultra*, never proved Bay yet,[1] and who hath named the same, might as well be deceived here as at other places by fogs bankes; for, if this part be protracted, I cannot see that there is any discovery made at all on both sides (betweene *Hubarts vaine hope*[2] and *Swannes Nest*) worth the noting.

Therefore it must be confest that this Tyde doth come from the West, so inclining to that shore; and that it is a Tide, hath been proved; for I doe not thinke that there's any that will pretend inundating, impulsing, or ingulfing; and that it doth proceed from some great Ocean, is without all contradiction; for, comming to this West side, I found great store of fish playing at the crust[3] of the water, and of great fish, which is a maine argument; for there was Whales, Sea-mors, and Seales, of which there are infinite [numbers], which fish doe not live in Winter but in deepe

---

[1] See pp. 179 and 413.—C.
[2] See p. 335.—C
[3] Perhaps *crest*, meaning the *surface* of the water.—C.

Oceans[1]; and that those Whales must come from the West, is certaine; for, all the way from Cape *Farewell*, in all that distance of neere 500 leagues, we did not see one untill I came there; which, if there had beene any lying so long becalmed and amongst the ice, having light nights, we should have seene them, for they are fish that affect to play and breath above the water.

The main land was high within Sir *Thomas Roes Welcome*, as in all the straights besides, with deepe water [? close] to shore; whereas, discovering Southwards, it fell to bee low land with shallow shore; at 11 fathoms, wee could but see it upon the hatches. This is much contrary to the Oceans, who are bounded with high mountainous climes, steepe Promontories, ragged Rockes, and inamoled[2] Ilands, subsisting upon insearchable deepes, salt and greene-coloured waters, wherein live the great fishes.

Now let us compare this Tyde with some others, neerer our own home, with which we are the most familiar; as to begin at the mouth of the River *Thames*, towards which two Tydes resort.

And, at the mouth thereof, it floweth a S and N. Moone, at the S. Foreland, S.S.E.; in the Channell, of the *Ile of Wight*, S.E. or S E. by S.; at *Plimmouth*, E , at the Gulfe where the Ocean doth first enter our Channell, E.N.E. This reckoning goeth against the Sunne and Moone, yet this is the way to finde the Sea from whence the tide doth come.

Likewise, along the North coast, there commeth another tide to the saide River, bringing the like flowing, and almost answerable at the same distance; for, from off *Harwich*, it floweth S.S.E.; at *Yarmouth*, S.E., at *Laresnesse*, E. by N.; at *Whitby*, N.E.; at *Barwick*, N.N.E.; at *Buckham-*

---

[1] Of course, at the time Foxe wrote, whales, walruses, and seals were regarded as "great fish" (to use Foxe's own words), and not as mammals, as we now know them to be.—C

[2] Perhaps *enamelled*.—C.

nesse,[1] N. by E.; in *Orkney*, N. Now we know that both those Tydes, the one from the North, the other from the West, came both out of the Westerne Ocean, and that from the North, by the lands trenting his channell, his Current from the West Eastwards to S.E., as at *Timmouth*, to S.S E. as at *Laresnesse*,[2] to W. to S.E. as at *Halsbrough*,[3] to S. as at *Soale*,[4] to S.W. as at *Harwich*, and to W. into the said River of *Thames*.

So as here it is made manifest that, both Tydes comming out of the Western Ocean E., doth in the end goe or set just against themselves, as they set at their first comming from the Ocean. And, therefore, why may wee not thinke that the land to the West in this passage shall bend towards the South into *Mare del Zur*, as it doth here trent within this Bay, S.W. by S from latitude $64\frac{1}{3}$ to 59 But, to draw these points to a head, it is said these Tides met at the *Kentishe Knocke*,[5] and turne their streames into *Thames*. It not being able to retaine them both, the other parts are turned along the coast of *Flanders*, *Holland*, *Frisland*, and *Zutland*, where those Tides doe end, by reason of the *Baltickes* Seas bottome, it being farre unto beside the strait Channels betweene it and the sound. It is made now heare to appeare that he that will seeke the Ocean, as the Atlanticke to the West, or the *Hiperborian* to the North; for the mouth of the River of *Thames* must follow the Tyde; one thing is to be observed, that it floweth more

---

[1] See p. 269.—C.

[2] It is *St. Lawrence* in the text, but is altered in the Errata.—C.

[3] It is *Hambrough* in the text, but is amended to Halsborough in the Errata. Seller's *English Pilot* (1671) seems to identify it with Happisburgh, on the Norfolk coast.—C.

[4] It is printed *Hull* (which seems to be right) in the narrative, but is amended by the Errata.—C.

[5] A sandbank off the coast of Kent, near the estuary of the Thames.—C

water upon this coast of *England* then it doth upon the other coasts mentioned; the reason may be because *England* standeth nearer the West Sea.

Listen now againe how places farre remote from these our neighbour Channels doth correspond with them, as in *Groenland* it flowed E. and W Moone, and, following the tide 130 leagues to *Resolution*, it flowed E S.E. as before, and so the tide setting in with the Sunne untill it flowed S. by W. at *Swanne's Nest*, and there is lost in *Hudson's Bay;* so that it holds the same quality in the processe of time with the former from the West; and it is apparent that, to seeke the Ocean from the bottome of Rivers, deepe Bayes, or within lands (as the *Mediterranian* or the *Balticke*), we must find the flood tide, and follow it downe the hill of time I meane, proceeding against it, we shall shorten the flood, as this day we shall be where it floweth a S Moone, which we account to bee 12 of the clocke; to-morrow we shall be where the same Tyde flowed but 9. So that I, being but allowed what experience doth make due unto me, both neare home and else-where, I make no doubt but to prove this passage

It followeth now to parrallell this supposed passage with those formerly declared and certainly knowne. Beginning at *Port Nelson*, where I had the exactest account of his flowing point, and climing the flood (for so he must conceive that sayleth against Tide), [I] found that it flowed there a South East Moone, at the Checks, where I was on land, it flowed E S.E ; at *Brigges* his Mathematickes, East, at *Brooke Cobham*, E. by N.; at Sir *Thomas Roes Welcome*, E.N.E. Now it is prooved that the course time and change of this Tyde doth correspond with all other Ocean Tydes, it running also halfe Tyde (which is the floods running still the way of flood, untill it be halfe ebbe on shore, the ebbe running likewise his course in continuance, untill the water be halfe flowed upon the shore), so as it cannot be said to want any joynt or member of an Ocean's flood, but may rightly bee tearmed a limme thereof.

It may be objected that, although by all likelyhood that is a passage, yet it may prove to be a great distance to saile through; and how shall a man doe to know when he is thorow, that thereby he may direct his course Southward?

I answere: it can be no great distance, for that the water doth heighten in Spring-Tydes almost as much water at Sir *Thomas Roe's Welcome* in the Spring Tydes as at C. *Warwicke*, which standeth in the edge of the *Hyperborion* Ocean; and, therefore, how can this Tyde come farre from his sea, and bring constantly as much water as it floweth in any place that standeth neere the Ocean's lips? How can then the *Mare del Zur* be farre from hence? for the distance betweene Cape *Warwicke* and *Swan's Nest* is not above 200 leagues, where this Tyde's quite consumed; so, at the like distance from Sir *Thomas Roe's Welcome*, this new Tyde along that Bay holds the same untill in the bottome thereof it be consumed. For I have heard from some that, if North winds doth not inforce the Tydes, that they doe not flow above two foot in *Hudson's* E. and W. Bay.[1]

Me thinketh there is three materiall proofes that maketh better for our purpose, for to answere and free this doubt, though all the rest of Sir *Humphrey Gilbert* and Master *Wills* makes for the passage.

The first is, that the Cosmographers of *China* doe extend their coasts to the N.E., even to the 50 d. of latitude, and may doe further for any thing they know.

The second is *Paulus Venetus*, that lived there, and

---

[1] He must have heard this either from Bylot or Prickett, or from some of Captain James's crew.—C.

sayled from *Cattaia* 1,500 leagues North-East, and might have gone further for any land he see.

The 3rd is *Barnard la Tore*.

The 4th may be the ships found by *Francis Wasques* at *Sierra Nevada*, not being of *America*, but were a moneth in comming thither from *Asia;* all making that this passage cannot be long, for that they of *Asia* extend the breadth of their country so farre to East.

Beside, *Francisco Gaule*, the Spanish Pylot, reports of a high set of a Sea from the Northward in his passage from *Japon* to *Callyfornia*, which, he sayth, continued howsoever the windes blew. This doth shew the Sea to be open to the N.; for the like may be observed upon our N. coast, about *Whitby*, where the highest set of the Sea commeth from the N.N.W, although that poynt bloweth oblicke to the coast, yet there is more Sea therwith then the N.E. wind bringeth, that blowes opposite. The reason is, that the land to the N.N.W. is the furthest remote, all open towards the Pole, where these windes Eastwards off N. doe blow; but from *Greeneland* and the N. Cape at furthest, whose greatest distance being not above 370 leagues, must want space to raise his swelling motion. But, contrary, at the entrance into our Channell from W., you shall have a cõtinuall set into *Sleeve*,[1] which showes the distances of land to be far to the W. and S.-wards; and the like must be granted to this set of *Francis Gauls*, and also by that current that set *la Tore* to *Tidore:* it must come out of a wide Sea from the N.E.

And, for knowing when thou art through, be assured thou shalt have as great a Sea from the *del Zur* as from the W. into our Sleeve; and the strength of tide along

---

[1] A translation, apparently, of the French name for the English Channel—La Manche.—C. Betweene England and France.—F.

the coast will leave thee; then thou shalt not feare to direct thy course to *Tartaria, Cataia*, or *Japon*.

It may also be said that the Articke Circle is farre N., and that it will be frost, Icy, and cold, and that there is but two moneths in the yeare to make this triall, for in the rest it will not be nauigable.

I answere. that the Articke circle is not so farre N. as the Cape of *Finmarke*, neere in 73 d., where there is few or no Ice[1] at any time, and thereby it is Navigable at all times, but that there is no trading in winter; besides, the Sunne having great declination South, it is all night. But what is this to the Sea that is cleare of Ice; the like may this be for anything yet knowne; for, after I went from *Swanne's Nest*, I see no yce to the N.; nor doe I thinke there was any to the West, for, the winde blowing from [thence,] the ayre was as warme as in *England* in the latter end of *August*, and the land had no snow thereon, although it be very high land, and surely is inhabited, for else how could there have beene so many corps inwalled at Sir *Thomas Roe's Welcome*[2]? Yet, passing from hence S.-ward into the bay, it was colder, and yet warme enough.

And, for those Ice which are ingendred in this shallow sandy Bay, [it] is but as in other places in *Europe* neare the same Latit.; for those that have gone timely into the *Balticke* Sea hath found yce comming out of the Sound, and it is no marvaile to see the same froze over, which in those parts is as usuall as to have a noose,[3] to have the shipping froze all the whole winter therein, and for waggons to goe in winter where Ships saile in Sommer for many miles; for it is well knowne that those Sandy Easterne low coun-

---

[1] Throughout his narrative, Foxe uses the word *ice*, as though it were in the plural (see p. 281).—C.

[2] See p. 319.—C.

[3] I can only surmise that this expression means *to be entrapped* or *entangled*, as in a noose.—C.

treys (as *Sprutia, Denmarke, Frisland,* and the *Neatherlands*) are in winter subiected to violent frost; then why should not wee allow this low sandy countrey and Bay the like, being, about the same parallel, and a Bay as the Balticke is also from thence; which Latit where it freezeth so hard is from 52 to 57d.; but elevate the Pole to 73 d., there, at that time of winter in the same continent, there is no yce, but that you may saile Sea-free into the coast of *Russia*? Why should then this our Westerne passage be denyed of as good an opinion, but that it may be Sea-free as well as theirs to saile into the *Mare del Zur* to *Cathaia* (being doubtlesse to the Southward of that parallell), these 2 places of *Europe* and *America* thus answering one another both in quality and clime?

Goe to *Iseland,* as the Fishers doe now, in *March,* the North part lying in the Articke circle, and yet those Fishermen are not so troubled with Ice but that they can saile about it; and, [as] for the yce they finde there, they conceive [it] to be ingendred in the Bayes, Rivers, and Inlets of *Groneland,* and not about the Iland, nor in the Sea. It now appeares, as I said before, that this country doth but comply with those countries Eastward, and the like may be expected by them that is found by the other; nor can this channell be narrow that, in 6 poynts of the compasse (being but 4 howres ½ of time, to wit, from Sir *Thomas Roes* Iland to Port *Nelson*), doth send a flood and ebbe it backe againe along the coast, for 150 leag. knowne in so short time, and this to accord with the Moone.

To demonstrate this by example: Admit I was sent out of *Russia* to discover a land that I have heard lyeth farre S.W., which suppose to be *Atlantis* or *America.* Now it must be thought that I know of no land to the W. of *Europe's* continent; and, therefore, when I am come about the C. of *Finmarke,* I direct my course to the S. and W.-wards, as soone as the land will give me leave. For I doe know that it doth trent so, and that the coast of *Norway* is bonded with an Ocean. Now, bending towards, to the W of S., not knowing of Great *Brittaine*, I direct my course at gainest,[1] as I conceive, imagining that I shall meet with no land to the W. of *Europe;* but, thinking thus to proceede, I finde the land to meet mee to the W. as I thought to have sailed, to wit, the coast of Great *Brittaine;* and there I finde a tide going along the land to the S.-ward, I follow this coast, hopeing it may cast about to the W.; and, as I proceede, so doth this tide, keeping the height of his water still; so, by this ebbing and flowing, course and Latit., I doe assure it to my selfe that it cannot be any part of the maine continent of *Europe*, nor adioyning thereunto. And, thus persuing to the S, in long distance, I finde that this tyde doth still continue his height of water, so by that I speede on with more comfort. At length, I come betwixt two main lands[2], and, doubting some alteration or imbayment, I keep still the W. side, for thereby I must obtaine my intent, if at all, but now, when I come to make triall of my tyde, I find it hath left mee, which before convayed me many leag. along this unknowne coast; and now my tide of flood commeth from the W.-ward, and against me as I should sayle Shall I not then assure my selfe that, in pursuing against this tyde, that it will bring me into a new Ocean, by which I shall obtain my desire, which is the Atlanticke Sea? Yea, and I shall find it so, for, as that tide which came along with me from the N. out of the Sea which I have sailed from, will direct me backe againe into the same Sea, so shall this new tide from the W., in following his ebbe, bring me into his Ocean, or the Atlantic, which I desire.

Even so may this tide of mine, in persuing his ebbe

---

[1] In Yorkshire, whence Foxe came, the *gainest way* is the shortest way.—C.
[2] Calis and Dover.—F.

from the place where I found it first, bring me into the *Mare del Zur*.

Againe a Comparison fained to be sailed into a Sea through, our owne Kingdome from the East Sea to the West.

ADmit I come from *Hambrough*,[1] or the Easterne Sea, to expediate a Voyage through a great Ocean in a Country I have heard to lye far to the W. Directing my course W.-ward, I met with land sooner then I did expect In coasting this land W.-wards, I find an entrance, which I follow, for, by my account, I am but newly come to Sea, and must be farre shorte of my intent, but, following this entrance, I finde there is ebbing and flowing, which I pursue, and finde it to be a River, which conceive to be the river of *Thames* I goe therein with the tide, without debarre or hinderance, yet, finding the further up that I do proceede, the tide heightneth lesse water and runeth lesse time, so as knowing I goe from the East W.-ward, as I desire, yet I doe not know what will become of this hazard; but, not knowing how to mend my selfe, I must now play the game this way At length, I come to the head of this river, which conceive to be at *Kingston*, there I finde this tide which I followed out of the Eastern Sea to fall into a spacious and large *Mare* or *Ponte*, which *Mare* I enter Now it must be conceived that all the Country betweene *Kingston* and *Severne*, neere *Bristow* (as part of *Surry*, part of *Hampshire*, *Wiltshire*, *Glostershire*, *Oxford*, *Buckingham*, and part of *Middlesex*), to be ingulfed and turned into an inland Sea round about. Being entred in this *Ponte*, I begin to circuit about by the S S.W., and comes to W. side, where I finde an Inlet (to wit, the river at *Barkly*[2]) comming from the W. Sea, out of *Severne*, ebbing

---

[1] Hamburg.—C.   [2] Berkeley, in Gloucestershire.—C

and flowing into the *Mare*, as that did on the E. side by which I entred. Now I intend to venter into this ebbing and flowing of waters from the W., and thus persisting against the tyde by observation, as yesterday it flowed a W. Moone, this day it flowed a W. by N. Moone, keeping this constant fluxe and refluxe from the W. Eastward, so as sayling I shorten the tyde and is come in short distance to the place where it flowed S W. The same tide I tooke at my entring this river or inlet to flow W. I may now assure my selfe that those tyde streames are supported by waters from an Ocean, which, by pursuite, I find to be the *Atlanticke*.

It is to be observed in discoveries, as is found in other places by experience, that, in sayling against the flood-tide, wee shorten the time of flowing, and, in sayling therewith, we lengthen the same.

This comparison standeth thus :—

Hambrough is *England*, from whence we saile to *Fretum Hudson*, which here is conceived to be the *Thames*, whose head, as *Kingston*, is *Cary Swan's Nest;* the Country, Pont, or Mare so ingulfed, is *Hudson's* or *Button's* Bay; the W. Tide coming out of the Ocean at *Severne* is that new Tide I found at Sir *Thomas Roe's* Ile, which, pursued, will bring me into the *Mare del Zur*.

Let it not now be said that there is no passage by the N.W. into *India;* for that the best *Cosmographers*, those learned in Mathematickes and all Arts, have in former time consented that *America* is an Iland, and separated from any other continent. By which, great *Princes* have been perswaded to adventure and countenance [voyages for discovering a passage to the North-west] with great Summes (nor were their hopes mistaken, although as yet God hath not appoynted the time), as also the Nobility, Gentry, and

Merchants, when in the Voyage of Sir *Thomas Button* were about 160 adventurers.[1]

The fifth of the knowne (and supposed) passages to that rich *Indies* is by the Pole itselfe, yet never attempted, the gainest[2] and most hopefull of those three, yet unknowne, and the shortest of them all, as, from our N. parts of *Scotland's* Iles, from the latit. of 60 d to the Pole it selfe is but 600 leag., of which it hath beene sayled to the $82\frac{1}{2}$ d. by Captaine THOMAS MARMADUKE of *Hull*,[3] his furthest visible marke to the N. From thence was certaine Ilands he named *Sheffield's Orcades*, in duty to his most noble favourer in his Northerne designes, [who] was *Edmond* Lord *Sheffield*, now Earle of *Mulgrave*,[4] and at that time Lord President of the North, by whose great assistance, charge, and countenance, with the Merchants of the same Corporation, he was still set forth.

By which meanes, in his discoveries N-ward towards the Pole, it was his good fortune to enter into a harbour in *Greenland*, where he found one *Jonas Poole*, and *Nicholas Woodcocke*, with others, in a ship of *London*, distressed, for that a fall of an Ice had sunke their Ship. Which subjects, with their oyles, whale-finnes, and mors-teeth (who must have miserably perished there if he had not brought them home) to this noble Lord's perpetuall honour, and the future incouragement of that trade, now the most rich and safest that wee have. And this is the best by prescription or any other claime the City of Yorke and the Corporation of *Kingston* upon *Hull* can plead for the continuance of their Trade thither I make no doubt but

---

[1] See Introduction, p. xx.—C.   [2] See p. 437.—C.

[3] A reference to Captain Marmaduke, his northern voyages, and his rescue of Jonas Poole, is to be found in *Purchas his Pilgrimes* (vol. iii, pp. 707-715).—C.

[4] This was Edmund Sheffield, third Baron Sheffield, who was created Earl of Mulgrave in 1626, and died in 1646.—C.

that they doe acknowledge his Lordship for the same, with all thankfulnesse. This *Greeneland* was first seene by Mr. *Hudson*, who was countenanced by Sir *John Wolstenholme*, in his N E. coursaries.

There may be something objected against this passage, wch may with ease be answered, and this Treatise better supplied; but this I leave to Capt. Goodlade,[1] whose great experience this way, and to the E.-ward thereof, is the best able to supply or confute, if he be pleased so to shew himselfe

From the Pole to the knowne Coast of *China* in *Asia*, latit 50 d , is but 800 leag more, and yet the most Cosmographers have extended the land of *Tartaria* and *Scythia* N -ward to the 60, 70, and 80 Parralell, Septentrionall latitude; and on the America side is discovered to the 50 d.; so that the greatest distance is but 1,400 leag, nearer by one third part then any other of the S.

My comfort is that the quantity of Whales and Sea Mors that place affordeth (although it may be thought that I did not see the 100 part[2]) will (when Whale oyle comes into request[3]) drive the Merchant to send the Marriner to visit the Ile of *Brooke Cobham* for the Whale, and with their shallops range N.-wards to search for Vnicorne horne, Mors teeth, and Whale-finne, to come where Sir *Tho Roe* will bid them *Welcome*[4]; and, by these inticements,

---

[1] Probably he refers to Captain William Goodlard, a whaling captain, and no doubt a friend of Foxe's, a letter from whom appears in *Purchas his Pilgrimes* (vol. iii, p. 735).—C.   [2] See p. 326.

[3] At the time Foxe wrote, the northern whale-fishery was still in its infancy, though it had been prosecuted with energy, both by the English and Dutch, since Hudson's first voyage to Greenland and Spitzbergen in 1607, to which it owed its origin.—C.

[4] He means, of course, that they would come to the island he had named Sir Thomas Roe's Welcome. Foxe has previously expressed his belief that a Passage would be found in the position indicated, if found at all (see p. 370) —C.

they will be perswaded to inquire after this tyde, and at length bring home the good newes (which I expect) of this so long sought for [Passage].

For my part, I have now washt the Black-moore[1] these five yeares, having yet received neither sallery, wages, or reward, except what som few Gentlemen hath (I know not whether in curtesie or charity) bestowed upon me; having [here] to fore had my meanes taken from me in the time of warres betwixt *France*, *Spaine*, and us, so as I am utterly unable to prosecute the same, though I wish well thereto, knowing it is now to be done at very small charge

And this is more for their great comfort that it hath pleased Almighty God, of his great mercy, alwayes so to preserve those imployed this way to search in this discovery that no ship ever perished, but, howsoever they suffered, the account was brought home and wee made acquainted with their actions, all which wee must acknowledge to be the providence of Almighty God, who hath thus preserved those seeds we have sowne, and will doe still, untill the time come which he hath appoynted to send some happy man to plucke the fruite. Heere lyeth the way to *Colcos*, and he that finds the same brings home the *Golden Fleece!*[2]

My pen and selfe now is growne weary; and, hoping some other brave Spirit will enter the Lists and attempt the Enterprize, I rest.

---

[1] Laboured in vaine.—F. See the Introduction, p cxxii.—C.

[2] The three preceding paragraphs appear to have been misplaced by an error of the printer in Foxe's work, wherein they precede the four which they herein follow.

FINIS.

To the Worp[full], the Masters, Wardens, and Assistants of the Trinity-Houses, but especially to these of *Dedford-Strand* and *Kingstone* upon *Hull*, with their whole Corporations.

Worshipfull Gentlemen,

Nd Foster Fathers of my Academie, I present you heere neither with Jason's voyage to Colcos, nor the Golden fleece as yet, but with the best of my endeavours to the North-West, which we poore Discoverers are so jeered about (with so much Phylosophy) as though these Voyages have spent so much time and treasure as it is not able to redeeme it selfe by being guld with the false Sea cards or fabulous reports of strangers; for no Nation in the World knoweth so much of this as yourselves; nor neede wee neither the arguments of Phylosophy to examine so much variety, and that so various as the Schoole-men finde out, nor (for their inquisitions or disquisitions their) Mr. Aristotle did not know what Time, since his, hath brought forth; and, since him, we have almost found out the reason for the Tide, about which some of them have writ he drowned himself because he could not; nor you neede not goe to the N.W. passage to seeke the Philosopher's stone, having one of your owne by which you have angled, levelled, and brigged over the ocean from this Monarch to the furthest East and West. The touch thereof hath made you attended home (as the shadow the substance) with the Tawny Peruian and the Sunne-burnt Blackmoore, Affrican's gold, the rich Sparkling Diamond, the night-shining Carbunkle, the Physicall Beager, the Emerald, Saphire, and the Orient Indian Pearle, adorning the Lilly necks of the most daintiest Ladies, with other of

pleasure and price, besides the Drugges, Vigitables, Simples, and Balsoms for health, and all these and farre more Jemms of wealth and treasure hath the vertue of your Ademant stone exported hither, to the enriching and honouring of our Nation

I pray that, when this abortive [book] shall come to your view, that you passe over its deformity and imperfections (which Nature, in haste, stampt into it, in which it still remayneth, both for want of meanes and Art), and your private admonition shall cause me [to] amend it at the next Edition; for with this I am glad I have not overcharged the presse (as fearing), the worst part of which is already befalne (in Erataes), for which, if I should excuse myselfe, I know both the Compositor and the correcter will witnesse with not[1] in taking the fault upon themselves. I have done my endevour to correct the most palpable, as mistaking words or non-sense; which, not being acquainted with our Sea termes, they might easily commit, and, for the faults in letters, I know your Arithmetick can make whole numbers of Fractions If these faults had beene committed by myself in the Copie, I might with some reason have pleaded an excuse, being no Scholler, and having had no helpe, which I did know was very needfull, but [I] was not able to buy it, and I was told it would not be had for naught, especially by[2] the Scholler that was acquainted with the language of the Sea. Therefore, now I feels the want of Mr. Hackluit (and so I doubt will others in time to come), who, for the good of his country, stored those Journals at his owne charge.

Whereupon, not knowing otherwise how to proceede, I was enforced, with such Tackling, Cordage, and Raftage as I had, to Rigge and Tackle this ship my selfe. I hope she

---

[1] Apparently this is a misprint for *me*.—C.
[2] *From* makes better sense than *by*.—C.

will saile the better in this Trimme if you be pleased to conduct her, which I doubt not but you will, having heretofore observed your favours in cherishing and preferring young Sea-men, with your charity to others, not onely in your Almes-deeds to the Fatherlesse and Orphans, but your continuall maintenance, with all necessaries, to aged poore Widdowes and decayed Mariners; your compassion and reliefe to the distressed ship-wrackt Seamen farre from home, and others; your priviledge to maimed Men; with the right in Justice you doe to those that are not able to wage law for the same, deserveth to be inrolled amongst the greatest acts of Christian charitie.

And, for that your helpefull care towards my furnishing forth with all materials for this service, your loving aspects and bounty since my home comming, hath obliged me to acknowledge your favours with thanks, [for which] I desire your kind acceptance, and the rather because it is the Present of your younger Brother,

LUKE FOXE.

Resensui librum hunc, cui titulus est (*North-West Foxe*), in quo nihil reperio quò minùs cum utilitate publicâ Imprimatur, modò intra sex menses proximè sequentes typis mandetur.

Decemb 1,
1634.

SA. BAKER R.P.D. Episcopo
Londinensis Cap domest.

THE
STRANGE AND DANGEROUS VOYAGE
OF
CAPTAIN THOMAS JAMES.

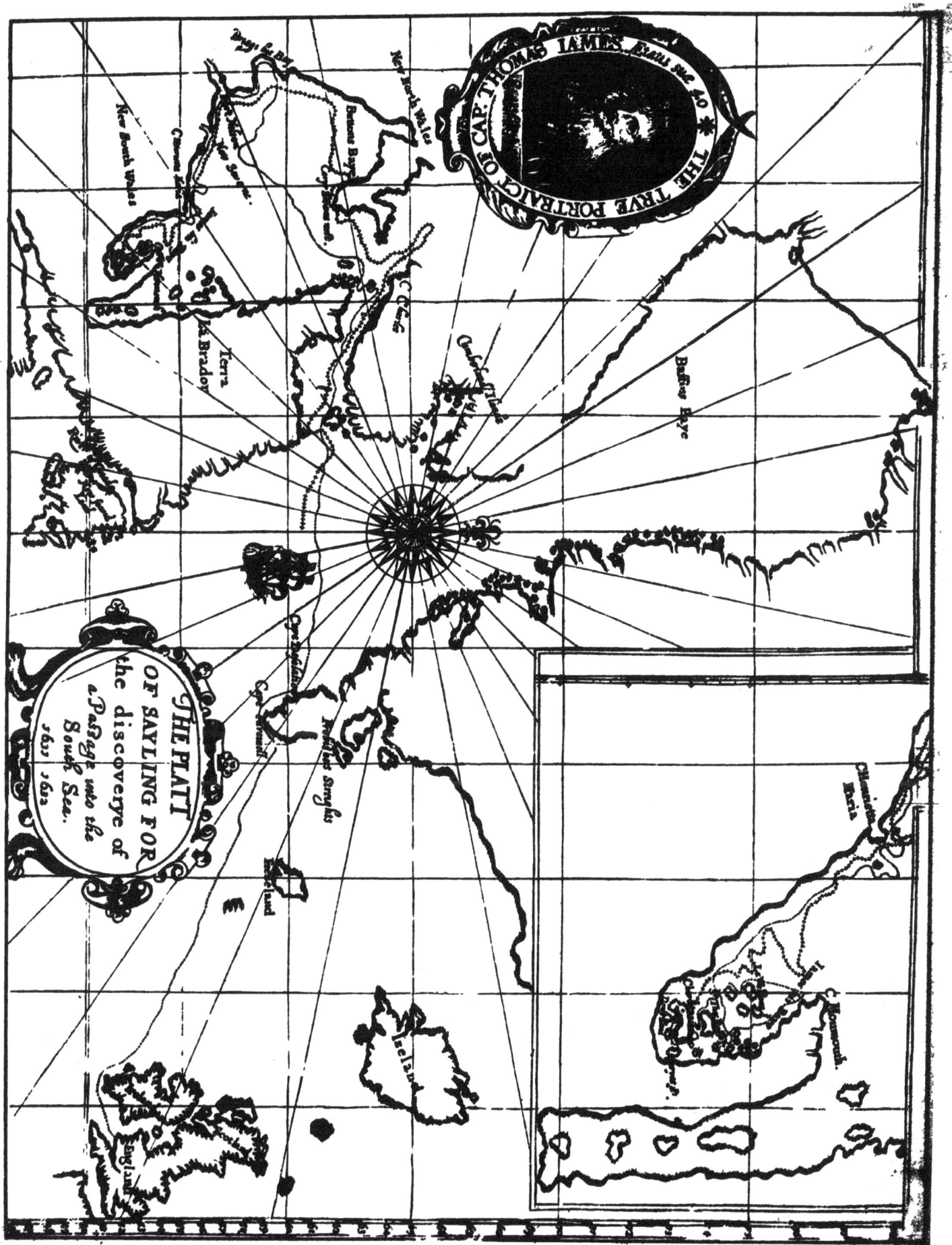

THE STRANGE AND DANGEROVS VOYAGE OF

Captaine THOMAS IAMES, in
his intended Discouery of the Northwest
Passage into the South Sea

VVHEREIN

THE MISERIES INDVRED, BOTH
Going, Wintering, Returning; & the Rarities
observed, both *Philosophicall* and *Mathematicall*,
are related in this Iournall of it

Published by His MAIESTIES
command.

To which are added, A Plat or Card for the
Sayling in those Seas.

Divers little Tables of the Author's, of the Variation of the Compasse, &c

VVITH

An Appendix concerning *Longitude*, by Master
Henry Gellibrand, Astronomy Reader,
of *Gresham* Colledge in *London*.

AND

An Aduise concerning the Philosophy of these late
Discoueryes, By W. W

LONDON:
Printed by *Iohn Legatt*, for *Iohn Partridge*.
1633.

To my worthy friend and fellow-Templar, Captaine IAMES.

 *HAVE perused your Iournall. To commend it, were to dispraise it; Good Wine needs no Ensigne*[1]*: Mos est fæda coloribus abdere: Yet this I must needs say, you have shewed your-selfe to be a Master of your Art.* The Worth of a Warrier and Pylot is never discouered but in stormes and skirmishes[2]; *and how many skirmishes of storms and tempests you have past, this Iournall of yours doth sufficiently manifest. Go on then, as you haue begun, so, when any good occasion is offered, second your good beginnings with sutable proceedings; and let not the cold entertainment you have had in the frozen Seas, freeze up your affections in undertaking other worthy employments So may you deserue, with* Columbus, Drake, *and* Frobusher,

---

[1] A bush, as the sign of a wine-shop, is one of the most ancient of signs, having been in use among the Romans and other nations of antiquity. In the Middle Ages, it was a very common inn-sign, and is still popular Hence the above very old proverb.

[2] Miles in acie probatur ; Gubernator in tempestate dignoscitur.

to haue the remembrance of you smell sweetly in the nostrils of posteritie when you are in the dust. Farewell,

From the Inner Temple,

THOMAS NASH[1]

---

[1] This, of course, was not the famous satirist of this name, who had died about thirty years before. He does not seem to have been a man of any special distinction, and I have failed to discover anything relating to him, except that he published in 1633 (the year in which James' work appeared) a very learned theological discourse entitled, *Quaternio, or a fourefold way to a Happie Life, set forth in a Dialogue between a Countryman and a Citizen, a Divine and a Lawyer* The author is described on the title-page as "Tho Nash, Philopolitem", and the preface is dated from the Inner Temple. Later editions (apparently identical, except in the title-page) appeared in 1636 and 1639

The Printer desires to be excused to the Courteous Reader if, in an Argument of this Nature, the Compositer, not throughly acquainted with termes of Nauigation, hath sometimes, which he feareth, and in some words, mistaken the Authors minde; as in *stowed* for *stood*, &c, promising a future amends (if Occasion profer it selfe) by a more exact Impression

Farewell.

TO THE KING'S MOST
EXCELLENT AND SACRED
MAIESTIE

Most Dread Soueraigne,

THAT my vnskilfull selfe was made choyce of for this imployment, and my undertaking in it encouraged by Your gracious commandement, I must ever account of for the greatest honour that ever yet befell mee. Many a Storme, and Rocke, and Mist, and Winde, and Tyde, and Sea, and Mount of Ice, haue I, in this Discouery, encountered withall; many a despaire and death had almost ouerwhelmed mee; but still the remembrance of the accompt I was to giue of it to so gracious a Maiesty, put me in heart againe; made mee not to giue way to mine owne feares, or the infirmities of humanitie. Your Maiesty, in my employment (like a true Father of your countrey), intended the good of your subjects; and who is not bound to blesse God for your Royal care in it? Had it now beene my fortune to have done my countrey this seruice (as to have brought home the newes of this supposed and long-sought-for Passage), then should the Merchant have

enjoyed the sweetnesse of the hoped profit, and the Subject haue beene sensible of the benefit of your Majesties royall intentions in it. I have done my good will in it; and, though [I have] not brought home that newes, yet shall I here divulge those observations, which may (I hope) become some way beneficiall vnto my countrey. The Accompt of them, I here, in all humilitie, offer unto your iudicious Majesty. Your gracious acceptance of what I had done, though I had not done what was expected, emboldeneth me to doe so; and, since your Majestie was pleased to signifie your desires of hauing a Briefe of my Voyage presented unto you, that word became a command unto mee to draw this rude abstract of it. Your Majestie will please to consider that they were rough elements which I had to doe withall; and will, with fauour, vouchsafe to pardon if a sea-man's style be like what he most converseth with. In the plainenesse, therefore, of well-meaning (since your Majestie hath beene so gracious to mee, as to appoint mee your seruant), I am now bound to vow you my seruice; and it shall be my honour to be commanded it; and I shall account no dangers too great in the going thorow it. These are the resolutions of

Your Majesties humblest Subject
and Seruant,

THOMAS IAMES.

THE PREPARATIONS TO THE VOYAGE.

*Auing bin for many yeeres importuned by my honorable and worshipfull friends to vndertake the discouery of that part of the world which is commonly called* The North-west Passage *into the* South Sea, *and so to proceed to* Iapan, *and so round the world to the Westward; Being prest forward withall by signifying to mee the earnest desire the King's most excellent Maiestie had to be satisfied therein: I acquainted my much Honoured friends, the Merchants of* Bristoll, *therewith, who (as euer they haue bin Benefactors and Aduancers of them that pursue the wayes of Honour, together with the enlargement and benefit of his Maiesties Kingdomes) did freely offer to bee at the charge of furnishing forth shipping for this purpose.*[1] *And now, being thus enabled, I addresse my selfe to the Honourable Sir* Thomas Roe, Knight (*as to a learned, and furthest employed traueller by Sea and Land this day in* England[2]), *who ioyfully presented*

---

[1] For remarks on the incentives to James' voyage, see the Introduction.

[2] This eminent statesman and traveller was also one of those who helped forward Captain Foxe in the preparations for his voyage. For a brief biographical notice of him, see the Introduction, p. lxxv.

theirs and mine owne voluntary willingnesse to doe his Maiesties Seruice in this kinde, who most graciously accepted of the offer, and encouraged mee by many fauours in my weake vndertakings. Wherefore, with all speed, I contriued in my mind the best modell I could, whereby I might effect my designe. The Adventurers' monies were instantly ready and put into a Treasurer's hand, that there might be no want of present pay for anything I thought necessary for the Voyage.

I was euer of the opinion that this particular action might be better effected by one ship then by two consorted, because, in those Icie Seas, so much subiect to fogs, they might be easily separated. I forbeare to speake of stormes and other accidents, as that a Rendezvous in discoueries cannot surely, or without much hinderance, be appointed, and that speedy perseuerance is the life of such a businesse Wherefore I resolued to haue but one Ship, the Ship-boate, and a Shallop.

A great Ship (as by former experience I had found[1]*) was vnfit to be forc'd thorow the Ice, wherefore I made choice of a well-conditioned, strong Ship, of the burthen of seuentie Tunne*[2]*; and in God and that only Ship to put the hope of my future fortunes*

The Ship resolued vpon, and [it having been decided] that in lesse time then 18 moneths our voyage could not be effected, I next considered how our Ship of seuentie Tuns in bulke and weight might now be proportioned—in victuals, namely, and other necessaries. This was all done as contractedly as

---

[1] Probably James does not mean *personal* experience The matter is referred to in the Introduction.

[2] This was about the burthen of Foxe's ship, the *Charles*. Rundall states (*Voyages towards the North-west*, p 187) that she "had been expressly built for the service", but James himself says nothing to this effect, and I cannot discover whence Rundall obtained his information. She had, however, been re-named the *Henrietta Maria*, after the Queen.

we could; and the number of men it would serue, at ordinary allowance, for the forementioned time, was found to be twenty-two[1]—*a small number to performe such a businesse, yet double sufficient to sayle the Ship with prouident carefulnesse.*

The Baker, Brewer, Butcher, and others, vndertake their Offices vpon their credits, knowing it to be a generall businesse and their vtter vndoing if they fayled in performance; but truly they prooued themselues Masters in their Arts, and haue my praise for their honest care, in them consisting a great part of the performance of the voyage.[2]

The Carpenters goe in hand with the Ship, to make her as strong and seruiceable as possibly in their vnderstandings they could.

Euery thing being duly proportioned, and my small number of men knowne, I began to thinke of the quality and abilitie they should be of.

Voluntary loyterers I at first disclaimed, and published I would haue all vnmarried, approoued, able, and healthy Seamen. In a few dayes, an abundant number presented themselues, furnished with generall sufficiencie in marine *occasions. I first made choice of a* Boate-swayne, *and some to worke with him for fitting the rigging of the Ship, and, as things went forward, shipt the* subordinate Crue; *and, all things being perfectly ready, I shipt the* Master's mates, *and, last of all, the* Master *of my Ship, and my* Liefetenant.

---

[1] Foxe also had a crew of twenty-two. From what James says in the letter he left at Charleton Island (see *post*), we learn that the crew consisted of Captain James himself, nineteen "choice able men", and two boys ("younkers", as he calls them). A list of their names and positions, so far as these can be ascertained from James' narrative, is given in the Introduction.

[2] Foxe's remarks on the competency of his culinary officers (see p. 265) show that he had read the above passage, and, as a rough seaman, despised the tone of it.

The whole company were strangers to me, and to each other (as by way of familiaritie), but yet [*they were all*] *priuately recommended by worthy Merchants for their abilitie and faithfulnesse I was sought to by diuers that had bin in places of the chiefest command in this action formerly, and others also that had vsed the* Northerly Icie Seas, *but I vtterly refused them all, and would by no meanes haue any with mee that had bin in the like voyage or aduentures, for some priuate reasons vnnecessary here to be related. Keeping thus the power in my owne hands, I had all the men to acknowledge immediate dependance vpon my selfe alone, both for direction and disposing of all, as well of the Nauigation as all other things whatsoeuer*[1]

In the mean time, the better to strengthen my former studies in this businesse, I seeke after Iournals, Plots,[2] Discourses, *or what-euer else might helpe my vnderstanding.*[3]

I set skilfull workemen to make me Quadrants, Staues, Semicircles, *&c, as much, namely, as concerne the Fabricke of them, not trusting to their Mechannicke hands to* diuide *them, but had them diuided by an ingenious practitioner in the* Mathematicks.[4] *I likewise had* Compasse-needles *made*

---

[1] Foxe and James were, therefore, similarly situated, in that they both sailed with crews not a single member of which had had any previous experience of navigation in Arctic seas; but there is this difference between them that, whereas Foxe had wisely endeavoured to secure men with Arctic experience, James "utterly refused" all such, though he had been expressly advised to the contrary by his employers (see Introduction), and though he says some offered him their services This he did "for some private reasons" which he thought unnecessary to state, but which (one cannot help thinking) would have seemed very inadequate, had he ventured to state them.

[2] *Plat* (also spelled *plot*) is an old name for a map or chart

[3] Foxe had an advantage over James, in that he had been collecting and studying these for twenty years before he sailed (see p. 262).

[4] One may surmise that it was Henry Briggs (see p. lx), or Henry Gellibrand (see *post*).

after the most reasonablest and truest wayes that could be thought on[1]; *and, by the first of* April, *euery thing was ready to be put together into our hopefull Ship*

In the meane space, I made a Iourney vp to London *to know his Maiesties further pleasure, and to make knowne to him my readinesse*[2]; *who, calling for the forementioned Honourable Knight, I speedily after receiued his Maiesties Royall Letters, with directions for proceeding in my voyage, and my discharge*[3]; *whereupon I had foorth the Ship into the Rode, expecting a faire winde to begin the voyage.*

---

[1] At the end of his book, James gives a very full list of the instruments he took with him on his voyage. They were probably made for him by Andrew Wakely of "Redriff Wall, near Cherry-garden Stairs", as a page of advertisements of nautical instruments for sale by him follows the title-page in some copies of James's work that I have seen.

[2] The circumstances connected with James's visit to London are set forth in the Introduction

[3] As with Foxe, so also with James, we have no information as to the precise tenour of the Letter of Instructions given him by the King There can be little doubt, however, that the Instructions given to James were to much the same effect as (if not identical with) those given to Foxe. At the same time, it is not easy to infer this from anything the former actually says in his narrative, which is not the case with the latter. The matter has been discussed in the Introduction, p. xcvi

A Voyage for the discouering
a Passage to the South Sea.

THE second of *May*, 1631,[1] I tooke my leaue of the Worshipfull Merchant Aduenturers in this Action, in the Citie of *Bristoll*; and, being accompanied with a Reuerend Diuine, one Master *Thomas Palmer*,[2] and diuers of the Merchants, with others of my kindred and natiue Countrey-men, I repaired aboord. Here Master *Palmer* made a Sermon, exhorting vs to continue brotherly loue amongst vs, and to be bold to professe the true *Christian* Religion where-euer we should happen, in this our perigrination. After they had receiued such entertainment as my estate could affoord them, they departed for *Bristoll*. This afternoone, I made reuiew of all things, as well of clothes, and other necessaries, as of victuals; and, where there was found any want, wee were presently furnished.

The third of *May* (after Prayer for a prosperous suc-

---

[1] Foxe sailed three days later. Rundall incorrectly states (*Voyages towards the North-west*, p. 187) that the two navigators sailed on the same day.

[2] I have failed to discover any information as to the history or position of this reverend gentleman. No doubt he was a prominent divine at the time in Bristol.

cesse to our endeauours), about three a clocke in the afternoone, we came to Sayle and Stode downe the Channell of *Seuerne*, with little winde, but slowly got forward to the Westward of *Lundie;* and then the winde opposed it selfe so strongly against vs that wee were driuen to beare vp and come to an Anker in *Lundie*-Rode, the fifth in the euening, where we remained vntill the eighth in the morning.

Now, hoping the winde would fauour us, wee came to Sayle, but wee were forc'd to put into *Milford*,[1] where we came to an Anker about mid-night.

Here we remained till the seuenteenth, in the morning, when, with the first fauouring winde, wee proceeded and doubled about Cape *Cleere*, of *Ireland*.

The two and twentieth, we were in *Latitude* 51. 26, and the *Blaskes*[2] did beare of vs North-east, about twelue leagues off; which *Blaskes* is in *Lat* 52 4. Here I ordred the course that should bee kept, which was generally West North-West, as the winde would giue leaue, which in this Course and distance is very variable and vnconstant.

The fourth of *Iune*, we made the land of *Groynland*. Standing in with it, to haue knowledge of the trending of it, it prooued very thicke foule weather.

And the next day, by two a clocke in the morning, we found our selues incompassed about with Ice; and, endeauouring to cleere our selues of it (by reason we could not see farre about vs), we were the more ingaged, and strooke many fearfull blowes against it. At length we made fast to a great piece (it blowing a very storme), and,

---

[1] Now known as Milford Haven, the magnificent harbour on the coast of Pembrokeshire.

[2] The Blaskets, a group of rocky islands off the entrance to Dingle Bay, on the coast of Kerry.

with poles, wrought day and night to keepe off the Ice, in which labour we broke all our poles.

The sixth, about two a clocke in the morning, we were beset with many extraordinary great pieces of Ice that came vpon vs, as it were, with wilfull violence, and doubtlesse had crushed vs to pieces if we had not let fall some Sayle, which the Ship presently felt. In scaping that danger, we ran against another great piece, that we doubted whether our Ship had not bin stav'd to pieces; but, pumping, we found she made no water The former pieces of Ice had crushed our Shallop all to pieces[1]; wherefore I caused our long Boate speedily to be had vp from betwixt the Decks and put ouer Boord, by helpe whereof we againe recouered our broken Shallop, and had her vp on the Decks, intending to new build her. All this day, we did beat, and were beaten fearfully amongst the Ice, it blowing a very storme. In the euening, wee were inclosed amongst great pieces, as high as our Poope, and some of the sharpe blue corners of them did reach quite vnder vs. All these great pieces (by reason it was the out-side of the Ice) did heaue and set, and so beat vs that it was wonderfull how the Ship could indure one blow of it; but it was God's only preseruation of us, to whom be all honour and glory In this extremitie, I made the men to let fall, and make what Sayle they could, and the Ship forced herself thorow it, though so tossed and beaten as I thinke neuer Ship was. When we were cleere, we sayed[2] the pumps and found her stanch, vpon which we went instantly to prayer, and to praise God for his mercifull deliuery of vs.

The seuenth and eighth dayes, we indeauoured to double about *Cape Farewell*, being still pestered with much Ice

---

[1] This was but the first of Captain James' innumerable misfortunes.
[2] *To say* is an old and contracted form of *to assay* or *essay*, meaning *to try.*

The ninth, we were in *Lat.* 59. 00, and we made account the *Cape Farewell* bare of vs due East, and some ten leagues off The *Blaskes* in *Ireland* is in *Lat* 52 4, and *Cape Farewell* in *Lat.* 59 00 The course is West-North-west, and the distance about 410 leagues. I know very well these *Latitudes*, courses, and distances doe not exactly agree with Mathematicall conclusions, *but thus we found it by practice*. The variation of the Compasse in *Lat.* 52. 30, and 30 leagues to the Westward of *Ireland*, is about 3. 00 to the Eastward; in *Lat.* 57. 00, about 310 leagues West Northwest from the *Blaskes*, the Compasse doth vary 9. 00 to the West-ward; in *Lat.* 59. 15, some 40 leagues to the East-ward of *Cape Farewell*, the variation is about 14. 45. In this course, I haue bin obseruant whether there were any Currant that did set to the N E., as some haue written there did, and that as well in calme weather as otherwayes, but I could not perceiue any. The windes here are variable, and the Sea of an vnsearchable depth. We haue not seen, from *Ireland* hitherto, any Whales or other Fish. The weather, for the most part, was foggie and mistie that wets as bad as raine.

The tenth, all the morning, was very foule weather, and a high-growne Sea, although we had Ice not farre off about vs, and some pieces as high as our Top-mast-head. Our long Boate, which we were faine to Towe at Sterne (by reason we were building our Shallop on our Decks), broke away and put vs to some trouble to recouer her againe. This we did, and made meanes to haue her into the Ship, though very much bruised, and that I had two men sore hurt, and like to be lost in the hauing of her in. By eight a clocke this euening, we were shot vp as high as *Cape Desolation;* for, finding here the Land to trend away North and by East, we certainly knew it to be the *Cape*. It stands in *Lat* 60. 00, and the Land from *Cape Farewell* to it trends N.W., the distance about 40 leagues. The distance from *Cape Desolation* to the South end of the Iland of *Resolution* is about 140 leagues, the course West halfe a point North. The *Lat.* of the South end of the Iland being 61. 20; some 12 leagues to the Westward of *Cape Desolation*, the variation is 16 00. In this course, we were much tormented, pestered, and beaten with the Ice, many pieces being higher then our Top-mast-head. In our way, we saw many Grampusses[1] amongst the Ice, and it seemeth the Sea is full of them The weather, for the most part, a stinking fogge, and the Sea very blacke, which I conceiue to be occasioned by reason of the fogge

The seuenteenth, at night, we heard the rut of the shoare, as we thought; but it prooued to be the rutt against a banke of Ice that lay on the shoare[2] It made a hollow and a hideous noyse, like an ouer-flow of water, which made vs to reason amongst our selues concerning it, for we were not able to see about vs, it beinge darke night and foggie. We stood off from it till breake of day, then in againe, and about 4 a clocke in the morning wee saw the Land aboue the fogge, which we knew to be the *Iland* of *Resolution*.[3] This last night was so cold that all our Rigging and Sayles were frozen Wee endeauoured to compasse about the Southern point of the Iland, for that we were so much pestered with the Ice, and blinded with a very thicke fogge. Here runnes a quicke tyde into the Straight, but the ebbe is as strong as the flood The fogge was of such a piercing nature that it spoiled all our Compasses, and made them flagge, and so heauy withall

---

[1] See p. 274.

[2] The *rut of the shore*, in nautical parlance, is the dashing of the sea upon the coast. James, of course, means that he heard the waves dashing against a bank of ice.

[3] This island lies on the northern side of the entrance to Hudson's Strait, and was, doubtless, so named by Sir Thomas Button in 1612 (see p. 283, *note*).

THE OUTWARD VOYAGE. 465

that they would not trauerse. Wherefore I would aduise any that shall Sayle this way hereafter to prouide Compasses of *Muscouia* Glasse, or some other matter, that will endure the moisture of the weather.[1] As the fogge cleered vp, we could see the entrance of the Straight to be all full of Ice close thronged together Indeauouring to goe forward, wee were fast inclosed amongst it; and so droue to and againe with it, finding no ground at 230 fad., 4 leagues from the shoare.

The twentieth, in the morning, we had got about the Southerne point of the Iland,[2] and the winde came vp at West, and droue both vs and the Ice vpon the shoare. When we were driuen within two leagues of the shoare, we came amongst the most strangest whirlings of the Sea that possibly can bee conceiued. There were diuers great pieces of Ice aground in 40 fad. water; and the ebbe, comming out of the broken grounds of the Iland amongst these Iles of Ice, made such a distractiō that we were carryed round, sometimes close by the Rocks, sometimes close by those high pieces, that we were afeard they would fall vpon vs.[3] We were so beaten likewise with the encountering of the Ice that we were in a most desperate estate. We made fast two great pieces of Ice to our sides with our Kedger[4] and Grapnels[5] that drew 9 or 10 fad., that so they might be a-ground before vs, if so be we were

---

[1] Foxe was troubled by the inactivity of the needle when he was in Hudson's Strait. He attributed it to cold (see p. 309, *note*).

[2] Now known as Hatton Headland. Foxe did not pass this point until three days later.

[3] These were the strong overfalls and ripplings in the sea which are met with at the mouth of the Hudson's Strait. The phenomenon was first remarked by Davis, who called it the "Furious Overfall", and is mentioned by many later navigators. Foxe passed through the current on June 18th.

[4] See p. 71.   [5] See p. 254.

driuen on the shoare. But that designe fayled vs; and now, from the top, seeing in amongst the Rocks, I sent the Boate (for now wee had finished her) to see if shee could find some place of securitie; but shee was no sooner parted but shee was inclosed and driuen to hale vp on the Ice, or else shee had beene crushed to pieces. They ranne her ouer the Ice, from piece to piece; and, in the meane space, with the whirling and incountring of the Ice, the two pieces brake away from our sides, and carryed away our Kedger and Grapnels Then we made signes to the Boate to make all the haste shee could to vs, which shee, perceiuing, did, the men being, with much difficultie, inforced to hale her ouer many pieces of Ice In the meane space, we made some Sayle, and got to that piece of Ice that had our Grapnell on it, which wee againe recouered. By this time was our Boate come, and we put afresh Crue into her, and sent her to fetch our Kedger, which shee endeauoured with much danger of Boate and Men. By this time, the Ship was driuen so neere the shoare that we could see the Rocks under vs and about vs, and we should be carryed with the whirlings of the waters close by the points of Rocks, and then round about backe againe, and all this, notwithstanding the Sayle we had abroad, that we expected continually when shee would be beaten to pieces. In this extremetie, I made them to open more Sayle, and to force her in amongst the Rocks and broken grounds, and where there was many great pieces of Ice aground. We went ouer Rocks that had but 12 or 13 foot water on them, and so let fall an Anker. This Anker had neuer bin able to winde vp the Ship, but that (by good fortune) the Ship ranne against a great piece of Ice that was aground. This rush brake the Mayne knee of her Beake head, and a corner of it tare away 4 of our maine Shrouds, and an Anker that we had at the Bowe fastened into it, and so stopt her way that she did winde vp to her Anker.[1] Wee saw the sharp Rocks vnder vs and about vs, and had but 15 foot water, being also in the tides way, where all the Ice would driue upon vs. Our Boate we could not see, which made us doubt shee had bin crushed to pieces. In her was the third part of our company; but, by and bye, we saw her come about a point amongst the Rocks. Shee had recouered our Kedger, which made us something ioyfull. With all speed, we laid our Hawsers to the Rocks, and euery one did worke to the best of his strength to Warp her out of this dangerous place to the Rocks side, where wee had 3 fad. water and were vnder the shelter of a great piece of Ice that was a-ground, which should keepe off the Ice that otherwise would haue driuen vpon vs. Here wee lay very well all the ebbe; but, when the flood came, we were assaulted with pieces of Ice that, euery halfe houre, put vs into despayrable distress. We did worke continually, and extremely, to keepe off the Ice. At full Sea, our great piece of Ice (which was our Buckler) was afloate, and (doe what wee could) got away from vs, and left vs in a most eminent danger, by reason of the Ice that droue in vpon vs. But the ebbe being once made, this great piece of Ice came a-ground very fauourable to vs, and sheltered vs all the rest of the ebbe. All night, we wrought hard to shift our Cables and Hawsers, and to make them fast aloft on the Rocks, that the Ice might the better passe vnder them. All day and all night, it snowed hard and blew a very storme at West, which droue in all the Ice out of the Sea vpon vs. In working against the violence of the Ice, the flooke of our Kedger was broken, two armes of

---

[1] This is the second of Capt. James' many misfortunes. A little later we hear of more injuries to the ship Foxe also was enclosed among the ice at this place (see p. 284).

our Grapnels, and two Hawsers, our Shallop being againe very much bruised, whereupon to work we goe on all hands to repaire it.

21. This tyde, the Harbour was choaked full of Ice, so that it did seeme firme and vnmoouable; but, when the ebbe was made, it did mooue. Some great pieces came a-ground, which did alter the course of the other Ice, and put vs on the Rocks. Here, notwithstanding all our vttermost endeauours, she settled vpon a sharpe Rocke, about a yard aboue the Mayne Mast, and, as the water ebbed away, she hung after the Head, and heeld to the Offing. We made Cables and Hawsers aloft to her Masts, and so to the Rocks, straining them tough[1] with our tackles; but shee, as the water ebbed away, sunk still, that at length she was so turned ouer that wee could not stand in her. Hauing now done all to the best of our vnderstandings (but to little purpose), we went all vpon a piece of Ice and fell to prayer, beseeching God to be mercifull vnto vs   It wanted yet an houre to low-water, and the tyde did want a foot and a halfe to ebbe to what it had ebbed the last tyde We were carefull obseruers of the low-waters, and had marks by stones and other things which we had set vp, so that we could not be deceiued. The Ship was so turn'd ouer that the Portlesse of the Fore-castell[2] was in the water, and we did looke euery minute when she would ouer-set. Indeed, at one time, the Cables gaue way, and shee sunke downe halfe a foot at that slip; but vnexpectedly it began to flow, and sensibly wee perceiued the water to rise apace, and the Shippe withall   Then was our sorrow turned to ioy, and we all fell on our knees, praising God for his mercy in so miraculous a deliuerance.

---

[1] *Taut*, the nautical form of *tight*.
[2] No doubt he means the *gunwale* of the forecastle, portlast or portoise being synonymous with gunwale.

As soone as she was freed from this Rocke, we wrought hard to get her further off All the flood, we were pretty quiet from the Ice; but, when the ebb was made, the Ice came all driuing againe vpon vs, which put vs to a great extremity. We got as many pieces betwixt vs and the Rockes as we could, to fence vs from the Rockes. There came a great piece vpon our quarter, which was aboue 300 of my paces about, but it came aground. Thus did diuers great pieces besides, which was the occasion that this tyde the Harbour was quite choakt vp, so that a man might goe any way ouer it, from side to side. When it was three-quarters ebbe, these great pieces that came aground began to breake with a most terrible thundering noyse, which put vs in a great feare that those about vs would breake vs all to pieces. But God preserued vs.

22 This morning, the water veer'd to a lower ebbe then the last tide it had done by two foote, whereby we saw God's mercies apparent in our late extremity That flood we had some respit from our labours; but, after full sea, our hopes ebde too. The great peece that was by vs so stopt the Channel that the Ice came all driuing vpon vs, so that now vndoubtedly we thought wee should haue lost our Ship. To worke thereupon we goe, with axes, barres of iron, and any thing proper for such a purpose, to breake the corners of the Ice, and to make way for it to driue away from vs. It pleased God to giue good successe to our labours; and we made way for some, and fended off the rest, and got so much of the softer sort of the Ice betwixt vs and the Rockes, that we were in pretty security. But, at low water, those peeces that were aground, breaking, kept a most thundering noyse about vs. This day, I went ashore and built a great Beacon with stones vpon the highest place of the Iland, and put a Crosse vpon it, and named this

H H

Harbour *The Harbour of God's Prouidence*.[1] In the Euening, the Harbour was fuller of the Ice then euer it had beene since we came hither, and the greater peeces grounded and stopt the rest, that none went out the ebbe, but the Ship lay as if shee had laine in a bed of Ice.

The three and twentieth day, in the morning, with the flood, the Ice droue vp amongst the broken grounds, and with the ebbe droue all out (it being then very calme) except one extraordinary great peece, which, comming aground not farre from vs, settled itselfe in such a manner that we much feard him But there came no more great Ice after him · otherwise we must haue expected as great danger as at any time heretofore I tooke the boate and went ashore vpon the Easterne side, to see if I could finde any place freer from danger then this vnfortunate place, where, amongst the Rockes, I discried a likely place From the top of the Hill where I was, I could see the Ship. It was now almost lowe water, at which instant the fore-mentioned piece of Ice brake, with a terrible noyse, into foure pieces, which made me doubtfull it had not spoyled the Ship, it being full halfe mast high. I made what haste I could to the boate, and so to the Ship, to be satisfied, where I found all well ; God be thanked ; for that the Ice had broken from the Ship-ward I instantly sent away the boate to sound the way to a Coue that I had found, which was a very dangerous passage for the boate. At her returne, we vn-moord the Ship, and, with what speede possible, warpt away from amongst this terrible Ice. We were not a mile from them, but they brake all to pieces, and would surely haue made vs beare them company, but

---

[1] This was the first point named by James, but the name has not been retained, for the cove he was in is nameless on the latest charts. This is the first time we read of anyone having landed on Resolution Island Foxe, who passed at this time, saw the smoke of Capt. James's fires while he was in this harbour there (see p. 286).

that God was more mercifull vnto vs. We got about the Rocks, and so into this little Coue which I had so newly discouered. Here we made fast to the Rockes, and thought ourselues in indifferent safety; which, being done, I went ashoare againe, to wander vp and downe, to see what I could discouer. I found it all broken Rockie grounds, and not so much as a tree, herbe, or grasse vpon it. Some Ponds of water there were in it, which were not yet thawed, and therefore not ready for the fowle. We found not in the snow any footing of Deere or Beares, but Foxes we saw one or two.

We found where the Saluages had beene; but it was long since They had made fiue hearths; and we found a few fire-brands about them, and some heads of Foxes, and bones of Foxes, with some Whale-bones. I could not conceiue to what purpose they should come thither; for we could finde none, or very little, wood on the shoares side, and no fish at all, though we did dayly indeauour to take some. But it may be the season was not yet come. I named this Coue by the Master's name of my Ship, *Price's Coue*.[1] The Latitude of it is 61 24.; the Variation[2] . The firebrands and chips which I spake of had beene cut with some hatchet or other good instrument of iron.[3] From the top of the hills, we could see the Ilands that are on the South shore, and commonly called *Sir Thomas Button's Iles*; they did beare South and by East halfe a point Easterly, some 14 or 15 leagues distant; vpon the change

---

[1] This name has not been retained.

[2] Here, and in several other places hereafter, the figures stating the latitude or the variation of the compass have been left blank by some oversight

[3] There was nothing remarkable in this, as several of the earlier explorers who sailed through the Straits tell us that they traded with the natives, and there can be little doubt that the hatchets used were so obtained; but, when James afterwards met with the same thing in the bottom of James's Bay, the occurrence was worthy of note.

day, it flowes here seuen a clocke and a halfe; and the tyde highest at most three fad. The flood comes from the Eastwards, and thither it returnes I haue beene obseruant from the top of the hills, whence I might descry the great pieces of Ice, 2 or 3 leagues from the shoare, driue to and againe with the flood and ebbe indifferently. Hence I collected that assuredly there is no currant sets in here, but that it is a meere tyde[1]   Neere the shoare, the eddies whirle into twenty manners when the ebbe is made, which is because it comes out of the broken ground amongst the Ice that is aground neere the shoare; besides which reason, there be diuers Rockes lying vnder water, on which you shall haue now 30, then 12, and anon but 8, and then 20 fad ; and these vncertainties occasion such distractions. I would therefore aduise none to come too neere those dangerous shoares, for feare hee lose his ship, and so, by consequence, all.   The last night, we tooke better rest then we had done in tenne nights before.

And this morning, being the 24, there sprung vp a faire gale of wind at East ; and, after prayer, we vnfastened our Ship and came to saile, steering betwixt great pieces of Ice that were a-ground in 40 fad., and twice as high as our top-mast head.

Wee went forth of this Coue vpon the flood, and had none of those whirlings of the waters as we had at our going into it   We indeauored to gaine the North shoare, kept our selues within a league of the shoare of the *Iland of Resolution*, where we had some cleere water to saile thorow   In the Offing, it was all thicke throngd together as might be possible.   By 12 a clocke, we were fast inclosed ; and, notwithstanding it blew very hard at East,

---

[1] Foxe's wisdom in not seeking a harbour in this neighbourhood (see p 284) is shown by the difficulties James met with as a result of approaching the shore. However, his doing so enabled James to make this interesting observation.

yet we could make no way through it; but the hard corners of the Ice did grate vs with that violence as I verily thought it would haue grated the plankes from the Ship's sides.

Thus we continued in torment till the 26 day, driuing to and againe in the Ice, not being able to see an acre of sea from top-mast head This 26 was calme Sun-shine weather; and we tooke the Latitude and Variation. The Latitude is[1] ; the Variation[1] ; we sounded and had ground at 140 fad., small white sand. I caused the men to lay out some fishing lines, but to no purpose, for I could not perceiue that baite had beene so much as touched. The nights are very cold, so that our rigging freezes, and the fresh ponds of water stand vpon the Ice, aboue halfe an inche thicke

The 27, there sprung vp a little gale at South-East, and the Ice did something open. Hereupon, we let fall our foresayle and forced the Ship thorow the throng of Ice In the Euening, the winde came contrary at W.N W. and blew hard, which caused vs to fasten to a great piece, to which we remained moord till the 29.

I am resolued that here is no currant, and that by many experiments which I haue made Namely, by taking markes on the land, and [by] noting our drift to and againe with the ebbe and flood, for many days together, as well in calme weather as otherwayes. By all these experiments, I found exactly that the tide was no stronger there then that betwixt *England* and *France*

29. This morning there sprung vp a fine gale at E., and the Ice did open something, so that we did force the Ship thorow it with her fore-saile. By 12 a clocke, we were gotten into some open water, with a fine gale of wind at East, and so cleere weather that we could see the *Iland of*

---

[1] See note 2 on p. 471.

Resolution. The North end did beare of vs E.N E., some 12 leagues off

From this 29 till the 5 of *July*, wee sayled continually thorow the Ice, with variable windes and fogges, and sometimes calme. The 5, at noone, we had a good *observation*, and were in *Latitude* 63 15, and then wee saw *Salisbury Iland*, bearing W. by N., some 7 leagues off, with much Ice betwixt it and vs, to weather which we were driuen to stand to the Northward. Soone after, we saw *Prince Charles his Cape*[1] and *Mill Iland*, and, to the North-north-west (and, indeed, round about vs), the Sea most infinitely pestered with Ice This did grieue me very much, for, whereas I had determined to prosecute the discouery to the North-westward, I saw it was not possible this yeere[2] Wee were, moreouer, driuen back againe with contrary windes, still closed and pestered with ice, and with all the perils and dangers incident to such aduentures, so that we thought, a thousand times, that the Ship had bin beaten to pieces

By the fifteenth day of *July*, we were got betwixt *Digges Iland* and *Nottingham's Iland*,[3] not being able to get more Northward. There, for an houre or two, we had some open water.

---

[1] This was not the Cape Charles on the southern side of Hudson's Strait, which was presumably so named by Hudson in 1610, but it was the Cape which, according to Foxe (p 395), was named Prince Charles's Foreland by Bylot, though I cannot find any other record of his having so named the Cape. It does not appear under this name on modern charts, but was undoubtedly one of the Capes near to (or, perhaps, identical with) that still known by Foxe's name of King Charles's Foreland Foxe reached the spot where James seems now to have been on the 11th, or six days later, and was also much pestered by the ice.

[2] Foxe had exactly the same intentions, but was prevented by the ice from carrying them out (see Introduction, p. xcvi, and p. 364)

[3] Foxe also seems to have been very near the same place on the same date, but the two captains saw nothing of each other there.

But, before I proceed further, it were not amisse in some manner to describe the *Straight*, which begins at the *Iland of Resolution*, and ends here at *Digges Iland*. If you goe downe into the *Bay*, the *Straight* is about 120 leagues long, and trends W.N.W. and E.S E generally In the entrance, it is about 15 leagues broad ; and then on the Southward side is a great *Bay*.[1] About the middest, it is likewise about 15 leagues broad, and then the Land opens something wider; so that, betwixt *Digges Iland* and *Cape Charles*,[2] it is about 20 leagues broad ; betwixt which two stands *Salisbury Iland* and *Nottingham Iland*. If it be cleere weather, you may see both the South and the North shoares ; ordinarily, the depth in the middle of the Straight is 120 faddomes, white sand. A certaine tyde runnes in it, and no current.[3] The North shoare is the straightest, and the cleerest from Ice too Alongst the North shoare, you haue many low small Ilands, which cannot be seene farre off from the land, and, in many places, the land makes as if it had small sounds into it. The Maine land on both sides is indifferent high land. And so much for discourse may suffice ; referring you to the *Plot*[4] for the particulars.

16. Being now resolued of the impossibilitie to doe any thing to the North-westward, for the reasons aforesaid : I gaue order to the Master of my Ship to Steere away W S W , to haue a sight of *Mansfeild's Iland*[5] ; which, the next day, by three a clocke in the after-noone, we had,

---

[1] Ungava Bay.

[2] Here, again, of course, he refers to the Prince Charles' Cape of Bylot, mentioned on the preceding page.

[3] See pp. 472 and 473.

[4] He means his map (see p. 458).

[5] This island, wrongly called *Mansfield* Island, was named by Button in 1612 after his eminent kinsman and neighbour, Admiral Sir Robert *Mansell*, Kt. (see p. 188).

hauing had so much dangerous foule weather amongst the Ice, that we strooke more fearfull blowes against it then we had euer yet done This was the first day that wee went to halfe allowance of bread Flesh dayes, and I ordered things as sparingly as I could. Two of our men complaine likewise of sicknesse, but soone afterward recouered. In the euening, wee came to an Anker, and I sent the Boate ashoare to try the tydes. They brought mee word that, whilest the Boat was ashoare, it flowed about some three foote; and, as wee found by the Ship and by the Ice, the water at that time came from the W S.W., and that the highest tydes (so farre as they could perceiue) it had not highed aboue two fadome They found that the Saluages had been vpon it, by certaine fires which they found, and heapes of stones, tracks of other beasts, but Foxes they could not finde. The winde was so contrary, and the weather so foggie, that wee were faine to spend some powder to recouer our Boate againe.

Next morning, being the 17, the winde came something fauourable, and wee wayed. The shoare being something cleere of Ice (though very thicke all to the Offing), wee stood alongst it S. and S. by W., some 10 leagues In the after-noone, the winde came contrary, and we came againe to an Anker within a mile of the shoare, for to Sea-boord was all thicke Ice, and vnpassable. I went ashoare my selfe to be resolued of the tyde, and found, whilest I was a shoare, that it did flow two foote, and at that time the flood came from the S W. by W. I doubted it was an halfe tyde, which afterwards I found to be true. I found where the Saluages had beene vpon the Iland, but could see little or no drift wood on the shoare, no beasts on the Iland, nor fishes in the Sea. It flowes on the change day about eleuen a clocke We saw some fowle on it, of which we killed one, and returned aboord.

This Iland is very low land, little higher then a dry sand-banke. It hath Ponds vpon it of fresh water, but no grasse, and is vtterly barren of all goodnesse.

The 18, in the morning, the winde came something fauourable; and we weyed and came to Sayle, for the Ice was all comne about vs We endeauoured to proceed to the Westward, intending to fall with the Westerne land, about the *Latitude* 63. 00.[1] By twelue a clocke (hauing beene much pestered), we were comne to a firme range of Ice, but it pleased God that the winde larged, and wee stowed[2] away S.S.W. At noone, in *Lat* 62 00, by 4 in the euening (hauing scaped dangerous blowes), wee were come (as wee thought) into an open Sea, and ioyfully steered away West and W. by N., although that Ioy was soone quayled. By ten at night, we heard the rut of the Ice, and it grew a thicke fogge, and very darke with it. Neuerthelesse, we proceeded, and the neerer we came to it, the more hideous noyse it made.

By three in the morning, the 19, we were come to it; and, as it did cleere a little, we could see the Ice, which were as thicke rands[3] of Ice as any we had yet seene. These being vnpassable, and, moreouer, the winde at N W., we stowed[2] alongst it, hoping to weather it to the Southward; but, at last, we became so blinded with fogge, and so incompassed with Ice, that we could goe no further.

---

[1] Foxe, we know (see pp 321 and 318), had exactly similar intentions, but he succeeded in carrying them out with ease, and even in attaining a more northerly latitude, whereas James was only able to reach the western shore of the Bay, two degrees further south (Lat 61°)

[2] Undoubtedly a misprint for *stood* (see the printer's apology on p. 452).

[3] James afterwards makes frequent use of this word. There can be no doubt that it comes from the A -S *rand*, meaning *edge* or *border*. Halliwell defines *rand* as meaning *border* or *edge* in old English.

The 20, in the morning (notwithstanding the fogge), we endeauoured to get to the Westward, our ship beating and knocking all this while most fearefully.

In this wilfulnesse, we continued till the 21, when, being fast amongst the Ice, I obserued we were in *Lat* 60 33, and then, looking what damage our Ship might haue receiued, we could perceiue that, below the plate of Iron which was before her Cut-water, shee was all bruised and broken, the two knees she had before to strengthen her, spoyled and torne; and many other defects, which we could not by any meanes come to mend. Notwithstanding all this, and the extraordinary thicke fogge (that we could not see a Pistoll-shot about vs), we proceeded with the hazzard of all.

Till the 27, which was the first time we had cleere weather to looke about vs. The winde withall came vp at South, and the Ice did open something, so that we made some way thorow it to the Westward. In the euening, we were fast againe and could goe no further, the winde veering from the South to the East, and blowing a fresh gale. This occasioned our griefes the more, that with a good winde wee could not goe forward. Putting, therefore, a Hawser vpon a piece of great Ice, to keepe the Ship close to it, we patiently expected for better fortune. Since we came from *Mansfield's Iland*, our depth was commonly 110 and 100 fad., oozye ground. Now the water begins to showlde, for this present 27, driuing fast to and againe in the Ice, we haue but 80 fad., ground as before.

The 28 and 29, we were so fast inclosed in the Ice that, notwithstanding we put abroad all the sayle that was at yards, and that it blew a very hard gale of winde, the Ship stirred no more then if shee had beene in a dry Docke. Hereupon, we went all boldly out vpon the Ice to sport and recreate ourselues, letting her stand still vnder all her Sayles. It was flat, extraordinary large Ice, the worst to deal withall that we had yet found. I measured some pieces, which I found to be 1000 of my paces long. This was the first day that our men began to murmure, thinking it impossible to get either forwards or backe-wardes. Some were of the opinion that it was all such Ice betwixt vs and the shoare. Others that the Bay was all couered ouer, and that it was a doubt whether we could get any way, or to any land to winter in. The nights were long, and euery night it did so freeze that we could not sayle amongst the Ice by night, nor in the thicke foggie weather. I comforted and incouraged them the best I coulde, and, to put away these cogitations, wee drank a health to his Maiestie on the Ice—not one man in the Ship, and shee still vnder all her sayles. I most ingeniously confesse that all their murmuring was not without reason, wherefore, doubting that we should be frozen vp in the Sea, I ordered that fire should be made but once a day, and that but with a certaine number of shides[1] that the Steward should deliuer to the Cooke by tale, the better to prolong our fewell, whatsoeuer should happen

The 30, we made some way thorow the Ice, we heauing the Ship with our shoulders, and, with Mawles and Crowes of Iron, breaking the corners of the Ice to make way. As we got forwards, the water shoaled apace, so that I beleeue it to be some Iland   At noone, we *obseru'd* thorow the fogge, with the Quadrant, vpon a piece of Ice, and were in *Lat* 58. 54; our depth 30 fad. We put out hookes to try to catch some fish, but to no purpose, for there is not any in this Bay.

The 31, we laboured as aforesaid, and got something forward. At noone, we were in *Lat.* 58. 40; our depth

---

[1] Halliwell gives shide, *a billet of wood.* James, no doubt, means he ordered that not more than a certain number of logs were to be used daily.

23 fad. It was very thicke hazye weather, or else I thinke we should haue seene the land.

The first of *August*, the winde came vp at West, which droue vs to the Eastward, where our depth increased to 35 fad. At noone (by obseruation with the Quadrant on the Ice), we were in *Lat* 58 45 At sixe a clocke this euening, we might perceiue the Ice to heaue and set a little, which was occasioned by a swelling Sea, that came out of the South-West. This did comfort vs very much, hoping shortly we should get out of the Ice.

The second, it did blow hard at South-West, and yet we could not feele the forementioned swelling Sea, which did againe quench the hopes we had formerly conceiued.

The third, wee did see a little open water to the North-westward, and did feele a swelling Sea from the West, which doth assure vs that there is an open Sea to the Westward.

The fifth, we saw the Sea cleere; but could by no means worke ourselues to it with our sayles, wherefore, about sixe in the euening, wee let fall an Anker in 50 fad water, and stood all with poles and oares to fend off the Ice and let it passe to Leewards. We continued this labour all night.

6. In the morning, the winde came vp at North-West, and we wayed with much ioy, as hoping now to get into an open Sea to the Southward This, by noone, we had done, and were in *Lat*. 58. 28, very free of Ice. The winde did large vpon vs, so that we stood away North-West, to get vp as high to the Northward as we could, and so to come coasting to the Southward We went to prayer, and to giue God thanks for our deliuery out of the Ice [1]

The ninth (being in *Lat*. 59. 40), we came againe to the Ice, which lye very thicke to the North. Since we came out

---

[1] There is apparently no record for the 7th and 8th.

of the Ice, our depth increased to 110, and now decreaseth againe; so that I thinke we approached towards the shoare.

The tenth prooued very thicke foggie weather; the winde [being] contrary, and the water showlding apace, we came to an Anker in 22 fad

The eleuenth, in the morning, we wayed and made in for the shoare, and, about noone, saw the land; our depth being 16 fad. in *Lat.* 59. 40. The land to the North of vs did trend North by East, and so made a point to the Southward, and trended away West by South, which we followed, making it for that place which was formerly called *Hubbert's Hope*.[1] And so it prooued indeed, but it is now hopelesse.

Two or three words now concerning the Bay that we haue past ouer It is, from *Digges Iland* to this Westerland (in latitude aforesaid), about 160 leagues; the course, West South West; the variation[2] .

The tydes doe set, in the middle of the Bay, East and West, as we haue often tryed by our ledde aground, but, neerer the shoares, as they are forced by the land. I am of the opinion that, in the *Ocean*, or in large *Bayes*, the tydes doe naturally set East and West, and that this doth giue little hope of a passage. The greatest depth we had in the Bay was 110 fad, and so shoalding as you approach to land, we coasted round about this forementioned little Bay,[3] which is some 18 leagues deepe, in 8 and 6 fad., and, in the bottome of it, we were in two faddome and a halfe water, and saw the firme land almost round about vs. Then we proceeded to the Southward, sixe and seuen faddome

---

[1] We are to a large extent in the dark as to exactly what "Hubbert's Hope" was (see p. 331) On his map, James calls it "Briggs his Bay", which supports the belief that it was Briggs who had hoped the passage would be found here (see Introduction, p. cvi, note 1).

[2] See note 2, p. 471.

[3] Apparently he means Hubbart's Hope: that is, Churchill Bay.

water, within sight of the breach of the shoare, keeping the lead continually going, and in the night we would come to an Anker. This night, being little winde, we came to an Anker with our Kedger; but, in waying of him, we lost him, hauing no more aboord vs.

The 12, we were in *Lat.* 58. 46, some two leagues from the shoare. The variation is about 17 deg.

The 13, in the afternoone (it being something hazye), we saw some breaches ahead vs; our depth was 9 and 10 fad, and, luffing to cleere our selues of them, we suddenly strooke vpon the Rocks,[1] the Ship then being vnder our two Topsayles, Foresayle and Spreetsayle, with a fresh gale of winde. In this fearefull accident, wee strooke all our sayles amaine, and it did please God to send two or three good swelling Seas, which did heaue vs ouer the Rocks into 3 fad., and presently into three faddome and a halfe, where we chopt to an Anker,[2] and sayed[3] the pumps; but we founde shee made no water, although shee had three such terrible blows that we thought her Mast would haue shiuered to pieces, and that she had bin assuredly bulged. Wee hoyst the Boate ouer-boord and double man'd her, to goe seeke and sound a way out of this perilous place. Shee was no sooner gone but there rose a fogge, so that we were faine to spend some powder that shee might heare whereabouts we were. The winde duld something: otherwise it had beene doubtfull whither shee could euer haue recoured to vs againe. After shee had beene absent two houres, she brought vs word that it was all Rocks and breaches round about vs; and that withall shee had found a way where there was not lesse then two fad. and a halfe, and that afterwards the water did

---

[1] This was, no doubt, Nelson Shoal, as remarked by Foxe (see p. 337).

[2] This expression, which is still in use, means that they came suddenly to an anchor.   [3] See p. 462.

deepen. We did presently way and follow the Boate, and past ouer two ledges of Rocks, on which there was scarce 14 foot water. Then it did deepen to 3, 4, and so to 14 fad.; then it shouldest againe to 9. It being now night, we came to an Anker, where we ride indifferent well all the night. In the morning, the winde came contrary, so that wee could not goe that way we intended to cleere our selues; and therefore we went to worke to fit our holds, to splise our Cables, and made ready two shot, and so placed them in the Hold, that they might vpon all occasions runne cleere, the ends of them being fastened to the maine Mast. We likewise lookt to our Ankers, and fitted our spare ones. We got out our long Boate from betwixt the decks, which was very much broken and bruised. The Carpenter went to worke to fit her (for I intended to tow the Shallop at Sterne), and so to haue the Boats ready at an instant, either to lay out Ankers, or to be seruiceable to what God should be pleased to try our faith and patience withall; for in him was our only trust and our hope vpon his fauour in our honest endeauours. At noone, in *Lat.* 57.45, wee could see the land from the N.W. to the S.E. by E., with Rocks and breaches; and the Rocks that we came ouer, dry aboue water, whereby I knew it flowes here two faddomes at least. At noone, I sent the Boate off to sownd to the Eastward, because the water shoulded when we came to an Anker. Shee brought vs word the shouldest water she had beene in was 7 fad. We intending thereupon to way, the winde came Easterly, so that we could not budge, but lay here the 14 all night, with a stiffe gale of winde.

The 15, in the euening, our Cable galded off,[1] by reason of which perilous and sudden accident, in which wee had

---

[1] Probably he means that it was so badly cut or injured by friction (*galled*) that it broke.

not time to put a Buoy to it, we lost our Anker, and were driuen into 4 fad. water before we could set our sayles This when we had done we stowed[1] South-South-East, the winde being at East, but the water shoulded to 3 fad Then wee stowed[1] North north-east, and it did deepen by degrees to ten fadd , and, because it grew daike, we came to an Anker, and rid a good stresse all night

In the morning, the 16, the winde came vp at North, a fresh gale, and we wayed and came to sayle By nine a clocke, it grew to be a very storme, and we turned to and againe in 10 fad water. In the euening, the winde duld, and wee stood South-west to haue a sight of *Port Nelson*, which course we stood all night, by the Starres, being in *Lat* 57 25 ; the variation about 17 degrees.

The 17, in the morning, we stood South, and our depth decreased by degrees to 8 faddomes. At noone, we had good obseruation, being in *Latitude* 57. 15 , and wee make account that we are some 6 or 7 leagues of the Southerne side of *Port Nelson*. Here the colour of the water changed, and was of a puddlelish and sandy red colour.[2] We stood into 6 fad , and could not see the land from Top-mast-head ; so, night comming on, and it beginning to blow hard at East by South, we stood off againe into 10 and 12 fad-domes, where the water was againe of the colour of the Sea.

The 18, as the winde and weather fauoured vs, and the storme was broken vp, we stood in againe South, and came againe into thicke puddleish water, into 8, 7, and 6 fad , and then off againe, for that it grew thicke foggie

---

[1] See p. 477.

[2] Foxe was at this time in Port Nelson, building his pinnace and rummaging his ship, but he left a couple of days later. From his latitude, and the fact that he was sailing in the muddy water of the estuary, James was probably at this time a little to the west of Cape Tatnam.

weather, keeping our lead continually going night and day

The 19, being fine cleere Sun-shine weather, we stood in againe, into the thicke puddelish water, into 8 fad, where we came to an Anker to try the tydes, for that from Top-mast-head we could not now see the land. We were at noone (by good obseruation) in *Latitude* 57. 20,[1] and the tyde did set N.W. by W. and S.E. by E. It did runne two knots and a halfe in two glasses. I resolued that this was nothing but shoalds to the land. In the after-noone, it began to snuffle and blow, so that we had much adoe to get vp our Anker. This being done, we stood East-South-East, but the water shoalded apace. Then we stood East, and it deepened a little. In the euening, the winde came vp at West, and then we stood East South-east into 10 and 8, and afterwards South-East, as our depth did guide vs by our lead, and the colour of the water, into 7 and 6 faddomes.

The 20, at 6 in the morning, we saw the land, it being a very low flat land. Wee stood into 5 faddomes to make it the better, and so stood alongst it. At noone wee were in lat 57 00. We named it *The new Principality of South Wales*[2], and drank a health in the best liquor we had to

---

[1] James was now, simultaneously with Foxe, exploring the then-totally-unknown southern shore of the Bay, between Button's easternmost point at Port Nelson and Hudson's presumed westernmost at Cape Henrietta Maria (as he says in his letter left at Charlton Island). The honour of having accomplished this piece of geographical discovery belongs equally to the two captains.

[2] Button, in 1612-13, had already named the whole of the west coast of his Bay (now called Hudson's Bay) New Wales (see p. 170), so that James' claim to have bestowed the name upon it was rather absurd. Foxe, a day or two earlier (see p. 357), had named the same coast New Yorkshire, after his native county, but the name was never used. The region in question was for long after generally known by a combination of the names bestowed upon it by both Button and James, that part to the north of Port Nelson being

Prince *Charles* his Highnesse, whom God preserue. We stood alongst it, and came to a point where it trends to the Southward, neere to which point there are two small Ilands.[1] In the euening, it was calme, and we came to an Anker. The tyde set as aforesaid There we rid all that night and the next day, by reason the winde was contrary There went a chopping short Sea, and the Ship did labour at it exceedingly, leaping in Spreet-sayle yard, Forecastell, and all; for, as yet, we had not trimmed her well to ride About nine at night, it was very darke, and it did blow hard Wee did perceiue by the lead the Ship did driue, wherefore bringing the Cable to Capstang to heaue in our Cable (for we did thinke we had lost our Anker), the Anker hitcht againe, and, vpon the chopping of a Sea, threw the men from the Capstang A small rope, in the darke, had gotten foule about the Cable, and about the Master's legge too; but, with helpe of God, hee did cleere himselfe, though not without sore bruising The two Mates were hurt the one in the head, the other in the arme One of our lustiest men was strooken on the brest with a bar, that he lay sprawling for life Another had his head betwixt the Cable, and hardly escaped. The rest were flung where they were sore bruised But our Gunner (an honest and a diligent man) had his legge taken betwixt the Cable and the Capstang, which wrung off his foote, and tare all the flesh off his legge, and crushed the bone to pieces, and sorely withall bruised all his whole body; in which miserable manner hee remained crying till we had recouered ourselues, our memory, and strengths to cleere him Whilest we were putting him and the rest downe to the Chirurgion, the Ship droue into shoalde water,

---

known as New North Wales, and that to the south of Port Nelson as New South Wales, but both names alike have now been discarded.

[1] Perhaps the East and West Pens.

which put vs all in feare, we being so sorely weakened by this blow, which had hurt eight of our men. It pleased God that the Anker held againe, and shee rid it out all night By midnight, the Chirurgion had taken off the Gunners legge at the gartering place, and drest the others that were hurt and bruised; after which we comforted each other as well as we could.

The 22, wee weyed and stood a little off into deeper water, expecting a better winde, which, in the afternoone, fauoured vs. Wee stood in againe for the shoare, and alongst it wee proceeded It is very shoald about foure leagues off, and full of breaches

The 23, at noone, we were in latitude 56. 28. In the euening, the winde came contrary, and we were faine to turne to and againe. All this moneth, the winde hath beene very variable, and continued not long vpon one point; yet it happened so that we can get but little forward

The 26, there sprung vp a fine gale at West, but very thicke weather, neuerthelesse, wee stood into 7 and 6 fad., the water very thicke and puddlelish At noone, it cleered and we could see that we were imbayed in a little Bay, the land being almost round about vs.[1]

We stood out of it, and so alongst it, in sight, till the 27, in the morning, when we came to higher land then any we had yet seene since we came from *Nottingham Iland* We stood into it, and came to an Anker in 5 faddome. I sent off the Boate, well man'd and arm'd, with order in writing what they were to doe, and a charge to returne againe before Sunne-set. The euening came, and

---

[1] Without doubt, they were now in the estuary of the Severn river, which James must have named, as it appears as "New Severne" on his map, though he does not say he did so in his narrative. James had, of course, sailed out of the Severn. The "thick and puddleish" water was, of course, river-water.

no newes of our Boate We shot, and made false fires,[1] but had no answer, which did much perplex vs, doubting that there had some disaster befalne her through carelessnesse, and in her we should lose all Wee aboord at present were not able to wey our Anker nor sayle the Ship. At last, we saw a fire vpon the shoare, which made vs the more doubtfull, because they did not answer our shot nor false fires with the like. Wee thought withall that it had beene the Saluages, who did now triumph in their conquest. At length they came, all safe and well, and excused themselues in that, vpon their comming ashoare, it did ebbe so suddenly that a banke of sand was so presently dry without them as they could not come away till that was couered againe, and with that they pacified mee. They reported that there was great store of drift-wood on the shoare, and a good quantitie growing on the land, that they saw the tracks of Deere and Beares, good store of Fowle (of which they had killed some), but no signe of people; that they past ouer two little riuers, and came to a third, which they could not passe, that it did flow very neere three faddomes sometimes, as appeared by the shoare; that it was low water at foure a clocke, that the flood came from the North-west, and that it flowed halfe tyde, which both they and we had perceiued by the Ship At low water, we had but three faddome where we did ride. The winde began to blow hard at East, whereupon we weyed and stood to the Northward till midnight Then in againe, and, in the morning, wee saw the land, and then it began to blow hard; and, as we stood off, it increased to a very storme, so that at length wee could not maintaine a payre of courses, but tryed vnder our Maine

---

[1] False-fires or blue-lights burn several minutes, and are used at sea as night-signals.

THE OUTWARD VOYAGE. 489

course, all day and all night, sometime turning her head to the Landward, sometime to the Offing.

The 29, in the morning, we made account we had drouen backe againe some 16 or 18 leagues; and, in the morning (as it cleered), wee saw a Ship to Leeward of vs, some three or foure leagues. So wee made sayle and bore vp with her. Shee was then at an Anker in 13 fadd. It was his Maiesties Ship [the *Charles*], and Captaine *Foxe* commanded in her.

I saluted him according to the manner of the Sea, and receiued the like of him. So I stood in to see the land, and thought to tacke about and keepe weather of him, and to send my Boat aboord of him; but the winde shifted, so that for that time I could not. In the euening, I came to weather of him, and sent my Boat aboord of him, who presently weighed and stood off with mee till midnight, and then we stood in againe.

In the morning, Captaine *Foxe* and his friends came aboord of mee, where I entertained them in the best manner I could, and with such fresh meat as I had gotten from the shoare. I told him how I had named the land *The South Principality of Wales*. I shewed him how farre I had beene to the Eastward,[1] where I had landed, and, in briefe, I made knowne to him all the dangers of this Coast, as farre as I had beene. He told mee how himselfe had beene in *Port Nelson*, and had made but a Cursory discouery hitherto, and that he had not beene aland, nor had not many times seene the land. In the euening, after I had giuen his men some necessaries, with Tobacco and other things which they wanted, hee departed aboord his Ship, and, the next morning, stood away South-South-west, since which time I neuer saw him. The winde some-

---

[1] This must be a misprint for *Westward*.

thing fauouring mee, I stood in for the shoare, and so proceeded alongst it, in sight.[1]

This moneth of *August* ended with Snow and Haile, the weather being as cold as at any time I haue felt in *England*.

September 1. We coasted alongst the shoare in 10 faddomes, and, when it cleered, in sight of land. At length the water shoalded to 6 and 5 fadd , and, as it cleered, we saw it all breaches to Leeward So we hull'd off[2] North-North-east, but still raised land. By night, we had much adoe to get safely out of this dangerous Bay[3] At midnight, the winde came vp at South, and so we tooke in our sayles, and let the Ship driue to the Northward into deeper water. This day was the first time the Chirurgion told mee that there were diuers of the men tainted with sicknesse. At noone, we were in latitude 55 12.

The second, we stood in againe for the shoare, but, as we came into shoald water, it began to blow, the weather being winterly and foule, threatning a storme, wherein we were not deceiued, for that, in standing off, wee had a violent one

By midnight, it broke vp , and the third, in the morning, wee stood in againe, and by a 11 wee saw it. Here wee found the land to trend South South-east and South, so that we knew we were at a *Cape Land*, and named it *Cape Henrietta Maria*,[4] by her Maiesties name, who had before named our Ship. At noone, we were in latitude 55 05, and that is the height of the Cape.

From *Port Nelson* to this Cape, the land trends (generally)

---

[1] Foxe's contemptuous account of his meeting with James appears on p. 355. [2] Query, *hauled off*.

[3] It is not at all clear what bay he was in

[4] Foxe, on the very same day, named this cape Wolstenholme's Ultimum Vale (see p. 367), but this cumbrous name has not been retained

East South-east, but makes with points and Bayes, which in the particulars doth alter it a point two or three. The distance is about one hundred and thirtie leagues. The variation at this Cape, taken by Amplitude, is about sixteene degrees A most shoald and perilous coast, in which there is not one Harbour to be found.

The third day, in the afternoone, we had a tearing storme at North, which continued till midnight in extreme violence.

The fourth, in the morning (the storme being broke vp), we stood in againe, South-West. The weather was very thicke, and we sounded continually; but by noone it cleered, and wee saw the land Here it did trend South by East, and the tydes did set alongst it with a quicke motion In the euening, there came a great rowling Sea out of the North North-east, and by eight a clocke it blew very hard at South-east; and, by reason of the incounter of the winde and this great Sea, the Sea was all in a breach; and, to make vp a perfect tempest, it did so lighten, snow, raine, and blow all the night long, that I was neuer in the like. We shipt many Seas, but one most dangerous, which rackt vs fore and aft, that I verily thought it had sunke the Ship, it strooke her with such a violence. The Ship did labour most terribly in this distraction of winde and waues, and we had much adoe to keepe all things fast in the hold and betwixt decks.

The fifth, in the morning, the winde shifted South-West, but changed not his condition, but continued in his old anger and fury In the afternoone, it shifted againe to the North-west, and there showed his vttermost malice, and in that tearing violence that nor I, nor any that were then with mee, euer saw the Sea in such a breach. Our Ship was so tormented, and did so labour, with taking it in on both sides and at both ends, that we were in a most miserable distresse, in this so vnknowne a place. At eight a clocke in the euening, the storme brake vp, and we had some quietnesse in the night following, not one hauing slept one winke in 30 houres before. If this storme had continued Easterly, as it was at first, without God's goodnesse, we had all perished.[1]

The sixth, the winde was at South-west, so that wee could do no good to the Westward. We spent the time therefore in trimming of our Ship; we brought all our coales (which for the most part was great Coale) aft, as we also did some other things, and all to lighten her afore.[2] Others did picke our bread, whereof there was much wet; for, doe what we could, we shipt abundance of water betwixt decks, which ranne into the hold, and into our bread-roome; for the Sea, indeed, so continually ouer-rackt vs that we were like *Ionas* in the Whales belly. We ouer-looked our Tacks and Shoots, with other Riggings of stresse, because that henceforward we were to looke for no other but Winter weather. This euening, our Boat-swayne (a painefull man, and one that had laboured extremely these two or three dayes) was very sicke, swouning away three or foure times; insomuch that wee thought verily he would presently haue dyed.

The seuenth, in the morning, the winde came vp at South-east, and we stood away South-west, vnder all the sayle we could make.[3] In this course, we saw an Iland and

---

[1] Foxe, also (p. 368), mentions this violent storm.

[2] Foxe, also (p. 371), curiously enough, on the very same day, mentions having been troubled by the coals he had on board.

[3] James was now commencing what may almost be called a piece of original discovery, for the honour of having explored the southern coastline of Hudson's Bay, between Port Nelson and Cape Henrietta Maria, belongs jointly to both Foxe and he. But he was now cruising in the Bay which has ever since borne his name, and which had certainly never before been entered, except by Hudson and his surviving mutineers, while the account they gave of their discoveries in it is so vague that we can only guess at the amount of it they explored.

came close aboord it, and had twentie fadd water, which was some comfort to vs, for hitherto we could not come within foure or fiue leagues of the shoare at that depth. This Iland stands in 54. 10.[1] The afternoone, we stood away South-west, and in the euening had the shoalding of the Westerne shoare, in 10, 8, and 7 fadd., but it was so thicke that we could not see the land. It is about 14 leagues betwixt this Iland and the Maine.

The eight was thicke, foggie, and calme, which so continued till the ninth, about sixe in the morning. The winde then comming vp at South South-west (though very foggy), we stood to the Eastward, keeping our lead going continually. In the euening, the water shoalded to 10 and 9 fadd, wherefore we stood off and on all night

The tenth we made it, finding it an Iland of about 8 or 9 leagues long. It stands in latitude 53. 5, and about 15 leagues from the Westerne shoare   The part of it that we coasted trends West North-west. I named it my Lord *Westons Iland*[2] We stood still away to the Eastward, it being

---

though there is reason to believe (see p 131) that they partially explored the whole of it   Captain James, notwithstanding the amount of time he spent in his bay, cannot be credited with having made a much more precise geographical survey of it than did Hudson or his mutineers, twenty years earlier   He did not even ascertain sufficient to controvert the erroneous idea that it was divided into *two bays* by a long narrow tongue of land, ending in what appears on his map as "Cape Monmouth", though he gives no clue as to who gave this name to this imaginary Cape, or as to whom it was named after   Sir Robert Carey, Chamberlain to the Household of the Prince of Wales, first Baron Carey of Leppington, co York (created February 1622), was created Earl of Monmouth in February 1626, and died in 1639, but it does not appear that he had any connection with James's voyage.

[1] This was undoubtedly Bear Island, which is about in the latitude mentioned by Captain James (54° 10'). It seems strange that James did not name it, either on his chart or in his narrative, as it is certain that no one had previously done so.

[2] This was, almost certainly, Agoomska Island of the Admiralty Charts. James named it after Richard Weston, first Baron Weston,

broken foggie weather. In the afternoone, we discryed land to the Eastward of vs, which made like three hils, or hummockes.[1] Towards them we sayle, keeping our lead still going, and very circumspect. At length, wee also saw land to the Southward of vs,[2] whereupon we loofe vp, and now make for that, by course, as we had set it in the thicke darke fogge. We came in amongst such low broken grounds, breaches, and rockes, that we knew not which way to turne vs; but, God be thanked, it was but little winde, and so we came to an Anker. Soone after, it cleered, at which time we could see nothing but sands, rocks, and breaches round about vs, that way onely excepted which we came in. I sent presently the Boate to sound amongst the shoalds and rocks, that, if wee should be put to extremitie, we might haue some knowledge which way to goe. This night prooued calme and faire weather, and we rid quietly.

The eleuenth, in the morning, I went in the Boate ashoare myselfe, and, whilst I was a land, I sent the Boate

---

who was afterwards created Earl of Portland, and after whom Foxe had named a cape on the eastern side of Foxe's Channel (see p. 388) He was Lord High Treasurer at the time, and James had had at least one interview with him whilst making preparations for his voyage (see Introduction) James's name for the Island has not been retained, although, on the latest Admiralty Chart, the name of Weston Islands is applied to a small group further to the S E Agoomska, as well as Danby Island, Cary Island, and most of the other islands mentioned by James hereafter, are fully described by Mr. A P Low, of the Canadian Geological Survey (*Report of Progress for 1887-88*, Sec. J), who gives the best account extant of James's Bay. Captain Coats's information, given in his *Geography of Hudson's Bay* (Hakluyt Society, 1852), though of much interest, is now largely superseded by the above It seems likely that the Admiralty Chart of James's Bay is by no means accurate in detail.

[1] This was probably the group of islands named Solomon's Temples on the Admiralty Chart.

[2] This must have been the group marked as Weston Islands on the Admiralty Chart. They are about in the latitude given by James.

about amongst the broken grounds to sound. I found this Iland vtterly barren of all goodnesse; yea, of that which I thought easily to haue found, which was Scuruy-grasse, Sorrell, or some herbe or other, to haue refreshed our sicke people. I could not perceiue that the tyde did flow here (ordinarily) aboue two foot. There was much drift-wood on the shore, and some of it droue vp very high on the North side of the Iland; whereby I iudged that the stormes were very great at North in the Winter. Thus I returned aboord, and sent many of our sicke men to another part of the Iland, to see if they themselues could fortunately finde any reliefe for their griefes. At noone, by good obseruation, we were in latitude 52. 45. In the euening, our men returned comfortlesse, and then we weyed and stood to the Westward, comming to an Anker vnder another Iland,[1] in 20 faddomes.

The twelfth, in the morning, it began to blow hard at South-east, which was partly of the shoare, and the Ship began to driue, it being soft oozie ground. We heaued in our Anker thereupon, and came to sayle vnder two courses. Whilest the most were busie in heauing out of Top-sayles, some that should haue had speciall care of the Ship ranne her ashore vpon the rocks out of meere carelesnesse in looking out and about, or heauing of the leade, after they had seene the land all night long, and mought[2] euen then haue seene it, if they had not beene blinded with selfe conceit, and beene enuiously opposite in opinions. The first blow stroke me out of a dead sleepe; and I, running out

---

[1] Probably this was one of the nameless group lying between Solomon's Temples and the East Main; or, perhaps, it was one of the Weston Island group, or one of the shoals marked in this neighbourhood. In his narrative, James does not mention having named this island; but, in the letter left at Charlton Island, he says he called it the Isle of God's Favour.

[2] An old form of *might*.

of my Cabbin, thought no other, at first, but I had beene wakened (when I saw our danger) to prouide myselfe for another World.

After I had contrould a little passion in myselfe, and had checkt some bad counsell that was giuen me to reuenge myselfe vpon those that had committed this error, I ordered what should be done to get off these Rockes and stones First, we halde all our sayle abacke-slayles[1], but that did no good, but make her beate the harder. Whereupon we strooke all our sayles amaine, and furdeld[2] them vp close, tearing downe our sterne to bring the Cable thorow the Cabbin to Capstang, and so laid out an Anker to heaue her asterne I made all the water in hold to be stau'd, and set some to the pumpes to pumpe it out, and did intend to doe the like with our Beere. Others I put to throw out all our Coles, which was soone and readily done We quoyld[3] out our Cables into our long boate, all this while the Ship beating so fearefully that we saw some of the sheathing swim by vs. Then stood we, as many as we could, to the Capstang, and heaued with such a good will that the Cable brake, and we lost our Anker Out, with all speede, therefore, we put another. Wee could not now perceiue whether she did leak or no, and that by reason we were imployed in pumping out the water which we had bulged in hold, though we much doubted that she had receiued her deaths wound. Wherefore we put into the Boate the Carpenters tooles, a barrell of bread, a barrell of powder, sixe muskets, with some match,[4] and a tinder-boxe, fish hookes and lines, pitch and okum, and, to be breefe, what-euer could be

---

[1] No doubt he put his sails aback.

[2] That is, *furled* To furl is a contracted form of the obsolete *to furdle*, or *fardle*, meaning to pack or roll up.

[3] A form of *coiled*

[4] Match was the piece of slow-burning rope by means of which match-lock guns were fired.

thought on in such an extremity   All this, we sent ashoare to prolong a miserable life for a few dayes   We were fiue houres thus beating, in which time she strooke 100 blows; insomuch that we thought euery stroke had bin the last that it was possible she could haue endured   The water we could not perceiue in all this time to flowe any thing at all   At length, it pleased God, she beat ouer all the Rockes; though yet wee knew not whether she were stanch   Whereupon, to pumping we goe on all hands, till we made the pumpes sucke, and then we saw how much water she did make in a glasse.   We found her to be very leakie, but wee went to prayer and gaue God thankes it was no worse, and so fitted all things againe, and got further off, and came to an Anker   In the Euening, it began to blow very hard at W S W ; which, if it had done whilest we were on the Rockes, we had lost our Ship without any redemption. With much adoe, we wayde our Anker, and let her driue to the Eastward amongst the broken grounds and Rockes, the boate going before sounding   At length, we came amongst breaches, and the boate made signes to vs that there was no going further.   Amongst the Rockes, therefore, we againe came to an Anker, where we did ride all night, and where our men, which were tyred out with extreme labour, were indifferent well refreshed   Here I first noted that, when the wind was at S , it flowed very little, or no, water at all , so that we could not bring our Ship aground to looke to her, for we did pumpe almost continually

The 13, at noone, we wayed, and stood to the Westward; but, in that course, it was all broken groundes, shoaldes, and sunken Rockes, so that we wondered with our selues how we came in amongst them in a thicke fogge. Then we shapte our course to the North-ward , and, after some consultation with my associates, I resolued to get about this land, and so to goe downe into the bottome of

Hudson's Baye,[1] and see if I could discouer a way into the Riuer of *Canada*[2]; and, if I failed of that, then to winter on the maine Land, where there is more comfort to be expected then among Rockes or Ilands. We stood alongst the shoare[3] in sight of many breaches. When it was night, we stood vnder our fore-sayle, the leade still going. At last, the water shoalded vpon vs to 10. fad., and it began to blow hard. We tackte about, and it did deepen to 12 and 14 fad., but, by and by, it shoalded againe to 8 fad. Then we tackte about againe; and suddenly it shoaled to 6 and 5 fad.,[4] so wee strooke our sayle amaine, and chopt to an anker, resoluing to ride it out for life and death. We ridde all night a great stresse, so that our bittes[5] did rise, and we thought they would haue been torne to pieces.

At breake of day, the 14, we were ioyfull men, and, when we could looke about, we discried an Iland some 2 leagues off, at W. by N[6]; and this was the shoald that lay

---

[1] He means into Hudson's *East* Bay (see p. 131), for he imagined himself to be in Hudson's so-called *West* Bay.

[2] Hudson was supposed to have wintered in the bottom of his so-called *East* Bay, and it was to this point that James was anxious to get. His chart shows that he believed it to be only a very short distance north from the River St Lawrence, "the River of Canada," as he here calls it, and as it was then commonly called. On a large chart published in Paris in 1715, it is marked as "La Grande Rivière de Canada, appellée par les Européens le St Laurens." Accordingly, as we learn from p. 500, James endeavoured to work to the northward, in order to round the imaginary "Cape Monmouth" of his chart (see p 493, *note*), and to get into the equally non-existent "East Bay" of Hudson.

[3] Probably this was the shore of some island.

[4] Probably he was now again among the islands known as Solomon's Temples, but his course is very difficult to follow.

[5] See p 390.

[6] So far as one can make out, this must have been the southern end of the southernmost of the two Twins. This is rendered the more probable by the subsequent mention of an opening between two

about it. Here did runne a distracted, but yet a very quicke, Tyde, of which we taking the opportunity, got vp our Anker and stood N W, to cleere our selues of this shoald In the afternoone, the wind came vp at N E, and we stood alongst the Easterne shoare in sight of a multitude of breaches. In the Euening, it began to blow a storme not sayle-worthy; and the sea went very high, and was all in a breach. Our shallop, which we did now towe at sterne, being moord with two hawsers, was sunken, and did spine by her moorings with her keele vp, 20 times in an houre This made our ship to hull very broad, so that the sea did continually ouer-rake vs; yet we indured it, and thought to recouer her. All night, the storme continued with violence, and with some raine in the morning; it then being very thicke weather. The water shoalded apace, with such an ouer-growne sea withall that a sayle was not to be endured; and, what was as ill, there was no trusting to an Anker Now, therefore, began we to prepare our selues how to make a good end of a miserable tormented life About noone, as it cleered vp, we saw two Ilands vnder our lee,[1] whereupon we bare vp to them; and, seeing an opening betwixt them, we indeauored to get into it before night, for that there was no hope of vs, if we continued out at sea that night Therefore, come life, come death, we must runne this hazzard. We found it to be a good sound, where we ridde all night safely, and recouered our strengths againe, which were much impared with continuall labour But, before we could get

---

islands, in which he sought shelter, but it seems clear that he was wrong in saying that he had formerly coasted the western side of the island, and had named it Lord Weston's Island. Apparently he was confusing the Twins with Agoomska, on which he did bestow the above name. The same misconception is shown in the letter left at Charlton Island (see *post*)

[1] As explained above, these were apparently the two Twins.

into this good place, our shallop broke away (being moord with 2 hawsers), and we lost her, to our great griefe. Thus now had we but the Ship boate, and she was all torne and bruised, too. This Island was the same that we had formerly coasted the Wester side of, and had named my Lord *Westons Island*[1]. Here we remained till the 19, in which time it did nothing but snow and blow extremely, insomuch that we durst not put our boate ouerboord.

This 19. the wind shifted N.N.E., and we wayde and stood to the Southward; but, by noone, the wind came vp at S, and so we came to an Anker vnder another Iland, on which I went ashoare, and named it *The Earle of Bristols Iland*[2]. The Carpenter wrought hard in repairing our boate. Whilest I wandered vp and downe on this desart Iland, I could not perceiue that euer there had been any Saluages on it; and, in briefe, we could finde neither Fish, Fowle, nor Hearbe upon it; so that I returned comfortlesse aboord againe. The tydes doe high about some 6 Foote, now that the wind is Northerly. The flood comes from the North, and it doth flow halfe tyde, the full sea this day was at one a clocke. Here, seeing the windes continue so Northerly that we could not get about to goe into *Hudsons Baye*,[3] we considered againe what was best to doe to look out for a wintering place. Some aduised me to goe for *Port Nelson*, because we were certaine that there

---

[1] Apparently this was an error, as stated above.

[2] So far as one can follow the narrative, this was not "another" island, but still the southernmost of the two Twins, which he had confused with the island (Agoomska) he had named Lord Weston's. The latitude he gives for it (53° 10') seems to show this. James, no doubt, intended to honour John Digby, first Baron Digby, who was created Earl of Bristol in September, 1622, and died in 1653. It is not clear what connection he had with James's voyage. He was living in retirement at the time.

[3] See p. 498, *note*.

was a Coue where we might bring in our Ship. I likte not that counsell; for that it is a most perilous place, and that it might be so long ere we could get thither that we might be debard by the Ice. Moreouer, seeing it was so cold here as that euery night our rigging did freeze, and that sometimes in the Morning we did shouelle away the snow halfe a foote thicke off our deckes; and in that Latitude, too, I thought it farre worse in the other place. I resolued thereupon to stand againe to the Southward, there to looke for some little Creeke or Coue for our Ship.

The 21, the winde came vp at N., and we wayde, although it was a very thicke fogge, and stood away S.W. to cleere our selues of the shoalds that were on the point of this Iland. This Iland is in Lat. 53 10. When we were cleere, we steerd away S. At noone, the fogge turned into raine, but very thicke weather; and it did thunder all the afternoone, which made vs doubt a storme, for all which wee aduentured to proceed In the euening, the winde increased and blew hard, wherefore we tooke in all our sayles and let her driue to the Southward, heauing the lead euery glasse. Our depth, when we tooke in our sayles, was 30 fadd., and it did increase to 45, which was a great comfort to vs in the darke. At midnight, our depth began suddenly to decrease; and, as fast as the lead could be heaued, it shoalded to 20 fadd., wherefore we chopt to an Anker, and trimmed our Ship *aft* to mount on the Sea, and fitted all things to ride it out. There was no need to bid our men watch: not one of them put his eyes together all the night long. We rid it out well all the night, although the Sea went very loftie, and that it did blow very hard.

The 22, in the morning, when we could looke about vs, we saw an Iland vnder our Lee, some league off, all being shoalds and breaches betwixt vs and it. At noone (with the helpe of the windward tyde), we attempted to haue vp our Anker, although the Sea still went very loftie Ioyning all our strengths therefore, with our best skils, God be thanked, we had it vp; but, before we could set our sayles, wee were driuen into nine fadd. Indeauouring thereupon to double a point, to get vnder the Lee of this Iland, the water shoalded to 7, 6, and 5 fadd.; but, when we were about, it did deepen againe, and we come to an Anker in a very good place; and it was very good for vs that we did, for the winde increased to a very storme. Here wee rid well all the night, tooke good rest, and recouered our spent strengths againe. The last night and this morning it did snow and hayle, and was very cold; nevertheless, I tooke the Boate and went ashoare to looke for some Creeke or Coue to haue in our Ship; for shee was very leaky, and the company becomne[1] sickly and weake with much pumping and extreme labour This Iland, when wee came to the shoare, it was nothing but ledges of rocks and bankes of sand, and there went a very great surfe on them. Neuerthelesse, I made them rowe thorow it; and ashoare I got with two more, and made them rowe off without the breaches, and there to come to an Anchor and to stay for mee. I made what speed I could to the top of a hill to discouer about, but could not see what we looked for: thus, because it began to blow hard, I made haste towards the Boate againe. I found that it had ebbed so low that the Boate could not by any meanes come neere the shoare for mee, so that we were faine to wade thorow the surfe and breaches to her, in which some tooke such a cold that they did complaine of it to their dying day. But now it began to blow hard, so that we could not get but little to windward toward our Ship, for the wind was shifted since we went ashoare; and return to the shoare we could not, by reason of the surfe. Well, we

---

[1] Probably a form of the earlier word *becomen* (see also p. 477).

row for life; they in the Ship let out a Buoy by a long warpe; and, by God's assistance, we got to it, and so haled vp to the Ship, where we were well welcom'd, and we all reioyc'd together   This was a premonition to vs to be carefull how we sent off the Boate, for that it was winter weather already. I named this Iland *Sir Thomas Roe's Island:* it is full of small wood, but in other benefits not very rich, and stands in latitude 52. 10.[1] At noone, we weyed, seeing an Iland that bare South South-east of vs some foure leagues off, which was the highest land we had yet seene in this Bay[2], but, as we came neere it, it suddenly shoalded to 6, 5, and 4 fadd   Wherefore we strooke our sayles amaine, and chopt to an Anker; but it was very foule ground, and, when the Ship was winded vp, we had but three fadd. at her Sterne. As it cleered, we could see the breaches all alongst vnder our Lee, holding it safe,[3] therefore, to stay long here, we settled euery thing in order for the Ship to fall the right way. We had vp our Anker, got into deeper water, and stood ouer againe for *Sir Thomas Roe's Iland*, which by night we brought in the winde of vs, some two leagues off, which did well shelter vs. The tydes runne very quick here amongst these shoalds; and their times of running ebbe, or flood, be very vncertaine. Their currants are likewise so distracted that in the night there is no sayling by the Compasse; wherefore we were faine to seeke euery night some new place of securitie to come to an Anker.

---

[1] As James says this island was in 52° 10', it was probably the nameless island a little to the north of Charlton Island; or it may have been one of the Tiders. In any case, James marks it on his map very much bigger than it really is. Foxe had previously named an island Sir Thomas Roe's Welcome (see p 321)—for both the captains were largely indebted to the learned Knight.

[2] Possibly this was one of the Strutton group, but the mention of high land points to its having been Charlton Island

[3] Apparently he means *not safe.*

The 24, in the morning, it did lower and threaten a storme, which made vs, with the windward tyde, wey to get neerer vnder the Iland. It was very thicke foggie weather; and, as we stood to the North-eastward, we came to very vncertaine depths: at one cast, 20 fadd, the next 7, then 10, 5, 8, and 3; and, comming to the other tacke, we were worse then we were before, the Currants making a foole of our best iudgements in the thicke fogge when we could see no land-marks It pleased God that we got cleere of them, and endeauored to get vnder the Lee of the Iland. This being not able to doe, wee were faine to come to an Anker in 35 fadd, some two leagues off the shoare. All this afternoone (and, indeed, all night too), it did snow and hayle, and was very cold.

The 25 wee weyed, and thought to get to the East-ward; but, as we tackte to and againe, the winde shifted so in our teeths, that it put vs within a quarter of a mile of the very shoare, where we chopt to an Anker and rid out for life and death. Such miseries as these we indured amongst these shoalds and broken grounds, or, rather, more desperate then I haue related (very vnpleasant perchance to be read), with snow, haile, and stormy weather, and colder then euer I felt it in *England* in my life. Our shoote-Anker[1] was downe twice or thrice a day, which extreme paines made a great part of the company sickly. All this lasted with vs vntill the 30 of this moneth of *September*, which we thought would haue put an end to our miseries; for now we were driuen amongst rocks, shoalds, ouer-falles, and breaches round about vs, that which way to turne we knew not, but there ride amongst them in extremitie of distresse. All these perils made a most hideous and terrible noyse in the night season, and I hope it will not be accounted ridiculous if I relate with what meditations

---

[1] Sheet-Anchor (see Skeat's *Etymological Dictionary*, p. 546).

I was affected, now and then, amongst my ordinary prayers, which I here affoord the Reader, as I there conceiued them, in these few ragged and teared Rimes[1]:—

> OH, my poore soule, why doest thou grieue to see
> So many Deaths muster to murther mee?
> Looke to thy selfe, regard not mee; for I
> Must doe (for what I came), performe, or die.
> So thou mayst free thy selfe from being in
> A dung-hill dungeon: a meere sinke of sinne,
> And happily be free'd, if thou beleeue,
> Truly in God through Christ, and euer liue.
> Be therefore glad; yet, ere thou goe from hence,
> For our ioynt sinnes, let's doe some penitence
> Vnfainedly together. When we part,
> Ile wish the Angels Ioy, with all my heart.
> We haue with confidence relied vpon
> A rustie wyre, toucht with a little Stone,
> Incompast round with paper, and, alasse,
> To house it harmelesse, nothing but a glasse;
> And thought to shun a thousand dangers by
> The blind direction of this senselesse flye.
> When the fierce winds shatter'd blacke nights asunder,
> Whose pitchie clouds, spitting forth fire and thunder,
> Hath shooke the earth, and made the Ocean roare;
> And runne to hide it in the broken shoare
> Now thou must Steere *by faith*, a better guide;
> 'Twill bring thee safe to heauen, against the tyde
> Of Satan's malice. Now let quiet gales
> Of sauing grace inspire thy zealous sayles.

October 1. The first of *October* was indifferent faire weather; and, with a windward tyde, out went out Boate to sound a channell to help vs out of this perilous place. The Boat within two houres shee returned, and told vs how shee had beene away where there was not lesse then 12 fadd. We presently thereupon weyed, but found it otherwise, and came amongst many strange races and ouer-falles, vpon which there went a very great and break-

---

[1] These lines are referred to in the Introduction.

ing Sea. As we proceeded, the water shoalded to 6 fadd. Well, there was no remedy, we must goe forward, happy be luckie. seeing there neither was any riding, and as little hope to turne any way with a sayle, but that there appeared present death in it. It pleased God so to direct vs that we got thorow it, hauing no lesse then fiue seuerall and all very vncertaine depths. The water sometimes deepened to 20 fadd.; then vpon a sudden it shoalded to 7, 6, and 5 faddomes; so we strooke all our sayles amaine, and chopt to an Anker, where wee rid till midnight for life and death, it blowing a mercilesse gale of winde, and the Sea going very loftie, and all in a breach The ground was foule ground, too, insomuch that wee doubted our Cable euery minute.

The second, in the morning, was little winde; wherefore, taking the opportunitie of the tyde, the Boate went forth to sound, which, returning againe in two houres, told vs how they had sounded about that shoald, and had found a place of some safetie to ride in, and had beene in no lesse water then fiue faddome We weyed, and found our Cable galled[1] in two places, which had soon failed vs if the foule weather had continued. We stood the same way that the Boat did direct vs, but it prooued so calme that wee came to an Anker in 18 faddome. I tooke the Boate, and went ashoare on an Iland that was to the Southward of vs, which I named *The Earle of Danbyes Iland.*[2] From the highest place in it, I could see it all broken grounds and

---

[1] That is, cut or injured by friction (see p. 483).

[2] This was apparently one of the small islands lying just to the S.E of Charlton Island; or it is possible that it may have been Jacob Island. On his map, James shows it a good deal larger than it really is. James named it after Sir Henry Danvers, K.G., first Baron Danvers, who was created Earl of Danby in February 1625-6, who had been instrumental in arranging for Captain James to have an audience of the King (see Introduction). He died *s.p* in 1644, when all his honours became extinct.

shoalds to the Southward, and rather worse (then any thing better) then that which we had beene in. I found that the Saluages had beene vpon it, and that it was full of wood. I made haste to the Boate to sound the Baye, for feare of shoalds and sunken Rockes, but found it indifferent good. Toward the Euening, it began to blow hard; wherefore we made towards the Ship. She put forth a Buoy and a warpe; and we, rowing for life to recouer her, were put to Lee-ward of her; but, by getting hold of the warpe, we halde vp to her. The boate we left halfe full of water, our selues being as wet as drown'd rats, and it made vs the more reioyce that we had escapt this great danger. All night, we had a very hard rode-steede, it blowing a most violent gale of wind, with snow and haile.

The third, about noone, the wind duld, and we had vp our Anker, standing in further in the Baye into foure fad and a halfe water. Here we came againe to an Anker, with our second Anker; for many of our men are now sicke, and the rest so weakened that we can hardly way our shoote-Anchor. I tooke the Boate and went presently ashoare to see what comfort I could find. This was the first time that I put foote on this Iland, which was the same that we did after winter vpon.[1] I found the tracks of Deere, and saw some Fowle; but that that did reioyce me most was that I did see an opening into the Land, as if it had beene a riuer. To it we make with all speede, but found it to be barr'd; and not 2 foote water at full sea on the Barre; and yet within a most excellent fine Harbour, hauing 4 fad. water. In the Euening, I return'd aboord, bringing little comfort for our sicke men more then hopes.

The 4, it did snow and blow very hard; yet I got ashoare, and appointed the boate to goe to another place

---

[1] Charlton Island, not Danby Island.

(which made like a Riuer), and to sound it In the meantime, I went with foure more some 4 or 5 miles vp into the Countrey, but could find no releefe all that way for our sicke, but a few Berries onely. After we had well wearied ourselues in the troublesome woods, wee return'd to the place I had appointed the boate to tarry for me; where at my comming I still found her, she hauing not beene where I had ordered her, for it had blowne such a fierce gale of wind that she could not row to wind-ward. Thus we return'd aboord with no good newes. It continued foule weather, with snow and haile and extreme cold, till the 6, when, with a fauouring winde, we stood in neerer to the shoare, and here moord the ship.

The 7, it snow'd all day, so that we were faine to cleare it of the Decks with shouels; and it blew a very storme withall It continued snowing and very cold weather, and it did so freeze that all the bowes of the Ship, with her beake-head, was all Ice; about the Cable also was Ice as bigge as a man's middle. The bowes of the boate were likewise frozen halfe a foote thicke, so that we were faine to hew and beate it off. The Sunne did shine very cleere, and we tore the top-sayles out of the tops, which were hard frozen in them, into a lumpe, so that there they hung a Sunning all day in a very lumpe, the Sunne not hauing power to thawe one drop of them. After the boate was fitted, we rowed towards the shoare, but could not come neere the place where we were vsed to land, for that it was all thickned water with the snow that had fallen vpon the sands that are dry at low water This made it so difficult to row that we could not set through it with 4 oares; yet something higher to the Westward we got ashoare. Seeing now the winter to come thus extremely on vpon vs, and that wee had very little wood aboord, I made them fill the boate, and went aboord and sent the Carpenter and others to cut wood, others to carry it to the water side, whilest the boate brought it aboord; for I doubted that we were likely to be debar'd the shoare, and that we should not goe to and againe with the boate. It was miserable and cold already aboord the Ship; euery thing did freeze in the Hold and by the fire side. Seeing therefore that we could no longer make vse of our sayles (which be the wings of a Ship), it raised a many of doubts in our mindes that here we must stay and winter. After we had brought so much wood aboord as we could conueniently stowe, and enough (as I thought) would haue lasted 2 or 3 moneths, the sicke men desired that some little house or houell might be built a shoare, whereby they might be the better sheltered, and recouer their healths. I tooke the Carpenter (and others whom I thought fit for such a purpose) and, choosing out a place, they went immediately to worke vpon it. In the meane space, I myselfe, accompanied with some others, wandered vp and downe in the Woods, to see if we could discouer any signes of Salvages, that so we might the better prouide for our safeties against them. We found no appearance that there was any on this Iland, nor neere vnto it.[1] The snow by this time was halfe-legge high; and, stalking through it, we returned comfortlesse to our Companions, who had all this time wrought well vpon our house. They aboord the Ship tooke downe our topsayles in the meane while, and made a great fire vpon the hearth in the hatch way; so that, hauing well thaw'd them, they folded them vp, and put them betwixt deckes, that, if we had any weather, they might bring them againe to yard. Thus, in the Euening, we returned aboord.

The 12, we tooke our maine sayle from the yard, which was hard frozen to it, and carried it ashoare, to couer our

---

[1] There is confusion here; for, just before (p. 507), he had said: "I found that the savages had been upon" the neighbouring island, which he named the Earl of Danby's Island. Later on, he makes the same apparently-contradictory statement.

house withall, being first fain to thawe it by a great fire. By night, they had couered it, and had almost hedged it about, and the six builders did desire to lye in it ashoare that night, which I condiscended vnto, hauing first fitted them with Muskets and other furniture, and a charge to keepe good watch all night. Moreouer, they had a shoare 2 Greyhounds (a dogge and a bitch) which I had brought out of *England* to kill vs some Deere, if happily we could finde any.

By the 13, at night, our house was ready, and our sixe builders desired they might trauell vp into the Country to see what they could discouer.

The 14, betimes in the morning, being fitted with munition and their order to keepe together (but especially to seeke out some Creeke or Cove for our Ship), they departed. We aboord tooke downe our two top-masts and their rigging; making account, if we did remooue, to make vse of our fore-sayle and mizzen.

The 15, in the Euening, our hunters returned very weary, and brought with them a small, leane Deere,[1] in 4 quarters, which reioyced vs all, hoping we should haue had more of them to refresh our sicke men withall. They reported that they had wandered about 20 miles, and had brought this Deere aboue 12 mile, and that they had seene 9 or 10 more. The last night, they had a very cold lodging in the woods; and so it appeared, for they lookt almost starued, nor could they recouer themselues in 3 or 4 dayes after. They saw no signe of Salvages, nor of any rauening wild beasts, nor yet any hope of harbour.

The 17, my Lieutenant and 5 more desired they might try their fortunes in trauelling about the Iland. But they had farre worse lucke then the others, although they

---

[1] This was, no doubt, a cariboo or reindeer, as no other species of deer would be likely to be found so far north.

endured out all night, and had wandered very farre in the snow (which was now very deepe), and returned comfortlesse and miserably disabled with the coldnesse. But, what was worse then all this, they had lost one of their company, *Iohn Barton*, namely, our Gunners mate, who, being very weary, meerly to saue the going about, had attempted to goe ouer a pond that was a quarter of a mile over, where, when he was in the very middest, the Ice brake and closed vpon him, and we neuer saw him more. Considering these disasters, I resolued to fish no more with a golden hooke, for feare I weakned myselfe more with one hunting then 20 such deare Deeres could doe me good. Being now assured that there was no Salvages vpon the Iland, nor yet about vs on the other Ilands, no, nor on the maine neither, as farre as we could discouer (which we further proued by making of fires), and that the cold season was now in that extremity that they could not come to vs if there were any, we comforted and refreshed ourselues by sleeping the more securely. We changed our Iland garrison euery weeke; and, for other refreshing, we were like to haue none till the Spring.

From this 10 to the 29, it did (by *interims*) snow and blow so hard that the boate could hardly aduenture ashoare, and but seldome land, vnlesse the men did wade in the thicke congealed water, carrying one another. We did sensibly perceiue withall how wee did daily sinke into more miseries. The land was all deepe couered with snow, the cold did multiply, and the thicke snow water did increase; and what would become of vs, our most mercifull God and preseruer knew onely.

The 29, I obserued an *Eclipse* of the Moone with what care possibly I could, both in the tryall of the exactnesse of our instruments, as also in the obseruation. I referre you to the *obseruation* in the latter end of this

Relation, where it is at length described.¹ This moneth of *October* ended with snow and bitter cold weather.

The first of November, I cast vp accounts with the Steward concerning our victuall, the third part of our time being this day out.² I found him an honest man, for he gaue me an account euery weeke what was spent, and what was still in the hold, remaining vnder his hand. I would take no excuse of leakage or other waste, vnlesse he did daily show it to me. Euery month, I made a new suruey, and euery sixe moneths put what we had spared by itselfe, which now was at least a moneths prouision of Bread, and a fortnights of Pease and Fish, etc.³

The 3 day, the boate indeauored to get ashoare, but could not set thorow the thicke congealed water.

The 4, they found a place to get ashoare, and so once in 2 or 3 dayes, till the 9, bringing Beere to our men ashoare in a barrell, which would freeze firmely in the house in one night. Other prouision they had store. The Ice Beere, being thaw'd in a kettell, was not good, and they did breake the Ice of the pondes of water to come by water to drinke. This pond-water had a most lothsome smell with it, so that, doubting lest it might be infectious, I caused a Well to be sunke neere the house. There we had very good water which did taste (as we flattered ourselues with it) euen like milke.

The 10 (hauing store of boordes for such a purpose), I put the Carpenter to worke to make vs a little boate, which we might carry (if occasion were) ouer the Ice, and make vse of her where there was water. At noone, I tooke the Latitude of this Iland by 2 *Quadrants*, which I found to be

---

¹ See *post*.

² He means that they had been victualled for eighteen months, and had now been out six, or one-third of the time.

³ No doubt he means what they had *saued*, over and above thei allowance.

52. 00.¹ I vrged the men to make traps to catch Foxes, for we did daily see many. Some of them were pied, blacke and white, whereby I gathered that there was some blacke Foxes, whose skinnes, I told them, were of a great value, and I promised that whosoeuer could take one of them, should haue the skinne for his reward. Hereupon, they made diuers traps, and waded in the snow (which was very deepe) to place them in the woods.

The 12, our house tooke a fire, but we soone quenched it. We were faine to keepe an extraordinary fire, night and day; and this accident made me order a watch to looke to it continually; seeing that, if our house and clothing should be burnt, that all we were but in a woefull condition. I lay ashoare till the 17, all which time our miseries did increase. It did snow and freeze most extremely. At which time, we looking from the shoare towards the Ship, she did looke like a piece of Ice in the fashion of a Ship, or a Ship resembling a piece of Ice. The snow was all frozen about her, and all her fore-part firme Ice, and so was she on both sides also. Our Cables froze in the hawse,² wonderfull to behold. I got me aboord, where the long nights I spent with tormenting cogitations; and, in the day time, I could not see any hope of sauing the Ship. This I was assured of: that it was most impossible to endure these extremeties long. Euery day the men must beate the Ice off the Cables, while some within boord, with the Carpenter's long Calking Iron, did digge the Ice out of the hawses; in which worke, the water would freeze on their clothes and hands, and would so benumme them that they could hardly get into the Ship, without being heau'd in with a rope.

The 19, our Gunner (who, as you may remember, had his

---

¹ He seems to have calculated his latitude with absolute precision.

² Hawse-holes are the holes in a vessel's bows through which the cables pass.

legge cut off[1]) did languish vnrecouerably, and now grew very weake, desiring that, for the little time he had to liue, hee might drinke Sacke altogether, which I ordered hee should doe.

The 22, in the morning, he dyed; an honest and a strong-hearted man. Hee had a close-boorded Cabbin in the Gunroome, which was very close indeed, and as many clothes on him as was conuenient (for we wanted no clothes), and a panne with coales a fire continually in his Cabbin. For all which warmth, his playster would freeze at his wound, and his bottle of Sacke at his head. We committed him at a good distance from the Ship vnto the Sea.

The three and twentieth, the Ice did increase extraordinarily, and the snow lay on the water in flakes as it did fall; much Ice withall droue by vs, yet nothing hard all this while. In the euening, after the watch was set, a great piece came athwart our hawse, and foure more followed after him, the least of them a quarter of a mile broad; which, in the darke, did very much astonish vs, thinking it would haue carried vs out of the Harbour vpon the shoalds Easter point, which was full of rocks. It was newly congealed, a matter of two inches thicke, and wee broke thorow it, the Cable and Anker induring an incredible stresse, sometimes stopping the whole Ice. We shot off three Muskets, signifying to our men ashore that we were in distress, who answered vs againe, but could not helpe vs. By ten a clocke, it was all past; neuerthelesse, wee watched carefully, and the weather was warmer then wee had felt it any time this moneth. In the morning, at break of day, I sent for our men aboord, who made vp the house, and arriued by 10, being driuen by the way to wade thorow the congealed water, so that they recouered to the Boate with

---

[1] See p. 487.

difficultie. There droue by the Ship many pieces of Ice, though not so large as the former, yet much thicker. One piece came foule of the Cable and made the Ship driue.

As soon as we were cleere of it, we ioyned our strengths together, and had vp our Eastermost Anker; and now I resolued to bring the ship aground, for no Cables nor Ankers could hold her; but I will here show you the reasons why I brought her no sooner aground: First, it was all stony ground, some stones lying dry three or foure foote aboue water, so that it was to be suspected that it was the like all about vs; secondly, it did ordinarily flow but two foot and a halfe here, and, if shee should bed deepe in the sands, we could not euer come to digge her out againe, for that shee would not be dry by foure or fiue foot; thirdly, it was a loose sand, which might rise with the surfe, or so mount about her that all our weake powers could not heaue it away in the next spring time; fourthly, we doubted the tydes would not high so much in the summer as they did now; fifthly, we could not bring her out of the tydes way, which doth runne something quicke here, and the Ice, besides, might driue and mount vp vpon her, and so ouerset her, or teare her, and carry away her plankes, iron workes, and all, so that we should haue nothing left to finish our Pinnasse with[1]; sixtly, if it did blow a storme at North-west, or thereaboutes, the water would flow ten foot and vpwards, and that winde (being of the shore) it would blow away all the Ice, and there would come in an extraordinary great surfe about the shoald Ester-point, which was occasioned by a deep ouerfall. Moreouer, shee would beate extremely; and, if shee were put vp by the Sea or that surfe, it was very doubtfull that we should neuer haue her off againe. For these reasons, we endured all the extremitie, still hoping vpon some good and fortunate accident. But now all our

---

[1] He means the pinnace they afterwards decided to build.

prouident designs we saw to become foolishnesse, and that a great deal of miserable labour had been spent in vaine by vs. With the flood, wee weyed our Westermost Anker, perceiuing Gods assistance manifestly, because it happened to be fine warme weather: otherwise we had not beene able to worke The winde was now South, which blew in vpon the shoare, and made the lowest tydes We brought the Ship into 12 foot water, and layd out one Anker in the Offing, and another in shoald water, to draw her aland at command. Our hope also was that some stones that were to the Westward of vs would fend off some of the Ice. We then being about a mile from the shore, about ten a clocke in the darke night, the Ice came driuing vpon vs, and our Ankers came home. She droue some two Cables length, and, the winde blowing on the shoare, by two a clock she came aground, and stopt much Ice; yet shee lay well all night, and we tooke some rest

The fiue and twentieth, the winde shifted Easterly, and put abundance of Ice on vs. When the flood was made, we encouraged one another, and to worke we goe, drawing home our Ankers by maine force vnder great pieces of Ice, our endeuour being to put the Ship to the shoare. But, to our great discomforts, when the halfe tyde was made (which was two houres before high water), the Ship droue amongst the Ice to the Eastward (doe what we could), and so would haue [driven] on the shoald Rockes As I haue formerly said, these two dayes and this day was very warme weather, and it did raine, which it had not yet but once done since wee came hither: otherwise it had been impossible we could haue wrought Withall, the wind shifted also to the South, and, at the very instant, blew a hard puffe, which so continued for halfe an houre I caused our two Top-sailes to be had vp from betwixt deckes, and wee hoyst them vp with ropes in all haste, and we forst the Ship ashoare, when she had not halfe a Cables length to driue on the Rocky shoalds. In the Euening, wee broke away thorow the Ice, and put an Anker to shoareward in fiue foot water to keep her to the shoare, if possible it might be. Here Sir *Hugh Willoughby*[1] came into my mind, who, without doubt, was driuen out of his Harbour in this manner, and so starued at sea. But God was more mercifull to vs. About nine a clocke at night, the winde came vp at North-West, and blew a very storme. The winde was of the shoare, which blew away all the Ice from about vs long before we were afloat. There came in a great rowling Sea withall, about the point, accompanied with a great surfe on the shoare And now were we left to the mercy of the Sea, on the ground. By tenne, she began to rowle in her docke, and, soon after, began to beate against the ground. We stood at the Capstang, as many as could, others at the Pumpes, for we thought that euery fift or sixt blow would haue staued her to pieces. We heaued to the vttermost of our strengths, to keepe her as neere the ground as we could. By reason of this wind, it flowed very much water, and we drew her vp so high that it was doubtfull if euer we should get her off againe. She continued thus beating till two a clocke the next Morning, and then she againe settled; whereupon wee went to sleepe, to restore nature, seeing the next tyde we expected to be againe tormented.

The sixe and twentieth, in the morning tyde, our Ship did not floate, whereby we had some quietnesse. After

---

[1] Sir Hugh Willoughby sailed with three ships in May 1553, on an expedition in search of a North-East Passage, but the voyage ended disastrously. One ship, under Richard Chancellor, was separated from the rest in a storm, and eventually returned home; but Willoughby, with the other two ships, attempted to winter in a harbour on the coast of Lapland, where he and all his men perished of cold and starvation. Their fate was not ascertained until some time after

prayers, I cald a consultation of the Master, my Lieutenant, the Mates, Carpenter, and Boat-swayne, to whom I proposed that now we were put to our last shifts, and, therefore, they should tell me what they thought of it, namely, whether it were not best to carry all our prouision ashoare, and that, when the wind should come northerly, it were not safest to draw her further off and sinke her. After many reasonings, they allowed of my purpose, and so I communicated it to the Company, who all willingly agreed to it. And so we fell to getting vp of our prouisions, first our bread, of which we had landed this day two Dryfats[1] with a Hogshead of Beefe, hauing much adoe to set the Boate thorow the thicke congealed water In the Euening, the winds came vp at North-East and East, and fild the Bay choakefull of Ice.

The twenty seuenth, the Bay continued full of Ice, which I hoped would so continue and freeze, that we should not be put to sinke our Ship This day we could land nothing

The twenty eighth, at break of day, three of our men went ashoare ouer the Ice vnknown to mee; and the winde, comming vp at West, droue the Ice from betwixt vs and the shoare, and most part of the Bay also, and yet not so that the Boate could goe ashoare for any thing I made the Carpenter fit a place against all sudden extremities; for that, with the first North-West or northerly wind, I meant to effect our last proiect. In the runne of her, on the starboord side, he cut away the sealing and the planke to the sheathing, some four or fiue inches square, some foure foote high from the keele of her, that so it might be boared out at an instant. We brought our bread, which was remayning in the Bread-roome, vp into the great Cabbin,

---

[1] Halliwell says dryfats were strong boxes, casks, or packing-cases.

and likewise all our powder, setting much of our light dry things betwixt deckes.

The nine and twentieth, at fiue a Clocke in the Morning, the winde came vp at West North-West, and began to blow very hard. It was ordinary for the wind to shift from the West by the North round about. So first I ordered the Cooper to goe downe in hold and looke to all our Caske: those that were full, to mawle in the bungs of them,[1] those that were empty, to get vp, or, if they could not be gotten vp, to staue them. Then to quoile[2] all our Cables vpon our lower tyre,[3] and to lay on our spare Ankers, and any thing that was weighty, to keepe it downe from rising. By seuen a Clocke, it blew a storme at North-West, our bitter enemy. The Ship was already bedded some two foote in the sand, and whilst that was a flowing shee must beate. This I before had in my consideration, for I thought she was so farre driuen vp that we should neuer get her off Yet we had bin so ferrited[4] by her last beating, that I resolued to sinke her right downe, rather then runne that hazzard. By nine a clocke, she began to rowle in her docke with a most extraordinary great Sea that was come, which I found to be occasioned by the forementioned ouer-fall. And this was the fatall houre that put vs to our wits end. Wherefore, I went downe in hold with the Carpenter, and tooke his auger and board a hole in the Ship, and let in the water. Thus, with all speed, we began to cut out other places to boare thorow,

---

[1] Probably he ordered the men to *hammer* in the bungs, a *maul* being a heavy iron hammer used for driving tree-nails or bolts.

[2] See p. 496.

[3] A *tyre* (now spelled *tier*) is a range of guns, all placed on a level in a ship's side; also a range in a ship's hold, or the casks or goods stowed away there.

[4] Presumably this means *frighted*, but the dictionaries give no such form of the word Ash's *Dictionary* (1775) gives *ferit*=a blow (a cant word), which may have some connection.

but euery place was full of nailes By tenne, notwithstanding, the lower tyre was couered with water; for all which, she began so to beate in her docke more and more, that we could not worke nor stand to doe any thing in her. Nor would she sinke so fast as we would haue her, but continued beating double blowes, first abaft, and then before, that it was wonderfull how she could indure a quarter of an houre with it. By twelue a clocke, her lower Tyre rose, and that did so counter-beate on the inside that it beat the bulke heads of the Bread-roome, powder-roome, and fore piece all to pieces; and, when it[1] came betwixt deckes, the chests fled wildly about, and the water did flash and flie wonderfully, so that now we expected euery minute when the Ship would open and breake to pieces. At one a clocke, she beat off her Rudder, and that was gone, we knew not which way. Thus she continued beating till three a clocke, and then the sea came vp on the vpper decke; and, soon after, shee began to settle. In her, wee were faine to sinke the most part of our bedding and clothes, and the Chirurgions Chest with the rest. Our men that were ashoare stood looking vpon vs, almost dead with cold and sorrowes, to see our misery and their owne. We lookt vpon them againe, and both vpon each other, with woefull hearts. Darke night drew on, and I bade the Boate to be haled vp, and commanded my louing companions to goe all into her, who (in some refusing complements[2]) expressed their faithful affections to mee, as loth to part from me. I told them that my meaning was to goe ashoare with them. And thus, lastly, I forsook the Ship.

We were seuenteene poore soules now in the Boate, and

---

[1] Apparently *it* here means the water.
[2] Possibly he means they refused to leave him, which, in a way, he considered complimentary to himself.

we now imagined *that we were leapt out of the Frying pan into the fire.* The ebbe was made, and the water extraordinary thicke congealed with snow, so that we thought, assuredly, it would carry vs away into the Sea. We thereupon double-mand foure oares, appointing foure more to sit ready with oares, and so, with the helpe of God, we got to the shoare, haling vp the Boate after vs. One thing was most strange in this thicke water, namely, that there went a great swelling Sea. Being arriued vpon the land, we greeted our fellows the best we could, at which time they could not know vs, nor we them, by our habits nor voyces, so frozen all ouer wee were, faces, haire, and apparell. And here I meane to take breath awhile, after all this long and vnpleasant Relation of our miserable endeauours, crauing leaue first of all to speake a word or two in generall.

The winds, since we came hither, haue been very variable and vnconstant; and, till within this fortnight, the Southerly winde was the coldest. The reason I conceiue to be, for that it did blow from the Maine land, which was all couered with snow, and for that the North winds came out of the great Bay which hitherto was open. Adde to that, we were now vnder a South Banke, which did shelter vs, so that we were not so sensible of it.

A North-west, a North-west by North, and a North-North-west winde (if it blew a storme) would raise the Tydes extraordinarily; and, in briefe, from the West North-west to the North North-east, would raise the tydes in proportion, as they did blow from the middle point. The wind being on the opposite points (if it blew), it would flow very little at all. The harder it blew, the lesse water it would flow. If it were little winde or calme, it would flow indifferently. The tydes doe high ordinarily (without being forced) about three foot, but, being forced with the forementioned winds, vpward of ten foot.[1] I could perceiue no difference betwixt Neape and spring tydes. It flowes halfe tyde; that is, the flood comes from the Northward, and thither returnes againe, two houres before it be high water; and it is commonly so seene in most *Bayes* or *Inlets*.

---

[1] The Admiralty Chart says that, in James's Bay "North or west winds will make a rise of tide of 12 or 14 feet."

The VVintering.

Fter we had haled vp the Boate, we went alongst the breach side in the darke, towards our house, where we made a good fire, and, with it and bread and water, we thawde and comforted our selues, beginning after that to reason one with another concerning our Ship. I requir'd that euery one should speak his mind freely. The Carpenter (especially) was of the opinion that she was founderd and would neuer be seruiceable againe. He alledged that she had so beaten that it was not possible but that all her Ioints were loose and seams open, and that, by reason it flowed so little water, and no Creeke nor Coue being neere, wherein to bring her aground, he could not deuise how he might come to mend it. Moreouer, her Rudder was lost, and he had no Ironworke to hang on another. Some alledged that we had heaued her vp so high vpon the sands that they thought we should neuer haue her off againe, and that they were assured she was already dockt three foote. Others, that she lay in the Tydes way, and that the Ice might teare her to pieces off the ground; besides which, two of our Ankers we could not now get from vnder the Ice, which, when the Ice brake (which would be of a great

thicknesse by the Spring), would breake our Ankers to pieces, and then we should haue no Ankers to bring vs home withall, supposed[1] we got off the Ship and that she proued sound also. I comforted them the best I could with such like words: My Masters and faithfull Companions, be not dismaide for any of these disasters, but let vs put our whole trust in God It is he that giueth, and he that taketh away; he throwes downe with one hand, and raiseth vp with another. His will be done. If it be our fortunes to end our dayes here, we are as neere heauen as in *England;* and we are much bound to God Almighty for giuing us so large a time of repentance, who, as it were, dayly calls vpon vs to prepare our selues for a better life in heauen. I make no doubt but he will be mercifull to vs, both here on earth and in his blessed Kingdome, he doth not in the meane time deny but that we may vse all honest meanes to save and prolong our naturall liues withall; and, in my Iudgement, we are not yet so farre past hope of returning into our natiue Countries but that I see a faire way by which wee may effect it. Admit the Ship be foundered (which God forbid; I hope the best), yet haue those of our owne nation, and others, when they haue beene put to these extremities, euen out of the wracke of their lost Ship, built then a Pinnasse, and recouered to their friends againe. If it be obiected that they haue happened into better Climats, both for temperatenesse of the ayre and for pacificke and open Seas, and provided withall of abundance of fresh victuall, yet there is nothing too hard for couragious minds, which hitherto you have showne, and I doubt not will still doe to the vttermost.

They all protested to worke to the vttermost of their strength, and that they would refuse nothing that I should order them to doe, to the vttermost hazzard of their lives.

---

[1] *Supposing* makes better sense.

I thanke them all; and, to the Carpenter, for his cheerefull vndertaking, I promised to giue him so much plate presently as should be worth ten pound sterling; and, if so be I went to *England* in the Pinnasse, I would giue her him freely, and fifty pounds in mony ouer and aboue, and would, moreouer, gratifie all them that I should see painefull and industrious. Thus we then resolued to build vs a new Pinnasse with the timber we should get vpon the Iland, that so, in the spring, if we found not the Ship seruiceable, wee might teare her vp, and planke her with the Ships planks And so, for this night, we settled our selues close about the fire, and tooke some rest till daylight.

The thirtieth, betimes in the morning, I caused the Chirurgion to cut the haire of my head short, and to shaue away all the haire of my face, for that it was become intolerable, and that it would be frozen so great with Icesickles. The like did all the rest, and we fitted our selues to worke. The first thing we were to doe was to get our clothes and prouisions ashoare; and, therefore, I deuided the company. The Master, and a conuenient company with him, were to goe aboord, and to get things out of Hold. The Cock-swaine, with his ging,[1] were to goe in the Boate to bring and carry things ashoare. My selfe, with the rest, to carry it halfe a mile thorow the snow vnto the place where we intended to build a Store-house. As for the heauier things, we purposed to lay them vpon the Beache. In the afternoone, the winde was at South South-west, and the water veerd to so low an ebbe that we thought we might get something out of our Hold. We lanched our Boate, therefore, and, with oares, set thorow the thicke congealed water. It did freeze extreme hard,

---

[1] This is an Anglo-Saxon word, meaning a *crew* or company of persons, but Halliwell says it is not a corruption of *gang*

and I did stand on the shoare with a troubled mind, thinking verily that, with the ebbe, the Boate would be carried into the Sea, and that then wee were all lost men. But, by Gods assistance, they got safely to the Ship, and made a fire there to signifie their arriuall aboord. They fell presently to worke, and got something out of the Hold vpon the decks; but, night comming on, they durst not aduenture to come ashoare, but lay on the bed in the great Cabbin, being almost starued.

The first of *December* was so cold that I went the same way ouer the Ice to the Ship where the Boate had gone yesterday. This day, we carried vpon our backs in bundles 500 of our fish, and much of our bedding and clothes, which we were faine to digge out of the Ice.

The second was milde weather, and some of the men, going ouer the Ice, fell in, and very hardly recouered, so that this day we could land nothing, neither by Boate nor backe.[1] I put them therefore to make vs a Store-house ashoare. In the euening, the winde came vp at West, and the Ice did breake and driue out of the Bay. It was very deepe and large Ice, that we much doubted it would haue spoyled the Ship.

The third day, there were diuers great pieces of Ice that came athwart the Ship, and shee stopt them, yet not so that we could goe ouer them. We found a way for the Boat; but, when shee was loaden, shee drew foure foot water, and could not come within a flight-shot[2] of the shoare. The men, therefore, must wade thorow the thicke congealed water, and carry all things out of the Ship vpon their backs. Euery time they waded in the Ice, it so gathered about thē that they did seeme like a walking piece of Ice, most lamentable to behold. In this extreme

---

[1] He means neither by boat nor on the backs of his men.
[2] See p. 207

cold euening, they cut away as much Ice from about the Boate as they could, and pickt it with hand-spikes out of her, and endeauouring to hoyse her into the Ship, there being small hope that shee could goe to and againe any more. But, vse what meanes they could, shee was so heauy that they could not hoyse her in, but were faine there to leaue her in the tackles by the Ships side.

The fourth, being Sunday, we rested, and performed the Sabbath duties of a Christian.

The fift and sixt were extreme cold, and wee made bags of our store shirts,[1] and in them carried our loose bread ouer the Ice ashoare vpon our backs. We also digged our clothes and new sayles, with hand-spikes of iron, out of the Ice, and carried them ashoare, which we dryed by a great fire.

The seuenth day was so extremely cold that our noses, cheekes, and hands did freeze as white as paper.

The eighth and ninth, it was extreme cold, and it did snow much, yet we continued our labour in carrying and rowling things ashoare. In the euening, the water raised the Ice very high, and it did breake two thoughts of our Boat, and breake in the side of her; but, for that time, we could not helpe it.

The tenth, our Carpenter found timber to make a Keele and a Sterne for our Pinnace. The rest wrought about our prouisions vntill the 13 day, and that we spent in digging our boate out of the Ice, which we were faine to doe to the very Keele, and dig the Ice out of her; and then we got her vp on the Ice, in which doing many had their noses, cheekes, and fingers frozen as white as paper. The cold now increased most extremely. By the 19, we could get no more things out of our Hold, but were faine to leaue 5 barrels of Beefe and Porke, all our

---

[1] The spare shirts for his men he had among his stores.

Beere, and diuers other things, which were all firme frozen in her.

The one and twentieth was so cold that we could not goe out of the house.

The three and twentieth, we went to haue our boate ashoare, running her ouer our oares; but, by 10 a clocke, there came such a thicke fogge that it was as darke as night. I made them giue ouer, and make what haste we could to the shoare, which we had much adoe to finde, for the time losing one another. At the last, we met all at the house, the miserablest frozen that can bee conceiued. Vpon divers had the cold raised blisters as bigge as wall-nuts. This we imagined to come by reason that they came too hastily to the fire. Our Well was now frozen vp, so, digge as deepe as we could, we can come by no water. Melted snow-water is very vnwholsome, either to drinke or dresse our victualls. It made vs so short-breathed that we were scarce able to speake. All our Sacke, Vineger, Oyle, and euery thing else that was liquid, was now frozen as hard as a piece of wood, and we must cut it with a hatchet. Our house was all frozen on the inside, and it froze hard within a yard of the fires side. When I landed first vpon this Iland, I found a spring vnder a hils side,[1] which I then obseruing, had caused some trees to be cut for markes to know the place againe by. It was about three quarters of a mile from our house. I sent 3 of our men, which had beene formerly with me, thither vpon the 24. These, wading thorow the snow, at last found the place; and, shoueling away the snow, they made way to the very head of it. They found it spring very strongly, and brought me a Can of it, for which I was right ioyfull. This spring continued all the yeere, and did not freeze but that we could breake the Ice and come to it. We labor'd very hard these three

---

[1] See p. 566.

or foure dayes to get wood to the house, which we found to be very troublesome, through the deepe snow.

Wee then settled our bedding and prouisions, providing to keepe *Christmas* day holy, which we solemnized in the ioyfullest manner we could. So, likewise, did we *Saint Iohns day*, vpon which we named the wood we did winter in, in memory of that Honourable Knight, *Sir Iohn Winter, Winters Forrest*.[1] And now, in stead of a *Christmas Tale*, I will here describe the house that we did liue in, with those adioyning.

When I first resolued to build a house, I chose the most warmest and conuenientest place, and the neerest the Ship withall. It was amongst a tuft of thicke trees, vnder a South banke, about a flight-shot from the Seas side. True it is that at that time we could not digge into the ground to make vs a Hole or Caue in the earth (which had been the best way), because we found water within 2 foote digging; and, therefore, that proiect fail'd. It was a white light sand, so that we could by no meanes make vp a mud-wall. As for stones, there were none neere vs, which, moreouer, were all now couered with the snow. We had no boords for such a purpose, and, therefore, we must doe the best we could with such materials as we had about vs.

The house was square, about 20 foote euery way; as much, namely, as our *mayne-course* could well couer. First, we droue strong stakes into the earth round about, which

---

[1] Sir John Winter (concerning whom I have been able to obtain very little information) was knighted at Belvoir on August 7th, 1624 (Metcalfe's *Book of Knights*, p. 183). In what way Captain James was connected with him does not appear. In a pamphlet published in November 1642, he is described as "Her Majesties principall Secretary and Master of Requests". From another pamphlet, published in the same year, we learn that he was examined, with certain other knights, at the Bar of the House of Commons, and committed to the Tower for treason, they having illegally raised troops in Somersetshire.

we watteled with boughes, as thicke as might be, beating them downe very close. This, our first worke, was six foote high on both sides, but, at the ends, almost vp to the very top. There we left two holes for the light to come in at; and the same way the smoke did vent out also. Moreouer, I caused at both ends three rowes of thick bush trees to be stuck up as close as mought be possibly. Then, at a distance from the house, we cut downe trees, proportioning them into lengths of sixe foote, with which we made a pile on both sides, sixe foote thicke, and sixe foote high, but, at both ends, tenne foote high, and sixe foote thicke We left a little low doore to creepe into, and a portall before that, made with piles of wood, that the wind might not blow into it We next of all fastned a rough tree aloft ouer all, vpon which we laid our rafters, and our Mayne Course ouer those againe, which, lying thwartwayes ouer all, did reach downe to the very ground on either side. And this was the Fabricke of the out-side of it. On the inside, we made fast our bonnet sayles round about. Then we droue in stakes and made vs bed-stead frames, about three sides of the house, which bedsteads were double, one vnder another, the lower-most being a foote from the ground. These we first fild with boughes; then we layd some spare sayles on that, and then our bedding and clothes We made a Hearth or Causie[1] in the middle of the house, and on it made our fire; some boords wee layd round about our Hearth to stand vpon, that the cold dampe should not strike vp into vs. With our Wastclothes,[2] we made vs Canopies and Curtaines; others did the like with our small sayles. Our second house was not

---

[1] Probably he means *causeway*, formerly spelt *causey*, as it is sometimes pronounced locally.

[2] Waist cloths are the painted canvas coverings of the hammocks, which are stowed in the waist-nettings, between the quarter-deck and forecastle

past 20 foote distant from this, and made, for the watteling, much after the same manner; but it was lesse, and couered with our fore-course. It had no pyles on the South side, but, in liew of that, we pilde vp all our Chests on the inside; and, indeed, the reflexe of the fire against them did make it warmer then the Mansion house.[1] In this house, we drest our victuall, and the subordinate crue[2] did refresh themselues all day in it. A third house (which was our store-house), we likewise made, some twenty paces off from this, for feare of firing This house was onely a rough tree fastened aloft, with rafters layd from it to the ground, and couered ouer with our new suite of sailes. On the inside, we had laid small trees, and couered them ouer with boughes, and so stor'd vp our Bread and Fish in it, about two foote from the ground, the better to preserue them. Other things lay more carelessely.

Long before *Christmas*, our mansion house was couered thicke ouer with Snow, almost to the very roofe of it. And so, likewise, was our second house; but our Storehouse all ouer, by reason we made no fire in it. Thus we seemed to liue in a heape and wildernesse of Snow; forth adores[3] we could not go, but vpon the snow, in which we made vs paths, middle-deepe in some places, and, in one speciall place, the length of tenne steps. To doe this, we must shouell away the Snow first; and then, by treadding, make it something hard vnderfoote. The Snow in this path was a full yard thick vnder vs. And this was our best gallery for the sicke-men, and for mine owne ordinary walking And, both houses and walkes, we did daily accommodate more and more, and make fitter for our vses.

---

[1] This expression, which is now seldom used in its old sense, formerly meant a house in which one resided, as distinguished from a storehouse or workshop.

[2] No doubt he means the seamen, other than the officers.

[3] *At doors*, meaning out of doors.

The twenty seuenth, we got our Boate ashoare, and fetcht vp some of our prouisions from the beach side into the Store-house; and so, by degrees, did we with the rest of our prouisions, with extremity of cold and labour, making way with shouells thorow the deepe Snow, euen from the Sea-side vnto our Store-house. And thus concluded we the old yeere, 1631.

January, 1632.

The first of *January* (and, for the most part, all the moneth) was extreme cold.

The sixth, I obserued the latitude with what exactness I could (it being very cleere Sun-shine weather), which I found to be 51. 52. This difference[1] is by reason that here is a great *Refraction.*[2]

The one and twentieth, I *obserued* the Sunne to rise like an *Ouall* alongst the *Horizon*. I cald three or foure to see it, the better to confirme my Iudgement, and we all agreed that it was twice as long as it was broad. We plainly perceiued withall that, by degrees, as it got vp higher, it also recouered his roundnesse.

The sixe and twentieth, I *obserued*, when the Easterne edge of the *Moone* did touch the Planet *Mars*, the Lions heart was then in the East quarter, 21. 45 aboue the *Horizon;* but all this was not done with that exactness that I haue done other *obseruations*.

The thirtieth and one and thirtieth, there appeared, in the beginning of the night, more Starres in the firmament then euer I had before seene by two thirds. I could see the *Cloud* in *Cancer* full of small Starres, and all the *via*

---

[1] For other observations on the latitude of the spot, see pp. 513 and 555.

[2] This phenomenon is commented upon by Captain Parry (*Journal of a Third Voyage, etc*, p. 66), who gives illustrations of abnormal shapes of the moon from drawings made by Mr. Head.

lactea nothing but small Starres; and, amongst the *Pylades*, a great many small Starres. About tenne a Clocke, the Moone did rise, and then a quarter of them was not to be seene. The wind, for the most part of this month, hath beene Northerly and very cold, the warmest of which time wee imployed our selues in fetching Wood, working vpon our Pinnasse, and other things that happened. In the beginning of this moneth, the Sea was all firmely frozen ouer, so that we could see no water any way. I hope it will not seeme tedious to the Readers, if I here deliuer mine owne opinion how this abundance of Ice comes to be ingendered.

The Land that encircles this great *Bay*[1] (which lyes in a broken irregular forme, making many little shoald Bayes and Guts, being, moreouer, full of Ilands and dry sands) is, for the most part, low and flat, and hath flat shoalds adioyning to it, halfe a mile or a mile, that are dry at low water. Now you must know that it flowes halfe tyde (as I haue often experienced); that is, from whence the flood commeth, the water thither returneth, two houres before it be high water or full Sea. It seldome raines after the middle of *September*, but snowes, and that Snow will not melt on the Land nor Sands. At low water, when it snowes (which it doth very often), the sands are all couered ouer with it, which the halfe tyde carries officiously[2] (twice in twentie foure houres) into the great Bay, which is the common Rendezvous of it. Euery low water are the sands left cleere, to gather more to the increase of it. Thus doth it daily gather together in this manner, till the latter end of *October*; and, by that time, hath it brought the Sea to that coldnesse that, as it snows, the snow will lye vpon the

---

[1] That is, Hudson's (now called James's) Bay.
[2] This seems a somewhat unusual use of the word, but it may probably be regarded as synonymous with regularly or busily.

water in flakes without changing his colour, but, with the winde, is wrought together; and, as the winter goes forward, it begins to freeze on the surface of it, two or three inches in one night, which, being carried with the halfe tyde, meets with some obstacle (as it soone doth), and then it crumples and so runnes vpon itself that, in a few houres, it will be fiue or sixe foote thicke. The halfe tyde, still flowing, carries it so fast away that, by *December*, it is growne to an infinite multiplication of Ice. And thus, by this storing of it vp, the cold gets the predomination in the Sea (which also furnisheth the Springs and water in the low flat lands) that it cools it like it selfe. This may appeare by our experience, though in all this I freely submit my selfe vnto the better learned Our men found it more mortifying cold to wade thorow the water in the beginning of *Iune*, when the Sea was all full of Ice, then in *December*, when it was increasing. Our well, moreouer, out of which we had water in *December*, we had none in *Iuly*.

The ground, at ten foote deepe, was frozen. The quantitie of the Ice may very easily be made to appeare by *Mathematicall Demonstration*, and yet I am not of the opinion that the *Bay* doth freeze all ouer. For, the one and twentieth, the winde blowing a storme at North, we could perceiue the Ice to rise something in the *Bay*.

February, 1632.

The cold was as extreme this moneth as at any time we had felt it this yeere, and many of our men complained of infirmities; some of sore mouthes, all the teeth in their heads being loose, their gums swolne, with blacke rotten flesh, which must euery day be cut away. The paine was so sore on them that they could not eate their ordinary meat. Others complained of paine in their heads and their brests; some of weaknesse in their backs; others of aches in their thighs and knees; and others of swellings in their legges. Thus were two thirds of the company vnder the Chirurgions hands. And yet, neuerthelesse, they must worke daily, and goe abroad to fetch wood and timber, notwithstanding the most of them had no shooes to put on. Their shooes, vpon their comming to the fire, out of the snow, were burnt and scorcht vpon their feete, and our store-shooes[1] were all sunke in the Ship. In this necessitie, they would make this shift: To bind clouts about their feet; and endeauoured, by that poore helpe, the best they could, to performe their duties Our Carpenter likewise is by this time falne sicke, to our great discomforts I practised some *obseruations* by the rising and setting of the Sunne, *calculating* the time of his rising and setting by very true running glasses. As for our Clocke and Watch, notwithstanding we still kept them by the fire's side, in a Chest, wrapt in clothes, yet were they so frozen that they could not goe. My obseruations by these Glasses, I compared with the Stars comming to the *Meridian*. By this meanes, wee found the Sunne to rise twentie minutes before it should, and, in the euening, to remaine aboue the Horizon twentie minutes (or thereabouts) longer then it should doe. And all this by reason of the *Refraction*.

Since now I haue spoken so much of the cold, I hope it will not be too coldly taken if I, in a few words, make it someway to appeare vnto our Readers.

Wee made three differences of the cold, all according to the places. In our house; in the woods; and in the open Ayer, vpon the Ice, in our going to the ship.

For the last, it would be sometimes so extreme that it was not indurable; no Cloathes were proofe against it; no motion could resist it. It would, moreouer, so freeze the

---

[1] The spare shoes he had in store (see p. 527).

haire on our eye-lids that we could not see; and I verily beleeue that it would haue stifled a man in a very few houres. We did daily find by experience that the cold in the Woods would freeze our faces, or any part of our flesh that was bare, but it was yet not so mortifying as the other. Our house, on the out-side, was couered two third-parts with Snow, and, on the inside, frozen & hang with Icesickles.[1] The Cloathes on our beds would be couered with hoare frost, which, in this little habitacle,[2] was not farre from the fire. But let vs come a little neerer to it. The Cookes Tubs, wherein he did water his meate, standing about a yard from the fire, and which he did all day plye with melted Snow-water, yet, in the night season, whilst he slept but one watch, would they be firme frozen to the very bottome. And, therefore, was hee faine to water his meate in a brasse Kettle, close adioyning to the fire, and I haue many times both seene and felt, by putting my hand into it, that side which was next the fire was very warme, and the other side an inch frozen. I leaue the rest to our Cooke, who will almost speake miracles of the cold. The Surgeon,[3] who had hung his bottles of sirrops and other liquid things as conueniently as he could to preserue them, had them all frozen. Our Vineger, Oyle, and Sacke, which we had in small Caske in the house, was all firme frozen. It may further in generall be conceiued that, in the beginning of Iune, the Sea was not broken vp, and the ground was yet frozen; and thus much wee found by experience, in the burying of our men, in setting vp the King's Standard towards the latter end of Iune, and by our Well,

---

[1] Although Foxe also spells this word *ice-sickle*, Skeat (*Etymological Dictionary*, p. 280) cites no instance of its use elsewhere.

[2] A small dwelling or habitation.

[3] Elsewhere, James speaks of the Chirurgion, which shows that the word was in his day undergoing the change to its present form, as here used.

at our comming away in the beginning of *Iuly*, at which time, vpon the land, for some other reasons, it was very hote weather.

March, 1632.

The first of this moneth, being Saint *Dauids* day,[1] we kept Holyday, and solemnised it in the manner of the *Ancient Britaines*, praying for his Highnesse happinesse, *Charles* Prince of *Wales*.

The fifteenth, one of our men thought he had seene a Deere, whereupon he, with two or three more, desired that they might go to see if they could take it. I gaue them leaue; but, in the Euening, they returned so disabled with cold, which did rise vp in blisters vnder the soales of their feete, and vpon their legges, to the bignesse of Walnuts, that they could not recouer their former estate (which was not very well) in a fortnight after.

The sixe and twentieth, three more desire that they also might goe out to try their fortunes, but they returned worse disabled, and euen almost stifled with the cold.

This Euening, the *Moone* rose in a very long Ovale alongst the Horizon.

By the last of this moneth, the Carpenter had set vp 17 ground timbers, and 34 Staddles,[2] and (poore man) hee proceedeth the best he can, though he be faine to be led vnto his labour.

In briefe, all this moneth had beene very cold; the wind about the N.W.; the snow as deepe as it hath beene all this winter; but, to answer an obiection that may be made:

---

[1] St. Dauid, the patron saint of Wales and Archbishop of Caerleon, died about the year 544. Captain James doubtless kept the day as a west-country festival. Probably, too, there were Welshmen among his crew.

[2] These were part of the pinnace they were building for the return voyage, in the event of their being unable again to raise the ship. No doubt *staddles* here means the upright timbers (see p. 347).

You were in a wood (may some men say vnto vs), and therefore you might make fire enough to keepe you from the cold. It is true, we were in a wood, and vnder a South banke too, or otherwise we had all starued.[1] But I must tell you withall how difficult it was to haue wood in a wood; and, first, I will make a muster of the tooles we had. The Carpenter, in his Chest, had 2 Axes indeed; but one of them was spoyl'd in cutting downe wood to pile about our house before Christmas. When we came first a land, we had but two whole hatchets, which in a few dayes broke 2 inches below the Sockets. I cald for 3 of the Cooper's hatchets; the Carpenters axe and the Coopers best hatchet, I caused to be lockt vp; the other 2 hatchets to be new helu'd; and the blades of the 2 broken hatchets to be put into a cleft piece of wood, and then to be bound about with rope yarne, as fast as might be, which must be repaired euery day. And these were all the cutting tooles we had; moreouer, the 6 of *February*, the Carpenter had out his best axe about something, and one of the company, in his absence, by his vndiscreete handling of it, brake that too, two inches below the Socket; we must henceforth order these pieces of tooles the best we could; wherefore I gaue order that the Carpenter should haue one of the Coopers hatchets; they that lookt for timber in the woods, the other; and they that cut downe wood to burne were to haue the 2 pieces. And this was before Christmas.

The three that were appointed to looke crooked timber[2] must stalke and wade (sometimes on all foure) thorow the snow; and, where they saw a tree likely to fit the mould, they must first heaue away the snow, and then see if it would fit the mould; if not, they must seeke further. If it

---

[1] The expression, *starved with cold*, which James often uses, still survives; but starving is now more usually associated with hunger.

[2] Of course, for use in the pinnace.

did fit the mould, then they must make a fire to it, to thawe it: otherwise it could not be cut. Then [they must] cut it downe, and fit it to the length of the mould, and then, with other helpe, get it home a mile thorow the snow.

Now, for our firing, we could not burne greene wood; it would so smoke that it was not indurable; yea, the men had rather starue without in the cold then sit by it. As for the dry wood, that also was bad enough in that kinde; for it was full of Turpentine, and would send forth such a thicke smoke that would make abundance of soote, which made vs all looke as if we had beene free of the Company of Chimney-Sweepers. Our cloathes were quite burnt in pieces about vs; and, for the most part, we were all without shooes; but to our Fuellers againe. They must first (as the former) goe vp and downe in the snow till they saw a standing dry tree, for that the snow couered any that were fallen. Then they must hacke it downe with their pieces of hatchets, and then others must carry it home thorow the snow. The boyes with Cuttleasses must cut boughes for the Carpenter; for euery piece of timber that he did worke must first be thaw'd in the fire, and he must haue a fire by him, or he could not worke. And this was our continuall labour throughout the forementioned cold, besides our tending of the sicke, and other necessary imployments.

Aprill, 1632.

The first of this moneth, being Easter-day, we solemnised as religiously as God did giue vs grace. Both this day and the 2 following Holy-dayes were extreme cold; and now, sitting all about the fire, we reasoned and considered together vpon our estate. We had 5 men (whereof the Carpenter was one) not able to doe any thing. The Boateswayne, and many more, were very infirme; and, of all the rest, we had but 5 that could eate of their ordinary allowance. The time and season of the yeere came forwards apace, and the cold did very little mitigate. Our Pinnace was in an indifferent forwardnesse, but the Carpenter grew worse and worse. The Ship (as we then thought) lay all full of solid Ice, which was weight enough to open the seames of any new and sound vessel, especially of one that had layne so long vpon the ground as she had done. In briefe, after many disputations, and laying open of our miserable and hopeless estates, I resolued vpon this course: that, notwithstanding it was more labour, and though we declined weaker still and weaker, yet that, with the first warm weather, we would begin to cleere the Ship; that so we might haue the time before vs to thinke of some other course. This being ordered, we lookt to those tooles we had to digge the Ice out of her; we had but 2 Iron barres ashoare, the rest were sunke in the Ship, and one of them was broken too. Well, we fell to fitting of those barres, and of 4 broken shouels that we had, with which we intended (as after we did) to digge the Ice out of her, and to lay that Ice on a heape vpon the Lar-boord bowe, and to sinke downe that Ice to the ground so fast that it should be a Barricadoe to vs when the Ice brake vp, which we feared would teare vs all to pieces.

The 6 was the deepest snow we had all this yeere, which fild vp all our pathes and wayes by which we were vsed to goe vnto the wood. This snow was something moyster and greater than any we had had all this yeere, for formerly it was as dry as dust, and as small as sand, and would driue like dust with the winde.

The weather continued with this extremitie vntill the 15, at which time our spring was harder frozen then it had beene all the yeere before. I had often obserued the difference betwixt cleere weather and mistie *Refractious* weather, in this manner, from a little hill which was neere adioyning to our house. In the clearest weather, when the

Sunne shone with all the purietie of ayre that I could conceiue, we could not see a little Iland, which bare off vs South South-east, some foure leagues off; but, if the weather were mistie (as aforesaid), then we should often see it from the lowest place. This little Iland I had seene the last yeere, when I was on *Danby Iland*. The 13, I tooke the height of it *instrumentally*, standing neere the Sea side, which I found to be 34 minutes, the Sunne being 28 degrees high. This showes how great a *Refraction* here is. Yet may this be noted by the way: that I haue seene the land eleuated by reason of the refractious ayre, and neuerthelesse the Sunne hath risen perfect round.

The sixteenth was the most comfortable Sun-shine day that came this yeere, and I put some to cleere off the snow from the vpper decks of the Ship, and to cleere and dry the great Cabbin, by making fire in it. Others I put to digge downe thorow the Ice to come by our Anker that was in shoald water, which, the 17 in the afternoone, we got vp and carried aboord.

The eighteenth, I put them to digge downe thorow the Ice, neere the place where we thought our Rudder might be. They digged downe and came to water, but no hope of finding of it; we had many doubts that it might be sanded,[1] or that the Ice might haue carried it away already the last yeere; or, if we could not recouer it by digging before the Ice brake up and droue, there was little hope of it.

The nineteenth, wee continued our myning worke aboord the Shippe, and returned in the Euening to Supper ashoare. This Day, the Master and two others desired that they might lye aboord, which I condiscended to; for indeed they had laine very discommodiously all the winter, and with sicke bed-fellowes, as I myselfe had done, euery one in that kinde taking their fortunes. By lying aboord, they

---

[1] Probably he means *imbedded in the sand*.

auoyded the hearing of the miserable groanings, and lamenting of the sicke men all night long, enduring (poore soules) intolerable torments.

By the one and twentieth, we had laboured so hard that we came to see a Caske, and could likewise perceiue that there was some water in the Hold. This we knew could not be thawed water, because it did still freeze night and day very hard aboord the Ship, and on the land also.

By the three and twentieth, in the Euening, wee came to pierce the forementioned Caske, and found it was full of very good Beere, which did much reioyce vs all, especially the sicke men, notwithstanding that it did taste a little of bulge-water. By this we at the time thought that the holes we had cut to sinke the Ship were frozen, and that this water had stood in the Ship all the Winter.

The foure and twentieth, we went betimes in the morning to worke, but found that the water was risen aboue the Ice where we had left work aboute two foot, for that the wind had blowne very hard at North the night before. In the morning, the wind came about South and blew hard; and, although we had little reason for it, we yet expected a lower veere of the water. I, therevpon, put them to worke on the outside of the Ship, that we might come to the lower hole which we had cut in the Sterne-Shootes. With much labour, by night, we digged downe thorow the Ice to it, and found it vnfrozen (as it had bin all the Winter); and, to our great comforts, we found that on the inside the water was ebd euen with the hole, and that on the outside it was ebd a foot lower. Hereupon, I made a shot-boord[1] to be naild on it, and to be made as tight as might be, to try if the water came in any other way. To the other two holes, we had digged on the inside and found them frozen. Now, I

---

[1] Probably he means such a board as might be nailed over a shothole, made in a ship's side, as a "shot-plug" might be used to plug it.

did this betimes that, if we found the Ship foundered, we might resolue of some course to saue or prolong our liues, by getting to the maine before the Ice were broken vp; for, as for our Boate, it was too little, and bulged besides that. Our Carpenter was by this time past hope, and therefore little hope had we of our Pinnasse. But, which was worst of all, we had not foure men able to trauell through the Snow ouer the Ice; and in this miserable estate were we at this present.

The 25, we satisfied our longing; for, the winde now comming about Northerly, the water rose by the Ships side (where we had digged downe) a foot and more aboue the Hold,[1] and yet did not rise within boord. This did so incourage vs that we fell very lustily to digging, and to heaue out the Ice out of the Ship. I put the Cooke and some others to thaw the pumps, who, by continuall powring of hot water into them, by the 27, in the morning, they had cleered one of them, which we say-ing,[2] found that it did deliuer water very sufficiently. Thus we fell to pumping, and, hauing cleered two foot water, we then left to haue a second tryall. Continuing our worke thus, in digging the Ice, by the 28, we had cleered our other pumpe, which we also found to deliuer water very well. We found, likewise, that the water did not rise anything in Hold.

The 29, it rained all day long, a sure signe to vs that winter was broken vp.

The 30, wee were betimes aboord at our worke, which day, and the one and thirtieth, were very cold, with snow and haile, which did pinch our sicke men more then any time this yeere. This euening, being *May* Euen, we returned late from our worke to our house, and made a good

---

[1] Apparently a misprint for *hole*, meaning the one he had bored in his ship's bottom (see p. 519).
[2] See p. 462.

fire, and chose Ladies, and did ceremoniously weare their names in our Caps, endeauouring to reuiue ourselues by any meanes. And, because you heare vs in this merry humour, I will make knowne to you what good cheere we kept at Christmas and Easter, and how we had dieted ourselues all the winter.

At our comming foorth of *England*, we were stored with all sort of Sea prouisions, as Beefe, Porke, Fish, etc.; but, now that we had little hope of refreshing, our Cooke did order it in this manner —

The Beefe which was to serue on Sunday-night to Supper, he did boyle on Saterday-night in a Kettle full of water, with a quart of Oatemeale, about an houre. Then, taking the Beefe out, he boyled the rest till it came to halfe the quantitie And this we called porridge, which, with bread, we did eate as hot as we could, and, after this, we had our ordinary of fish. Sunday dinner, wee had Porke and Pease, and at night the former boyled Beefe made more porridge. In this manner, our Tuesdayes Beefe was boyled on the Munday nights, and the Thursdayes vpon the Wednesdayes; and thus all the weeke (except Friday night) we had some warme thing in our bellies euery supper. And (surely) this did vs a great deale of good. But, soone after Christmas, many of vs fell sicke, and had sore mouthes, and could neither eate Beefe, Porke, Fish, nor Porridge. Their dyet was onely this: they would pound Bread or Oatmeale in a mortar to meale, then fry it in a frying panne with a little oyle, and so eate it. Some would boyle Pease to a soft paste, and feed as well as they could vpon that. For the most part of the winter, water was our drinke. In the whole winter, we tooke not aboue a doozen Foxes, many of which would be dead in the traps two or three dayes, oftentimes, and then when the blood was settled they would be vnwholesome. But, if we tooke one aliue that had not bin long in the trap, him we boyled, and made broth for the weakest sicke men, of him; the flesh of it, being soft boyled, they did eate also.

Some white partridges we kild,[1] but not worth the mentioning towards any refreshing.

We had three sorts of sicke men: those that could not moue, nor turne themselues in their Beds, who must be tended like an Infant; others that were, as it were, creepled with scuruy Aches; and others, lastly, that were something better. Most of all had sore mouthes. You may now aske me how these infirme men could worke? I will tell you: Our Surgeon (which was diligent, and a sweet-conditioned man as euer I saw) would be vp betimes in the mornings, and, whilest he did picke their Teeth, and cut away the dead flesh from their Gummes, they would bathe their owne thighes, knees, and legges. The manner whereof was this: there was no tree, bud, nor herbe but we made tryall of it; and this, being first boyled in a Kettle, and then put in a small Tubs and Basons, they put it vnder them, and, couering themselues with Cloathes vpon it, this would so mollifie the grieued parts that, although, when they did rise out of their Beds, they would be so crippled that they could scarce stand, yet after this done halfe an houre, they would be able to goe (and must goe) to wood thorow the Snow, to the Ship, and about their other businesse. By night, they would be as bad againe, and then they must bee bathed, anoynted, and their mouthes againe drest, before they went to Bed. And with this dyet, and in this manner, did we goe thorow our miseries.

I euer doubted that we should be weakest in the Spring, and therefore had I reserued a Tun of Alegant Wine vnto this time. Of this, by putting seuen parts of water to one

---

[1] This was the Willow Ptarmigan (*Lagopus lagopus*), of which both Hudson and Button killed such large numbers during their wintering in the Bay (see pp. 134 and 167).

of wine, we made some weake Beuerage, which (by reason that the wine, by being frozen, had lost his Vertue) was little better then water. The sicker sort had a Pint of Alegant a day by it selfe, and of such poore Aqua vitæ too, as we had, they had a little dramme allowed them next their hearts euery morning; and thus wee made the best vse of what we had, according to the seasons.

May, 1632.

The first, we went aboord betimes to heaue out the Ice.

The second, it did snow and blow, and was so cold that we were faine to keepe house all day. This vnexpected cold at this time of the yeere did so vexe our sicke men that they grew worse and worse. We cannot now take them out of their beds but they would swound,[1] and we had much adoe to fetch life in them

The third, those that were able went aboord betimes to heaue out the Ice. The Snow was now melted in many places vpon the Land, and stood in plashes.[2] And now there came some Cranes and Geese to it

The fourth, while the rest wrought aboord, I and the Surgeon went, with a couple of pieces, to see if we could kill any of these fowle for our sicke men; but neuer did I see such wild-fowle · they would not indure to see anything mooue. Wherefore we returned within 2 houres, not being able to indure any longer stalking thorow the snow and the wet plashes. I verily thought that my feet and legs would haue fallen off, they did so torment me with aking.

The 6, *Iohn Wardon*, the Master of my Ship's chiefe Mate, dyed, whom we buried in the Euening (in the most

---

[1] *Swoon.* Halliwell says "swound" is still in common use in East Anglia.

[2] See p. 315.

Christian-like manner we could) vpon the top of a bare hill of sand, which we cald *Brandon Hill*[1]

The weather continued very cold, freezing so hard in a night that it would beare a man.

By the 9, we were come to, and got vp, our fiue barrels of Beefe and Porke, and had found 4 Buts of Beere, and one of Cydar, which God had preserued for vs. It had layne vnder water all the winter, yet we could not perceiue that it was any thing the worse. God make vs euer thankefull for the comfort it gaue vs.

The 10, it did snow and blow so cold that we could not stirre out of the house. Yet, neuerthelesse, by day the snow vanisheth away apace on the land

The 11, we were aboord betimes, to heaue out Ice. By the 12, at night, we had cleered out all the Ice out of the Hold, and found likewise our store-shooes which had layne soakt in the water all the winter; but we dried them by the fire, and fitted our selues with them. We strooke againe our Cables into the Hold; there stowed we a But of Wine also, which had beene all the Winter on the vpper decke, and continued as yet all firme and frozen. We fitted the Ship also, making her ready to sinke her againe when the Ice brake vp We could hitherto find no defect in her, and therefore well hoped that she was stanche. The Carpenter, neuerthelesse, did earnestly argue to the contrary, alleadging that now she lay on the ground in her Docke, and that the Ice had fild her defects, and that the Ice was the thing that kept out the water; but when she should come to labour in the sea, then doubtlesse she would open. And, indeed, we could now see quite through her seames betwixt wind and water. But that which did

---

[1] Brandon Hill is a conical elevation forming a portion of Bristol. It was formerly fortified. From its summit may be obtained a very fine view of the city and surrounding country.

trouble vs as ill as all this was the losse of her Rudder, and that she now lay in the very strength of the Tyde, which, when euer the Ice droue, might teare her to pieces. But we still hoped the best.

The 13, being the Sabbath Day, we solemnized, giuing God thankes for those hopes and comforts we dayly had The weather by day-time was pretty and warme, but it did freeze by night; yet now we could see some bare patches of land.

The 14, we began a new sort of worke. The Boateswaine and a conuenient number sought ashoare the rest of our Rigging, which was much spoyled by pecking of it out of the Ice, and this they now fell to fitting and to seruing of it I set the Cooper to fit our Caske, although (poore man) he was very infirme, my intent being to passe some Cables vnder the Ship, and so to Buoy her vp with these Caskes, if otherwise we could not get her off. Some others I ordered to goe see if they could kill some wild-fowle for our sicke men, who now grew worse and worse. And this is to be remembred: that we had no shot but what we did make of the Aprons of our Gunnes[1] and some old pewter that I had; for the Carpenter's sheet-lead, we durst not vse.

The 15, I manured a little patch of ground that was bare of snow, and sowed it with Peason,[2] hoping to haue some of the hearbs of them shortly to eat; for, as yet, we can finde no greene thing to comfort vs.

The 18, our Carpenter, *William Cole*, dyed, a man generally bemoaned of vs all, as much for his innate goodnesse as for the present necessity we had of a man of his quality. He had indured a long sicknesse with much

---

[1] The apron of a gun is a small piece of sheet-lead laid over the touch-hole to exclude damp.

[2] An old collective name for *peas*, or pulse in general (see Nares's *Glossary*).

patience, and made a very godly end. In the Euening, we buried him by Master *Wardon*, accompanied with as many as could goe, for 3 more of our principall men lay then expecting a good houre. And now were we in the most miserable estate that we were in all the voyage. Before his extreme weaknesse, he had brought the Pinnace to that passe that she was ready to be boulted and trenneld,[1] and to be ioyn'd together to receiue the planke, so that we were not so discouraged by his death but that we did hope of our selues to finish her, if the Ship proved unseruiceable.

This our Pinnace was 27 foot by the Keele, 10 foot by the Beame, and 5 foot in Hold. She had 17 ground timbers, 34 principall Staddles, and 8 short Staddles.[2] He had contriued her with a round sterne to saue labour; and, indeed, she was a well-proportioned Vessell. Her burthen was 12 or 14 Tunne.

In the Euening, the Master of our Ship, after buriall, returning aboord Ship and looking about her, discouerd some part of our Gunner vnder the Gun-roome ports. This man we had committed to the Sea, at a good distance from the Ship, and in deep water, neere 6 moneths before.

The 19, in the morning, I sent men to dig him out. He was fast in the Ice, his head downewards and his heele vpward (for he had but one legge), and the plaster was yet at his wound. In the afternoone, they had digd him cleere out; after all which time, he was as free from noysomenesse as when we first committed him to the Sea. This alteration had the Ice and water and time onely wrought on him: that his flesh would slip vp and downe vpon his bones like a gloue on a man's hand. In the Euening, we

---

[1] *Trennels*, or *tree-nails*, are stout cylindrical pins of hard wood driven through the planks and timbers of a vessel to fasten he together.

[2] See p. 347.

buried him by the others. This day, one *George Vgganes* (who could handle a toole best of vs all) had indifferent well repaired our boate; and so we ended this mournefull weeke. The snow was by this time pretty well wasted in the woods, and we hauing a high tree, on the highest place of the Iland, which we called our watch-tree, from the top of it we might see into the sea, but found no appearance of breaking vp yet.

This 20, being Whit-Sunday, we sadly solemnized, and had some taste of the wilde-fowle, but not worth the writing.

The one and twentieth was the warmest Sunne-shine-day that came this yeere. I sent 2 a fowling, and my selfe taking the Master, the Surgeon, and one more, with our pieces and our Dogs, we went into the woods to see what comfort we could finde Wee wandred from the house eight miles, and searcht with all diligence, but returned comfortlesse, not an herbe nor leafe eatable that we could finde. Our Fowlers had as bad success. In the woods, wee found the Snow partly wasted away, so that it was passable. The ponds were almost vnthawd, but the Sea from any place we could see all firme frozen.

The snow doth not melt away here with the Sunne or raine, and so make any land-floods, as in *England;* but it is exhaled vp by the Sunne, and suckt full of holes, like honeycombs, so that the land whereon it lyes will not be at all wetted. The like obseruation wee also had: that, let it raine euer so much, you shall see no land-floods after it.

The two and twentieth, we went aboord the Ship, and found that she had made so much water that it was now risen aboue the ballast, which made vs doubt againe of her soundnesse. We fell to pumping, and pumpt her quite dry. And now by day sometimes we haue such hot gloomes[1] that we cannot indure in the Sunne, and yet, in the night, it would freeze very hard. This vnnaturalnesse of the season did torment our men, that they now grow worse and worse daily.

The three and twentieth, our Boat-swayne (a painefull man) hauing beene long sicke, which he had heartily resisted, was taken with such a painefull ache in one of his thighs, that we verily thought he would haue presently dyed. He kept his bed all day in great extremitie; and it was a maxim amongst vs that, if any one kept his bed two dayes, he could rise no more. This made euery man to striue to keepe vp, for life.

The foure and twentieth was very warme Sun-shine, and the Ice did consume by the shore's side, and crackt all ouer the Bay with a fearefull noyse. About three in the afternoone, we could perceiue the Ice, with the ebbe, to driue by the Ship. Whereupon I sent two with all speed vnto the Master with order to beate out the hole, and to sinke the Ship, as likewise to looke for the Rudder betwixt the Ice. This he presently performed, and a happy fellow, one *David Hammon*, pecking betwixt the Ice, strooke vpon it, and it came vp with his lance, who, crying that he had found it, the rest came and got it vp on the Ice, and so into the Ship. In the meane space, with the little drift that the Ice had, it began to rise and mount into high heaps against the shoald shores and rocks, and likewise against the heape of Ice which we had put for a Barricado to our Ship, but with little harme to vs. Yet we were faine to cut away 20 faddome of Cable which was frozen in the Ice. After an houre, the Ice settled againe, as not hauing any vent outwards. Oh! this was a

---

[1] *Glum*, as applied to weather, means overcast or sullen; but, from the context, one may assume "gloomes", as here used, to be a form of *gleams* or *glows*.

ioyfull day to vs all, and we gaue God thanks for the hopes we had of it.

The fiue and twentieth was a fine warme day, and, with the ebbe, the Ice did driue against the Ship, and shake her shrowdly [1]

The sixe and twentieth, I tooke the Chirurgion with mee, and went againe to wander the woods, and went to that Bay where last yeere wee had lost our man *Iohn Barton*. But we could see no signe of him, nor of other reliefe.

By the eight and twentieth, it was pretty and cleere betwixt the Ship and the shoare, and I hoped the Ice would no more dangerously oppresse vs Wherefore I caused the lower hole to be firmely stopt, the water then remaining three foot aboue the Ballast.

The nine and twentieth, being *Prince Charles his birthday*, we kept Holy-day, and display'd his Maiesties colours, both aland and aboord, and named our habitation *Charles Towne*, by contraction *Charlton;* and the Iland, *Charlton Iland*.

The thirtieth, we lanched our Boate, and had intercourse sometimes betwixt the Ship and the shoare by Boat, which was newes[2] to vs.

The last of this moneth, wee found, on the Beach, some Vetches[3] to appeare out of the ground, which I made the men to pick vp and to boyle for our sicke men.

This day, we made an end of fitting all our Rigging and Sayles; and, it being a very hot day, we did dry and new

---

[1] Perhaps *shrewdly*, meaning maliciously (see Skeat's *Etymological Dictionary*).

[2] *News* (formerly spelled *newes*), now meaning new tidings, is merely the plural of *new*, treated as a substantive. James means it was a fresh or novel means of communication.

[3] Probably either *Astragalus alpinus* or *Lathyrus maritimus*, both of which Mr. J. M. Macoun found on Charlton or the adjoining islands in the summers of 1885-87.

make our Fish in the Sunne, and ayred all our other prouisions. There was not a man of vs at present able to eate of our salt prouisions, but my selfe and the Master of my Ship. It may be here remembred that, all this Winter, wee had not beene troubled with any rhumes nor flegmaticall diseases. All this moneth, the winde hath beene variable, but for the most part Northerly.

Iune, 1632.

The foure first dayes, it did snow, haile, and blow very hard, and was so cold that the Ponds of water did freeze ouer, and the water in our Cans did freeze in the very house; our clothes also, that had beene washed and hung out to dry, did not thaw all day.

The fift, it continued blowing very hard in the broad side of the Ship, which did make her swag and wallow[1] in her Docke, for all shee was sunken, which did much shake her. The Ice withall did driue against her, and gaue her many fearfull blowes. I resolued to endeauour to hang the Rudder, and, when God sent vs water (notwithstanding the abundance of Ice that was yet about vs), to haue her further off. In the afternoone, we vnder-run our small Cable to our Anker, which lay a-Sterne in deepe water; and so, with some difficultie, gate[2] vp our Anker. This Cable had laine slacke vnder-foot, and vnder the Ice, all the Winter, and wee could neuer haue a cleere flatch[3] from Ice, to haue it vp, before now. We found it not a iot the worse. I put some to make Colrakes,[4] that they might goe into the water, and rake a hole in the sands to let downe our Rudder.

---

[1] *Swag* (now obsolete) = to hang loose, to swing about: whence *swagger*. *Wallow* has much the same meaning.

[2] *Got*. See p. 373.

[3] Possibly a misprint for *platch* = a clear space (now obsolete). Ash's *Dictionary* (1775) gives *flack:* a body of water driven by violence.

[4] These were undoubtedly *rakes* of some kind.

The sixth, we went about to hang it; and our young lustiest men tooke turnes to goe into the water, and to rake away the sand; but they were not able to indure the cold of it halfe a quarter of an houre, it was so mortifying; yea, vse what comforts we could, it would make them swound and dye away. We brought it to the Sternepost, but were then faine to giue it ouer, being able to worke at it no longer. Then we plugg'd vp the vpper holes within boord, and fell to pumping the water againe out of her.

The seuenth, we wrought something about our Rudder, but were againe forced to giue ouer, and to put out our Cables ouer-boord, with *Messengers* vnto them, the Ankers lying to that passe that we might keepe her right in her docke, when we should haue brought her light.

By the eighth, at night, we had pumpt all the water out of her, and shee, at a high water, would fleet in her docke, though she were still dockt in the sands almost foure foot. This made vs to consider what was to be done. I resolued to heaue out all the Ballast, for that the bottome of her, being so soakt all the winter, I hoped was so heauy that it would beare her. If we could not get her off that way, I then thought to cut her downe to the lower decke, and take out her Masts, and so, with our Caske, to Buoy her off.

The ninth, betimes in the morning, wee fell to worke. We hoyst out our Beere and Cydar, and made a raft of it, fastning it to our shoare-Anker. The Beere and Cydar sunke presently to the ground, which was nothing strange to vs, for that any wood or pipe-staues[1] that had layne vnder the Ice all the winter would also sinke downe so soone as euer it was heaued ouer-boord. This day, we heaued out tenne tunne of Ballast. And here I am to remember God's goodnesse towards vs, in sending those

---

[1] See p. 343.

forementioned greene Vetches. For now our feeble sicke men, that could not for their liues stirre these two or three months, can indure the ayre and walke about the house; our other sicke men gather strength also, and it is wonderfull to see how soone they were recouered. We vsed them in this manner: Twice a day we went to gather the herbe or leafe of these Vetches, as they first appeared out of the ground; then did we wash and boyle them, and so, with Oyle and Vineger that had been frozen, we did eate them. It was an excellent sustenance and refreshing; the most part of vs ate nothing else. We would likewise bruise them, and take the Iuyce of them, and mixe that with our drinke. We would eate them raw also with our bread.

The eleuenth was very warme weather, and we did hang our Rudder. The tydes did now very much deceiue vs, for a Northerly wind would very little raise the water. This made vs doubt of getting off our Ship.

The thirteenth, I resolued of the Latitude of this place; so that, hauing examined the Instruments, and practised about it this Fortnight, I now found it to be in 52 degrees and 3 minutes.[1]

The foureteenth, wee had heaued out all the Ballast, and carried all our Yards and euery thing else of weight a-shoare, so that we now had the Ship as light as possible it could be.

The fifteenth, we did little but exercise our selues, seeing that by this time our men that were most feeble are now growne strong, and can runne about. The flesh of their gummes became settled againe, and their teeth fastned, so that they can eat Beefe with their Vetches.

This day I went to our *Watch-tree;* but the Sea (for any thing I could perceiue to the contrary) was still firme

---

[1] See p. 532.

frozen, and the Bay we were in all full of Ice, hauing no way to vent it.

The sixteenth was wondrous hot, with some thunder and lightning, so that our men did goe into the ponds ashoare, to swimme and coole themselues; yet was the water very cold still. Here had lately appeared diuers sorts of flyes, as Butterflyes, Butchers-flyes, Horse-flyes, and such an infinit abundance of bloud-thirsty Muskitoes, that we were more tormented with them then euer we were with the cold weather.[1] These (I thinke) lye dead in the old rotten wood all the winter, and in summer they reuiue againe. Here be likewise infinite company of *Ants*, and Frogs in the ponds vpon the land; but we durst not eate of them, they lookt so speckled, like Toads. By this time, were there neither Beares, Foxes, nor Fowle to be seene: they are all gone.

The seuenteenth, the wind came Northerly, and wee, expecting a high Tyde, in the morning betimes, put out our small Cable asterne out at the Gun-roome-port; but the morning Tyde we had not water by a foot. In the Euening, I had laid markes, by stones, &c., and mee thoughts the water did flow apace. Making signes, therefore, for the Boate to come ashoare, I tooke all that were able to doe any thing with me aboord; and, at high water (although she wanted something to rise cleere out of her docke), yet we heau'd with such a good will that we heaued her thorow the sand into a foot and a halfe deeper water. Further then so, we durst not yet bring her, for that the Ice was all thicke about vs. After we had moor'd her, we went all to prayers, and gaue God thankes that had giuen vs our ship againe.

---

[1] Bad as are the torments of mosquitoes, James must surely have been exaggerating when he describes them as worse than the cold, though he afterwards (p 563) repeats the statement.

The 18th, we were vp betimes: the Cooper, and some with him, to fill fresh water: my selfe, with some others, to gather stones, at low-water; which we, pyling vp in a heape, at high water, the Cock-swaine and his Ging[1] fetcht them aboord, where the Master with the rest stood[2] them. The Ship, at low water, had a great lust[3] to the offing, by which meanes we could the better come and stop the two vpper holes firmely; after which, we fitted other conuenient places, to make others to sinke her, if occasion were.

The nineteenth, we were all vp betimes to worke, as afore specified These two dayes, our Ship did not fleet; and it was a happy houre when we got her off, for that we neuer had such a high Tide all the time we were here. In the Euening, I went vp to our *Watch tree;* and this was the first time I could see any open water any way, except that little by the shoare-side where we were. This put vs in some comfort that the Sea would shortly breake vp, which wee knew must bee to the Northward, seeing that way we were certaine there was aboue two hundered leagues of Sea.

The 20, we laboured as aforesaid; the winde at N.N.W. The tyde rose so high that our Ship fleeted, and we drew her further off, into a foote and a halfe deepe[4] water. Thus we did it by little and little, for that the Ice was still wonderfull thicke about vs.

The 22, there droue much Ice about vs and within vs, and brought home our Sterne-Anker. At high water (notwithstanding all the Ice), we heau'd our Ship further off, that so she might lie aflote at low-water.

---

[1] *Gang;* see p. 525.

[2] Probably *stowed* is meant, as *stood* is in several places printed *stowed* (see p. 477).

[3] Smythe (*Sailors' Word-Book*) gives "*Lust* = an archaism of *list*", meaning to incline to one side. [4] Query, *deeper*.

The next low-water, we sounded all about the Ship, and found it very foule ground; we discouered stones 3 foote high aboue the ground, and 2 of them within a Ships breadth of the Ship: whereby did more manifestly appeare Gods mercies to vs; for if, when we forced her ashoare, she had strooken one blow against those stones, it had bulged her. Many such dangers were there in this Bay, which we now first perceiued by the Ices grounding and rising against them. In the Euening, we tow'd off the Ship vnto the place she rid the last yeere, and there moord her, shering the Ship, night and day, flood and ebbe, amongst the disperst Ice that came athwart of vs.

The 23, we laboured in fetching our prouisions aboord; which to doe we were faine to wade, to carry it to the boate, a full flight-shot,[1] and all by reason the winde was Southerly. This morning, I tooke an *Obseruation* of the *Moones* comming to the South, by a *Meridian line* of 120 yards long, which I had rectified many weeks beforehand.[2]

The 24, I tooke another *Obseruation* of the *Moones* comming to the *Meridian*, for which I referre you to the obseruations in the latter end of this Iournall.[3]

Whereas I had formerly cut downe a very high tree, and made a Crosse of it, to it I now fastned (vppermost) the Kings and Queenes Maiesties Pictures, drawne to the life, and doubly wrapt in lead, and so close that no weather could hurt them. Betwixt both these, I affixed his Maiesties Royall Title, Viz., *Charles the First, King of England, Scotland, France, and Ireland, as also of New-found-land, and of these Territories, and to the Westward,*

---

[1] See p. 207.   [2] See p. 606.
[3] See the details of all James's observations, given at the end of his book (p. 617).

as farre as Nova Albion, and to the Northward to the Latitude of 80 degrees, &c.

On the out-side of the lead, I fastened a shilling and a sixepence of his Maiesties Coyne; vnder that, we fastened the *Kings Armes*, fairely cut in lead; and, vnder that, the *Armes* of the City of *Bristoll*. And, this being *Midsummer-Day*, we raised it on the top of the bare Hill where we had buried our dead fellowes[1]; formally, by this ceremony, taking possession of these Territories to his Maiesties vse.

The winde, continuing Southerly and blowing hard, put all the Ice vpon vs, so that the Ship now rid amongst it in such apparent danger that I thought verily we should haue lost her. We laboured, flood and ebbe, both with poles and oares, to heaue away and part the Ice from her. But it was God that did protect and preserue vs; for it was past any mans vnderstanding how the Ship could indure it, or we by our labour saue her. In the night, the winde shifted to the Westward, and blew the Ice from vs, whereby we had some rest.

The 25, in the morning, the Boate-swayne, with a conuenient crue with him, began to rigge the Ship, the rest fetching our prouisions aboord. About 10 a clocke, when it was something darke, I tooke a Lance in my hand, and one with me with a Musket and some fire, and went to our watch-tree, to make a fire on the eminentest place of the Iland, to see if it would be answered. Such fires I had formerly made, to haue knowledge if there were any Saluages on the maine or the Ilands about vs. Had there beene any, my purpose was to haue gone to them, to get some intelligence of some *Christians* or some Ocean Sea thereabouts. When I was come to the tree, I laid downe my Lance, and so did my Consort his Musket; and, whilest

---

[1] Brandon Hill; see p. 547.

my selfe climed vp to the top of the tree, I ordered him to put fire vnto some low tree therabouts. He (vnadvisedly) put fire to some trees that were to windward, so that they (and all the rest, too, by reason it had beene very hot weather), being seare and dry, tooke fire like flaxe or hempe; and, the wind blowing the fire towards me, I made haste downe the tree. But, before I was halfe way down, the fire tooke in the bottome of it, and blazed so fiercely vpwards that I was faine to leape off the tree and downe a steepe hill; and, in briefe, with much adoe, escapt burning. The mosse on the ground was as dry as flaxe; and it would runne most strangely, and like a traine, along the earth. The Musket and the Lance were both burnt. My Consort, at last, came to me, and was ioyfull to see me, for he thought verily I had bin burned. And thus we went homeward together, leauing the fire increasing, and still burning most furiously. We could see no answer of it. I slept but little all night after; and, at breake of day, I made all our Powder and Beefe to be carried aboord. This day, I went to the hils, to looke to the fire, where I saw how it did still burne most furiously, both to the Westward and Northward. Leauing one vpon the hils to watch it, I came home immediately, and made them take downe our new suite of sayles and carry them to the seaside, ready to be cast in if occasion were, and to make haste to take downe our houses. About noone, the winde shifted Northerly, and our Sentinell came running home, bringing vs word that the fire did follow him at hard heeles,[1] like a traine of powder. It was no neede to bid vs take downe and carry all away to the sea-side. The fire came towards vs with a most terrible rattling noyse, bearing a full mile in breadth; and, by that time wee had vncouered our houses, and laid hand on to carry away our

---

[1] Halliwell gives "at hard heels", meaning close to his heels.

last things, the fire was come to our Towne[1] and seazed on it, and (in a trice) burnt it downe to the ground. We lost nothing of any value in it, for we had brought it all away into a place of security. Our dogges, in this combustion, would sit downe on their tayles and howle, and then runne into the Sea, on the shoalds, and there stay. The winde shifted Easterly, and the fire ranged to the Westward, seeking what it might deuoure. This night, we lay all together aboord the Ship, and gaue God thankes that had Shipt vs in her againe.

The twentie seuen, twentie eight, and twentie nine, wee wrought hard in fetching our things aboord, as likewise our water, which we must towe off with the ebbe, and bring it to the Ship with the flood. Moreouer, we must goe about the Easter-point for drift-wood; for our tooles were all so spent that we could cut none. Wherefore, about some three dayes agone, I had caused our Pinnace to be sawed to pieces, and with that we stowed our Caske, intending to burne it at low waters, and such other times as we could not worke in carrying things aboord. I employed the men in fetching stones; and we did build three Tombs ouer our three dead fellowes, filling them vp with sand in a decent and handsome fashion. The least Tombe had two tunnes of stone about it.

The thirtieth, we most earnestly continued our labour, and brought our sayles to yard; and, by eleuen a clocke at night, had made a *priddy*[2] Ship, meaning to haue finished our businesse with the weeke and the moneth, that so we might the better solemnize the Sabbath ashoare to morrow, and so take leaue of our wintering Iland.

---

[1] The "towne" consisted of three houses. Skeat says the original sense of the word was simply an enclosure, and in Lowland Scotch it was often applied to a single farmhouse.

[2] This is perhaps a form of *pretty*. Halliwell gives *pridy* = proud (Cornwall).

The winde hath been variable a great while, and the Bayes are now so cleere of Ice that we cannot see a piece of it, for it was all gone to the Northward. Hoping, therefore, that it giue content to some Readers, I will relate the manner of the breaking of it vp. It is first to be noted that it doth not freeze (naturally) aboue sixe foot · the rest is by accident. Such is that Ice that you may see here, sixe faddome thicke. This we had manifest proofe of, by our digging the Ice out of the Ship, and by digging to our Ankers, before the Ice broke vp.

In *May*, when the heate increaseth, it thawes first on the shoald by the shoare side; which, when it hath done round about, then the courses of the tydes (as well by the ebbe and flood, as by their rising and falling) doe so shake the maine Ice that it cracks and breakes it. Thus, when it hath gotten roome for motion, then runnes one piece of it vpon another, and so bruises and grinds it selfe against the shoalds and rocks that it becomes abbreuiated, insomuch that a Ship may haue well passage thorow it. Besides this, much of it is thrust vpon the shoalds, where it is much consumed by the heate of the Sunne. The season here in this Climate is most vnnaturall; for, in the day time, it will be extreme hot, yea, not indurable in the Sunne, which is by reason that it is a sandy countrey. In the night, againe, it will freeze an inch thicke in the ponds, and in the tubs about and in our house; and all this towards the latter end of *Iune*.

The *Muskitoes*, vppon our comming away, were most intolerable. Wee tore an old Auncient[1] in pieces, and made vs bagges of it to put our heads in; but it was no fortification against them. They would finde wayes and meanes to sting vs, that our faces were swolne hard out in

---

[1] Auncient or ancient is an old name for a ship's flag or colours (Smythe's *Sailors' Word-Book*, p. 40).

pumples, which would so itch and smart that we must needs rubbe and teare them. And these flyes, indeed, were more tormenting to vs then all the cold we had heretofore indured.[1]

Iuly, 1632.

The first of this month, being Sunday, we were vp betimes. And I caused our Ship to be adorned the best we could, our Ancient on the Poope, and the Kings Colours in the maine top. I had prouided a short briefe[2] of all the passages of our voyage to this day. I likewise wrote in what state we were at present, and how I did intend to prosecute the discouery, both to the Westward and to the Southward, about this Iland. This Briefe discourse, I had concluded with a request to any Noble minded Trauaylor that should take it downe, or come to the notice of it, that, if we should perish in the Action, then to make our indeuours knowne to our Soueraigne Lord the King. And thus, with our Armes, Drumme and Colours, Cooke and Kettle,[3] we went ashoare; and, first, we marcht vp to our eminent Crosse, adioyning to which we had buried our dead fellowes. There we read morning prayer, and then walked vp and downe till dinner time. After dinner, we walkt to the highest Hils, to see which way the fire had wafted. We descryed that it had consumed to the Westward sixteene miles at least, and the whole bredth of the Iland. Neere about our Crosse and dead, it could not come, by reason it was a bare sandy Hill. After Euening prayer,

---

[1] See p 556, *note*

[2] Originally any short abstract, statement, or epitome. The word is still used in this sense among lawyers.

[3] Clearly the crew intended to dine on shore, and this may have been their reason for taking "cooke and kettle"; but, from the context, it seems possible that some punning reference is intended to the man who carried the kettle-drum.

I happened to walke alongst the Beach side, where I found an herbe resembling Scuruy-grasse. I made some to be gathered, which we boyld with our meate to supper. It was most excellent good, and farre better then our Vetches. After supper, we went all to seeke and gather more of it, which we did to the quantity of two bushels, which did afterwards much refresh vs. And now the Sunne was set, and the Boat comne[1] ashoare for vs; whereupon we assembled our selues together, and went vp to take the last view of our dead, and to looke vnto their Tombes and other things. Here, leaning vpon mine arme on one of their Tombes, I vttered these lines,[2] which, though perchance they may procure laughter in the wiser sort (which I shall be glad of), they yet moued my young and tenderhearted companions at that time with some compassion. And these they were:

> I Were vnkind vnlesse that I did shead,
>   Before I part, some teares vpon our dead;
> And, when my eyes be dry, I will not cease
> In heart to pray their bones may rest in peace.
> Their better parts (good soules) I know were giuen
> With an intent they should returne to heauen.
> Their liues they spent, to the last drop of bloud,
> Seeking Gods glory and their Countries good
> And, as a valiant Souldier rather dyes
> Then yeelds his courage to his Enemies,
> And stops their way with his hew'd flesh, when death
> Hath quite depriu'd him of his strength and breath,
> So haue they spent themselues; and here they lye,
> A famous marke of our *Discovery*
> We that suruiue perchance may end our dayes
> In some imployment meriting no praise,
> And in a dung hill rot; when no man names
> The memory of vs, but to our shames.

---

[1] See p. 502.

[2] One authority states that Southey quotes these lines, with the remark that they show "a strain of fine and manly feeling" (see Introduction).

THE WINTERING.

> They haue out-liu'd this feare, and their braue ends
> Will euer be an honour to their friends.
> Why drop ye so, mine eyes? Nay, rather powré
> My sad departure in a solemne showre.
> The Winters cold, that lately froze our bloud,
> Now were it so extreme, might doe this good,
> As make these teares bright pearles, which I would lay,
> Tomb'd safely with you, till Doomes fatall day
> That, in this solitary place, where none
> Will euer come to breathe a sigh or grone,
> Some remant might be extant of the true
> And faithfull loue I euer tenderd you
> Oh, rest in peace, deare friends, and let it be
> No pride to say the sometime part of me.
> What paine and anguish doth afflict the head,
> The heart, and stomake, when the limbes are dead
> So, grieu'd, I kisse your graues, and vow to dye
> A Foster-father to your memory.
>   *Farewell*

So, fastning my briefe to the Crosse, which was securely wrapt vp in Lead, we presently tooke Boat and departed, and neuer put foote more on that Iland.[1] This Iland, and all the rest (as likewise the maine), is a light white sand, couered ouer with a white mosse, and full of shrubs and low bushes, excepting some bare hils and other patches. In these bare places, the sand will driue with the wind like dust. It is very full of trees, as Spruse and Iuniper; but the biggest tree I saw was but a foote and a halfe ouer.[2]

---

[1] A copy of this letter which he left at Charlton Island James prints at the end of his narrative (see p. 594), though it is omitted from the second (1740) edition. It is an interesting document, as it supplements the fuller narrative here reprinted, and gives information on several minor points as to which the main text is silent (see p. 495).

[2] Dr. Bell's Map showing the General Northern Limits of the Principal Forest Trees of Canada (*Report of the Geological Survey of Canada for 1879-80*) shows that a number of trees (namely, the balsam fir, canoe birch, aspen, balsam poplar, larch, and the spruces), if they do not actually grow on Charlton Island, at least have their northern limits on the mainland far to the north of it.

At our first comming hither, we saw some Deare, and kild one; but neuer any since. Foxes, all the winter, we saw many, and kild some dozen of them; but they went all away in May Beares we saw but few, but kild none: we saw some other little beasts In May, there came some fowle, as Duckes and Geese, of which we kild very few White Partridges we saw, but in small quantities, nor had we any shot to shoot at them. Fish we could neuer see any in the Sea, nor no bones of fish on the shoare side, excepting a few Cockle-shels, and yet nothing in them neither. Other things remarkeable I haue before mentioned.[1]

---

[1] The latest and best account of Charlton Island is that by Mr A. P. Low, of the Geological Survey of Canada (*Report of Progress for 1887-88*, p. 28 J), who explored James's Bay on behalf of the Survey in 1887. From the following statements made by Mr. Low, it appears that Captain James was singularly fortunate in the precise spot in which circumstances obliged him to winter, for he can scarcely be said to have selected it of his free will. Mr Low says: "At House Point, the water is deep close along the shore, and it was here that Captain James wintered his ship in 1631 Here also, in 1675, the Hudson's Bay Company's ships discharged their cargoes from England, and took in the furs brought from the different forts on the Bay in sloops. In 1695, this depôt was abandoned, and the anchorage has since been used only by the Company's ships when obliged to winter in the Bay, as it is the only moderately-safe place in the southern part of James Bay where a ship may winter and allow the crew to obtain good water and fuel. The last ship wintered here in 1884. The remains of the low huts (partly built in the ground) for the officers and crew, are to be seen about one quarter of a mile south of House Point, on the first plateau inland, near a fine large spring of clear water, which never dries or freezes, and is consequently available throughout the year." This spring is, of course, that James speaks of on p 528

OVR DISCOVERY
and comming Home.
Iuly, 1632.

Vnday, being the second of *Iuly*, we were vp betimes, about Stowing and fitting our Ship, and waying of our Ankers, which, when the last was a-trippe, wee went to prayer, beseeching God to continue his mercies to vs, and rendering him thanks for hauing thus restored vs. Our Ship, we found no defect in; we had abundance of such prouisions as we brought out of *England*; and we were in indifferent health, and did gather strength daily. This being done, we wayed and came cheerefully to sayle, the winde at North-West; bad to get away. Wherefore we stood ouer to *Danby Iland*, to take in more wood, and there to be ready to take the opportunitie of a faire winde. I went ashoare my selfe with the Boate, for that some of the company had told me they had seen some stakes the last yeer, drouen into the ground. When we came ashoare, whilest some gatherd wood, I went to the place, where I found two stakes drouen into the ground about a foote and a halfe, and firebrands where a fire had beene made

by them. I puld vp the stakes, which were about the bignesse of my arme, and they had beene cut sharpe at the ends with a hatchet, or some other good Iron toole, and driuen in, as it were with the head of it. They were distant about a stones-throw from the water-side. I could not conceiue to what purpose they should be there set, vnlesse it were for some marke for boats. This did augment my desire to speake with the Saluages; for, without doubt, they could haue giuen notice of some Christians with whom they had some commerce.[1] About 4 in the

---

[1] James had previously found "firebrands and chips .... cut with some hatchet", but this was Resolution Island, where it was in no way remarkable (see p. 471). Foxe, too, on an island in Sir Thomas Roe's Welcome, had met with flattened iron nails and a copper dart-head, which was an interesting occurrence (see p. 320); but James's discovery, on Danby Island, of stakes as thick as his arm, sharpened to a point by "a hatchet, or some other good iron tool", and apparently driven into the ground by the head of the same, was in every way a more remarkable occurrence. Presumably, it is to these relics that James alluded when, on landing upon Danby Island on October 2nd, 1631, he says (p. 507). "I found that the Salvages had been upon it"; but, from what he himself says, we may infer with fair certainty that these stakes had not been prepared and driven into the ground by savages. Yet there are only two suppositions by which it is possible to account for their being the work of white men. They may have been the relics of overland traders from Canada; but, as I have already pointed out (p. 321, *note*), there is no record of any white men reaching Hudson's Bay from Canada until at least thirty years later; and, even supposing some earlier explorers had accomplished the overland journey, it is difficult to see how they could have reached Danby Island, which lies twenty miles from the mainland The only other probable theory is that the stakes had been placed there by some earlier explorers by sea; but we know that no earlier expedition had been in this part of the Bay, with the exception of Hudson's; and I fail to see that it is by any means impossible that these stakes had been placed there by Hudson and his deserted companions. So far as it is possible to identify the spot wnere Hudson was aoandoned, it probably lay within twenty miles of the spot where these stakes were discovered. Hudson was abandoned on the 21st of June 1611, or twenty-one years previously (within a few

Euening, I returned aboord with a boats lading of wood; and, the winde something fauouring, we wayde, with our lead seeking out a Channell amongst these perilous shoalds. In the Euening, the winde opposing it selfe, we came to Anker betwixt *Charleton Iland* and that *Iland* we named the last yeere (in memory of that Honourable Gentleman Master *Thomas Carie*, one of the Bed-chamber to the King) *Caries Iland*,[1] where we rid all night.

The 3, at breake of day, we wayde with a bare winde; and, sounding vp and downe for a Channell, we were many times in 5 and 4 fad. water. The winde larging vpon vs, we stood away West: by noone, we saw all Ice to the North-ward of vs. Indeauouring, therefore, to compasse about the Wester-point of *Charleton Iland*, and so to seeke to the South-ward, we found it all shoalds, Rockes, and breaches. By 4 in the afternoone, we saw the Western-land, but all full of Ice; whereupon, as the wind fauoured vs, we stood alongst it in sight to the North-ward.

The fourth was calme, but so very thicke fogge withall that we could not see a Pistoll-shot about vs. Wherefore

---

days), and it is not impossible that the stakes might have existed so long Moreover, we know from Prickett's most explicit statement, (see p. 144) that, when Hudson's carpenter was put with the others into the shallop, he had with him his chest of tools. It is in no way remarkable that the idea of these stakes being relics of Hudson and his abandoned companions did not occur to Captain James; for we know that James believed Hudson to have been abandoned in *another bay*, many leagues to the westward of that in which he was himself sailing (see p 498) The whole is, however, an interesting speculation, incapable of proof

[1] James may have named this island in the previous year, but he makes no mention of having done so. Although the name does not appear on the Admiralty Chart, it is still retained, and is used by both Captain Coates and Mr. A. P. Low It is the southernmost of the two small islands lying just to the south-east of Charlton Island, the northernmost being Danby Island. It is marked on James's map much larger than it really is. For a reference to Cary, see the Introduction, p. cxliv and p. 165.

we came to an Anker, and there rid all this day and the next night.

The fift, at three in the morning, we waide; but, Ice being all about vs, we knew not which way to turne vs. Now (to avoide telling the same thing 20 times), we were continually, till the 22, so pestered and tormented with Ice that it would seeme incredible to relate it. Sometimes we were so blinded with fogge that we could not see about vs; and, being now become wilfull in our indeauours, we should so strike against the Ice that the fore-part of the Ship would cracke againe, and make our Cooke and others to runne vp all amazed and thinke the Ship had beene beaten all to pieces. Indeed, we did hourely strike such vnavoidable blowes that we did leaue the hatches open; and, 20 times in a day, the men would runne downe into the hold to see if shee were bulged.

Sometimes, when we had made her fast in the night to a great piece of Ice, we should haue such violent stormes that our fastning would breake, and then the storme would beate vs from piece to piece most fearefully. Other-while, we should be fast inclosed amongst great Ice as high as our poope. This was made (as I haue formerly said[1]) by one piece running vpon another, which made it draw 8 or 10 fad. water. Besides which, the lowermost would rise from vnderneath, and strike vs vnder the bulge, with pieces of 5, 6, yea 8 tunne, that many times we haue pumpt cleere water for an houre together before we could make the pumpe sucke. Amongst these seuerall and hourely dangers, I ouer-heard the men murmure, and say that they were happy that I had buried, and that, if they had a thousand pounds, they would giue it, so they lay fairely by them; for we (say they) are destined to starue vpon a piece of Ice. I was faine to indure all this with

---

[1] See p. 533

patience, and to comfort them vp againe when I had them in a better humour

The 22, hauing been vext with a storme all last night, and this morning with a thicke fogge, we droue in 13 faddome water. About noone, it cleer'd, and we saw the land, and at the instant had a good obseruation; whereby we knew it to be *Cape Henrietta Maria*. I made the Master stand in with it; and, in the meane time, we fitted a Crosse, and fastened the *Kings Armes* and the *Armes* of the City of *Bristoll* to it We came to an Anker within a mile of the shoare, in 6 fadd water: so we hoyst out the boate, and tooke our Armes and our Dogs, and went ashoare. Vpon the most eminent place, we erected the Crosse; and then, seeking about, we soone saw some Deere,[1] and by and by more and more We stole to them with the best skill we had, and then put our Dogs on them; but the Deere ranne cleere away from them at pleasure We tyred the Dogs, and wearied our selues, but to no purpose; neither could we come to shoote at them. I saw in all about a dozen (old and young), very goodly beasts. We tooke halfe a doozen young Geese on the pooles, by wading in to them; and so returned to our Boate, vext that now we had found a place where there was refreshing, and we could get none of it. Whereas, therefore, we had kept our Dogs, with a great deale of inconuenience, aboord the Ship all the winter, and had pardoned them many misdemeanors (for they would steale our meate out of the steeping tubs) in hope they might hereafter doe vs some seruice; and, seeing they now did not, and that there was no hope they could hereafter, I caused them to be left ashoare. They were a Dogge and a Bitch, Bucke Dogs, of a very good race The Dogge had a collar about his necke, which, it may be

---

[1] Probably cariboo or reindeer.

hereafter, may come to light. I did see no signe at all of any Saluages, nor could we finde any hearbs or other refreshing here

In the Euening (being returned aboord), and the winde blowing faire at South, I caused the Master to weigh and come to saile, and to lose no time; for we did hope for an open Sea to the North-west. This *Cape* hath a very shoald point that lies off it, which we indeauoured to compasse about.

Sayling, therefore, amongst shattered Ice, we came to very shoald water (4 and 5 faddome deepe), and could not auoyde it. At length, standing North, the water deepened; but we came withall amongst great pieces of Ice, which, by reason of some open water, there went a pretty sea. These hard pieces of Ice made a most fearefull noyse. It proued a faire Moone-shine night: otherwise it had gone ill with vs. We turned amongst this Ice, staying the Ship sometimes within her length of great pieces as bad as Rockes; but, by reason we were often forst to beare vp, we did sagge vpon the maine rand of Ice[1], and that, we thought, would it be worse for vs, wee let fall an Anker, and stood all on the decks to watch the Ices, sheering of the Ship (to and againe) to auoyd it. Thus, hauing poles and oares to fend it, we could not keepe our selues so cleere but many pieces came foule of vs. We brake two of our great poles with it, which were made to be handled by foure men, besides some other dammages. At breake of day, we wayed and sought all wayes to cleere our selues of Ice, but it was impossible I conceiue it impertinent[2] to relate every particular dayes passages, which was much alike to vs. Our endeauours were sometimes with our

---

[1] See p 477.

[2] This word has, of course, now entirely lost its old meaning—*not pertinent.*

sayles, giuing and receiuing 500 fearefull blowes in a day. Sometimes we would stop at an Anker, when we could get a little open water, and so suffer the Ice to driue to Leeward. Other-whiles, we should be inclosed amongst it, and then it would so breake, and rise, and leape vp vnder vs, that we expected to be beaten every houre to pieces.

Moreouer, wee should haue such stormes in the darke nights that would breake the moorings we had made fast to some piece of Ice for securitie in the night season; and then we should beat most dangerously from piece to piece till daylight, that we could see to make her fast againe I forbeare to speake of thicke fogges, which we had daily, which did freeze our Rigging day and night. Besides all which, wee should come into most vncertaine depths, sometimes 20 faddome; next cast 10; next 15; then 9; rocky foule ground. The great deepe Ice withall, driuing on these vncertaine depths, did so distract the tydes, and deceiue vs so much in our accounts that, by the thirtieth, we were driuen backe so farre to the Eastward and to the Southward of the Cape that, at fiue a clocke in the Euening, it bare North-west of vs, some three leagues off, contrary to our expectations. With all these mischiefes, our Ship is now become very leaky, that we must pumpe euery halfe watch. Here I called a consultation; and, after consideration of all our experience, we were all of the same opinion, that it was impossible to get to the Northward, or to the Eastward, by reason of the Ice. Wherefore I resolued vpon this course: When the winde blew South, it would blow the Ice off the South shoare; then we would seeke to get to the Westward, betwixt it and the shoare. I must confesse that this was a desperate resolution, for all the coast we knew to be shoald and foule ground, all rocks and stones; so that, if the winde should shift to the Northward, there would be (without Gods mercies) little hope of vs. But here we must not stay.

The nights grew long; the cold so increased that, betwixt the pieces of Ice, the Sea would be frozen I caused the Ship to be fitted, and places conuenient againe prepared to sinke her the second time, if so be we were put to extremities. We presently put our proiect in execution (the winde being at South), and got about the shoalds of the Cape. Standing then into the shoareward, to get betwixt it and the Ice, we came into foure faddome water (very foule rocky ground), thinking to come to an Anker all night, and let the Ice driue to Leeward; but still there was so much Ice betwixt vs and the shoare, that we were faine to beare vp amongst it into deeper water, and to let the Ship driue amongst it. The winde increasing, we endured a most dangerous darke night of it. In the morning, we fell to worke to get the Ship againe out of the Ice into some cleere water, which we saw West by South of vs: some of our company out vpon the Ice, to heaue her with their shoulders, whilest others stood aboord with poles. The rest stood to spill[1] and fill the sayle. By nine in the morning, we had gotten into some cleere water, and stood West and by South, and into foure faddome water, foule ground; but, being not able to weather some rands of Ice which did driue, wee were faine to stand off againe, and (when the euening grew darke) to come to an Anker.

About midnight, there came a great piece of Ice (which we could not auoyd) athwart of our Cable, and made the Ship driue and dragge her Anker. This droue her into shoald water, it being very rocky and foule ground. We brought the Cable to Capstang, and heau'd with such a courage that we heau'd home our Anker from vnder it. Thus we did endeauour (the best we could) to keep our selues in eight and ten faddome water. It then pleased

---

[1] To spill a sail is to let the wind out of its cavity or belly, in order to furl it easily.

God that the wind blew alongst the shoare: otherwise it had gone far worse with vs

August, 1632.

The first of this moneth, at breake of day, when we could see a little about vs, we fell to struggle and striue againe with the Ice, and to get in neerer to the shoare. There, by reason the winde was opposite to come to an Anker, we let the Ice driue to Leeward, hoping that there was a cleere Sea to the Westward. The Ice droue very thicke vpon vs, and one piece came foule of vs, which did touch our Sprect-sayle Yard, and made the Ship driue. But we soon cleered our selues of it. Then we wayed, and stood in neerer to the shoare; but the water shoalded, and there were so many great rands of Ice betwixt vs and the shoare that there was no comming to an Anker. So wee turned betwixt the Ice, many pieces of it being aground in shoald water, and few pieces distant one from the other a Cables length. This day we saw two Sea Morses on the Ice.

The second, in the morning, we were glad of the breake of day, hauing most dangerously turn'd amongst the Ice all night, and endured many a heauy blow. We stood in againe to the shoare-ward, to see if we could get some cleere water, for to the Northward it was all impassable Ice. We stood into fiue and four faddome, but still all incompast with Ice. So we stood off againe into deeper water, and in the Euening we were inclosed amongst extraordinary great pieces. It was a very thicke fogge withall, so that we made fast the Ship to a great flat piece, and went to sleepe and refresh our selues after our extreme painestaking.

The third, fourth, and fift, wee were inclosed amongst very great Ice, and it blew such a storme of winde that we, sometimes indeuouring to get forward to the Westward, did strike such heauy blowes that made all the forepart of the Ship cracke againe. Then we would giue ouer working, and let her alone amongst it; but then the Ice would breake and rise vnder vs, that would indanger vs as bad as the former. Our ship doth make aboue a tun of water euery watch, which we must pumpe out, beside our other labour. God thinke on vs, and be mercifull to vs amongst all these dangers.

The fift, at noone, we were in Latitude 55. 30, the *Cape*[1] bearing off vs South-East by East, some twelue leagues off. And this is all we haue gotten since the two and twentieth of Iuly. All night it blew a violent gale of wind at West North-West; and, about midnight, our hawser (by which we had made fast to a piece of Ice) broke, and we lost 14 faddome of it. We beat all night most fearefully, being tost from piece to piece, because that in the darke we durst not venture our men to goe forth on the Ice, for feare of losing them.

All the sixth, the storme indured, and droue vs againe with the Ice almost to the *Cape*.

The seuenth was the most comfortablest day wee had since we came out of our wintering place; the wind came vp faire at East, and we got (although with our former inconueniences and dangers) neerer to the shoare, and into some open water, making good way to the West-ward. Moreouer, our leake now stopt of its owne accord, so that now we pumpt but little. We sayld all night, keeping good watch on the forecastle, bearing vp for one [piece of ice], and looffing for another.

Thus did we the eighth also, but then, the wind shifting to the North-west, it droue the Ice on the shoare, and we came to an Anker in eight faddom water. The maine Ice we had some two mile to windward of vs, but the set of

---

[1] Cape Henrietta Maria.

the tyde kept it off from vs. At noone, we were in Latitude 55. 34. In the Euening, a range of Ice droue vpon vs, which made vs weigh and stand in neerer the shoare, into sixe faddom, and there to come to an Anker. The wind increasing about midnight, the Ship did driue, and was quickly in fiue faddom water; wherefore wee let fall our Shoot-Anker, and both held her. But that that troubled vs was that we expected euery minute when the maine Ice would come vpon vs, and then there would be no hope but to be put ashoare.

The ninth, in the morning, we waide our second Anker, the Ice being within lesse then a mile of vs. About eight in the morning, a point of it came foule of vs, which we preuented by waying, and came to an Anker in three faddom and a halfe water. The wind continued North North-West, which was in on the shoare This morning, I caused all our empty Caske to be fild with water, and the Ship to be left vnpumpt, and the places lookt to that we had prepared to sinke her. For we were at present in as apparent danger as any time this voyage, and (to our great griefes) it was all foule rocky ground. The danger of this was, if we made fast to a piece of Ice that drew deepe water, then, as soone as it came to ground on these rockes, it would breake all to pieces and betray vs to our destruction. About noone, there came foule of vs the point of a range of Ice, which we resolued to indure the extremity of with an Anker, thinking to ride and breake through it, we now perceiuing some open water beyond it. Thrusting, therefore, and fending with our poles, at last a great piece came thwart our hawser, and there went a pretty Sea amongst it. The Ship did now fall vpon it so violently, that I expected euery blow she would beate out her bowes. At length she did driue with it, so that I thought the Cable had bin broken. We brought it to Capstang to heaue it in, but found that our Shoote-Anker was broken in the middle of the shanke We presently set our sayles thereupon, indeauouring that way to edge in amongst the Ice off of this perilous shoare. It pleased God to fauour our labour, so that, by eight in the Euening, wee got off into seuen faddom; and, a darke night comming on, we made fast to the biggest piece we could find. It blew fairely all night, but about midnight the wind came vp at North, which was more on the shoare then before. By breake of day, on the tenth, we were driuen into foure faddom, very foule ground, so that the lead did fall off the rocks three or foure foote; we set our sailes, and vsed our vttermost indeuours to edge off. Some of vs went vpon the Ice to hale her; others stood with poles to thrust by night. At night, we had gotten off into eight faddom, and made fast to the biggest piece we could find If any man should aske why we now kept so neere to the shoare in this continuall danger, I answer: Because that, in the offing, the Ice was so extraordinary thicke that we could make no way any way through it. Moreouer, when we were in that great thicke Ice, and that the winde came vp faire at South, or South-East, or East, we could not get out of it Wherefore we chose to runne this aduenture, and so preuent and ouercome all dangers with Gods assistance and our extreme labour.

The eleuenth, in the morning, was a thicke fog; yet there sprung vp a gale of wind at East, and we made in for the shoare.

From the eleuenth till the foureteenth, the winde continued faire, and we made all the saile we could (night and day), as the Ice would suffer vs. We had the shoare in sight by day on one side, and the Ice within two miles on the other, and we saild amongst disperst pieces, luffing for one, and bearing vp for another.

The 14, at noone, we were in Latitude 57. 55.[1] In the

---

[1] Probably at this time he was due north from Cape Tatnam.

Euening, we were imbayed in Ice, and stood S.W to cleere ourselues of it, but could not. But, seeing from top-mast head cleere water ouer it, we put into it; but there rose a very thicke fogge, and night came on withall, that we were faine to [make] fast to a piece of Ice, expecting day and better weather.

The 15, in the morning (although the fogge was very thicke), we indeauoured to get out of the Ice, and stood away West; but, within 2 houres, the water shoalded from 40 faddome to 25, whereby we knew that we had the shoalding of the Western shoare. Then we shapte our course to the Northward, the fogge continuing so thicke that we could not see a Pistoll-shot about vs. We had not stood this way 2 houres, but we heard the rut of the Ice ahead of vs, which made the most hideous noyse of any we had heard this voyage. We hal'd our tackes aboord, and stood to the West-ward in this day darknesse, hearing of it sometimes, and sometimes seeing of it, which was very large, deepe, and high Ice aboue the water. We weathered it all, except some few pieces, and got into open water. About Sunne-set, there came a sudden gust at N.N.W., and, before we could handle our sayles, it was with vs, and put vs to some trouble. It dallied with vs by gusts till 9 a clocke, and then it fell into a most violent storme. We considered where we might haue the cleerest drift, and so tooke in all, and let her driue, her head to the shoare-ward. Before mid-night, the water shoalded on vs to 15 fadd. Then we turned her head to the Eastward, and set our maine Course low set, but as much as she could indure. The water deepned but little, and we knew that we were on those rockie shoalds which we strooke on the last yeere.[1] God be mercifull to vs. Here was the first great breaking Sea that we had this yeere.

The 16, in the morning, we were driuen to a great Rand

---

[1] Nelson Shoal (see p. 482).

of Ice, to avoyde which we set our fore-course too, and stood to the shoare-ward, in 13 fad. water, and then about againe. We stood in a mile into the Ice, but there went such a great swelling Sea in it that it was not indurable, so we stood out againe. About 3 a clocke in the afternoone, the storme broke vp, and blew faire at N.W., which prooued good for vs, for we had not drift for 4 houres; besides, it was but two leagues betwixt the shoalds and the Ice. We set all our sayles, and indeauoured to weather the Ice, but in the Euening we were still pestered with it. By mid-night, we knew not which way to turne, nor what to doe, so we tooke in all our sayles and let her driue amongst it. The Ice beat vs on euery side, for there went amongst it a very great full Sea.

The 17, in the morning, when we could see about vs, we were in the middest of the Ice, but with the last storme it was all broken into mammocks[1] as big as a boate of 3 or 4 Tunnes, which did giue vs many a heauy blow in the darke night If this storme had taken vs amongst it, it had beaten vs all to pieces, without God's miraculous preseruation. We made sayle, and indeauoured to cleere ourselues of it to the North-ward, which, by 8 in the morning, we had done.

We then went to prayer, and gaue God hearty thankes that had deliuered vs out of it. For we were hourely, for the space of sixe weekes, as it were in the Iawes of death; yea, neuer any (that I haue heard of) haue beene so long, in such long nights, vpon a foule shoald shoare, tormented with Ice, as we haue now beene. At noone, we were in Latitude 58. 20.

Now, as touching the dissolution or ruining of the Ice: we found that this storme had torne and shattered this Rande of Ice, which was on the outside; although it must

---

[1] Halliwell gives *mammocks* = *fragments* (various dialects).

haue a long time to worke into the maine body of it. I haue, in *Iuly* and in the beginning of *August*, taken some of the Ice into the Ship, and cut it square 2 foote, and put it into the boate, where the Sunne did shine on it with a very strong reflex about it; and, notwithstanding the warmth of the Ship (for we kept a good fire), and all our breathings and motions, it would not melt in 8 or 10 dayes.

It was our practice, when we should be two dayes together fast to a piece of Ice, to set markes on it, to see how it did consume; but it yeelded us small hope of dissoluing. We could not in that time perceiue any diminution by the sinking of it or otherwise. Neuerthelesse, I thinke that it is ruined with stormes or consumed with heate some yeeres, or else the Bay would be fild choke-full. But I confesse that these secrets of nature are past my apprehension.

Being out of it (but no otherwaies then that we yet saw it from off the deckes all to the Eastward), I ordered the Master to stere away North and by East, keeping the shoalding of the Wester-shoare.

The 18, at noone, we were in Latitude 59. 30.

The 19, we continued our course betwixt the N.N.E. and the N. by E., and at noone were in Lat. 61. 7,[1] some 12 leagues off the shoare. I ordered the Master to shape his course North-East, to looke to that place betwixt *Caries Swans-nest* and *Ne Vltra*.[2]

The 20, we were in Latitude 61. 45. This day we saw some few Seales about the Ship.

The one and twentieth, the water shoalded, so that we made account we did approach the land; but, about noone, the wind came vp at N.E., our direct opposite. We looft

---

[1] He must have been off Cape Esquimaux.
[2] It is by no means clear what place James means to indicate by this expression.

as neere it as we could, and, as it larg'd, we came to stand East, and East and by North

The two and twentieth, we fell with the land to the Westward of *Caries Swans-nest*,[1] where we had forty faddome three leagues off. We stood in, within a league of the shoare, into thirteene faddome; and, seeing the land to the South-ward[2] of vs, we compast about it, it being *Caries Swans-nest*, which is in Latitude 52 degr. oo Minutes.[3]

All the 23, we sayled North-East, and for the most part in sight of land.

The foure and twentieth, at noone, (by Iudgement) we were in Latitude 63 30, having sayled a North-East course. All this day was a very thicke fog, which about one a clocke cleered a little, so that I expected to see the land. Some of our men, being better sighted, spyed it out about some two leagues off from vs I knew it could be no other then *Nottingham Iland*, though it was something contrary to the expectation of our best Marriners. We stood into it to make it. It was the North end of it, and it bare off vs due East. I was soone assured of it, and I ordered the Master to shape his course North-West and by North Both he and others were vnwilling, but, without much adoe, submitted themselues (how loth so euer), for that it was so very foule thicke weather.[4] The reasons of my resolution were these: the time of the yeere was far spent, and the discommodities of Winter came vpon vs, and therefore would I make the shortest way betwixt the lands already discouered. If I found an open Sea, I had my desire, and

---

[1] Probably Cape Southampton.

[2] Probably a misprint for *north*-ward.

[3] Undoubtedly a misprint for 62° oo', which is a little to the south ward of the true position.

[4] James was, of course, now about to explore to the north-west of Nottingham Island, which he had been prevented doing in the previous year (see p. 474).

did then intend to proceed to the vttermost of our power; if we met with the land, I should then finish the discouery, it being not passing fifteene leagues from land to land, and not passing tenne leagues from *Nottingham Iland* to the maine of the North shoare. We made what sayle we could, it blowing a very stiffe gale of wind, vntill eight in the Euening; then it began to blow fiercely, and we tooke in our topsayles, and stood vnder our two courses and Bonnets. At nine, it blew a violent storme at South South-East, so that we tooke in our fore-saile, and let her driue North-West. All night it continued an extraordinary storme, so that we heaued the Leade euery half watch; but the Ship did driue so fast that she would be past the Leade before there was twenty faddom of line out, all the night being exceeding cold withall.

The fiue and twentieth, the storme continued in his vttermost malice, and did so perplexe vs that there were but few that did sleepe or eate a bit these twenty foure houres. About sixe a clocke in the afternoone, the Storme began to slaken; yet blew there a fierce gale of wind betwixt the South and South-West. We stood West North-West, and made a North-West way, when suddenly the Sea became very smooth. We reasoned thereupon amongst our selues what might be the cause of it. We all thought it to be the Leeward tyde; nothing doubting what afterwards we encountered. The Ship had very quicke away in this smooth water.

The sixe and twentieth, by two a clocke in the morning, we were suddenly come in amongst the Ice; and it pleased God that the Moone at the instant gaue vs so much light that we could see a little about vs. We could haue staid the Ship, but it was so thicke to wind-ward, and so neere vs, that we durst not. Wee then bore vp in this vnexpected accident, and (I verily beleeue) did not scape striking the length of a foote against the Ice as hard as rockes two or three times, the Shippe now hauing way after twelue leagues a watch. Then wee stood close by a wind to the Eastward, expecting day, that wee might see about vs. Wee could, from top-mast head, see the Ice to the North North-West, the North-west, and so round about by the South, to the East, and some there was to Leeward of vs. It was all flat sound Ice, in maine rands, and the Sea as smooth as a well amongst it. This strooke vs all into a dumpe,[1] whereupon I called a consultation of my Associates, namely, *Arthur Price*, Master; *William Clements*, Lieutenant; *John Whittered*, Masters Mate; *Nathaniel Bilson*, Chirurgion; *John Palmer*, Boateswayne; requiring them to aduise and counsell mee how to prosecute our businesse to effect. These all went together and reasoned amongst themselues, and then brought me their opinions in writing vnder their hands:—

Videlicet, our aduice is that you repaire homeward from this present twentie sixth, and that for these reasons: First, for that the nights are long, and so extreme cold withall that we can hardly handle our sayles and riggings. Secondly, the times are now subiect to stormy and gusty weather, as witnesseth the present season, it hauing continued a storme euer since the twentie fourth, and doth yet continue no weather to discouer in. Thirdly, we doubt whether *Hudsons Straights* be so cleere of Ice that it may be passable in conuenient time (winter comming now on apace) before wee be frozen vp, seeing the Ice lyes here all ouer the Sea in rands and ranges. Fourthly, wee must haue a set of faire weather to pass the Straight, which we may stay a long time for, if we neglect the first oppor-

---

[1] This old term is by no means altogether obsolete. We still have the expression "down in the dumps"; but Skeat says the singular form is rare. Nares says a *dump* was formerly the received term for a melancholy strain in music.

tunity. Fiftly, for that our Ship is very leaky, so that in foule weather we are faine to pumpe euery glasse, which is great labour. Moreouer, we know her to be so sorely bruised with rocks, and blowes of the Ice, that shee is no more to be aduentur'd amongst it, but in sauing of our liues homewards. Besides all this, our men grow very weak and sickly with extreme labour.

Sixthly, the season of the yeare is so farre spent that we can expect no other weather then we have had, both lately and at present; that is to say, snow and fogge, freezing our rigging, and making euery thing so slippery that a man can scarce stand. And all this, with the winde Southerly, which, if it should come to the Northward, then we are to expect farre worse. Seuenthly, and lastly, that the Ice lyes all in thicke rands and ranges in the very way we should goe, as you and all men here may see. And, therefore, we conclude, as aforesaid, that there is no possibilitie of proceeding further; wherefore we here counsell you to returne homeward, hoping that God will giue vs a fauourable passage, and returne vs home safe into our natiue countreys, if we take time, and not tempt him too farre by our wilfulnesse.

Indeed, most of these reasons were in view, and I could not tell what to say to oppose them; no, nor any reason could I giue how we might proceed further; wherefore (with a sorrowfull heart, God knowes) I consented that the helme should be borne vp and a course shapte for *England*, well hoping that his Maiestie would graciously censure of my endeauours and pardon my returne. And, although wee haue not discouered populous kingdomes, and taken speciall notice of their Magnificence, power, and policies, brought samples home of their riches and commodities, pryed into the mysteries of their trades and traffique, nor made any great fights against the enemies of God and our Nation; yet I wish our willingnesse in these desart parts may be acceptable to our Readers. When we bore vp Helme, we were in Latitude 65. 30, at least, North-west and by North from *Nottingham Iland*. Some were of an opinion that we were further to the Northward; but, by reason it was by Iudgement, I chose to set downe the lesser distance.[1]

The twentie seuenth, the winde came vp at North-west, with which winde we could not haue gone on our designe. That winde made no great swelling Sea. By noone, we were athwart of *Cape Charles*,[2] so that we went in betwixt that *Cape* and *Mill Ilands*. The last night, it did snow very much, and was very cold, so that all our rigging and sayles were frozen, and all the land couered with snow. And here (sithence I haue formerly spoken that it snowes very much) it will not be amiss to consider of the reasons of it. When I was vpon *Charleton Iland* (our wintering place), and in *Iune*, when the snow was cleereliest gone off the ground, I have, in the nights (and some of them following the hottest dayes), obserued whether there fell any dew or no, but I could neuer perceiue any; and (vnder correction of the learned), from mosse and sand, little (mee thoughts) was to be expected. Now, of what was exhald from the snowy Ice and cold Sea, could there probably be returned but the like againe. Generally, we continued on

---

[1] This was James's most northerly point. For two days he had been sailing up the channel Foxe had explored in the previous year, and which is now known by his name. The ice James encountered was probably that lying along the western shore of the channel, probably about Lyon Inlet, near which Parry wintered in 1821-22, though it may have been further north. If the latitude in which James believed himself to be was correct, he did not reach so far north by considerably over one degree as Foxe had done in the previous year, and this must have been on the western side of the channel (although he did not see the shore), whereas Foxe only visited the eastern side.

[2] Prince Charles Cape of Bylot (see p. 474)

our course, blinded with foggie and durtie weather; and that, intermixt with snow and frost, amongst disperst pieces of Ice, many of them higher then our Top-mast head.

With great varietie of winds, we were also driuen within three leagues of both shoares, so that the last of this moneth we were in the narrow of the Straight, which is about fifteene leagues ouer. The South shoare was much pestered with Ice.

September, 1632.

The first and second, we continued our endeuour to get on our way. The third, in the euening, as the weather cleered vp, we did see the South end of the *Iland of Resolution*.

These three dayes and nights had beene extreme cold, with fogge and frost, insomuch that our men, in the euening, could hardly take in our Top-sayles and Spreet-sayle. We haue sayled thorow much mountainous Ice, farre higher then our Top-mast head. But this day we sayled by the highest that I euer yet saw, which was incredible, indeed, to be related.[1] Now, as the winde comes Easterly, wee feel another Sea out of the Ocean, and the Ship labours with another motion then she hath done with any that euer we obserued to come out of the Westward.

From the third to the eighth, we had varietie of winds, and were gotten cleere out of the Straights, but were now comne[2] into such a tumbling Sea (the weather durtie and gustie, and by *interims* calme againe) that the Ship did so labour and rowle that wee thought verily shee would haue rowled her Masts by the boord. This made her so leaky

---

[1] Doubtless this ice consisted of large Davis Strait bergs which the tide had carried within the entrance to Hudson's Strait.

[2] See p. 502.

that we were faine to pumpe euery glasse; yea, her seames did so open aloft that we lay all wet in her.

This was the last day that wee saw any Ice. The winde now fauouring vs, we made all the haste we could homeward. By the way (hauing endeauored, obserued, and experimented some things in my vnfortunate voyage), I perfected vp my said obseruations, which, being after commanded to publish,[1] I here most submissely offer vnto the Iudicious Readers,[2] and mine owne priuate opinion withall, concerning the faiseablenesse of the Action intended, which was to finde a passage into the South Sea.

What hath beene long agoe fabled by some *Portingales*, that should haue comne this way out of the South Sea, the meere shaddowes of whose mistaken Relations haue comne to vs, I leaue to be confuted by their owne vanitie. These hopes haue stirred vp, from time to time, the more actiue spirits of this our Kingdome to research that meerely imaginary passage. For mine owne part, I giue no credit to them at all, and as little to the vicious and abusiue wits of later *Portingals* and *Spaniards*, who neuer speake of any difficulties, as shoald water, ice, nor sight of land, but [write] as if they had beene brought home in a dreame or engine.[3] And, indeed, their discourses are found absurd, and the *plots* (by which some of them haue practised to deceiue the world) meere falsities, making Sea where there is knowne to be maine land, and land where is nothing but Sea.

Most certaine it is that, by the onely industry of our owne Nation, those Northerne parts of *America* haue beene discouered, to the Latitude of 80 degrees and vp-

---

[1] See Introduction.   [2] See p. 607.

[3] It is not easy to explain this use of the word engine. Probably its meaning is imagination or invention. Skeat gives "*Engine* = a skilful contrivance", which, he says, is an early form.

wards. And it hath beene so curiously done (the labours of seuerall men being ioyned together), that the maine land hath been both seene and searcht; and they haue brought this supposed passage to this passe: that it must be to the North of sixty sixe degrees of *Latitude:* a cold Clyme, pestered with Ice and other discommodities, and where the *Spaniards* dispositions, and their weake Speeke Ships,[1] can hardly long indure it. And, withall, it is thus knowne that the entrance of *Hudsons Straights* is but 15 leagues broad; in the middle, not so much; and, betwixt *Salisbury Iland* and the maine, that is but 8 leagues. Then, proceeding to the Northwards, towards the fore-mentioned *Latitude*, it is but 15 leagues from mayne to mayne. This, in length, is but about a hundred and forty leagues, as may more plainely appeare by the *Mappe*. Most infinitely pestered withall it is with the Ice vntill *August*, and some yeeres not passable then; yea, I beleeue the straight is neuer cleere of Ice thorowly.

Now, most probable it is that there is no passage,[2] and, that for these reasons following :—

First, that there is a constant Tyde, flood and ebbe, setting into *Hudsons Straights*, the flood still comming from the East-ward, which, as it proceeds (correspondent to the distance), it alters his time of full Sea. This also entering into Bayes and broken ground, it becomes distracted, and reuerses with halfe tydes.

Secondly, here is no small fish, as Cod, etc., and very

---

[1] Halliwell gives *speeke* = a kind of nail used in shipping. Presumably speeke-ships are ships built with such nails (? spike-nails).

[2] James's views as to the existence and commercial value of a North-West Passage, as expressed in this and the following pages, differ widely from those expressed by Foxe, Button, and other very experienced Arctic explorers of his day; but it must be confessed that time has shown his to be the sounder.

few great ones, which are rarely to be seen. Nor are there any bones of Whales, Sea-horses, or other great fish, to be found on the shoare, nor any drift-wood

Thirdly, that we found the Ice in the Latitude of 65. 30 to be lying all ouer the sea in rands, and I am most certaine that the shoaldes and shoald bayes are the mother of it. Had there now beene any *Ocean* beyond it, it would haue beene broke all to pieces, for so we found it comming thorow the Straight into the Sea, to the Eastward.

Fourthly, the Ice seekes his way to the Eastward, and so driues out at *Hudsons Straight*, which I haue often obserued, being aland vpon the *Iland of Resolution*, and driuing amongst the Ice in the *Straight*.

Now admit there were a passage, yet it is knowne that it is partly narrow for a hundred and forty leagues, and to be infinitely pestered with Ice, as euery one haue found, who haue gone that way Comparing, therefore, some obseruation taken at *Bantam*, *Gulolo*, and at *Firando*, in *Iapan*, and the distance betwixt *Iapan* and the Wester-part of *Califurnia*, with the obseruations taken at *Charleton Iland*[1] (referring all to the *Meridian* of *London*), and then the distance betwixt the *Meridians* of *Cape Charles*[2] and the Wester-part of *Califurnia* will be found to be about 500 leagues in the Latitude of 66. 00, where yet the *Meridians* incline very much together.

To this may be added that, neere about *Cape Charles*, the variation is 29 degrees to the West, which is a probable argument that there is much land to the Westward, and that this straight must be very long, and that you haue no time to passe it but in *August* and *September*, when the nights are so long and the weather so cold that it will not bee indurable.

---

[1] See p. 613   [2] Query, Charlton Island.

Adde to this, that neither can any great Ships, which are fit for carrying of Merchandize, indure the Ice and other discommodities, without extraordinary danger.

Moreouer, a thousand leagues is sooner sayled to the Southward, and about the *Cape de Bona Speransa*[1] (where the winds are constant), and that with safety, then a hundred in these seas, where you must dayly runne the hazzard of losing Ship and liues. Put hereunto, that comfort for the sicke, or refreshing for your men, here is none to be had in these quarters.

Towards the latter end of *August*, and in *September*, the weather growes tempestuous, and the winds incline to be Westerly, that there will be but small hope of performing your voyage this way.

But let vs (by way of imagination onely) inlarge this Straight, in this *Latitude*, and free it of Ice; yet what aduantage, in speedy performance, will be gotten by this passage, if the winds be withall considered? To *Iapan*, *China*, and the Northerne parts of *Asia*, it may be the neerer cut; but, in Nauigation, the farthest way about is well knowne in fewer dayes to be performed; yea, with lesser paines, and more safety of Ship and goods.

Againe, to the East Indies and other parts where we haue the greatest Commerce and imployment of shipping, the other way is as neere. What benefit of Trade might haue been obtained in those Northerne parts of *Asia*, I will not presume to speak of, holding that there is a great difference betwixt those parts and the Northerne parts of *America*; whereas I am sure that there is none in any place where I haue beene all this voyage.[2]

---

[1] The Cape of Good Hope.

[2] James is in error here. Ever since 1669, the Hudson's Bay has carried on a very extensive trade of a kind from the region James visited on his voyage

The two and twentieth of *October*, we arriued in the Rode of *Bristoll*, hauing been hindered and crost with much contrary tempestuous windes and weather. The Ship being brought into Harbour, and halde dry aground to looke to her, it was there found that all her Cut-water and Sterne were torne and beaten away, together with fourteene foote of her Keele, much of her sheathing cut away, her bowes broken and bruised, and many timbers crackt within boord ; and, vnder the Star-boord bulge, a sharpe Rocke had cut thorow the sheathing, the planke, and an inch and a halfe into a timber that it met withall. Many other defects there were besides, so that it was miraculous how this vessell could bring vs home againe. Being all here arriued, we went all to Church, and gaue God thankes for his preseruation of vs amidst so many dangers

I very well know that what I haue here hastily written will neuer discourage any noble spirit that is minded to bring this so long tryed Action to absolute effect. And it is likely, withall, that there be some who haue a better vnderstanding, and a surer way of prosecuting of it, then my selfe haue, to whose designes I wish a happy successe. And, if they doe but make a reuiew of what hath beene done, and giue more certaine *Cœlestiall obseruations, Hydrographicall descriptions*, or exacter practice in *Nauigation*, it will be a most commendable labour. For, although I haue spent some yeeres of my ripest age in procuring vaine intelligence from forraine Nations, and haue trauailed vnto diuers Honourable and Learned personages of this kingdome for their instructions, haue bought vp whateuer I could find in print or manuscript, and what plot or paper soeuer conducing to this businesse that possibly I could procure, and haue serued voluntary besides, and spent some time in rendring a relation (since my comming home), and expended withall of my owne

monies, in my foresaid indeauours, and in furnishing of
extraordinary necessaries, aboue two hundred pounds in
ready money; yet I repent not my selfe, but take a
great deale of comfort and ioy, in that I am able to
giue an account (in some reasonable way) of
those parts of the world, which heretofore I
was not so well satisfied in.

FINIS.

THE COPIE OF THE
Letter I left at CHARLETON,
fastened to the Crosse, the first of
July, 1632.

BE it knowne to any that shall haply arriue here, on this *Iland of Charleton*, that, whereas our Soueraigne Lord, *Charles* the first, King of *England, Scotland, France, and Ireland, Defender of the faith,* etc., hauing a desire to be certified whether there were any passage or not by the North-west or North-westward, thorow these Territories, into the South Sea; some of the better-minded Merchants of the Worshipfull Company of Merchant-aduenturers of the Citie of *Bristoll*,[1] to satisfie his Maiestie therein, did voluntarily offer to set forth a conuenient Ship for that purpose, well man'd, victualed, and furnished with other necessaries. This free offer of theirs was not only commended, but graciously accepted of his Maiestie. Whereupon they fitted and furnished foorth a Ship, called the *Henrietta Maria*, of the burthen of seuentie Tuns, victualed for eighteene moneths. A number thought conuenient to mannage such a businesse was twentie two, whereof nineteene were choice able men, two yonkers, and my vnworthy selfe their Commander, all which the *Bristow* Merchants did most iudiciously and bountifully accommodate, and had in a readinesse the first of *May*, 1631.

The third of *May*, we began our Voyage out of the Rode of *Bristoll*, commonly called *Kings Rode*. Passing about the *Cape Cleere* of *Ireland*, vpon many courses, but reduced to

---

[1] See Introduction, p. cxxxiv.

a West North-west, we sayled along; and, vpon the 4 of *Iune*, wee made the land of *Groynland*, to the Northward of *Cape Farewell*, where, for the space of two dayes, we were dangerously ingagde amongst the Ice. Being cleere of it, we doubled *Cape Farewell* to the Southward, and so continued our course to the Westward, continually sayling and thrusting the Ship thorow much Ice. The 19 of *Iune*, we made the *Iland of Resolutiō*, and, endeuouring to cōpasse about it to the Southward, we were taken with a strong Westerly wind, which droue the Ice, and it vs, vpon the shoare. In that distresse (seeing it was broken grounds and maine inlets into it), I sent the Shallop to seek and sound a place for our refuge; but, when she was departed, she was in as great danger as we, and could not returne to vs by reason of the Ice. We, being now driuen very neere the rocks, were faine to set our Sayles and force the Ship into an opening, aduenturing her amongst vnknowne dangers to auoyd apparent, before we could *moore* her in a place (as we thought) safe from danger. The 22 of *Iune* (this inlet being full of Ice), that Ice vpon the ebbe so iambde one piece into another that it altred the ordinary course of it, and it came vpon the Ship and put her against the rocks, notwithstanding our vtmost resistance. As the water ebd away, the Ship hung by the Keele vpon a rocke, and heeld to the Offing. As soone as we perceiued this, we made fast some Hawsers to her Masts, and to the rocks, to hold her vpright. But all in vaine, she sunke still as the water ebb'd away, so that she was so turned ouer that we could not stand in her. Hereupon, we got all vpon a piece of Ice, looking vpon her, and praying God to be mercifull to vs. The rocke that she hung vpon was a little abaft the maine Mast, which made her hang after the head, and she sunk ouer so much that the *Portlasse* of the *Forecastell* was in the water. At length, it pleased God, the flood came, before it had ebd so low as the tyde before and after by a foote; and the Ship rose, and was safe and sound. And thus were we miraculously deliuered. With the first winde, we proceeded to the Westward, continually being pestred with so much Ice that it was about the middle of *Iuly* before we could attaine to *Sir Dudly Digges Iland*. And here I was put to my consideration; for whereas, by my directions,[1] I was to search especially two places (one from *Digges Iland* to the Northward, and, fayling there, to goe to the *Checks* and *Hubberts Hope*, and so to search it to the Southward), I now finding the Sea much pestred with Ice in the latitude of 64. 00, and as farre as we could see to the Northward, and that the time was farre spent as that before I could do any thing that way it would be *Aug*, and then as much trouble to returne againe to *Digges Iland*, and that by that time the yeere would be so farre spent, the nights so long and cold, that I feared I should be forced with shame to returne into *England* againe that yeere. Wherefore, I tooke my way to the Westward, by *Mansfields Iland*,[2] on which I landed twice, still hindred and incumbered with Ice. Thence I proceeded to the Westward, hoping for an open Sea in the Bay. We were there more troubled with Ice then in any place before, so that it was the eleuenth day of *August* before we had sight of the Western land, which we made in latitude 59. 30, something to the Southward of the *Checkes*.[3] Wee were not able to attaine thither by reason of the contrary winds and Ice, but were obseruant of the currant of the tydes, which after, by experience, we found to come from the Northward. We coasted along the shoare, in sight of land, and in 10 faddome water, to the Southward, and entred

---

[1] His Instructions for the Voyage have been discussed in the Introduction (see p. clix). [2] See p. 188.

[3] That is, the place Button named Hope's Check (see p. 165, *note*).

that Inlet, which heretofore was called *Hubberts Hope*,[1] which was the very place where the passage should be, as it was thought by the vnderstandingest and learnedest intelligencer of this businesse in *England*.[2] We sayld to the very bottome of it, into three faddom water, and found it to be a Bay of some 18 or 19 leagues deepe. From thence, we proceeded to the Southward, in sight of land for the most part; and, although I was as carefull to keepe the lead alwaies going (it blowing a fresh gale of winde, and a pretty bigge Sea), our depth, 8, 9, 10 faddome, yet, before the lead was vp, the Ship strook vpon a flat rocke (she then being vnder foresayle, fore top-sayle, maine top-sayle, and Spreetsayle) and gaue three sore knocks, and got ouer it. Being past this danger, we proceeded, and past by *Port Nelson*. Finding the land trend to the Eastward, wee began our discouery of it more carefully, because that no man (that euer I could heare or reade of) did euer see this land before.[3] Wee stood into sixe and fiue faddome, for it is very low land, and trends for the most part East Southeast, and East by South

The seuen and twentieth of *August*, I entred vpon it, and, in the name of the Merchants Aduenturers of *Bristoll*, tooke possession of it to his Maiesties vse, naming it *The New South-west Principalitie of Wales*. I brought from the land some small trees and herbs, and killed diuers sorts of fowle in signe of seysure, which I brought aboord.

---

[1] Churchill Bay (see p. 481).

[2] From a passage in a letter written by Sir Thomas Roe, and quoted in the Introduction (p. cvi), there can be little or no doubt that Henry Briggs is thus described, and that it was he who hoped to find a passage through "Hubbart's Hope" (Churchill Bay). Moreover, on James's chart, this place is marked as "Briggs his Bay", though neither in his narrative nor in the above letter does James state that he bestowed this name upon it.

[3] See notes on pp. 341 and 485.

Not long after (being put backe to the Westward with contrary winds), we spake with Captain *Fox*, in a Ship of his Maiesties set forth for the same purpose that we were. I inuited him aboord, and entertained him with such fare as we had taken in this new discouered land, and made him relation of all our endeauours. The like did he to vs, and, withall, told vs that he had beene in *Port Nelson*, where he had put vp a Shallop and found there many things which *Sir Thomas Button* had left there. The next day, he departed from vs, and stood to the Westward, and we neuer saw him since. His Ship, He, and all his Company, were very well. We continued our discouery to the Eastward, and came to the Easter point, which is in latitude 55. 06, which we named it *Cape Henrietta Maria*.[1] There the land trends to the Southward, and we followed it in sight, but were put off with foule weather, which being ouer-blowne, we stood in againe for the Wester-shoare (that we might leaue no part vnseene) and followed it againe to latitude 54. 40. The second time wee also put off with like foule weather, which made vs stand to the Eastward. In this way, we past by some Ilands, and happened amongst broken grounds and rockes, in latitude 53. 30, where wee came to an Anker, and sheltred our selues some few days, shifting Rodes. Now the winter began to come on, and the nights to be so long and cold that, amongst these dangerous places, wee were faine to spend the day to looke for securitie for the night. Here, by misfortune, our Ship came aground; and that amongst great stones, as bigge as a mans head, where shee did beate for the space of fiue houres most fearefully. In this time, we lightened her, and carried some of our things ashoare, so that, by the great fauour of God, we got her off againe, whereupon we named this Iland the *Iland of*

---

[1] See p. 490.

Gods fauour.[1] After that, againe, amongst those Rockes, we were put to many extremities. At length (hauing a gentle Southerly winde), we stood alongst the Easter-shoare to the Northward, now looking for a conuenient place to winter in. And here againe were we assaulted with a violent storme, in which we lost our Shallop, and were driuen amongst diuers dangers, and, seeing an opening betwixt two Ilands, we ventered to goe in, in very foule weather. We found it to be a very good Sound, and there we came to an Anker. We landed on one of them, which we named the *Lord Westons Iland*,[2] and man'd out our old Ship-boate vpon it. The other Iland we named my *Lord of Bristols Iland*. Parting from hence, wee stood to the South-ward to looke for a wintering place, because the time of discouery was past for this yeere. Many were our troubles amongst these Ilands, shoalds, and broken grounds, which made vs straine our ground-tackle for life many a time.

The 6 of *October*, we arriued in this Bay, it seeming a very likely place to finde a Harbour in; but, searching the likeliest places, we found it all so shoald flats and Rocks, and stony by the shoare side, that we could by no meanes bring our Ship neere the shoare, but were forced to ride a league off, in 3 faddome and a halfe water.

The winter came on apace; the weather proued tempestuous; and the cold so multiplied that our sailes froze in lumps to the yards vnmanuable. Neither could our onely boate goe from the Ship, by reason of the weather. About the middle of *October*, I caused a house to be made ashoare, where our sicke men might the better recouer, but always with an intent to take it downe, if we found other-

---

[1] In the text, James does not mention having given this name (see p. 495, *note*).

[2] This is an error, which has already been explained (see p. 498, *note*).

where a place for our Ship. I sent, likewise, men afoote (seeing the boate could not goe) to discouer the Iland, and to see if they could finde some Creeke or Coue, but all in vaine. We spent the time, with hope of fairer weather, till now the Cables began to freeze in the house,[1] and the Ship to be frozen ouer with the sprewe of the Sea,[2] so that we were faine to shouell the snow off our decks. Moreouer, the water began so to congeale by the shoare side that the boate could hardly get ashoare. Yet, for all that, if the wind blew N.W., there went a very great surfe on the shoare and such a great Sea in the Bay that there was no bringing of our Ship aground. Besides this, she would haue then laine open to the E. and S.E. and S.; and, indeed, the neerest land all about that way was 2 leagues off. Hereupon, we continued out the extremity at an Anker.

The 29 of *Nouember*, the Ice came about vs on all sides, and put vs from our ground-tackle, and would haue driuen vs out of the Bay vpon Rockes and shoalds (where vn-doubtedly we had perished), but that, by Gods great good-nesse, it proued so warme a day (the winde at S.) that suddenly we brought vp some sayle, and hoyst it vp with ropes, and so forst her ashoare, where shee beat all that night very sorely. The Ship being now grounded and quiet, wee considered what was best to doe with her, and resolued to sinke her; but, the next tyde, before we had any of our prouisions ashoare, the winde came N.W., so that the Ship beat most fearefully. We got all our dry prouisions vp to the vpper decke, and made a hole to sinke her; but, before she was sunke, she beat so extraordinarily

---

[1] Hawse (see p. 513).

[2] There can be no doubt that this means the *spray* or *foam* of the sea; but the etymology of the word is not clear. Skeat says: "It is remarkable that the word [spray] does not appear in any early author."

that we all thought she had beene foundered. Being sunke downe so low that the water came on the vpper decke, we tooke our boate and went all ashoare, in such pittifull cold weather that we were all so white frozen that some sicke men that were ashoare before did not know vs one from another.

The next day, we fell to land our prouisions; first our Bread, Fish, and dry things, the men driuen to wade in the water vp to the middles, most lamentable to behold. Within 2 dayes, what with greate flat pieces that stucke about vs, and that which froze, it was becomne[1] firme Ice betwixt the Ship and the shoare, so that then we were faine to carry all things on our backs a mile from the Ship to the house. Within few dayes, the hold became so frozen that we could not get all our things out of it, but were faine there to leaue it frozen till the next yeere. Then we made vs 2 other houses. Our first house was our Mansion house, wherein we did all lye together; our other was to dresse our victuall; and the third [was] for a store-house, which we built a pretty distance off for feare of fire. And now we considered of the estate we were in. We all doubted that the Ship was foundered, especially our Carpenter. But, suppose she were sound, yet was it a question whether we could get her off in the Summer, when the tydes are low. Moreouer, she might be spoyled, lying in the tydes way, when the Ice brake vp, and then we should be destitute of any vessell to bring vs home. The Carpenter vndertooke to build a Pinnace, of the burthen of 12 or 14 tunnes, that should be ready by the Spring, that, if we found the Ship vnseruiceable, we might teare her vp and planke her with the Ships planke. Vpon this we resolued, and, by *May*, brought it to that passe that she was ready to be ioyned together to receyue the planke. But God

---

[1] See p. 502.

mercifully prouided otherwise for vs. We indured a bitter cold winter, in which it pleased God to visit vs with sicknesse, so that, in the beginning of *May*, 1632, there was but my selfe and the Master and Surgeon perfectly sound, and he began to finde some defect also. About the beginning of *April*, we began to digge the Ice out of our Ship, which, by the middle of *May*, we had effected.

The 24 of *May*, the Ice began to breake vp betwixt the Ship and the shoare, and, about the middle of *Iune*, we had off our Ship, and found her to be stanch and sound, contrary to all our expectations Before this time, about the middle of *May*, our Carpenter dyed, and, with him, the hope of our Pinnace; Master *Wardon* dyed the 6 of *May*; our gunner, *Richard Edwards*, had his legge broken (which was cut off) at the Capstang in *August*, 1631, and languished till the 22 of *Nouember*, on which day he dyed. These three men lye buried here vnder these Tombes of stones. We lost another man, one *Iohn Barton*, our Quarter-Master, who mis-carried in the little Bay that is due West from this Crosse 3 mile, the Ice breaking vnder him, so that he sunke downe, and we neuer saw him more. The two Pictures, which are wrapt in lead, and fastened vppermost on this Crosse, are the liuely pictures of our Soueraigne Lord and Lady, *Charles* the first, and Queene *Mary*, his wife, King and Queene of *England*, *Scotland*, *France*, and *Ireland*, *etc*. The next vnder that is his Maiesties Royall Armes, the lowermost is the Armes of the City of *Bristoll*.

And now we are in a readinesse to depart this day; and I intend to prosecute our discouery to the West-ward, in this Latitude of 52. 03, and to the South-ward also, although with little hope. Failing there, I meane to haste to *Diggs Iland*, and indeauour to discouer to the North-ward. Thus, hauing had some experience of the dangers of the Ice, shoalds, and Rockes of vnknowne places, I thought it necessary to leaue this testimony of vs and our indeauours, if God should take vs into his heauenly Kingdome, and frustrate our returne into our natiue Countrey. Wherefore I desire any noble-minded Trauailer that shall take this downe, or come to the knowledge of it, that he will make relation of it to our Soueraigne Lord the Kings Maiesty, and to certifie [to] his Grace that we cannot as yet finde any hope of a passage this way, and that I do faithfully perseuer in my seruice, accounting it but my duty to spend my life to giue his Maiestie contentment whom I beseech God to blesse with all happinesse; and that they would likewise aduertise our worshipfull Aduenturers of all our fortunes; and that, if (as afore-said) wee perish, it was not by any want or defect in Ship, or victuall, or other necessaries, all which we haue in abundance for foure moneths and aboue, which, if occasion be, wee can prolong to sixe moneths. Thus, being at present vnable to expresse a grateful mind otherwise but in my prayers to God, I heartily beseech him to powre out his bountifull blessing vpon all their honest indeauours, and to continue their noble dispositions in Actions of this kinde. And I faithfully promise that, if I shall come where the like Letters and Tokens shall be left, to make me a relation of it, as it shall be desired. So, desiring the happinesse of all mankinde, in our generall Sauiour, *Christ Iesus*, I end.

Charleton, Iuly the second, 1632.

Thomas Iames.

THE NAMES OF THE
seuerall Instruments I prouided
and bought for this *Voyage*.[1]

A *Quadrant* of old seasoned Peare-tree-wood, artificially made,[2] and, with all care possible, diuided with *Diagonals*, euen to minutes. It was of foure foote (at leaste) *Semi-diameter*.

An *Equilateral Triangle* of like wood, whose *Radius* was fiue foote at least, and diuided out of *Petiscus Table* of *Tangents*.

A *Quadrant* of two foote *Semi-d.*, of like wood, and with like care *proiected*.

The *Sights*, *Centers*, and euery other part of them lookt to, and tryed with conuenient *Compasses*, to see if they had been wrongd or altred; and this continually before they were made vse of.

Staues for taking *Altitudes* and *Distances* in the heauens.

A *Staffe* of seuen foote long, whose *Transome* was foure foote, diuided into equall parts by way of *Diagonals*, that all the *figures* in a *Radius* of tenne thousand might be taken out actually.

---

[1] This list of instruments is of considerable interest as showing the details of the outfit of a skilled nautical observer at the period. For remarks on the nature of the various instruments, and the manner of using them, the reader may be referred to Davis's *Seaman's Secret* (1607), which is reprinted in Admiral Markham's *Voyages and Works of John Davis the Navigator* (Hakluyt Society, 1880).

[2] James here uses the word in its old sense, that of *skilfully* made.

LIST OF JAMES'S INSTRUMENTS.

Another of sixe foote, neere as conuenient, and in that manner to be vsed.

Masters *Gunters Crosse-Staffe*.

Three *Iacobs Staues, proiected* after a new manner, and truly diuided out of the Table of *Tangents*.

Two of Master *Davis Backe-staues*, with like care made and deuided.

Of *Horizontall Instruments*.

Two *Semicircles*, two foote *Semi-diameter*, of seasoned Peare-tree wood, and diuided with *Diagonals* to all possible exactnesse.

Sixe *Meridian Compasses*, ingeniously made, besides some doozens of others more common.

Foure *Needles* in square boxes of sixe inches *Diameter*, and other sixe of three inches *Diameter*.

Moreouer, foure speciall *Needles* (which my good friends Master *Allen* and Master *Marre* gaue me) of sixe inches *diameter*, and toucht curiously with the best *Loade-stone* in *England*.

A *Loade-stone* to refresh any of these, if occasion were; whose *Poles* were marked, for feare of mistaking.

A *Watch-clocke* of sixe inches *Diameter*, and another lesser *Watch*.[1]

A *Table*, euery day *Calculated*, correspondent to the *Latitude*, according to Master *Gunters* directions in his booke[2]; the better to keepe our *Time* and our *Compasse*, to iudge of our *Course*.

---

[1] These are referred to on p. 535.

[2] Edmund Gunter, mathematician, was born in Hertfordshire in 1581, and died at Gresham College in 1626. He was a friend and colleague of Henry Briggs, and the honour of having introduced the use of logarithms belongs largely to him. He published the *Canon Triangulorum* (1620) and various other works, which were collected in 1624, and again several times reprinted before the end

A *Chest* full of the best and choicest *Mathematicall bookes* that could be got for money in *England*; as likewise Master *Hackluite* and Master *Purchas*, and other books of *Iournals* and *Histories*.

Study Instruments of all sorts.

I caused many small *Glasses* to be made, whose part of time I knew to a most insensible thing, and so diuided and appropriated the *Logg-line*[1] to them, making vse of *Wilbrordus Snellius* his numbers of feete answering to a *Degree*, and approoued of by Master *Gunter*.

I made a *Meridian-line* of 120 yards long, with sixe *Plumb-lines* hanging in it, some of them being aboue 30 foot high, and the weights hung in a hole in the ground to avoyde winde; and this to take the *Sunnes* or *Moones* comming to the *Meridian*. This line wee verified by setting it by the *Pole* it selfe, and by many other wayes.[2]

Two paire of curious *Globes*, made purposely, the workeman being earnestly affected to this Voyage.

---

of the century. He was one of the first to discover the variation of the needle; but he suspected some error in his observations, and discontinued them. His professional successor, Henry Gellibrand, however, continued them, and confirmed their accuracy.

[1] This shows that James was, like Foxe (see pp 297 and 371), one of the earliest navigators to make use of the log and line.

[2] This meridian-line he set up and used on Charlton Island (see p 558).

THIS WAS THE MANNER

that we took the variation of the Compasse, and that as often as conueniently we could; but diuers of the Tables (by negligence of my boy) are lost; but these (I hope) may suffice to giue satisfaction of our care in Nauigation.[1]

Iuly 13th, 1631.

These 13 *Azimuths*, with the *Altitu. Dec.*, were taken upon a great piece of Ice with three *Needles* together; then the *Declination* was not equated, the last three set forth by themselues prooues the rest, *viz.*, the *Azimuth* of West with his *variation*, the *Azimuth* at due West, and the *variation* by the *Altitude* and *Azimuth* at due West.

These were taken twentie leagues to the Eastward of

---

[1] These observations, which are of a highly technical nature, have been submitted to Mr John Coles, of the Royal Geographical Society, who has been good enough to supply the following critical note. He says "The same observations are used at the present day for determining Latitudes, Variation of Compass, and Longitude, but the means of arriving at results is different, as we now have accurate watches, which we use for determining the meridian distance of a heavenly body; whereas, in the case of James's observations, the meridian distance is determined from the observed altitude at the instant a certain phenomenon takes place. This is, at the present day, the common method of finding local time. As regards the Azimuths: they have been taken in precisely the same manner as they would be now, but have been computed in a roundabout way.'

Salisbury Iland,[1] and 2 *quad.*, one of 4, another of 2 foote *Semid.*, *Semicircle* of 2 foote *Semid.*

La.	De*cn*.	AL. ☉.	AZ. M.	F.	T. AZ	F.	Var.
63 01	20 14	39 42	77 50	S	50 11	S	27 39
63 01	20 14	35 33	90 00		62 12	S	27 48
63 01	20 14	34 24	76 30	N	65 07	S	27 23
63 01	20 14	31 24	80 18	N	72 12	S	27 30
63 01	20 14	30 57	78 53	N	73 21	S	27 46
63 01	20 14	29 00	74 50	N	77 28	S	27 42
63 01	20 14	27 10	71 00	N	98 42	N	27 42
63 01	20 14	25 52	68 28	N	96 02	N	27 34
63 01	20 14	25 00	66 40	N	94 16	N	27 36
63 01	20 14	24 00	64 50	N	92 16	N	27 26
63 01	20 14	23 30	64 00	N	91 18	N	27 44
63 01	20 14	22 50	27 35	N	89 58	N	27 33
63 01	20 14	22 30	61 24	N	89 18	N	27 44

The meane Var*on* is 27. 36

The variation of the Altit. and Azim. of West, 27. 33.
The variation of the Azimuth of West, 27. 48.
The variation by Azim. at due West, 27. 35.

The meane of these three is 27. 38.

Iuly 22, 1631.

These three *Azimuths* and *Altitudes* were taken vpon a piece of Ice, the *Magneticall Azimuths* by the Sunnes shade in the water, the ayre thicke of fogge, that the Sunne gaue no perfect shade otherwayes; 10 leagues West from *Mansfields Iland*.[2]

La.	Decl.	AL. ☉.	AZ. M.	F.	T. AZ.	Fr.	Var.
60 33	18 25	34 06	90 00	S	64 34	S	25 26
60 33	18 25	31 34	84 48	N	70 08	S	25 04
60 33	18 25	18 25	71 35	N	82 54	N	25 21

The meane is 25. 17.

---

[1] See p 474.   [2] See p 478.

Iuly 24, 1631.

These 11 *Azimuths* were taken vpon a piece of Ice about the middle of the great Bay,[1] some of them by the shade, and some by the sight of the Sunne in the water, the weather being thicke of fogge.

La.	Dec.	AL. ☉.	AZ. M.	F	T. AZ.	F.	Var.
59 20	17 40	36 44	82 50	S	59 04	S	22 46
59 20	17 40	35 44	83 40	S	61 18	S	22 22
59 20	17 40	33 02	90 00		67 14	S	22 46
59 20	17 40	29 49	84 25	N	73 40	S	21 55
59 20	17 40	27 25	79 50	N	75 10	S	22 00
59 20	17 40	26 27	78 10	N	87 14	S	22 14
59 20	17 40	23 48	72 35	N	84 38	S	22 47
59 20	17 40	21 16	68 47	N	88 38	S	22 35
59 20	17 40	20 40	67 30	N	90 00		22 30
59 20	17 40	20 10	67 00	N	89 00	N	22 12
59 20	17 40	19 34	66 00	N	88 10	N	22 10

The meane is 22^d. 23. 21.

Iuly 31th, 1631.

These several *Azimuths* were taken vpon a piece of Ice, 50 leagues off the Wester-shoare.[2]

AL. ☉.	AZ. M.	F.	T. AZ.	F.	Var.	
24 00	76 26	N	99 20	N	22 54	Latitude
23 35	76 00	N	98 38	N	22 38	58 43 43
22 50	75 00	N	97 18	N	22 18	
22 05	73 40	N	96 04	N	22 24	Declina.
20 32	71 20	N	93 32	N	22 12	15 43 43
18 40	67 55	N	90 24	N	22 29	
18 30	67 30	N	90 02	N	22 32	

The meane is 22. 29. 34.

---

[1] See p. 478.   [2] See p 479.

August 1, 1631.

These several *Asimuths* were taken vpon a piece of Ice, about 40 leagues off the Wester-shoare.[1]

AL. ☉.	AZ. M.	F.	T. AZ.	F.	Var	
26 36	83 05	N	104 36	N	21 31	Latitude
25 24	81 25	N	103 06	N	21 41	58. 45.
24 26	78 38	N	100 42	N	22 04	
22 30	75 16	N	97 22	N	22 06	
21 31	73 50	N	95 42	N	21 52	Declina.
20 10	71 27	N	93 24	N	21 57	15 25.
18 42	68 40	N	90 58	N	22 18	
18 07	67 25	N	89 56	N	22 31	

The meane is 22. 00

August 5th, 1631.

These *Asimuths* were taken vpon a piece of Ice, and calculated by all the figures of the Canon, about 40 leagues off the Wester-shoare.[1]

	AL. ☉.	AZ. M.	F.	T. AZ.	F.	Var.
	23 14	79 12	N	101 02	N	21 50
Latitude	22 11	76 40	N	99 12	N	22 32
58. 37	21 11	75 11	N	97 28	N	22 17
	20 00	73 02	N	95 48	N	22 46
	18 59	71 24	N	93 47	N	22 23
Declina.	17 15	68 35	N	90 53		22 18
14. 12	16 42	67 28	N	90 00		22 32
	15 39	65 32	N	88 18	N	22 46

The meane is 22. 25. 30.

These obseruations were taken the 10th of *November*, 1631, the Lat. 52. 03[2]; the difference may be conceiued to grow by reason of the Sunnes low Altitude and Refraction. The others about the Summer Solstice, where difference of Meridians is auoided, and are more exact.

---

[1] See p. 480. [2] See p. 512

Alt. ☉. G. M.	AZ. M. G. M.	T. AZ. G. M.	Var. West. G. M
14 25	42 25	26 11	16 14
14 00	45 25	27 30	17 55
13 15	47 25	29 54	17 31
12 18	48 10	32 33	15 37
12 03	49 20	33 16	16 04
11 41	51 07	34 15	16 52
10 57	53 25	36 04	17 21
9 42	55 25	38 58	16 27
9 15	57 45	40 00	17 14
8 50	58 37	40 52	17 45

The meane is 16. 57 West.

An Appendix touching Longitude.[1]

Latitude and Longitude are two primary affections of the Earth. By the helpe of these two, doth the Geographer striue to represent the parts of the Earth, that they may keepe Symmetry and Harmony with the whole. Latitude, then, is an arch of the Meridian, comprehended betweene the Æquator and a Paralell; but Longitude is an arch of the Æquator, intercepted by the Prime Meridian and the Meridian of a Place, the difference of Longitudes being the difference of two Meridians The measure of

---

[1] Henry Gellibrand, the author of this treatise, was Professor of Astronomy at Gresham College, London, where he succeeded Edmund Gunter He was born in London in 1597, and in 1615 was sent to Trinity College, Oxford, where he took his degrees He then entered into Orders; but, having conceived a passion for mathematics, through hearing one of Sir Henry Savile's lectures, he decided to devote himself entirely to the study of that science He became an intimate friend of Henry Briggs, and, upon the death of the latter, he was entrusted with the completion of the *Trigonometria Britannica*. The work was published at Gouda, in Holland, in 1633, with a preface containing an encomium of Mr. Briggs. Gellibrand wrote the second book, which was translated into English, and published in an English treatise with the same title. While engaged in this work he published an almanac, in which Popish saints were omitted for Protestant ones, as they stand in Foxe's *Book of Martyrs*. For this he was cited by Bishop Laud, but he was acquitted by Archbishop Abbot and the whole court, Laud only excepted, as it was proved similar almanacs had been published before. He afterwards published *A Discourse Mathematical, on the Variation of the Magnetic Needle* (London, 1635, 4to); *An Epitome of Navigation* (London, 1674, 1698, 8vo); and other works. His character was fuller of plodding industry than genius. He died of a fever in 1636, aged only thirty-nine.

the former is the Meridian; the Æquator of this latter. For the exact settling of Latitudes, we haue many and absolute helpes, so that the Error (if any happen) ought to be imputed to the imperfect handling of the Artist. But the Longitude of a Meridian is that which hath [wearied], and still wearieth, the greatest Masters of Geography. Neuerthelesse, hath not the wise Creator left Man vnfurnished of many excellent helpes to attaine his desire; for, besides Eclipses, especially of the Moone (whose leasure we must often waite, and, perhaps, goe without, if the Heauens be not propitious to vs), we haue the concurse of quickepac'd inferiour Planets with superiour slow ones, or their Appulses[1] with some fixed starre of knowne place, or else some other Artifice deriued from their Motions and Positions. As for the Magneticall Needle, to argue a Longitude from its Variation is altogether without ground. And, though well-furnisht Seamen are able by their dead Reckonings (as they tearme them) to determine the difference of Meridians somewhat neere, yet, by reason of the vnknowne quantity of a Degree in a giuen measure (which is the Rule of the Ships way), varieties of aduerse winds, different sets of Tydes, and other inuolued incombrances, they come often wide of the mark they aime at The best way yet knowne to the world is that which is deduced from the Cœlestiall Apparences, which, being performed by Iudicious Artists, may in short time rectifie our Geographicall and Hydrographicall Charts, hitherto in most places fouly distorted. It is my intent here to giue an instance from two seuerall obseruations, drawn from the Cœlestiall Bodyes by the Author of this discourse in his discouery for the N.W., at the bottome of the Bay, being

---

[1] Appulse is the near approach of two heavenly bodies, generally used with reference to stars or planets when the moon passes close to them without causing occultation.

his wintering place, and called by the name of *Charleton*, which, for Iudgement, Circumspection, and Exactnes, may compare with most: The first from the Eclips of the Moone; the second from the Moones Mediation of Heauen, or Her comming to the Plane of his Meridian of *Charleton*.

The Captaine, then, mindfull of the Lunar Eclips which was to happen October 29, Anno 1631,[1] was wayting on the Moone with his Instruments, but, by reason of the Interposition of the clouds, could make no Obseruation on the beginning of her Obscuration, but, at her Emersion or Totall Recouery of Light, the heauens being more Serene, he tooke the Altitude of the Superior Limb of the Moone, 29 gr. 11 m., the Latitude of Charlton being 52 gr. 3 min.

At that very time, my selfe, with some friends, found the exact time of the Moones Emersion at London in Gresham Colledge (by a Quadrant of sixe foot Radius, actually cut to each minute of the Quadrant) to be, Octob. 29, 13 h. 7 m. 28 sec., or, Octob. 30, d. at one of the clocke, seuen minutes and about a halfe in the morning.

Now, because the Tables of the Cœlestiall Motions lately published by that most Learned and Industrious

---

[1] See p. 511. The following observations are purely technical. Mr. Coles's remarks, given on p. 606, to some extent relate to them, while the valuable note on a somewhat similar observation made by Baffin in Hudson's Strait on June 21st, 1615, contributed by Mr. Coles to Mr. Clements R. Markham's *Voyages of William Baffin, 1612-1622* (Hakluyt Society, 1881, p 122), has also a bearing upon them. Readers desiring further information should consult Davis's *Seaman's Secret* (1607), and Hues' *Treatise on the Globes* (1592), both edited for the Hakluyt Society in 1880 and 1889 respectively. It is highly remarkable that, from these observations, the longitude of Charlton Island should have been calculated at the time with such accuracy, one observation making it 79° 30' (which is exactly correct) and the other only one degree different.

Lansberg[1] doe much amuse the world with that loftie title of Perpetuity, it shall not be amisse to enquire after the time of the Captaines Obseruation from them, that so, by comparing the one with the other, we may obtaine the difference of Meridians, which is the matter now sought after.

The middle motions of the Luminaries answerable to the equall time of the Emersion of the Moone, are these which follow:—

		Sex	Gr	M.	S.
The middle motion of the	Sunne	3	47	39	26
	Center of the ☉	3	15	49	58
	Apogæū of the ☉	1	35	45	44
The middle motion of the	Lōgitude of the ☽	2	59	29	1
	Anomaly of the ☽	0	5	11	30
	Latitude of the ☽	4	32	8	15
The Prosthaphæresis of the Æquinox		0	0	12	30

Being thus furnished with these middle motions, wee are next to enquire for the true places of the Luminaries, and their Concomitants, as their right Ascentions, the Declination, Latitude, Semidiameter, Parallax, and Refraction of the ☽, that so the true Altitude of the ☽ center, and consequently the time of the Emersion, may be had at *Charleton*.

For the Sunnes true Place.

	Sex.	Gr	M.	S.
The Middle Motion of the ☉ Center	3	15	49	58
The Prosthaphæresis of the Center add	0	1	37	0
The Proportionall Scruples,———1.				
The Middle Motion of the ☉ Apogæum	1	35	45	44
The True Motion of the Apogæum subtr.	1	37	22	44

---

[1] Philippus van Lansbergen, an eminent Dutch mathematician, was born in Zealand in 1561. He was a preacher at Antwerp and elsewhere, but ultimately retired to Middleburgh, where he died in 1632. He published numerous works on the Sacred Chronology, Astronomy, Mathematics, and kindred subjects. Henry Gellibrand made his acquaintance when on a visit to Holland

	Sex. Gr.	M.	S.
The Middle Motion of the ☉ is	3 47	39	26
The Anomaly of the ☉ Orbe	2 10	16	42
The Prosthaphæresis of the ☉ Orbe	0 1	32	43
The excesse to be added	0 0	0	20
The absolute Prosthaph. of the ☉ Orbe subtr.	0 1	33	3
The Midd. Mot. of the ☉ frõ the true Æqui.	3 47	51	56
The true Mot. of the ☉ from the true Æqui.	3 46	18	53
Therefore the ☉ true place was in ♍	0 16	18	53
And his right Ascention	223	49	53

For the Moones true Place.

	Sex. Gr.	M.	S.
The Anomaly of the ☽ Center	5 59	18	2
The Prosthaphæresis of the ☽ Center	0 0	5	36
The Proportionall Scruples—0.			
The Anomaly of the ☽ Orbe	0 5	11	30
The Æquated Anomaly of the ☽ Orbe	0 5	5	54
The Prosthaphæresis of the ☽ Orbe subtr.	0 0	24	4
The Midd. Mot. of the ☽ Longitude from the ☉	2 59	39	1
The true Motion of the ☽ Longit. from the ☉	2 59	14	57
The Midd. Mot. of the ☉ from the true æquin	3 47	51	56
The true Mot. of the ☽ from the true æqui	0 47	6	53
Therefore the ☽ true place was in ♉	0 17	6	53

For the ☽ Latitude.

	Gr.	M.	S.
The Middle Motion of the ☽ Latitude	4	32	8 15
The ☽ absolute Prosthaph. of her Orb subtr	0	0	24 4
The ☽ true motion of Latitude	4	31	44 11
The ☽ Northerne Latitude was	0	0	9 5
And her Reductiue Scruples subtr.	0	0	0 26
But the ☽ true motion in her proper Orbe was	0	17	6 53
Therefore the ☽ true place reduced to the Eclipt ♉		17	6 27
And, because the North Lat. of the ☽ was		0	9 5
Therefore will her Right ascens. be		44	35 10
And her Declination		17	7 49
And, because we have the Distance of the Moone from the earth in Semidiameters of the earth	64	15	
Therefore shall the ☽ apparent Semidiam. be		0	15
And her parallax of Altitude		0	47 0
Now, because the Altitude of the limbe of the ☽ was found by obseruation to bee			29 11
If we shall substract her Semidiameter			0 15
And the refraction			0 2
We haue the apparent Altitude of the ☽ center			28 54
To this, if we adde the parallax of Altitude			0 47
We shall haue the true Altitude of the ☽ center			29 41

Hauing thus the Latitude of the place, the ☽ true Altitude, with her Declination, by the resolution of a Sphæricall Triangle, according to the 11 Probleme, lib 2, Part 2, of our British Trigonometry, we haue the distance of the ☽ from the Meridian, 63 26

And, by comparing this Arch with the Difference of the ascentions of the Luminaries, the Time of the ☽ totall recouery of her light at *Charlton* will be 7 hou, 49 min., 28 sec.

Which subtr. from the time of the Emersion at *London*, 13 hou., 7 min., 28 sec

The difference of Meridians in respect of time will be 5 h, 18 m, 0. So that *Charlton* is remooud from *London* Westwards, 79 gr, 30 m.[1]

This may likewise be confirmed by a second different obseruation, made at the instant of the Moones Culmination or Mediation of Heauen, at which time the Altitude of the brightest Starre in the Asterisme of the Northerne Crowne (being of the second Magnitude) was found to be 33 gr, 27 m. Easterly, Ann 1632, *Iune* 23 [2]

It may be Problematically deliuered after this manner

> Hauing the Latitude of a Place, with the Altitude of a knowne fixed Starre, at the moment of the ☽ culmination, to find the Longitude.

This fixed Starre is of knowne longitude and latitude; therefore was his Declination 27 59, and right ascension 229 46. Now, by the resolution of a Sphæricall Triangle of 3 knowne sides, we haue the distance of this Star from the Meridian, and by consequence the right ascension of the ☽, whence we conclude her Culmination to be with the 28 10 m of ♑, but the Moones true place was much lesse.

---

[1] This is exactly the case, though, according to the latest Admiralty Chart, the precise spot at which James wintered lies 79° 15′ W.

[2] See p. 558.

Here note, that the scrupulosity of time is vnknown, and therefore we cannot argue the ☽ true place from thence, (though I grant it might be euinced), for that were to begge the Question, and to know that first, which we looke after

In the next place, we are to inquire with what point of the Ecliptique the ☽ did culminate with vs here at *London*, that so, from the difference of her places, of the like affection, we may deduce the difference of Meridians.

Observation on the ☽ Culmination here at *London*, wee made none; therefore must we have recourse to the aforesaid Tables of *Lansberg*, and from thence calculate the same. Now, because the ☽ was not farre remooud from the ☉ opposite point, it will not be amisse to enquire first the ☽ place at midnight.

	Sex	Gr	M.	S
The ☉ opposite place at midnight in ♑ . .	0	11	18	15
The ☽ true place at midnight reduced to the Ecliptique was in ♑	0	23	33	18
The South Latitude of the Moone was . . .	0	4	56	38
Therefore the difference of Ascensions will be .		14	6	0
The Diurnall motion of the Moone . .		14	24	0
Therefore the Moone proper Motion answerable to the difference of Ascensions is .		0	33	50
Which, added to the Moones true place at midnight		23	33	18
Gives vs the Moones true place reduced to the Ecliptique at her Culmination at London		24	7	8

Now, because the ☾ Southern Latitude was 4 · 56 38, the Arch therefore of the Ecliptique comprehended betweene the Moones true place and the culminating Point of the Ecliptique will Trigonometrically be found to be 54, 38, which, added to the ☾ true place before found, gives vs the culminating point of the Eclipti. 25 gr , 1 m., 46 s, which is lesse then that found at *Charleton;* the difference being 3, 8, 24, therefore is the place of Obseruation Westerly of *London*. Having, therefore, the ☾ Diurnall motion, and the difference of the seuerall culminating points, we conclude the Meridian of *Charlton* to be distant frõ this of *Lõdon*, 5 h., 14 m. of time, or 78 30. of the Equator.[1]

The difference betweene that of the Eclipse and this latter obseruation is only 4 minutes of time, or one degree, a difference easily pardoned, especially if wee shall compare the same with some other places, yea euen such as border neerely on each other. To giue an instance on 2 eminent places which lye in the heart of Europe, Rome and Norenberg: Their difference of Longitude Regiomontanus makes 36; Werner, 32; Appian, 34; Mæstlin and Origan, 33; Stofler, 18; Maginus, 26; Schoner, 12; Mercator and Hondius as much, Stadius, 13; Jansonius, 10; Kepler, by 2 obseruations on 2 Lunar Eclipses, but 4 minutes of time.

This varietie among these great Artists will, I hope, pardon vs this difference of 4 m., and be a means to incourage our English Sea-men and others to make such or the like obseruations in forraine parts, as the heauens shall be offred vnto them

H. GELLIBRAND.

---

[1] The results of this observation differ from those of the preceding one to the extent of one degree of longitude, which (as Gellibrand goes on to show) was exceedingly little difference for the period. That the results of one should have been quite correct, and those of the other so little out, prove James's accuracy as an observer.

TO THE VENERABLE
Artists and younger Students in
Divinity, in the famous University of
CAMBRIDGE.[1]

OV nobly-witted and ingenuously-studied *Academians*, whose excellency in all kinds of learning all forraigne *Vniuersities* doe admire, and none atteine vnto: I here present you a *Voyage* to *Cholcos*, though not the *Golden-fleece* with it: the *Searche*, I mean, but not the *finding*, of that so much talkt of, so often sought for, *North-*

---

[1] This very irrelevant discourse, which is described on the title-page as "an Aduise concerning the Philosophy of these late Discouereys", is signed in some copies "X Z", though on the title-page it is ascribed to "W. W." In one of the British Museum copies (C 32, d 9), however, it is signed in full "Yours, William Watts", though the initials only remain on the title-page. There is no very clear evidence who this man was; but it is in all respects likely that it was the Rev. William Watts, D D., who edited the works of Matthew Paris, in folio, in 1640 (later editions 1644 and 1684), and who also published a translation of *The Confessions of St. Augustine* (1650), which served as the basis of Dr. Pusey's edition (Oxford, 1838, 8vo). He also, in 1637, published a sermon, entitled *Mortification Apostolicall* (London, 4to), on the title-page of which he is described as "rector of St. Alban's, Wood Street, London". From the concluding sentence, we may gather that the author of the "Aduise" belonged to Cambridge, but, whoever he was, it cannot be maintained that his remarks have much value, either from the geographical or the theological points of view. They were omitted from the second ed.t.on of James's work (1740), and would not have

West Passage, and a neerer way into the *South Sea;* that, wherein so much *Time* and *Treasure* haue beene expended, so many braue Spirits employed, and yet none discouered. Perchance, there is no such *Passage* to be found, and that the *Spaniards*, by the gullery of their false *Sea-Cards*,[1] and the fable of an old *Greeke Pilote*,[2] have but diuerted our *English* and *Dutch* Sea-men from their golden *Indyes*. This plot of theirs hath taken for these many yeeres ; and it appeares to bee but a plot, for that themselves neuer make vse of this *Passage*. For mine owne part, I suppose that the *Philosophers stone* is in the *North-West Passage*. My argument for it is: For that theres so much *Philosophy* in the way to it.

So much and such variety : such variety; and that so various (I thinke) from what is receiued in the *Schooles :* that it were well worth the disquisition of an *Vniuersity* (and I wish you the first honour of it), either to find out how these *Obseruations* may bee reduced to *Aristotles Philosophy*, or whether they need any other enquiry, and ought to be examined by some other *Rules* then *Aristotle* hath yet light vpon. This is my purpose of inscribing it vnto you. Of this one thing am I confident: that you are all so *rationall* and *ingenuous* as to preferre *Truth* before *Authority*. *Amicus Plato, amicus Aristotles*, but *magis amica veritas*. Your *Sciences*, then, being *Liberall*, your *Studies*, I know, have so farre passed into your *maners* that your minds are so too, and that such as haue already profited beyond the credulity required in a yong learner, and are themselues promoted to be *Masters* of the *Arts*, though they still reuerence their *old Greeke Tutor*, yet they will not suffer that of *Pythagoras Schoole* so to domineere in *Aristotles* as to let an *Ipse dixit* goe away with it · much lesse allow it the authority of a *Mayors hammer*, with one *knocke* to silence all arguments.

Vpon this confidence, I, with all due respects, here

---

been here reproduced, but that their omission would have rendered the work incomplete. They are chiefly of interest as showing that the controversy as to the antagonism between established scientific facts and the Biblical narratives is by no means of modern origin. Concerning the "Advise", Harris says (*Navigantium, etc*, 2nd ed., vol. ii, p. 434) —"Who was the author of it, I cannot say ; but, whoever he was, it is plain that he had the correction of Captain James' work, and was himself (for those times) a person of surprising knowledge and freedom of thought."

[1] See p. 588.   [2] Juan de Fuca (see p. 244).

preferre two *Propositions* unto your discussing. The first this, *Whether those Rules of Aristotles Philosophy be to be allowed so Vniuersall that they hold all the world over.* The second this, *Whether they ought to be so magisteriall as to prescribe against all other examinations.* The first of these, I shall but *problematically* propound vnto you; but, in the second, I hope a man of my cloathing may be allowed the freedom of being something more earnest.

But, that I may not come with preiudice to the making of these motions, or bee thought (vpon some *ignorance* or *ambition*) to speake against the *incomparable Aristotle*, I shall desire all my *fellow Academians* to allow me so much descretion as to know that he that shall, in your hearings, oppose your *Aristotle*, does, like the ship here spoken of, runne against a Rocke, endanger his owne bulge, and the stauing of his vessell. No, I so farre honour the old *Aristotle* that I well allow him to bee *Master* and *Moderator of the Schooles;* and that there is the same respect due to him in the *Schooles* which, by *Reason* and *long Custome*, is due to one of the *Kings Ships* in the *Narrow Seas: That, in acknowledgment of a Soueraignty, every other name ought to strike sayle to him.* *Aristotle* (it must be confest) hath made all learning beholding to him: no man hath learned to confute him, but by him, and unless he hath plowed with his heyfer. He had the most incomparable wit, and was the most Logical and demonstratiue deliuerer of himselfe of all the Sonnes of nature: one who best of all deserued to be cald *Her Principall Secretary:* one who not onely *adornes a Library*, but *makes it: Qui habet Aristotelum, habet Bibliothecam*, is truer of him then of the *Great Comparer.* This is my opinion of him, and I wish him more studied.

1. Tis not, therefore, the name or the authority of the great *Aristotle* that my Propositions meddle withal; but, whether his obseruations, gathered out of this part of the world alone, could, like a royal *Passe* or a *Commission*, carry a man all the world over.

It must be confest that, in respect of the *Equinoctiall* and the *Latitude* that *Aristotle* liued in, hee was but a *Northern man;* and twas his owne Rule that, *Nihil agit extra Sphaeram actiuitatis suae.* So then it would bee put to voyces to consider whether he that knew but these Northerne parts and the *Mediterranean* Sea, could possibly make such collections, by what was here to be learned, as should bee vnfaileable in the *Southern Hemisphere* and the two Indyes. Plainely, those that are conuersant in the *nauigations* and *bookes of voyages* into those parts haue found so many contrarieties to obserue that it were rather *tedious* then difficult to fill vp a *Note-book* with them.

The Ancients, wee know (as if they had measured the world by the Yeard-wand), restrained the *limits* of *temperature* and *habitation* by the fiue *Zones*, without consideration of any interloping or concurring causes, which experience hath now found out to haue quite altered their obseruation. I adde that a good leisure and diligence might obserue how, in the contrary part of the world, there be found cleane contrary *Causes* and *Effects* vnto those in this part of the world. The *South-wind* there brings *cold* and *Winter;* and the *North* is the rainy wind. How will the *Thunder* and the *Wind* be made agree with Aristotles definition of a *Meteore?* In some places of the Mountaines *Andes*, by *Peru*, it thunders euer. The *East Indyes* haue their *Monsons* and their steady winds, constant for sixe moneths together; and who shall assigne their causes? Then the *doctrine* of the *Tydes*, nothinge so vncertaine, which *ebbe* and *flow* in some places *different*, and in others *contrary*, to the *Moone* and her *motions* This (as I remember) is *Aristotles* definition of a *Meteore*: That it is *An Imperfect mixt body, generated out of an infirme and inconstant concretion of the Elements, which therefore cannot be durable.* Now the *Monson* is both constant in his continuance this yeere, and in his returne next yeare, most constantly keeping his seasons halfe yeere one way and halfe yeere another way, for all ages : nothing more constantly or durably, and therefore nothing like *Aristotles Meteore.* And so for the *Thunder* vpon the *Andes.* it is first perpetuall; secondly, not caused by a *dry exhalation* (as *Aristotle* wills), but hanging ouer such hils as are couered with snow and a perpetuall winter. Witnesse the *Thunder* on the *Alpes* also: yea, and that in the middle of the Sea, 500 leagues from shoare or anything that is dry. Yea, it frequently both *Snowes* and *Thunders* vpon the *Andes* at one instant, and, in *dry* places that are hard by, scarce euer *Thundering.*

But, not to passe the *Line* for it, you see in this little Booke how *Charlton Island*, which is no more Northerly then your *Cambridge*, is yet so vnsufferably cold that it is not habitable; and that there encounter so many different (at least so seeming) occurrences of nature as were well worth the disquisition of a *Philosopher.* I could (in my smal reading) instance in many, many, other particulars, which I had rather should be found out by some industrious searchers after *Nature*, in the *Moderne Relations* of our *Discoverers*, then in this my short *Proposition.* Tis not to be doubted but that the careful reading of our *Books of Voyages* would more elucidate the *History of Nature*, and more conduce to the improuement of *Philosophy*, then any thing that hath beene lately thought upon. These *Nauigations* haue in part fulfilled that of the Prophet: *Many shall passe to and fro, and knowledge shall be increased.* This, I suppose, might be obserued from this study: That the great and infinite *Creator* hath so disposed and varied euery thing that it is impossible for mans reason and obseruation to conclude him; and, therefore, though vulgar and receiued *Philosophie* may giue a man a *generall* hint all the world over, yet no *Vniuersall* and vnfayling certainty.

2. This brings mee to my *Second Proposition:* That, seeing God will not haue his works, (no more then his Kingdome) to come by obseruation, *Whether, then, ought any humane dictates to bee so Magisteriall as to prescribe against all other examination?*

No humane study more conduces to the setting forth of Gods glory then the contemplation of his great workes, in *Philosophie*, for, though a smattering knowledge in *Second Causes* warps the mind towards *Atheisme*, yet a higher speculation of them brings about againe to Religion. No man, I beleeue, will thinke it fit for vs to haue a *Pope in Philosophie*, one that no body shall presume to censure of, but all be bound to aduance his *Decretalls* aboue the *Holy Scriptures.* This is the scandall that my selfe and diuers good men take at the vndue authority in some heates pinn'd upon the *Stagerite*.

I am sorry that the *Israelites* dotage vpon *Salomons Philosophy* should haue caused the zealous *Hezekiah* to call in and to suppresse those vnualuable *Physickes*, for feare, I suppose, lest their credit should haue as much derogated from the authority of the *Holy Scriptures* as the *brazen Serpent* (which he destroyed about the same time) had done from *Religion.* None will beleeue that *Salomons Philosophie* was contrary to the *Scriptures*, seeing the *Scripture* commends *Salomon* for them. Twas not *Hezekiahs* feare, therefore (or not onely), lest there might haue beene a competition betweene them, but a neglect of one of them: he was iealous lest the *Scripture* might haue any writing set vp by it, though not against it,

Can *Diuines*, then, be blamed for speaking when they heare *Aristotles Philosophy* to be solely magnified, and the study of the *Scripture Philosophy* disrespected? Or that when tis confest, That such a thing is true in *Diuinity*, and yet the *Moderating* of the point *determine* for *Philosophie?* Nay, to heare it cald *absurd* and *ridiculous*, to haue Scripture vrgd at all in point of *Philosophy?* No doubt there is, *But whatsoeuer is false in Diuinity is also false in Nature*, how much show of truth soeuer it passes with in *Philosophy*. *Philosophy* hath taken its turne in the *Schooles*, and the *holy Texts*, by the *Schoolemen*, have euen been submitted vnto *Aristotles:* yea, to the great corruption of *Theologie*, as the complaint is, hath this man been so farre aduanced, That *Contra est Philosophus, and Contra est Apostolus* haue familiarly passed vp and down for equall *Oppositions*, so that it hath been a *measuring cast* oftentimes betwixt the *Prophet* and the *Peripatetick;* and by foule play hath the measure beene made to stand the harder at the *Peripatetick*, for that the *Prophet* hath beene enforced to comply with him by a *wrested interpretation*. Thus had *S. Paul* need giue his caveat vnto *Theologie*, as well as vnto *Theologues, Beware lest any man spoyle you through Philosophy*

All this were to no purpose, unlesse the *Text of God* were excellent in this kinde, and embellished here and there with most admirable *Philosophy*. What incomparably rare foot-steps of it haue we in the Bookes of *Genesis, Iob*, and the *Psalmes?* How noble a Study then were it, and how worthy the leisure of some excellently learned, to bestow some time vpon it? *Valesius*, the *Physician*, hath, in his *Sacra Philosophia*, done something in this kinde: who yet might haue done better, here and there, for the honour of the Scriptures I am not so sottish to beleeue that every particular is to be drawn out of *Scripture:* tis none of my doteage, that. Or that God in Scripture did intend, euery where, the accuratenesse of Philosophy; or stand to be so curious in *definitions* and *decisions*. Nor so foolish would I be thought as to haue all *Philosophy* taken in pieces and new moulded by the *Scriptures* Nor, that nothing should be determined on till a *Text* confirmed it. But this, perchance, might profitably be thought vpon: That, where the *Scriptures* haue any thing in this kinde, it should more reuerently be esteemed; collections out of scattered places (as is done out of *Aristotle*) made : these compared, and their *Resultances* obserued. This, surely, would amount to more then is yet thought of: and, a-*Gods* name, let Schollers be so bold with *Aristotle* as to examine him vpon good assurance by what is *Truths Touch-stone*. Receiued *Philosophy* is a most necessary hand-maid to the *Scriptures*; but let her not be set aboue her Lady, nor no competition be maintained betwixt them.

Something else remaines to be thought of: That, seeing the same *God* who gave *Aristotle* these good parts hath, in like manner, raised vp many excellent Spirits more, whether it were not iniurious vnto what is done, and a discouragement to what might be done, to have the inuentions or obseruations of those excellent wits and great industries so abasht with *Aristotles* authoritie that they can haue no credit in the world, for that his *Dictates* haue pre-occupated all good opinion. Let it not, then, be thought vnequal to examine the *first cogitations* of the *old Philosophy* by the *second thoughts* of our more moderne *Artists;* for that the same improuement may by this meanes accrew vnto our *Physicks* that hath aduanced our *Geography*, our *Mathematicks*, and our *Mechanicks*. And let it not be thought so insolent to refuse *Aristotles* authoritie singly, where his reason is not so concluding; seeing other men haue taken the boldnesse to doe that before vs in severall kinds. Some haue perfected, and others controld, his *Ethicks* by the *Scriptures*, as *Scultetus*, *Wallæus*, and some others. *Iustin Martyr*, sir-named the *Philosopher*, hath purposely written *Contra dogmata Aristotelis: Basson* and *Gassendus* (two brave men) haue newly written point-blanck against him: nor haue they taken away all liberty from those that are to follow them.

And thus, with renewing my former protestation for mine owne respects to *Aristotle*, I conclude my two *Propositions;* which I desire may receiue a fauourable construction from all ingenuous, imcapricious *Schollers*. I meant them out of good will to promote learning; to encourage and countenance future vndertakings; and, in such a case, a little too much saying may be thought not to haue exceeded an *honest Rhetorication;* for I would not be thought too earnest in it. The hint for all this, I tooke from this booke; which, in mine owne and some better Iudgements, is (to say no more) as well done and enriched with as sure and vsefull obseruations as any in this kinde I was desired by the able Author, and some other friends, to ouer-look the written Copy of it, and to amend the

English here and there[1]; in which I did not despair of doing something, for that, in my younger time, I had a little acquainted my self with the *language of the Sea*. That which put me in the head to inscribe it vnto your Names (most excellently learned *Academians*) was for that the place of this *Wintering* was within a *minute* or two of the *heighth* of our *Cambridge*; which my prayer to God is that your Studies may make famous.

Yours,
X. Z.

---

[1] See note on p 621.

APPENDICES.

APPENDIX A.

COPY OF DEPOSITIONS, ETC, RELATING TO HUDSON'S EXPEDITION IN 1610-11, NOW PRESERVED AT THE TRINITY HOUSE.[1]

Trinity House Transactions, 1609 *to* 1625, fos 11-13.

[DEPOSITIONS]

24 Octob. 1611.

ROBART BILLET, who came home Mr., sayth that, going into the Straights, they weare 5 weekes in ther Passage to Cape Salisbery, but [that], in coming to the Eastward, they weare cleere of Cape Desolation in 16 days, as he conseaues

Men turned owte of the Ship, 23 June [1611[2]].

Henry Hudson, Mr.
John Hudson, his Son
Arnold Ladley
John King, q'Mr.
Michall Butt, Maried
Thomas Woodhowse, a mathematition put away in great distress.
Adame Moore.
Philip Staff, Carpenter.
Syracke ffanner, Maried.

John Williams dyed in 9 Octob. [1610].
Ivet dyed comming home.

---

[1] The general interest of the following documents has been explained in the Introduction (pp. xiv to xvi), and many of the details have been commented on in footnotes appended to Foxe's narrative of Hudson's expedition (see pp. 114-162). Here and there, largely owing to the use of contractions, the meaning is obscure.

[2] As to this date, see p. 145, *note*

Slaine.

Henry Greene.
William Wilson.
John Thomas.
Michaell Peerce.

Men that came home.

Robart Billet, Mr
Abecocke Pricket, a land man put in by the Aduenturers.
Edward Wilson, Surgeon.
ffrancis Clemens, Boteson.
Adrian Motter.
Bennet Mathues, a land man.
Nicholas Syms, Boy.
Silvanus Bond, Couper.

The Company remaining in the Ship after the Mr. was put owte, made choice of Billet for Master

They departed from London 18 Aprill, and fell with Cape Salsbery 2 August, victled for 8 monethes.

[Robert Billet]

ABACUCK PRICKET, sworne, saith: That the Shipp began to retorne about 12 of June, and [that], abowt 22 or 23, they put away the Master

Greene and Willson weare imployed to fishe for the Company, and, being at sea, combyned to Steale away the Shallope, but at last resolued to take away the Ship, and put the Mr. and other Impotent men into the Shallope

Vpon his othe, he cleers the now Mr. of any foreknowledg of this complot, but saith he assures him self they relyed on Iuett's Judgment and skill.

[Abacuck Prickett.]

SILUANUS BOND sayth that the certaine tyme of the Ship's comming owte of the wintring port, he remembreth not, but that it was in June But he saith that Wilson was the first that plotted the putting away of the Mr., and saith that, by the relation of William Wilson and Greene, the now Mr. was acquainted with the same, either the second or third man, and the rest that came home weare all likewise consenting to it.

Siluanus Bond.

EDWARD WILSON, surgeon, saith that they came owte of ther wintering Port abowt the 12 of June, but this deponent knew not of the putting the Mr. owte of the Ship untill he sawe the Mr. brought pinioned downe before his Caben dore: neither who weare to be put owte of the Ship with him.

Edward Wilson.

FRANCIS CLEMENS, ADRIAN MOTTER, BENNET MATHUES, all sworne, saith that the Mr. was put owte of the Shipp by consent of all that weare in health, in regard that ther victells was much wasted by him, and so to preserue life in the rest. The resolution was begun by W^m. Wilson, Greene, and others, and few or none against it; and some of those that weare put away weare directly against the Master, and yet, for safty of the rest, [were] put away with him: and all by thos men that weare slaine principally.

Bennet Mathue.
Fran. Clemence.
Adrian Motter.

[REPORT ON THE DEPOSITIONS.[1]]

24 Octob 1611.

By examination of Seauen of the Company of that Shipp that endeauored the Northwest discouery,[2] it plainly appeareth that the Mr and the rest of thos men which are lost weare put owte of the Ship by consent of all such as are come home and then were in health, and also not with owte the approbation of some of them that went with him, as Michaell Butt, who consented to ye same.

It appeareth, further, that the plot was begun by Henry Greene and Wm. Willson, and that by the privitie of Iuet, whome they presumed on for ther best Guide

Some of them confess that Robart Billet, who came home Mr., was acquainted with the same in the beginning. But Pricket cleers him therof, and saith he was chosen to take the charge after the Mr. was put away.

They all charge the Mr. to have wasted the Victells by a scuttle made owte of his Cabin into the hold, and it appears that he fedd his ffavorits, as the Surgeon, &c., and kept others at only ordenary allowance, w^{ch} [led] thos that weare not [thus] fauored to giue the attempt and to performe it so violently.

But all conclude that, to saue some from Starving, they weare content to put away so many; and that, to most of thos, it was vtterly vnknowne who should goe or who [should] tarry, but as affection or rage did guide them in that fury that weare authors and executors of that Plott.

---

[1] The following document is obviously what I have here described it as, namely, a report by the authorities of the Trinity House on the foregoing Depositions.

[2] The eighth survivor was a boy, Nicholas Syms, by name, as stated above.

NORTH WEST DISCOVERY.[1]

Owteward Bound. Course westerly.

On the Westerne side of ffretum Davies, they enter an Indraught the xxvjth of June; the Sea to sett S. W.; the land trending from N. to W.

27. Standing with it, they find it to sett more Westerly.

30. Anchoring on yce, they find a sett to West

6th of July. Fast to yce, they found, at 113 fad, green ose, and next day grose gravell sand at 116; then, losing, in three howers, osie sand at 120 fad. The morning drift was S E. b. E., by reason of the flodd from N W. b. W.

7 July. Standing N N.W., he found him selfe laid Sotherly by the fludd, and at afternoone the Tyde turned. At night, thē stop in 122 fād., 1 leage of an Isle of Yce aground, bearing W ; but, by 3 next morning, it bore E Sotherly.

9th. Ice driuing to the Westward   (*note the driuing.*)

10th. A strong sett of Yce to the West and W S W

11th. Imbayd, they find the fludd from the N. shole; sounding, 4 fadd., height and flud, 8 howers the chang day

12 and 13th. The North Coast fre from Ice.

17. 130 fadd. 145 fadd., and, by the lead, a drift N.N.W.; and, in 120 fadd. by the Ship's drift at haser and graple, the lead on ground finds the fludd to come from N.N.W.

19th. Betweene Hold with Hope and Cape Henry. No ground in 160 fadd. wthin 2 legues of shore. The flud from W. b. N.

21. A ground sea and way more westerly then accompt.

ffirst of August. No ground at 180 fadd.

2. Thē make Salisburyes I.; West south, and a faire sound West beffore thes the whirling sea either by ouer fale or meeting currant a streigh Passage S W. High land; 100 fadd. 2 legues ouer.

On the west land, they obserue the fludd to come from the north, heightening by shore 5 fadd.

In the Bay.

[*Outward Bound.*]   *Course Southerly.*

12 of August   They find White water, like Whaye.

13 They find strong fludd from N.W. b. N.; and the ebb from S.E. b. S. Yt flowd 9 a clock the 5 ☽ dayes and height 1½ fadd.

22. A Tyde from W. by N. from 8 till Noone.

---

[1] The foregoing appears to be an abstract of the log-book of the *Discovery*.

APPENDICES.

In the Bay.

Homewards Bound. Course N Easterly.

15 of July[, 1611.] Comming vp to the Straits mouth, they find a Sea comming from owte the North.

26. They run a ground on a Rock in the litle Streight mouth at 9 a.

Flat againe at 4 in the morning.

27. On the Wester side, they make land at N. by W., 8 legues of, not seene outwards bound. They take it to be ye Westerne Coast. Y^e tide came in W.S.W., and ye ebb E.N.E.

2 of August. [They passed] through the great Straighte; course Northeast and Westerly.

4. They make Islands of Yce, setting from East to West.

7. They see a Whale playing.

9. They make Hold wth Hope and the Northeren Cost both.

10 2 Islands of Yce, comming from the East into the Straights.

13. No ground at 80 fadd., yet [they] herd ye ratle of land ne^r at 85, among the Islands.

14. The set of Tyde from E. to West in 140 fadd. anchored.

15 Hope for a through faire, because the Yce draue from ye E. to W.

16. Cleare of the Straights.

GROUNDS FOR A CONIECTURE.[1]

The Streights lye from ffretum Dauis West and East, or neere at lest 200 l^e long, and 30 or 40 broade at most; sometymes very narrowe. The Soatheren Coast full of Bayes and pestered with yce; the Northeren, shorter and free.

At the Westerne mouth, the Northerne side opens to No. Northwest; the Great Billow comes in [here], Salsbury his Island being a head.

South[ward], the Great Bay enters and trends above 200 l^e. long.

The tyde setts into that Bay from No. and by W. into the Straight, ut Supra, yt setts more westerly, checking the current that comes from the East: and alwayes beares the Ice in to the West, as the whale plaid.

> Whether that great Bay must not be fedd from y [western] Oceans?

---

[1] This document may either have been supplied by the survivors of the expedition, or it may have been drawn up by the officials of the Trinity House for consideration. If the latter, we may regard the document following it as being their report after consideration.

Whether that Ocean lye not Norwest of Salsburyes Headland and the Straights?

Whether that Ocean can bee any other then ye South Sea?

[CONCLUSIONS]

Whereas it is enquired of us, the Mr., Wardens, and Assistants of the Trinity howse, what our opinion is concerning that discouery which is made in the Northwest: We, having deliberately herd the Mr. of the sayd ship that brought her home (who is the only man of that Company that can speake of Nauigation), doe conclude, for ought we can discerne by such Globes as we haue viewed: That the sayd Ship was neuer so far to the Westward to recou^r the South Sea as wee conceaue the land to be by many Leagues. And our opinion is that the same graund Bay in wch they sailed must be fedd from ye Ocean But [we] cannot coniecture that it is from the South Sea, but rather from the Ocean on the Northeast side of the Continent, because the currant did driue perpetually from the East But, whereas the Islands of Yce driue away from Cape Salsbury W N W., the land trending N.N.West, and that at the same Cape it heights 4 or 5 fadd water and keeps a trew course of Tyde, as he reports, we thinke that the Passage is to be found betwene the West and the N. West, and not more Northerly:

Yeouen vnder the Common Seale of our Corporation, the 26th of October, 1611.

APPENDIX B.

LETTER OF CREDENCE OF KING JAMES THE FIRST, AND PRINCE HENRY'S INSTRUCTIONS GIVEN TO SIR THOMAS BUTTON.[1]

James, by the Grace of the Most High God, Creator and only Guider of the Universal World, King of Great Brittaine, France, and Ireland, Defender of the Faith, &c.

Right high, Right Excellent, and Right mightie Prince, divers of our subjects, delighting in navigation and finding out of unknowne countries and peoples, having heard of the fame of you and of your people, have made a voyage thither of purpose to see your countries, and with your people to exercise exchange of Marchandize, bringing to you such things as our Realmes doe yeeld, and to receave from you such as y^{rs} affoord and may be of use for them, [it being] a matter agreeable to the nature of humane societye to have commerce and intercourse each with other. And, because, if they shalbe so happie as to arrive in yor Dominions, that you may understand that they are not persons of ill condition or disposition, but such as goe upon just and honest grounds of trade, Wee have thought good to recommende them and their Captain, *Thomas Button*, to your $favo^r$ and protection, desiring you to graunt them, while they shalbe in yor country, not only favor and protection, but also such kindness and entertainment as may encourage them to continue their travailles and be the beginning of further amitie between you and us. And we shall be ready to requite it with the like goodwill towards any of y^{rs} that shall have cause or desire to visit our Countries.

Geven under o^r Signet at o^r Pallace of Westminster, the twelveth day of Aprill in the year of o^r Lord God 1612.

JAMES R.

---

[1] These two documents have been discussed, and the latter of them summarised, in the Introduction (pp. xxvii-xxix). As there stated, the originals of both were in existence up to a quarter of a century ago, but their present whereabouts is unknown. The Letter of Credence has been reproduced from *The Athenæum*. The Instructions have been copied from one of the facsimiles of the original prepared by Mr. Hanrot, and now in the British Museum. In some minor respects, both *The Athenæum* version of the Instructions and Rundall's version differ from the facsimile.

Henry P.

CERTAINE ORDERS AND INSTRUCÕONS *set downe by the most noble Prince, Henry Prince of Wales, &c., this 5 of Aprill 1612 vnder his highnes signature and signe manuell and deliuered vnto his Seruant, Captaine Thomas Button, Generall of the Company now imployed about ye full and perfect discouery of the North-west passage for the better gouernment as well of the shipps committed to his charge as of the personns in them imployed vppon all occasions whatsoever.*

First therefore:

1. THAT it maie please Almightie god to preserue you and your charge from danger, and if it shall seeme good vnto his wisedome to giue a blessing of successe vnto this hopefull and important enterprize, LET there be a religious care dailie throughout your Shippes to offer vnto his divine Matie the Sacrifice of praise and thanks-giving for his fatherlie goodnes and protecc̃on. Especiallie prouide that the blessed daies wch hee hath sanctified vnto his service be christianlike obserued with godlie meditacions

2. LET noe quarrelling or prophane speeches, noe swearing or blaspheming of his Holie name, noe drunkennes or lewde behaviour passe vnpunished, for feare of his most heavie indignac̃on.

3. LET there be a perticuler note taken of all suche as shall shew themselves most willinglie obedient vnto you, most dilligent and industrious in their charges, most resolute and constant in the prosecution of this Acc̃on. That therebie we being informed at your returne, maie esteeme accordinglie of their deservings.

4. LET there be faithfull and true registring everie daie of all the memorable accidents of the voyage and that by as many as shalbe willing, especiallie by the most skilfull and discreete personnes, whome we would have once everie 10 or 12 daies to confer their Notes for the better perfecting a Jornall, wch we shall expect at your returne

5. MORE perticulerlie, when you shalbe cleare of the Landes end, be carefull to have kept a true accoumpt of yor waye to GROINLAND, and from thence to the STREIGHTS mouth, and to observe in what Latitude it lieth, what face the coast beareth, what Sea setteth into it, and, when you are within it, howe the coast doth trend, the contynuance and course of the Ebbe and ffludd, what height it riseth, from whence it cometh, and with what Moone, what Current, Eddie, or overfall you finde, what Islandes or Rockes, and howe bearing, and last of all your Soundings wch you must trie with good store of faddome once at least everie ffourth glasse, and oftener amongst broken landes, Rocks,

Shole and white waters. Yet, remembring that the waie is alreadie beaten to DIGGES ISLAND, rather then loose tyme, we would have you hasten thither, and leave the perfect observaĉon of theis thinges to the PINNACE in her returne.

6. As often as occasion offers it selfe, especiallie when you shalbe forced to sende on lande (for we would not [have] that you your selfe should quitt your Shippe), Let some skilfull man, with good instrument, obserue the ELEUATION, the DECLINATION, the VARIATION of the compasse and if you aryve time enoughe, the begynning and ending of the ECLIPSE that will happen on the 20th of Maye next. ESPECIALLIE, if you should winter, let there be carefull and painefull watching to obserue the instant of the coniunctions of anie of the planets, or the distance of the Moone from anie fixed starre or starres of note. All wch we would have entred into a Booke, and presented me at your returne

7. LET there be care by yor order and direction for keeping of your Shippes in consorte all your course, wherein we wishe you to make all the hast you can to the STRAIGHTS MOUTH, but we thinck your surest waie wilbe to stand vpp to ISELAND and soe over to GROINLAND in the heighte of 61 soe to fall downe with the current to the most Southerlie Cape of that land lyeing in about 59 called CAPE FARWELL, wch pointe as the Ice will give you leave, you must double, and from thence, or rather from some 20 or 30 L. to the Northward of it, if you shall fall over DAUIS his straights to the westerne Maine, in the height of 62 Degrees or thereabouts you shall finde HUDSONS streights, wch you maie knowe by the furious course of the Sea and Ice into it, and by certaine Islandes in the NORTHERNE SIDE thereof, as your CARDE shewes.

8. BEING in We holde it best for you to keepe the NORTHERNE side, as most free from [the] pester of Ice, at least till you be past CAPE HENRY, from thence, followe the leading Ice betweene KING JAMES and QUEEN ANNES forelands, the distance of wch two CAPES observe if you can, and what harbour or Rode is neir them, but yet make all the hast you maie to SALSBURY his Island, betweene wch and the Northerne continent you are like to meet a great and hollowe billowe from an opening and flowing Sea from thence. Therefore, remembring that your end is West, we would have you stand over to the opposite Maine, in the Latitude of some 58 degrees, where, riding at some Headland, observe well the flood, if it come in SOUTHWEST, then you maie be sure the passage is that waie; yf from the NORTH or NORTHWEST, your course must be to stand vpp into it, taking heed of following anie flood for feare of entring into BAIS, INLETS, or SANDS,[1] wch is but losse of time to noe purpose.

---

[1] Query, *Sounds.*

9. By the waie: if your SHIPPES within the STREIGHTS should sever, we thinck DIGGS ISLAND, for the good Rode and plentie of refreshing that is there, wilbe your fittest RANDE-VOUS. And, if it should fall out that the WINTER growe vppon you before your finding a thoroughe fare into the SOUTH SEA, we thinck your safest waie wilbe to seeke Southward for some place to winter in; for we assure our self by Gods grace you will not returne, without either the good Newes of a passage, or sufficient assurance of an impossibility.

10. YOU must be careful to prevent all Mutynie amongst yo[r] people, and to preserve them as muche as maie be from the Treacherie and villanie of the SALUAGES, and other Easterne[1] people Where ever you arrive, have, therefore, as little to doe with them as maye be, onlie, if the STRAGHTS it self afford noe sufficient strength,[2] you shalbe happie in finding out some convenient parte on the back of AMERICA, or some Island in the South Sea, for a haven or stačon for our Shippes and Marchaundizes hereafter, but yet spend as little tyme as maie be in this or anie other searche, saving of the Passage, till you have dispatched the PYNNACE wth advertisement of your entrie into the SOUTH SEA, w[ch] must be done as sone as you shalbe thereof assured.

11. LAST of all, see that you and all vnder yo[r] charge, doe faiethfullie obserue and followe all such further directions and instruccons as shalbe given by the ADVENTURERS. And, to the end it may appeare what care we haue of the Action, and howe acceptable everie mannes good indevour and service therin wilbe to Vs, LET theis be perticulerlie read once everie Moneth, if it can be, to your whole Companie.[3]

---

[1] This word is clearly "easterne" in the original, but its meaning is not obvious

[2] Again, although the word is clear in the MS., the meaning is obscure.

[3] The document concludes with a reproduction of the Prince's seal, with his monogram "H P.", and the legend, *Henricus Mag. Brit. et Hib. Principis Dux Walliæ.*

APPENDIX C.

Motiues

Inducing A Proiect for the discouerie of the North pole terrestriall: the streights of Anian into the South sea, & coasts thereof.[1]

All those Kingdomes are most complete, glorious, and doe best flourish wherevnto in abundance trade and traffique is performed. His Maties Kingdomes, being Ilandes whose traffique is to be mainteyned by Navigation of strong and fortified Shipps, with nomber of able Marriners, being otherwise secluded from all comerce with those of the mayne continent from exporting and importing of Marchandize, the furniture of Shipping consisting in many things wch England wants, as Masts, pitch, Tarr, Rosen, and cordage, wch now we enioy by ye favo^r of forraigne Pottentates.

The life of Navigation consisteth in ffishermen to begett shipps and Marriners: in Marchants to breed and mainteyne them and in Chieftaines to enable and encourage them. Otherwise, in Iland Kingdomes, the Citties, Burrowes, Port Townes, and Havens decay, wth all the whole people, where trade and traffique to proffitt is neglected

And, most notouriously, wee finde that trade and traffique with o^r neighbo^r countryes is in small request, the proffitt now seldome answering the Marchants adventure, whereby the poore ENGLISH Marchants, artificers, and Laborers can scarce gayne meate to their bellyes and clothes to their backs, so cunningly and disdainefully doe o^r neighbo^r contryes reiect o^r home commodities, to th'end to sett their owne people awork and to impoverish o^{rs.}

Wee shalbe of necessitie enforced to seeke out remote parts of ye world to vent o^r comodities of the[se] realmes at a higher rate than now we doe, whereby o^r people may live by their labo^{rs}, Shipping may be encreased, and that o^r Marriners be not enforced for want of entertaynem^t to runn dayly into the service of other Nations, to be imployed there, either their to serue or at home to starue.

More better it is and honorable for our State to vent o^r Comodities in Remote Regions, where wee may haue greate prizes for

---

[1] This document has been discussed and summarised in the Introduction (pp. xxxv-xxxviii). The following is an exact reprint of the original, the proof having been sent to America and there carefully corrected

them, and retourne nedefull Marchandizes at easy rates, being had at the first hand, by the same [means] encreasing o^r Shippes and Marriners, to ye good of all, and not to be beholding to o^r bad neighbo^{rs} or cold frendes from whome we receave nedelesse wares for o^r Staple comodities, importing much more thereof then we export of o^{rs}, giving o^r mony to the boote, to spoile of o^r land, mightily enriching o^r foresaide neighbo^{rs} and greatly impoverishing o^{r}selves, as doth manifestly appeare throughout all the Kingdome by the decay thereof.

A glorious state and renowned greate BRITTAYNE would be, had the same discovered the North pole & passage into ye South Sea [and] vnto the rich contryes of CHINA, CATAYA, and JAPON, with the Ilands of MOLUCCAS and PHILLIPPINAS, and many other [countries] bordering vpon the same Seas, there to sett forth the name of JESUS CHRIST and preach the gospell of Joy where multitudes of people are not yet called, and where plenty and abundance of many rich wares are to be had at lowe prizes and at the first hand, where all o^r home comodities might be vented at a greate rate, not only for the good and gaynes of the Gentleman, Marchant, tradsman, Artificer, and Laborere of all Greate BRITTAYNE, but also further would encrease Hundreths of Shipps & Thowsands of Marriners, making this land the Storehouse of all EUROPA, [which is] a matter of wonderfull greate importance.

The people of the North pole terrestriall haue but one day in the yeare.

Over & aboue [all this], within ye same passage doth growe in abundance all those things necessary for ye furnishing of Shipping, wch wee now haue out of POLONIA and RUSSIA, and there would be provided by the industery of such people as should be appointed therefore, wthout ye favo^r of those Pottentates aforesaide.

In the tyme of his Maties Royall Progenito^{rs}, the worthy Gentry of this land gave themselues to famous actions and were encouraged therevnto by the gratious favo^{rs} of his Highnes Progenito^{rs} respectiuely, according vnto their births, estates, and deserts, and so were taken and reputed with all the people accordingly, each man in his due ranck, by wch meanes honorable Justice and service was prosecuted to effect, and civill meetings [were] celebrated with loue and good liking, each man enioying his due right and dignitie. But, by mishap, many of ye foresaide haue lost that wch rightfully apperteyned vnto them, and so discouraged, although by no evell desert or dimerrit in themselues, but by error and impudent intrusion of some vnworthy men that haue gotten advantage to be placed in precedency at all publick meetings both for the execution of honorable services, as also at frendly enterteynments, wch causeth neglect of seruice and jvstice and breedeth envy, disagrement, and greivance in generall amongst the Gentry of the Kingdome, both men and weomen.

The King's Matie, for ye encouragement of worthy adventurers, and [for] contentment vnto the high Gentry of all his Kingdomes aforesaide, would be pleased to grace them with that favo^r by erecting an order of dignitie precedent in knighthood, or otherwise by what name or title shall seeme best to his Matie. There are many of noble births, greate livings, and due desert desirous of this society and to be adventurers, wch vpon their owne charges will prepare Shipps and men, with victualls and munition, for ye discovery aforesaide.

By wch his Matie shall not only giue Royall contentment to the worthy Gentlemen descended from auncient houses of all his Kingdomes (as John, the ffrench King, did in erecting the order of ST. OWEN: PHILIP, Duke of Burgundy, by instituting the order of the GOLDEN FLECE: and Lewes of ffraunce the Eleaventh by the order of ST MICHAELL), but in a higher degree eternizd, for that his intent is to advaunce the glory of God, enlarge his Territoryes, inrich his subiects, and make goode provision for the poore people of his Kingdomes, [which is] a work no doubt reserved of god for his Matie to performe in this his most prosperous and peaceable reigne: As well the planting as the discovery of the Northwest passage, All which is left vnto his Maties Prudency, with prayer to god for his highnes prosperitie.

Ffrom out of his Maties Three Kingdomes, ENGLAND, SCOTLAND, and IRELAND, theis Adventurers are to be selected, of noble birth descended; Or else in high Offices and worthy deserving; Or, at the least, of Two Thowsand Poundes of yearly revennewes   Theis Adventurers, in leiw of every Hundreth poundes adventured, shall haue One Thowsand acres of land where the plantačon shalbe seated, either on the North or South Sea, with further priviledges and benefitts at the discrete wisdome of the high person Parramounte, HENRIE PRINCE OF WALES.

The North pole terrestriall a Magnificent and pure Virgine yett vndiscouered.

The pith or spiritt of this proiect is not heere written: y^t resteth by speach to be deliuered, with the constant and secrett managinge thereof: for yor highnes great honour & present profitt: aboue 100,000^h. And heereafter much more.

In loue and dutie vnto your Highnes, I haue left wth Mr Wright[1] in yor librarie att St James a hand globe terrestriall for demonstračon of these.

---

[1] See p. xxxviii.

APPENDIX D.

A Charter granted to the Company of the Merchants Discoverers of the North-West Passage, July 26th, 1612.[1]

James R.

JAMES, by the grace of God, *King* of England, Scotland, ffraunce, and Ireland, Defendor of the faith, etc.

To ALL o[r] Officers, Ministers, and Subiects, and to all other people, as well w[th]in this o[r] Realme of *England* as elsewhere under o[r] Obeysance or Jurisdiccon, or in other parts, unto whom theis o[r] le[rs] Patents may appertaine and shalbee showen or redd, Greeting.

WHEREAS, wee are credibly informed that o[r] right trustie and welbeloved cozens and counsellors, Henry, Earle of Northampton, Keeper of o[r] privy Seale, Charles, Earle of Nottingham,[2] our Admirall of England, Thomas, Earle of Suff, o[r] Chamberlaine of our household, our right trusty and welbeloued Cozen, Henry, Earle of Southampton[3], William,[4] Earle of Salisbury; our right trustie and welbeloued Theophilus, Lo. Walden, S[r] Thomas Smith,[5] S[r] Robt. Maunsell,[6] S[r] Walter Cope, S[r] Dudley Diggs,[7] S[r] James Lancaster,[8] Knights; Rebecca, Lady Romney, ffrauncis Jones, one of the Aldermen of our Citty of London; John Wolstonholme, Esq.,[9] John Eldred, Robert Sandy, Will[m] Greenewell, Nicholas Leate, Hewett Stapers, Will[m] Russell, John Mericke, Abraham Chamberlaine, Philipp Burlomachie, mer-

---

[1] This long and interesting charter (which has never before been printed) is discussed and summarised in the Introduction (pp. xxxviii-xlii). It is an exact reprint from the original in the Public Record Office. It has here been broken into paragraphs and punctuated, in order to render its meaning clearer. Although the Sign Manual bears the above date, the Patent Roll (No 1950) bears date September 15th

[2] This is the man after whom Hudson or Button named Nottingham's Island.

[3] This is the man after whom Hudson or Button named Southampton Island.

[4] This should be Robert, Earl of Salisbury (see p. 304, *note*) After him, Hudson named Salisbury Island (see p. 117).

[5] See Markham's *Voyages of Baffin*, p. 11

[6] See p. 188, *note*

[7] See p. 118, *note*.

[8] See Markham's *Voyages of Baffin*, p. 3, *note* Foxe says (p. 368) that Hudson named certain islands after him,

[9] See Introduction, p. lxxvi.

chaunts of o^r Cittie of London; the Muscouia Companie; and the East India Companie[1] of the sixt voyage, did, in *Aprill* one thowsand six hundred and tenn, wth great chardge, sett fourth a shipp called the *Discouerye*, and certaine persons, under the commaund of Henry Hudson, to search and finde out a passage by the Northwest of *America* to the Sea of *Sur*, comonly called the south Sea, and have, in that voyage, found a streight, or narrowe *Sea*, by wch they hope and purpose to advaunce a Trade to the great Kingdomes of *Tartaria, China, Japan, Solomons Ilands, Chelie*, the *Philippins*, and other countryes in or upon the said sea:

FOR the better accomplishm^t and discovery whereof, o^r said sub^{ts} have sued unto us for our royall assent and licence to be graunted unto them, that they, and others that shall ioyne themselves unto them, at theire owne adventures, costs, and charges, might adventure, sett fourth, and make voyages wth shippes and pinaces for proceeding in the said discovery of the said Northwest Passage to the landes, territoryes, signioryes, and dominions aforesaid, and have likewise been Suito^{rs} unto us that, foras-

---

[1] Rundall (*Voyages North-westward*, p. 96) says that the Records of the East India Company for the period when the Company assisted in sending out Hudson are not accessible, and he appears to be correct, for I have carefully searched the Court Minute Books for any reference to the fact. It is recorded, however (*Court Minute Books*, vol iii, p 304), that, at a General Court held on December 6th, 1614, when there were present thirty-six members (most of whose names appear in the list of Members of the Company of Discoverers of the North-west Passage), that—

"M^r. Gou^{r}nor [Sir Thomas Smyth] . remembered them that 3 yeares since this company did aduenture 300^{li} p. annum for three yeares towards the discou^{ry} of the Nor'west passage, wch busines hath not succeeded accordinge to desire, thoroughe the negligence or ignoraunce of the Com'aunders; and, beinge retournd, there is somewhat brought home wch doth properlie belonge vnto this Company. The hopes and p'babilitie, notwthstandinge, of findinge yt hereafter doth incouradge many of the p'ticuler Aduenturers to proceede and vndertake a voyage this [coming] yeare, wch he thought fitt to acquainte this Company wthall, to knowe there opinions what they intend to doe therein, whether to ioyne in any parte of the said adventure, hopinge that they will not refuse to aduenture againe that remaynder wch is come home, and somewhat more, towards the said discouery. This Courte, consideringe that yt were dishonourable for such a body to wthdrawe their hands from soe worthie a worke for a small matter of charge, wch will not exceede a nobleman in their p'ticulers, and the honor and benefitt will be greate yf yt may bee found, They were, therefore, contented to ioyne for a certaine some, besyde the remaynder, wch they gave freelie by erection of hands. And, the question beeing putt likewise for three seuerall somes, They did, by the like erection of haunds, resolue upon the aduenturinge of twoe hundred pounds, so there may bee noe expectaĉon of any further supplie."

Apparently the particular voyage towards the expense of which this grant was made was that of Bylot and Baffin in 1615.

much as the successe of their charge and travells dependeth, next under the Providence of God and o^r favo^r, uppon the good order and governem^t wch shalbe used in the managinge of the said acčon, wee would be pleased to incorporate them into a Companye, as in case of other trades and discoveryes hath beene accustomed.

Wee have bin not onely willing to enclyne to theire petičon, but in regarde it is an enterprise tending to soe worthie an end, and wch now at last after manie proofes hath obtayned so happie and likely a begininge, Wee have thought of some extraordinarie meanes to grace and honor the same. And, therefore, conceiving hope that both the acčon it selfe willbe the more fortunate, and the undertakers thereof the more encouraged, if it shalbe countenaunced by o^r most deare and welbeloved sonne, *Henry, Prince of Wales*· KNOWE yee that wee doe first of all constitute and ordaine that o^r said deare sonne, ymediately under o^r selves (whose protecčon is universall), shalbe and be called Supreme Protector of the said Discovery and Company

AND, further, of o^r speciall grace, certain knowledge, and meere močon, and by the advise of our Priuie Councell, have given and graunted, and by theis p'nts for us, o^r heires and successors, wee doe give and graunt unto o^r right trusty and right welbeloved George, Archbishopp of Canterbury, Thomas Lo. Ellesmere, o^r Chauncellor of England, Henry, Earle of Northampton, Keeper of o^r Priuie seale, Lodovicke, Duke of Lenox; Charles, Earle of Nottingham, o^r Admirall, [Thomas[1]] Earle of Arundell, Thomas, Earle of Suff, our Chamberlaine of o^r howshold; Gilbert, Earle of Shrewsbury, Edward, Earle of Worcester; Willm, Earl of Pembrooke, Henry, Earle of South^{ton}, Willm,[2] Earle of *Salisbury*, Phillipp, Earle of Montgomery, Robert, Vicounte Lisle; Robert, Vicount Rochester; Thomas, Vicount ffenton; [William[1]] Lo. Mounteagle, [Thomas[1]] Lord Darcy; [William[1]] Lord Compton, William, Lord Cavendishe; [Thomas[1]] Lord Arundell of Wardour, Theophilus, Lo Walden, Edward Sackvile, Esquier; Sir Edward Cecill, Knight; [——[1]] Lord Rosse; Sr Julius Cesar, K^t, Chauncellor of o^r Excheq^r; Sir Edward Philipps, K^t, M^r of o^r Rolls; Sir John Harrington, Sir Willm Cavendishe; Sir Henry Huberd,[3] Knight and Baronett, o^r Attorney Generall; Sr Willm Maynard; Sr Thomas Puckering; Sr Henry Carie, M^r of o^r *Jewell Howse*, Sr George Moore; Sr Thomas Lake, Secretary for the *Latine Tongue*; S^r ffrauncis Bacon, o^r Sollicitor

---

[1] For some unexplained reason, blanks are, in the original, left for the Christian names of these noblemen.

[2] See p 642, *note* 4.

[3] This man was the sixth baronet, having been created among the first batch on May 22, 1611. He was afterwards Chief Justice of the Court of Common Pleas

APPENDICES.

Generall; Sr Thomas Challoner, Chamberlaine to o^r deare sonne, the Prince of Wales; Sr Charles Cornewallis; Sr John Digby; Sr Thomas Smith, Sr Robert Maunsell; Sr Walter Cope; Sr John Hollis; Sr David Murrey; Sr Henry Guilford; Sr John Sams, Sr Henry ffanshawe; Sr Arthur Manneringe; Sr Valentyne Knightley; Sr Richard Smith; Sr John Cutts; Sr George Haward, Sr William Paddy; Sr Thomas Hayes; Sr Dudley Diggs, Sr Willm Steede, Sr James Lancaster; Sr Hamon le Strange; Sr Henry Bowyer, Sr Edward Lewis; Sr John Howard; Rebecca, Lady Romeney; Adam Newton; Thomas Stephens, Attorney to o^r deare sonne, the Prince of Wales; Richard Connocke, sollicto^r and auditor generall to o^r said deare sonne, the Prince of Wales, Paule Baning; George Bowles, William Cockaine, ffrancis Jones, Aldermen of London, John Wolstonholme; John Eldred; Robt Sandy; Willm Greenewell; Nicholas Leate, Hewett Stapers; Willm Russell; John Merrick; Abraham Chamberlaine; Phillipp Burlomachie; John Smith, Thomas Digges, Thomas Smith, junior; John Digges; John Wolstonholme, junior; Henry Wolstonholme, Doctor Willm Barlowe; Olyver Styles; Thomas Culpeper; Robert Hunniwood, John ffowles; Willm Garway; Willm Quarles, John Eveline, Richard Chamberlaine, Thomas Watson; Henrie Twedy, Nicholas Salter; Willm ffanshawe, Captaine Thomas Button[1], Rowland Reynolds, Esquiers; Robert Middleton, Thomas Stone, Robert Bateman; Willm Burrell; Willm Millett, John Bancks; Thomas Westwray; Robt Goare; Morris Abbott; Richard Deane; Beniamine Decrowe; Richard Wyche; Richard Ironside; Humfrey Smith; Jefferey Kerby; Thomas Phettiplace; Humfrey Hanford; Henry Powlested; Thomas Garway; Robt Bell, Edmund Cryche; Edmund Scott; George Scott; Peter Chamberlaine; John Castelyne; Thomas Jeffereys; Arthure Robinson; Willm Evans, George Swinhowe, ffrancis Evington; John Cowchman, Robt Robinson, Humfrey Robinson; Richard Boorne; Robt Cox; Willm Payne; Gidian de Lawne; Christopher Alenson; Allen Cotton; Willm Bonham, John Milward; Richard Davyes; Richard Pointell; John ffletcher; Thomas Barber, Edward Allen; Thomasine Owfield; Willm Priestley; Humfrey Basse; Thomas Bostock; Robt Jenkinson, Thomas Johnson; John Connock ye younger, Robt Barley; George Holdman; Aden Perkins; Richard Champian; Willm Seracold; Lawrence Greene; Edward James; Robert Johnson; Willm Hasilden; John Jones; William Brewer; Thomas Chase, Willm Harrison; John Gearing; Walter Hartsfleete; Averie Drausfield; John Chambers, John Hide; Thomas Chapman; Henry Travice, John Busbridge; Richard Peate; Arnold Lulls; Raphe ffreeman; Hughe Hamersley; Willm Stone; Willm Tower-

---

[1] Button was away on his voyage at the time this charter was granted. Several of his companions are named hereafter.

son; John Hawkins; John Lee; Reynold Greene; Richard Maxlisden; Willm Allen; Raphe Allen; Richard Rogers; Christopher Goodlacke, Richard Hackett, Katherine Woodward, Willm Cockein jun^r; Richard Bull; John Burnell, Mathew Brownerigge; Daniell Gorsuche, Thomas Morley; Bernard Hyde; Henry Southworth; Bevell Molesworth; Thomas Southicke; Thomas Burnell; Thomas Dyke, George Chaundler, Abraham Jacob, Allen Cane; Raphe Hanson; John Holloway, Frauncis Garway; John Delberidge, Abraham Dawes; Robert Pennington; Willm Palmer; Samuell Hare; Thomas Whitley, Raphe Busby; John Hightlord jun^r; George Pitts; George Chamberlaine; Thomas Lever; John Morris; George Bennett, George Robins; Willm Ferryers; Isack Rumney, Willm Leveson, John Parham; Jervas Kirke; Christopher Clitherowe, Robt Papworth; Roger Dye; Thomas Covill; Peeter Humble, Thomas Jones; Gerrard Reade; Richard Hill; Thomas Juxon, ffrauncis West; Robt Offeley, Launcelott ffawkener, Nicholas Crispe, Ellis Crispe, Willm Cater, Edward Polhill, Humfrey Browne; Edward Higham; John Cason, Richard Edwards, Robt Mildmay; Edward Lutterforde; Anthonie Maydwell, Henry Brigges[1], Henry Wolstonholme; George Tucker; Willm Angell; Thomas Packington; Willm Willaston; Thomas Church, Willm Culpeper; Henry Timberlake, Richard Hackluytt[2], Richard Mountney, Robt Waldoe, Richard Penkavell; Peter Penkavell; ffrauncis Sadler; Thomas Stephens, Willm Pearepointe; Richard Atkinson, Gregory Allen, John Waldoe; John Adderley; David Watkins; Edmund Howe, John Ingram[3], Willm Gibbins[3], ffrauncis Nelson[4]; Robert Bylott[5]; Abacuck Prickett[5]; Edward Wilson[6]; George Iseham; Edmund Leaver, Charles Antonie, Robt Ray, Samuell Armitage, Benjamin Penkavill, Nicholas Penkavill, Digorie Penkavill,[7] and Edward Wright,[8] m'chaunts, that they

---

[1] See Introduction, p. lx.

[2] The celebrated author of the *Voyages*

[3] Ingram and Gibbins were companions of Button (see pp 174 and 195). It is curious that the name of Button's other companion Hawkridge (see p. 167) does not appear

[4] This is the man after whom Button named Port Nelson (see p. 166),

[5] These were two of the survivors of Hudson's expedition who accompanied Button (see p. 164, *note*).

[6] This was, no doubt, the surgeon who had accompanied Hudson's expedition, and returned home as one of the eight survivors (see p. 630). We may assume, from the fact that his name comes next to those of Nelson, Bylot, and Prickett, that he also accompanied Button. It is likely that some of those whose names follow his also formed part of Button's crews.

[7] Probably these were the heirs of Richard Penkavill, to whom, on January 19th, 1607, King James, in acknowledgment of his efforts to discover a North-West Passage, granted a charter (printed in Rymer's *Fœdera*, vol. xvi, p. 660) incorporating him and his associates as "The Collegues of the Fellowship for the Discoverie of the North Passage".

[8] See Introduction, p. xxxviii.

and everie of them[1] shalbe one body *Corporate* and *Politique* of themselves by the name of the GOUERNOR AND COMPANY OF THE MERCHAUNTS OF LONDON, DISCOUERERS OF THE NORTH-WEST PASSAGE, and them, by that name, for us, o^r heires and successors, wee doe incorporate as one body corporate and politique, really, fully, and wholly, by theis p'nts, and that by the same name they shall have perpetuall succession, and that they and theire successors, by the name of the Governor and Company of the Merchaunts of London, Discoverers of the Northwest passage, be, and at all tymes hereafter shalbe, persons able and capable in lawe to have, take, purchase, receive, possesse, and enioy mannors, messuages, landes, ten'ts, rents, lib'ties, priviledges, and hereditam^{ts} of whatsoever kinde, nature, or quality wch are not helde of us, o^r heires or successors in chief, or by knights service, to them and their successors not exceeding the value 200^{li} p. ann, the statute of landes and ten'ts not to be putt in Mortmayne, or anie other statute, act, ordinance, provision, or restrainte, or anie other matter, cause, or thing whatsoever to the contrary notwthstanding, and to alien and dispose thereof as they shall thinke fitte and convenient, and that they and theire successors, by the name of the Governor and Companie of the Merchaunts of London, Discoverers of the Northwest Passage, shall and may be persons able and capable in law to pleade and be impleaded, aunsweare and be aunsweared, defend and be defended, in whatsoever courts and places, and before whatsoever Judges, Justices, officers, and ministers of us our heires and successors, and in all and singular pleas, acc̃ons, suites, causes, and demaundes whatsoever, of whatsoever kind, nature, or sorte, in such manner and forme as anie other o^r leige people of this o^r Realme of *England*, or other o^r dominions, being persons able and capable in law, may impleade and be impleaded, aunsweare and be aunsweared, defend and be defended, have, purchase, receive, take, possesse, give, graunt, lett, or dispose, by anie

---

[1] The highly remarkable nature of the foregoing list of names has been already alluded to (Introduction, p. xxxix). A large proportion of the names appear also in the charter incorporating the East India Company, granted on December 31st, 1600; but, whereas the East India Company's list contains the name of only one man above the rank of a knight (George, Earl of Cumberland), while the great majority of the 216 members consisted of mere merchants, the above list is in every way the most remarkable of the two as regards the high rank and eminent position of those enumerated. Without doubt, the great success and large profits which had attended the early ventures of the East India Company had attracted the attention of many of the leading men of the day, and had made them anxious to participate in the still larger profits which were promised by Hudson's supposed discovery of a North-West Passage (see Introduction, p. xvi). In several other respects, the charter printed above resembles that granted to the East India Company.

lawfull waies or meanes whatsoever; To wch ende and purpose, it shall and may be lawfull for the said Governor and Companie of the Merchaunts of London, Discoverers of the Northwest Passage, to use and have a com'on seale or seales for all the causes and businesses of them and theire successors, wch seale or seales, o^r will and pleasure is, shalbe engraven and sett fourth in manner following, that is to saie, wth o^r Escouchion or coate at armes on the one side, rounded wth the title of the saide companie, and on the other side wth the three Estridge feathers, as o^r deare sonne *Henry*, Prince of Wales, doth give the same, yet wth this difference, that upon the feathers theis wordes be engraven, *Juuat ire per altum*,[1] and that the border be rounded with theis wordes, *Tibj seruiat ultima Thule*.[2]

AND, for the better ordering and governm^t of the said companie, wee will and by theis p'nts, for us, o^r heires and successors, wee doe ordaine and appointe that from hencefourth one of the same company shalbe elected and appointed in manner hereafter expressed, wch shalbe called the Governor of the said Company, And that from hencefourth there shalbe fower and twenty of the said companie, elected and appointed in manner hereafter expressed, who shalbe called Com'itties[3] or Directors of the said Companie, who, togither wth the Governor for the tyme being, shall have the direccon of the voyages and provision of the shipping, merchandises, and all other things thereunto belonginge, as also the sale of all goodes and marchandises wch shalbe retourned in any of theire shippes in any theire voyages, and the managinge of the trade, and orderinge of all theire busines and affaires belonginge to the said Company, for so much as they shall trade in ioynt stocke.

AND wee doe will and ordeine that the said Governor and Companie of the Merchaunts of London, Discoverers of the Northwest Passage, and theire successors, shall from hencefourth forever be ruled, ordered, and governed according to such manner and forme as in theis p'nts is expressed and no otherwise; And that they shall have, holde, and enioy all such liberties, priuileges, and jurisdiccons as are by theis p'nts graunted unto them.

---

[1] "He delights to go upon the Deep." This motto seems to have been adopted personally by Henry Prince of Wales, for it appears upon the excellent portrait of him in George Vertue's *Heads of the Kings of England* (Lond., fo., 1736).

[2] "The uttermost Thule shall serve thee".

[3] The modern meaning of the word "committee" is that of a *body of persons* to whom the management of certain business is committed, but it seems originally to have been applied to any individual to whom such work was committed, as now in law. Murray (*New English Dictionary*) cites the twenty-four "Committees" of the East India Company (founded 1600) as an instance.

FOR the better execuĉon of wch o^r graunt, and forasmuch as wee have bene credibly informed that the said Sr Thomas Smith, Sr Dudley Digges, Knights, and John Wolstonholme Esqr., have beene and were the first Movers and principall Instrum^ts of setting fourth of shippes to *Sea*, for accomplishing of the aforesaid discovery, Wee have therefore ordained, named, constituted, and appointed, and by theis p'nts doe ordaine, name, constitute, and appointe, o^r said welbeloved sub^t Sr Thomas Smith, Knight, to be the first and p'nte Governor in the said Companie, and [to] contynue governor thereof from the date of theis p'nts until the first daie of October next ensuing, if he so long live, and from thence untill a new Governo^r shalbee chosen and sworne in manner hereafter expressed.[1]

AND we doe by theis p'ntes, for us, o^r heires and successors, constitute and make Sr Robert Maunsell, Sr James Lancaster, Sr Dudley Digges, K^ts, Willm Cockaine, ffrauncis Jones, Aldermen of o^r Citty of London, John Wolstonholm Esqr, Willm Greenewell, John Eldred, Nicholas Leete, Nicholas Salter, Robert Offeley, Henry Stap,[2] Willm Russell, Richard Wyche, Ralphe ffreeman, Willm Stone, Robert Midleton, Willm Harrison, Morris Abbott, Humfrey Hanford, Philip Burlomache, Abraham Chamberlaine, Robert Bell, and William Burrell, Merchaunts of our saide Citty of London, the first and p'nte fower and twenty Com'itties and Directors of the saide Companie, to contynue therein from the date of theis p'nts till the first daie of October next ensuing, if they shall soe long live, and from thence untill fower and twenty Com'itties more, or Direct^rs, shalbe elected and sworne in manner hereafter expressed; And that it shall and may be lawfull for ye said Governor and Com'itties and [? *or*] Direct^rs, wth the generality or the greater part of the said Companie, being publiquely assembled, to elect, nominate, and appointe one of ye Companie to be deputy to the Governor, at wch tyme he shalbe publiquely sworne faithfully and truly to execute his office of deputy to the Governor; after wch oath so taken, it shall and may be lawfull for him, in ye absence of the Governo^r, to exercise his office in such sort as ye Governo^r ought to doe.

AND, further, wee graunt, for us, o^r heires and successors, unto the saide Governor and Companie of the Marchaunts of London, Discoverers of the Northwest Passage, and unto theire successors, that it shall and may be lawfull to and for ye said Governor and Companie, yearly and every yeere, on the first daie of *October*, or at any tyme w^thin thirty daies after that daie, to meete togither in some convenient place, there to choose and

---

[1] He was also at the time Governor of the East India Company. In the course of his life, he was also Governor of the Muscovy, Somer Island, and other incorporated trading Companies.

[2] Hewett Stapers is undoubtedly intended.

nominate one of the said companie who shalbe Governor for the yeere followinge, or till a new choyce; wch person, being so elected, before he be admitted to the execuc̃on of his office, shall take an oath before ye old Governo^r, his p'decessor, or his deputie, and six of the Com'itties and [? *or*] directo^rs for ye tyme beinge, well and truly to execute his office in all things concerninge the companie; At wch tyme, wee likewise will and graunt that it shall and may be lawfull to and for the said Governor and Companie, or the maior part of them then publiquely assembled, to nominate and elect fower and twenty of the said Companie, wch shalbe Com'itties or Directo^rs of the said Company for a yeere then next followinge, or till a new choyce be made, who shall likewise be sworne before the Goveno^r or his deputy, that they and every of them shall well and faithfully execute their place and office in all things concerninge the same.

But, if it shall fortune ye said Governo^r, deputy, or com'itties, or anie of them, to dye, or otherwise, in respect of theire misbehavio^r or ill governm^t, to be duly removed out of his place or office, (wch Governo^r, deputy, and com'itties our will and pleasure is shalbe removeable at ye pleasure and discrec̃on of ye Governo^r, deputy, com'itties, and generality then publiquely assembled, or ye greater part of them), that then and so often it shall and may be lawfull to and for ye Governo^r and Companie to assemble themselves togither and to make a new elecc̃on of any such as shall soe dye or be removed; wch p'son or p'sons, being soe elected, shall and may use and exercise ye place whereunto he or they shalbe so elected, during ye residue of ye yeare then to come, or till another elecc̃on, hee or they first takeing a corporall oath for the due execuc̃on of his or theire place as aforesaid.

And wee doe by theis p'nts, for us, o^r heires and successo^rs, graunt unto the said Governo^r and Companie of ye Merchaunts of London, Discoverers of the Northwest passage, and unto theire successors, full power and authority at all tymes convenient to assemble themselues in any place or places convenient for or about the affaires and busines of ye said Companie, and there to holde co^rte, and to make, ordeine, and constitute such and so manie laws, ordinances, and constituc̃ons as to ye greater p't of them so assembled shall seeme necessary and convenient for the good governem^t of the said companie, and of all such factors, maisters, marryners, and all other as they shall ymploy in any of their voyages or other their busines concerning ye said Companie, and ye same lawes and ordinances to putt in execuc̃on at their pleasure, to revoake and alter ye same as they shall thinke fitt and expedient; And, as often as ye said Company shall ordeine and establishe anie such lawes and orders as foresaide, it shalbe likewise lawfull for them to impose and inflict punishem^t upon ye offendors and breakers thereof, either by imprisonem^t or fine, as in ye discrec̃on of ye Governo^r and com'itties for ye tyme being shalbe thought reasonable; wch fines o^r will and pleasure is shalbe levyed and receiued to ye use of ye Governo^r and Company aforesaid, w^thout makeing anie accompt thereof unto us, o^r heires and successors, for ye same; All wch lawes and ordinances and constitucõns so to be made as aforesaid wee will and commaund to be observed and kept, so as ye said lawes, ordinances, and constitucõns, orders, imprisonem^ts, fines, and amerciam^ts[1] be reasonable and not repugnant to ye lawes of o^r realme.

AND, further, of o^r speciall grace, certaine knowledge, and meere mocõn, wee have given and graunted, and by theis p'nts for us, o^r heires and successors, wee doe give and graunt, unto ye said Governo^r and Companie of ye Merchaunts of London, Discoverers of the Northwest passage, that they and every of them, theire successors and assignes, shall and may from hencefourth at any tyme and from time to time after ye date of theis o^r l'res patents, use, prepare, and sett to sea such and so many shippes, barkes and pinaces and such number of men to saile therein, for ye discovery of the said Northwest passage, and of all such lands, territories, and dominions abovesaid, as they shall thinke fitt and necessarie.

AND, of o^r more ample and aboundant grace, certaine knowledge, and meere mocõn, wee have graunted and authorised, and by theis p'ntes for us, o^r heires and successors, wee doe graunt and authorise, ye said Governor and Company of the M'chaunts of London, Discoverers of the Northwest passage, and their successors, and unto all other theire assignes, that from tyme to time hereafter it shall and may be lawfull for them, ye said Governo^r and Companie, theire successors and assignes, and no other, to sett to sea such and so manie shippes, pinaces, and barkes as shalbe thought fittinge by ye said Governo^r and Com'itties, or ye maior p't of them assembled, and shall forever hereafter have use and enioy ye whole, entyre, and onely trade, lib'tie, use, and priuiledge of trading unto ye said North-west passage, and unto ye landes, territories, and dominions aforesaide.

AND, of o^r further royall favour, wee have graunted, and for us, o^r heires and successors, wee doe graunt, unto ye said Governo^r and Companie of M'chaunts of London, Discoverers of ye Northwest passage, and their successors, that ye said northwest passage, nor ye lands, signiories, and dominions thereunto adioyning, nor anie of them, shall not be visited, frequented, or traded unto, by or through ye said Northwest passage, by any other of o^r sub^ts, or ye sub^ts of o^r heires or successors, or by the sub^ts of anie other forreigne

---

[1] *Amerciaments.* Fr. *merce*, the pecuniary punishment of an offender, who is found to stand *in misericordia, i.e.*, to have offended and stand at the mercy of his superior. A more merciful penalty than fine, and differing from it in that it is arbitrarily imposed. (Jacob's *Law Dictionary.*, 1729.)

prince or state, either from any ye ports or havens belonging unto us and o^r successors, or from any ye ports or havens belonging or appertayning to any forreine Prince or Potentate whatsoever, any l'res Patents heretofore made by o^r late deere sister Queen Elizabeth,[1] or any o^r l'res Patents heretofore graunted,[2] to ye contrary notw^{th}standing; And, by vertue of o^r prerogative royall, wee straightly charge, commaund, and prohibite all ye sub^{ts} of us, o^r heires and successors, of what degree or quality soever they be, that none of them, directly or indirectly, p'sume to visitt, frequent, trade, or adventure to traffique into or from the said Northwest passage or into or from any ye said landes and dominions by the said Northwest passage, other than the said Governo^r and Companie and theire assignes, unles it be by and wth ye consent and license of the saide Governor and Companie first had and obtained in writing under theire com'on seale, upon paine of o^r indignačon and ymprisonem^t of theire bodyes during o^r pleasure, and the forfeiture and losse both of theire shippes and goodes, wheresoever they shalbe found, either w^{th}in o^r kingdome or in anie other places out of o^r dominions, or wheresoever the said Companie or their associats can or may come by or otherwise seize the same, The moyety of all wch forfeitures wee will shalbe come to us, o^r heires and successors, and the other moyety thereof wee, of our sp'ciall grace, doe wholly and cleerly, for us, o^r heires and successors, give and graunt unto ye said Governo^r and Companie, and unto theire successors, ye said parties so offending not to be released out of prison untill hee or they shalbe come bound wth sufficient suerties unto the Company at noe tyme thereafter to frequent or trade into any ye places aforesaid, contrary to o^r expresse commaundem^t in theis p'nts published and sett downe.

AND wee have likewise condescended and graunted, and by theis p'nts, for us, o^r heires and successors, wee doe condescend and graunt, unto ye said Governo^r and Company of the M'chaunts of London, discoverers of the North West passage, and unto theire successors, that wee, o^r heires and successors, will not give or graunt anie libertie, license, or authority to anie p'son or p'sons whatsoever to sayle, trade, or traffique unto the saide Northwest passage, or unto any the landes and terrytories above named by ye way of ye Northwest passage, w^{th}out the goodwill and liking of the saide Governo^r and companie, or the greater part of them[3];

AND, least anie question or doubt may hereafter arrise as touching the nominačon, boundes, limitts, and extent of the Northwest

---

[1] This doubtless refers to the charter granted to Adrian Gilbert and others (see Introduction, p. xl, *note*).

[2] Presumably the charter to Richard Penkavill (see p. 646) is here alluded to.

[3] It appears (see p. 664) that the foregoing clauses were, at the time, not regarded as conferring a monopoly.

passage, WEE doe hereby signifie and declare that ye same doth and shall beginne and hath it[s] entrance between ye headland of Groynland called y^e *Cape* of *Desolation*, and the cape or headland of *America* called *Labrodor*, in or about the Northerley latitude of fifty-eight degrees, and so extendeth itself into ye sea lying betweene those two Capes or lands of *America* and *Groinelande*, including not onely ye sea or streight called *Hudson's* streight, now newly discovered, but also that sea or streight called and knowne by ye name of *Fretum Davis*, and all other seas whatsoever lying and being betweene ye foresaid two Capes in and about ye height of fiftie eight degrees *Northerley* latitude, and from thence extending through or betweene ye said landes of *America* and *Groineland*, Northwardes, Northwestwardes, or westwards, unto ye verie territories of *Tartaria, China, Japan,* and *Coray*, and to all other coasts, countreys, or Islands, either knowne or unknowne, discovered or undiscovered, lying upon or in ye sea of *Sur*, either upon ye continent of *America* or *Asia*, or any Islandes lying and being in or upon ye said seas; And accordingly our will and pleasure is that the same shalbe so construed and understood in ye Article last precedent and use in and throughe all parts of theis our L'r^s Patents.

AND o^r will and pleasure is, and, for us, o^r heires and successo^{rs} wee doe further graunt to and wth ye said Governo^r and companie of ye M'chaunts of London, discoverers of the Northwest passage, that, as often as any custome, impost, or other deutyes shall growe due and payable unto us by reason of anie goodes or m'chandizes to be shipped forth, or any retourne to be made of any goodes or m'chandizes from ye said Northwest passage, or any the landes and territories aforesaid, that then, and in such case, o^r will and pleasure is that ye officers of o^r custome, or ffarmers of o^r customes, and every of them for the tyme being, upon request made unto them by ye said Companie, theire facto^{rs} and assignes, shall give and allowe unto ye said Governo^r and Companie six monethes tyme for ye paym^t of one half, and other six monethes then following for ye paym^t of the other half, of all such custome, subsidie, impost, and other dueties as shalbe due and payable unto us for ye same, for wch theis o^r l'res Patents, or ye duplicate or exemplificačon thereof, shalbe to such officers a sufficient warrant and discharge in that behalf.

AND, if it shall happen ye said Governo^r and companie to bring into this Realm either such or so great store of com'odities from anie landes, through and by ye said Northwest passage, as either cannott or will not be uttered or vented in theis o^r landes or dominions, wch they are or shalbe willing to transport into other countreys, then, and in such case, o^r will and pleasure is, and by theis p'nts, for us, o^r heires and successors, wee graunt that at all tymes during the space of thirteene monethes next after ye discharge of any such com'odities (o^r subsidie, custome, impost, and other dueties being first allowed and compounded for as aforesaid) it shall and may be lawfull to and for ye said Governo^r and Companie, or any of them, to transport and carry the same, in anie vessells or bottomes, out of this o^r Realme w^thout paying anie further custome, subsidie, or other duetyes for ye same; and that the Customer or other o^r officers to whom it shall in that behalf appertayne (upon proofe thereof made in o^r custome howse belonging to the Port of London, or any other port of o^r Realm of England), shall by vertue of theis o^r l'res Patents give them and every of them sufficient Cocketts[1] and certificats for the safe passing out of the same accordingly, w^thout paying anie other custome, subsidie, or other duety for ye same.

AND, for the better maintenance of the saide trade, wee are further pleased, and wee doe by theis p'nts graunt unto ye said Governo^r and companie of the Marchaunts of London, discoverers of the Northwest passage, and theire successors, that when and so often as any such com'oditie, being brought from anie the landes aforesaid through and by the said Northwest passage, wch cannott be vented here w^thin o^r owne dominions, shalbe transported over into other countreyes as aforesaid, in every such case it shall and may be lawfull to ye said Governo^r and Companie to receive and have backe againe so much impost onely as was payed and aunsweared inwards for the said comoditie so to be transported, The same to be repayed unto y^m by the Collecto^r of ye said impost inwardes, upon due proofe to be made (according to such order as is appointed by o^r l'r^s patents made for ye stablishinge of ye rates of ye new impost, bearing date ye sixt daie of September, in ye eight yeere of o^r raigne of Englande, ffraunce, and Ireland, and of Scotland the fower and fortyeth) by ye said Governo^r and Companie, both of the true paym^t of ye said impost inwardes, and also of ye true shippinge and transporting of the said Marchandizes outwardes; For ye repaym^t of wch impost and transportačon, in manner and forme aforesaide, theis o^r l'r^s Patents, or ye duplicates or exemplification thereof, shalbe unto ye said Collecto^rs of ye said imposts a sufficient warrant and discharge from time to time in that behalf.

AND our will and pleasure is that it shall and may be lawfull to and for ye said Governo^r and Companie, or ye most part of them, to admitt and take into theire compaine all and every such person or p'sons as to them, or the most part of them, shalbe thought fitt and agreable to the ordinances by vertue of theis p'nts to be made for the governm^t of the said company; ye said p'sons, and every of them so to be admitted, first payinge and allowing for

---

[1] A cocket was a scroll of parchment, sealed and delivered by officers of the Custom House to merchants, as a warrant that their merchandise was customed. Without a cocket, goods could not be re-transported.

theire and every of theire admissions unto the said Governo^r and Company, and unto theire successo^rs, for and in the name of a fine, the som'e of one hundred markes

AND our will and pleasure is that ye said Governo^r and Companie shall w^thout refusall admitt all and every such p'son and p'sons, aswell Aliens and denizens, as o^r naturall borne sub^ts, wch shall at any time duringe the space of seaven yeeres from and after the date of theis o^r l'res Patents seeke or desier to be admitted unto ye said company, whom ye first discoverers shall thinke fitt, so as they shall pay such fines and som'es of mony for theire said Admittances as are herein before sett downe, and doe and p'forme all other things as by theis o^r l'res patents shall thereunto appertaine

AND our further will and pleasure is that all and every ye sonnes of ye now Patentees wch now are or shalbe borne before the date of theis o^r l'r^s Patents, being under ye age of one and twenty yeeres, shall and may be admitted and incorporated into the saide company of the Merchaunts of London, discoverers of the Northwest Passage, at such tyme and tymes as they shall accomplishe theire severall ages of one and twenty yeeres, *Payinge* for theire admission or admissions onely twenty shillings a peece, and noe more; and that all such servaunts and app'ntices wch are or shalbe, at any tyme before ye date of theis o^r L'r^s Patents, bound as an app'ntice unto any ye above mencõned Patentees, shall and may likewise be admitted into ye said companie at th'ende and expiration of theire and every of theire Apprentishipps, *paying* and allowing unto ye said Governo^r and companie for theire and every of theire admissions the like severall som'es that theire severall Maisters payed, and noe more, nor otherwise, And, as touching the sonnes of anie the said company wch shall happen to be borne after the date of theis o^r L'r^s Patents, or after ye admission and freedome of theire fathers as aforesaid, and the servaunts and app'ntices wch shalbe bounde unto anie of ye said Company after ye date of theis our L'r^s Patents and after ye admission of theire Maisters, OUR will and pleasure is that all and every such sonnes so to be admitted unto ye said companie, haveing accomplished ye age of one and twenty yeeres, shall pay and allowe unto ye said companie for theire admittance ye some of twenty shillings; And that every servaunt and app'ntice, having so served his apprentishipp, shall pay and allowe for his admission twenty shillings likewise, and noe more, nor any greater some.

AND our further will and pleasure is that the sonnes of all such our loving sub^ts as shall at any tyme hereafter be admitted into the said company of the said Marchaunts of London, discoverers of the Northwest passage, as also all such app'ntices as shalbe bound unto them or any of them as their app'ntices, being borne or bounde before the admission of theire saide fathers or M^rs, shall and lawfully may be admitted and incorporated into the saide Companie at theire severall ages of one and twenty yeeres, and at the expiration of their severall apprentishipps, payinge and allowinge unto the said Governor and Companie such and the like fine and fines for their and every of theire admissions as their said father or M^r first payed and allowed unto the said companie for his admission, all wch fines and severall som'es of money so to be received and taken for the severall admissions as aforesaid, for and during the space of seaven yeeres next ensuing the date of theis p'nts, o^r will and pleasure is, shalbe and remaine to the use of the said Henry, Earle of Northampton, Charles, Earle of Nottingham, Thomas, Earle of Suffolke, Henry, Earle of South^ton, Willm, Earle of *Salisbury*, Theophilus, Lord Walden, Sr Thomas Smith, Sr Robt Maunsell, Sr Walter Cope, Sr Dudley Digges, Sr James Lancaster, Rebecca, Lady Romeney, ffrauncis Jones, John Wolstenholme, John Eldred, Robt Sandy, Willm Greenewell, Nicholas Leate, Hewett Stapers, Willm Russell, John Mericke, Abraham Chamberlaine, Philip Burlomachie, The Muscouia Company, and the East *India* Company of ye sixt voyage, being the first adventurers and discoverers of the said Northwest passage, their executo^rs, administrato^rs, and assignes, to be distributed and devided amongst them ratably, according to their severall adventures in ye first voyage set fourth in Anno one thousand six hundred and tenn, in liewe and satisfacčon of ye great costs and charges they have expended and disbursed in discovery of ye said passage; and, after ye said seaven yeeres expired, to be and remaine forever to ye use of the said Governo^r and Companie of the M'chaunts of London, Discoverers of the Northwest passage, in generall.

AND, forasmuch as wee greatly desier ye advauncem^t of the saide trade and benefitt of ye said Society, of o^r speciall grace, certaine knowledge, and meere močon, we have given and graunted, and, for us, o^r heires and successors, we doe give and graunt, full and free power and authority unto ye saide Governo^r and companie of ye Merchaunts of *London*, discoverers of the Northwest passage, and theire successors, that they, the said Governo^r and companie, or ye more part of them, shall and may from time to time admitt into ye freedome of the said Company all such Merchaunts, Aliens, denizens, and straungers as to them, or ye most part of them p'nte at anie court to be holden for ye said companie, shalbe thought fitt and agreable wth th'orders of the said companie, takeing of every such alien, denizen, and *Straunger* wch shalbe so admitted into ye said company, for theire and every of theire admittance, the some of one hundred markes, and noe more; And y^t all and every Merchaunt, Alien, denizen, and straunger, being admitted into the said society, shall and lawfully may use and have in ioynt stocke and trade wth ye said Governo^r and Companie (and not otherwise upon theire priuate adventure), all and every such ye same and yᵉ like lib'ties and priviledges, onely concerninge yᵉ said ioynt trade, and the Marchaundizes and other comodities to be brought from the Northwest passage and yᵉ lands and territories aforesaid, as anie yᵉ n'rall borne subᵗˢ of this oʳ Realme and being also of the Society, can, may, or ought to have and enioy by vertue of theis oʳ l'res patents, anie lawe, use, statute, custome, or other thing to the contrary notwᵗʰstanding.

AND, for the better encouragemᵗ of such well affected aliens, as well straungers as denizens, as shalbe willing to be admitted into yᵉ said society, to sett forward this so good and worthie an accõn for trade and traffique of such importaunce to the landes and territories aforesaide, *Wee* have further, of oʳ speciall grace, certaine knowledge, and mere mocõn, given and graunted, and, for us, oʳ heires and successors, do give and graunte, unto the said Governoʳ and Companie of yᵉ Marchaunts of London, discoverers of the Northwest passage, and unto theire successors, that all and every Marchaunts Aliens, both strangers and denizens, wᶜʰ shalbe admitted into yᵉ said companie by vertue of theis oʳ L'rˢ Patents, shall and may from time to time in ioynt and com'on stock wᵗʰ the said Companie, and not otherwise, trade and use the seale of Marchandize unto the saide landes and territoryes wᶜʰ now are, or hereafter shalbe, discovered by the saide companie, or by theire meanes or procuremᵗ, *paying* unto us, oʳ heires and successors, such customes, subsidyes, imposts, and other duetyes for such goods and m'chaundize as shalbe retourned from yᵉ said landes and territories aforesaide into oʳ Realme of *Englande*, as are due and payable unto us by *Englishmen* borne, and noe more or greater, anie lawe, statute, custome, usage, or other thing to the contrary in any wise notwᵗʰstanding.

AND whereas divers lawes have beene made concerninge the custome and other dueties wᶜʰ straungers ought to pay unto us in respect of the goodes and m'chaundizes wᶜʰ the saide Marchaunts, straungers and denizens, doe bring in and carrie forth out of this oʳ Realme, and also divers lawes and statutes have bene made inflicting divers punishmᵗˢ, penaltyes, and other forfeitures upon such of oʳ subiects as should collʳˡ[1] any straungers goodes, thereby to defraude us of oʳ dueties; For the avoyding of all doubts, daunger, and ympedimᵗˢ wᶜʰ might hinder the p'fect and good successe of oʳ gracyous intent and meaninge in this behalfe, *Wee* have hereby graunted, and by theis p'ntes, of our speciall grace, certaine knowledge, and meere mocõn doe declare, and, for us, oʳ heires and successors, doe graunt, that neither the said Governor and companie, nor anie member of the saide companie, being oʳ subiects, nor anie Merchaunts,

---

[1] To *colour strangers' goods* was to enter the goods of a foreign merchant under the name of a freeman, in order to avoid the payment of the extra duty.

denizens, Aliens, or straungers, wch are or shall hereafter be admitted into the said companie as is aforesaide, nor anie of them, nor anie the goodes, landes, or tenem^ts of o^r saide subiects, or of the saide Marchaunts, denizens, Aliens or strangers, or any of them, shall not hereafter be sued, arrested, seised, troubled, molested, or disquieted for or in respect of such trading as is aforesaid, under pretence of colouring straungers goodes traded in ioynt stock as aforesaid, because as well such straungers as Englishmen shalbe interested in such goodes and m'chaundizes, nor for or in respect of anie other matter or matters wch they or anie of them shall doe or suffer to be done by force and vertue, and according to the true intent and meaning of theis p'nts, but shalbe thereof cleereley acquited and discharged against us, o^r heires and successors, forever, anie lawe, statute, or anie other matter to the contrary notw^thstanding.

AND, of our more aboundant grace and favo^r, and to ye ende ye said Marchaunts, straungers, aliens, and denizens, may be more willing to advaunce ye benefitt and furtherance of the saide discovery, and the good of the trade wch may thereupon ensue, Wee have, for us, o^r heires and successors, given and graunted, and by theis p'nts, for us, o^r heires and successors, wee doe give and graunt, unto the said Governo^r and Companie, and theire successors, that at all tymes, and from tyme to tyme during ye space of thirteene monethes next after the discharge of anie such forreine goodes as shalbe brought into this Realme in ioynt and com'on stock by anie such straunger, denizen, and Englishman togither as aforesaid, or wch anie such Straunger shall have and buy of the said Companie, or any of them belonginge to their adventure (our customes, subsidies, and other dueties for the same being first payed or compounded for), it shall and may be lawfull for all and every denizen, straunger, or Alien, being, or wch hereafter shalbe, admitted into the said companie, to transporte the same in English bottoms out of this o^r Realme, w'thout paying anie more or further custome, subsedye, or other dueties for the same (the custome, subsidy, and other duetyes for the same being formerly payed as aforesaide, and soe proved), and that the customer and other officers to whom it shall and may [? *come*] shall, by vertue of theis o^r l'res Patents, and upon proof made as aforesaid, give them sufficient Cocketts or Certificats for the safe passing of ye same out accordingly, PROVIDED, nevertheles, that, if the said Marchaunts, Aliens, as well straungers as denizens, or anie of them, shall at anie tyme hereafter make, retourne, and bringe or carry out of this Realme anie Northwest goodes, wares, or comodotyes other than such as are or shalbe belonging ioyntly to the said Companie by reason of theire ioynt trade as aforesaid, that then, and in such case, every such Marchaunt, Alien, straunger, and denizen shall allowe and pay unto us, o^r heires and successors, all such customes and other dueties, both inward and outward, as Merchaunt strangers doe and ought for to pay unto us, for all other goodes whatsoever, anie thing before in theis p'nts conteined to the contrary notwthstanding.

AND, to the end it may appeare how acceptable ye said service hath bene unto us, and how willing wee are to gratifye and rewarde all such o^r loving sub^{ts} as by such or the like meanes endeavo^r themselves to advaunce o^r hono^r and dignity royall, and to sett open a trade of Marchaundizing and traffique for the benefitt of our com'onwealth, *Wee* have of o^r speciall grace, certaine knowledge, and meere moc̃on given and graunted, and, by theis p'nts, for us, o^r heires and successors, doe give and graunt, unto the said Henry, Earle of North^{ton}, Charles, Earle of Nottingham, Thomas, Earle of Suffolk, Henry, Earle of South^{ton}, Willm, Earle of Salisbury, Theophilus, Lord *Walden*, Sr Thomas Smith, Sr Robt Mawnsell, Sr Walter Cope, Sr Dudley Digges, Sr James Lancaster, Knights, Rebecca, Lady Romney, ffrauncis Jones, Alderman, John Wolstonholme, esq., John Eldred, Robt Sandy, Willm Greenewell, Nicholas Leate, Hewett Stapers, Willm Russell, John Merick, Abraham Chamberlaine, Phillipp Burlomachi, Marchaunts, the Muscouia Companie, and the East India companie of the sixt voyage, being the first adventurers and discoverers of the said Northwest passage, and their execut^{rs}, administrators, and assignes, all and all manner of Customes, subsidies, imposic̃ons and som'es of money, and dueties whatsoever they be, wch from and after ye fifteenth day of December wch shalbe in ye yeere of our Lord God one thousand six hundred and eighteene, untill the fifteenth day of December wch shalbe in ye yeere of o^r Lord God one thousand six hundred and nyneteene, shall, may, or ought to happen, come, arrise, growe, renewe, be due or payable to us, o^r heires and successors, or to any of them, by ye lawes, statuts, and customes of this Realme, or any of them, or by any other waies or meanes whatsoever, of, for, or by reason of all and all manner of wares, goodes, and marchaundizes, of whatsoever nature, kind, quality, or condic̃on they shalbe, wch at any tyme wthin the space of the said one yeere last above menc̃oned shalbe conveyed or brought to this o^r Kingdome of England, or any other o^r kingdomes, dominions, or territoryes, or anie of them, or any ports, havens, creekes, or place, to them or any of them belonging, from, by, or through the said Northwest passage, or proceeding of any voyage made out of this Realme by or through the said passage, or wch shalbe carryed out of this Realme of England, or any other o^r kingdomes, dominions, or territories, or shipped in any vessell or bottome whatsoever to th'intent to be conveyed out of this Realme, or anie other o^r dominions or territories, by way of marchaundize or trade, in, by, or throughe the said Northwest passage, into any countrey, coast, or place whatsoever, whether the same shall growe due for or in respect of theire owne proper goodes, or of the goodes of ye said company, or of anie other pertickler p'sons of ye said companye, wthout yeilding anie rent, accompt, or other thing to us, o^r heires and successors, for or in respect of ye same, to be distributed amongst them, ye said Henry, Earle of North^{ton}, Charles, Earle of Nottingham, Thomas, Earle of Suff, Henry, Earle of South^{ton}, Willm, Earle of Salisbury, Theophilus, Lord Walden, Sr Thomas Smith, Sr Robt Maunsell, Sr Walter Cope, Sr Dudley Digges, Sr James Lancaster, Knights, Rebecca, Lady Romeney, ffrauncis Jones, Aldermann, John Wolstonholme, Esq, John Eldred, Robt Sandy, Willm Greenewell, Nich'as Leate, Hewitt Stapers, Willm Russell, John Merick, Abraham Chamberlaine, Philip Burlomachie, Marchaunts, The Muscovia Company, and the East India Company of the sixt voyage, being ye first Adventurers and Discoverers of the said Northwest Passage, and theire executors, administrators, and ass^s, rateably, according to theire severall adventures in the said voyage sett fourth in ye yeare of o^r Lord God, one thowsand six hundred and tenn.

AND, further, of o^r sp'iall grace, certaine knowledge, and meere močon, we have given and graunted, and by theis p'nts, for us, o^r heires and successors, doe give and graunt, unto Thomas Button, Captaine of ye good shipp called y^e *Resolution*, and unto John Ingram, M^r of y^e *Discouery*, and to ye Marryners, Saylors, and to ye rest of his Companie in ye said shippes, being, and who are and have bin, ymployed and sett to sea in *Aprill* 1612, for the discovery of the said passage, and to theire executors and ass^s, all and all manner of customes, subsidies, ymposičons, and som'es of money and dueties, whatsoever they be, wch from and after the fiftenth daie of December wch shalbe in ye yeere of o^r Lord 1616, untill ye fiftenth daie of December wch shalbe in ye yeere of o^r Lord 1617, shall, may, or ought to happen, come, arrise, growe, renewe, be due or payable to us, o^r heirs and successors, or to any of them, by the lawes, statuts, and customes of this Realme, or any of them, or by anie other waies or meanes whatsoever, of, for, or by reason of all and all manner of wares, goodes, and marchandizes of whatsoever nature, kind, quality, and condičon they shalbe, or wch at any tyme wthin ye space of ye said one yeere last above menčoned, shalbe conveyed or brought to this o^r kingdome of England, or anie other o^r kingdomes or dominions, or into any o^r Ports, havens, Creekes, or places, to them or any of them belonging, from, by, or through ye said Northwest passage, or proceeding of anie voyage made out of this Realme of England, or any other o^r dominions, or shipped in any vessell or bottome whatsoever, to th'intent to be conveyed out of this Realme or any other o^r dominions, by or through ye said Northwest Passage, into any country, coast, or place whatsoever, whether ye same shall growe due for or in respect of theire owne prop^r goodes, or of the goodes of ye said companie, wthout yeilding anie rent, accompt, or other thing to us, o^r heires or successors, for or in respect of the same; the one half of all wch customes, subsidyes, imposiĉons, and som'es of money, and other ye duties before menĉoned, o^r will and pleasure is that ye said Captaine Thomas Button shall and may have and enioy to his owne proper use and behoofe; and th'other halfe thereof we will and ordaine that ye same shalbe distributed to and amongst ye said maisters, marriners, and saylors, and the rest of the companie aforesaide in ye said two shippes, as ye said Sr Thomas Smith and Sr Dudley Digges, Knights, and John Wolstenholme, esquier, shall in theire discreĉons order and appointe, and not otherwise.

AND wee are well pleased and contented, and of o^r sp'iall grace, certaine knowledge, and meere moĉon wee doe coven'nt and graunt, for us, o^r heires and successors, to and wth ye said Henry, Earle of North^ton, Charles, Earle of Nottingh'm, Tho. Earle of Suff., Henry, Earle of South^ton, Willm, Earle of Salisbury, Theophilus, Lo. Walden, Sr Thomas Smith, Sr Robt Maunsell, Sr Walter Cope, Sr Dudley Digges, Sr James Lancaster, knights, Rebecca, Lady Romeny, ffrauncis Jones, alderman, John Wolstenholme, esquier, John Eldred, Robt Sandy, Willm Greenewell, Nich'as Leate, Hewitt Stapers, Willm Russell, John Merick, Abraham Chamberlaine, Phillipp Burlomachie, marchaunts, The Muscouia Companie, and the East India Companie of ye sixt voyage, being ye first adventurers and discoverers of ye said Northwest passage, theire executors, adm^rs, and ass^s, and every of them, by theis p'nts, that, if we have heretofore made any graunt wch is now in force and shall continue in force untill ye said yeere betweene ye foresaid fifteenth day of December 1618, and the fifteenth daie of December 1619, or any p't thereof, to any other p'son or p'sons, of any ye customes, subsidies, Imposiĉons, som'es of money, or other dueties by theis p'nts graunted during ye yeere aforesaide, that then wee, o^r heires and successors, shall and will not onely discharge and save harmeles ye said Henry, Earle of North^ton, Charles, Earle of Nottingham, Tho. Earle of Suff., Henry, Earle of South^ton, Willm, Earle of Salisbury, Theophilus, Lo. Walden, Sr Thomas Smith, Sr Robt Maunsell, Sr Walter Cope, Sr Dudley Digges, and Sr James Lancaster, K^ts, Rebecca, Lady Romeney, ffrauncis Jones, Alderman, John Wolstonholme, Esq., John Eldred, Robt Sandy, Willm Greenwell, Nich'as Leate, Hewitt Stapers, Willm Russell, John Merick, Abraham Chamberlaine, Phillipp Burlomachie, m'chants, the Muscovia Company, and the East India Companie of the sixt voyage, and theire executors, adm^rs, and assignes, and every of them, against such former graunt, and all and every p'sons clayming by or under the same,[1] but also shall and will, for the better strengthening and corrobating of this o^r p'nte graunt unto all and every such p'son

---

[1] Probably this is in further allusion to the charter granted to Richard Penkavill (see pp. 652 and 646).

or p'sons, if anie rent be reserved upon any such o' graunt, a full and cleare declaračon, and allowaunce in theire rent of such som'es of money, or values, as are by theis p'nts graunted to ye said Henry, Earle of North^{ton}, Charles, Earle of Nottingham, Thomas, Earle of Suff., Henry, Earle of South^{ton}, Willm Earle of Salisbury, Theophilus, Lo. Walden, Sr Thomas Smith, Sr Robt Maunsell, Sr Walter Cope, Sr Dudley Diggs, Sr James Lancaster, Rebecca, Lady Romeney, ffrauncis Jones, John Wolstenholme, John Eldred, Robt Sandy, Willm Grenewell, Nicholas Leate, Hewett Stapers, Willm Russell, Jo. Mericke, Abraham Chamberlaine, Phillipp Burlomachie, ye Muscovia Companie, and the East India Companie of the sixt voyage, and their execu^{rs}, admi'strato^{rs} and ass^s, And also shall doe, performe, and make every such other act and acts, thing and things, assurance and assurances, as shall enable ye said Henry, Earle of North^{ton}, Charles, Earle of Nott., Tho. Earle of Suff., Henry, Earle of South^{ton}, Wm Earle of Salisbury, Theophilus, Lo Walden, Sr Tho Smith, Sr Robt Maunsell, Sr Walter Cope, Sr Dudley Diggs, Sr James Lancaster, Rebecca, Lady Romeney, ffrauncis Jones, John Wolstenholme, John Eldred, Robt Sandy, Willm Greenewell, Nicho's Leate, Hewett Stapers, Wm Russell, John Mericke, Abraham Chamberlaine, Phillipp Burlomachie, The Muscovia Company, and the East India Companie of ye sixt voyage and theire execut^{rs}, adm^s, and ass^s, to enioy ye full and absolute benefitt of this o^r graunt or otherwise to have, take, and r'ceyve [?] sufficient recompence for the same.

AND, to th'end that ye said Governo^r and Company may be truly informed from tyme to tyme of the successe and event of such voyages as shalbe sett fourth to and through the passage aforesaid, and nothing may be concealed from them wch may be fitt for them to knowe, either touching the said discovery and trade, or touching ye goodes that shalbe exported and imported by reason thereof, and the carryage and demeanor of any marchaunt, factor, marryner, or other person or p'sons ymployed by ye said Companie in anie of ye said voyages, or otherwise touching anie accident or circumstance materiall happening in, or about, or by reason of, ye said voyage, Wee doe give full power and authority by theis p'nts unto ye said Governo^r or his deputie, and anie six of ye said comittyes for the tyme being, to examine upon oath anie Captaine, M^r, Marchaunt, Marryner, or any other p'son imployed in or about any of ye saide voyages, upon anie such interrogatories, articles, or questions as to them shall seeme meete and conuenient concerning ye said voyage, discovery, trade, or goodes, or anie other materiall circumstance tending to the true and certaine informačon of the said Governo^r and Companie, And, if any person or p'sons, being thereunto called or required, shall refuse to take such oath, or, haveing received the same, shall refuse or neglect to aunsweare directly and effectually to such questions and Interrogatories concerning the p'misses as he shalbe exa'i'ed on, then to com'itt all and every such p'son and p'sons so refusing to take such oath, or refusing or neglecting to aunsweare such questions or Interogatoryes, to any o' prisons w^{th}in ye citty of London, there to remayne, w^{th}out bayle or manieprise, untill such person shall conforme himself, and be sworne and exa'i'ed as aforesaid.

AND, for that wee are credibly informed y^t in such and ye like interprises and voyages great losse and hinderance hath happened by the mutinous and disorderly carriage of the marryners and saylors shipped and ymployed in the said voyages, because none amongest them hath bene sufficiently authoryzed to punishe the offendors according to theire deserts; For ye reformacõn whereof the said Governor and Companie of ye Marchaunts of London, discoverers of the Northwest passage, have bene humble suitors unto us that such Generalls, and Captaines, and Commanders as shalbe ymployed by them in any of theire voyages might have power and authority to use and exercise Martiall lawe upon such mutinous and disordered p'sons as shall happen to be amongest them, Wee, gratiously tendring ye good successe of theire voyages, and to th'end that such as shall goe and be ymployed therein may be ye better ordered and governed, of o' speciall grace, certaine knowledge, and mere mocõn, have, for us, o' heires and successo^rs, given and graunted, and by theis o' l'res Patents, for us, o' heires and successo^rs, doe give and graunt, full power and authority unto all such generalls, captaines, and commaunders as are, or wch shalbe, admitted by the said Governo' and Companie to goe as generalls and captaines in their said voyages and shipping, having com'ission from the said Company under theire com'on seale aforesaid (unto whom likewise wee doe by theis p'nts, for us, o' heires and successors, give full power and authority to graunt com'ission or com'issions unto their generalls or captaines for the executing of Martiall lawe upon any offendors ymployed in their said shipping and voyages aforesaid, the said generalls, captaines, and commaunders to be made by the said Governo' and Companie in manner and forme aforesaid), that they, and every of them, shall and lawfully may use and execute such punishm^{ts}, correccõns, or execucõn upon him or them wch shalbe mutinous, seditious, disordered, or any way unruly in theire said voyages owtwards or homewardes, to ye p'iudice or hinderance of the successe in the attempt or prosecuting of this discovery or trade intended, as the cause shalbe found in Justice to require, according to Martiall lawe, and, nevertheless, by the verdict of twelve of the companie sworne thereunto for the tryall of such offendors as in such a case app'teyneth; The said power, use, and exercise of *Martial* discipline, by theis p'nts given, to contynue untyll the same shalbe revoaked by anie six of o' priuie *councell*, whereof the Lord Tr'er of *Englande* for the tyme being to be one.

AND our will and pleasure is, and by theis p'nts, for us, our heires and successors, Wee doe graunt unto the said Governo' and

Company of the Marchaunts of London, Discoverers of the Northwest passage, and theire successors, that theis our l'res Patents and all and singuler graunts and clauses herein conteyned, under the condicõns and limitacõns therein mencõned and expressed, shalbe and contynue firme, strong, sufficient, and effectuall in the lawe, and shalbe consieued, reputed, and taken aswell to the meaninge and intent as to the wordes of the same, most graciously, favourably, and to the benefitt of the said company and theire successors, any lawe, statute, act, proviso, order, ordinance, or restrainte, or anie omission or defect in the lawe, or anie other cause, matter, or thing to the contrary thereof in any wise notwthstanding, although expresse mencõn, &c

In Witness, etc.

It may please yor Excellente Maj^{tie}

This bill conteyneth your Ma^{ts} graunt unto the MARCHANTS OF LONDON, DISCOUERERS OF THE NORTHWEST PASSAGE, to be made and Treated a *Corporate Body*, and to be invested wth powers and capacityes thereunto incident, to th'end the Trade thorough that passage may be managed wth some order and governem^t, and not loosely at the discrecõn of every private *Aduenturer*.

The frame and constitucõn of this *Companye* is not restrained to anie number certaine, nor confined to any p'ticuler citty, towne, or place, nor tending to any degree of *Monopoly*[1]

The Prince is constituted *Supreame Protector* under yor Matie of this *Companie*

The custome, subsidie, and impost accruing to yor Matie of all goodes and m'chandize shipped outwardes and homewardes throughe the said passage, in ye 7th yeare after ye date of the l'res patents (by wch time it is conceiued the trade may settle and growe somewhat beneficiall) are therein graunted to ye first *Discouerers*, in consideracõn of theire charges in ye discovery; and the like graunt to Captaine *Button*, and the M^r and marriners in the two shippes lately sett fourth for the p'fecting of the said *Discouerye*, of the custome, subsidie, and impost happening in the 5th yeere after the date of the l'res patent (w^{ch}, as [is] supposed, will be a lesse matter), in consideracõn of theire services therein.

The whole policie hereof was digested into articles, and allowed by the Lords Commissioners for the Lord Tre'rs place, accõrding to whose direcčon and warrant I have putt it into forme.[2]

---

[1] If the clauses appearing on p. 652 were not held to confer a monopoly, it is hard to say what would have been held to do so.

[2] There appears to have been a signature to this summary, but it is illegible. It appears to have been that of Secretary Windebank, whose signature also appears upon the back of the charter, appended to an endorsement in Latin.

INDEX.

NOTE.—*In the following Index, the word "Adventurer" means that the man whose name it follows was one of the original members of the Company of Merchants of London Discoverers of the North-West Passage (see p. 642).*

Abbott, Morris, Adventurer, 645, 649
Adams, Clement, his map, 34
Address to the Divinity Students of Cambridge, *see* Watts, W.
Adderley, John, Adventurer, 646
Agoomska Island, Hudson reaches, 128 n.; James reaches, 493 n., 494 n., 499 n., 500 n.
Aide, Frobisher's ship, 43, 59
Akpatok Island, identified, 124 n.
Albany, frigate, ccxiv
Allen, Master, mathematician, 605
——— Edward, Adventurer, 645
——— Gregory ,, 646
——— Ralph ,, 646
——— William ,, 646
Allenson, Christopher, Adventurer, 645
Almacanter, 96, 275 n., 280, Bylot takes the sun's, 210
Alsop, Bernard, printer, cxxiii, cxxiv
Amplitude, 271, 274 n., 372, 491
Ancient Mariner, Coleridge's, partly derived from James's work, *see* Coleridge, S. T.
Angelica, plant, 100
Angell, William, Adventurer, 646
Anne Frances, the, 58 n.
Antonie, Charles, Adventurer, 646
Archbishop of Canterbury, George, 644
Arctic exploration, fever for, 1, *see also* North-West Passage.
Armitage, Samuel, Adventurer, 646
Arngrim Fitz Jonas, his description of Iceland, 17
Arundel, Thomas, Earl of, 644
Arundel of Wardour, Lord, 644
Astrolabe, description of, 250 n.
Atkinson, Richard, Adventurer, 646
Aurora, 313 n., 327 n., *see also* Harbours, Henbanes, and Pettie dancers.
Azimuth, 274, 280, 309, 607, 608, 609, 610

Bacon, Sir Francis, Solicitor-General, 644
Baffin, Susan, daughter of William Baffin, 202 n.
——— William, vi, born in London, 202 n.; pilot under Captain Hall, 96, 203 n., sails with Bylot, 202, his daughter Susan, 202 n., observation of the tide at Sea Horse Point, 217, 379, thinks there is no passage through Hudson's Strait, 220 n., letter to Sir John Wolstenholme, 233, thinks the Passage is not by Davis Strait, 234, death, 240, 370 n., *see also* Bylot.
Baker Foreland, 177 n., 179 n., 322 n., 426 n.
Ball, Richard, Adventurer, 96 n.
Baning, Paul ,, 645
Banks, John ,, 645
Barber, Thomas ,, 645
Barker, Andrew, of Hull, master under Captain Hall, 99
——— John, Alderman and Merchant of Bristol, cxliv, cxlix, cl, clxvi
Barley, Robert, Adventurer, 645
Barlow, Captain George, of the frigate *Albany*, ccxiv
——— Dr. William, Adventurer, 645
Barnard, Anne, Luke Foxe's marriage with, ccxxix
Barnett, Ann, *see* Barnard, Anne
Barton, John, gunner's mate of the *Henrietta Maria*, clvi, drowned, 511, 602
Basse, Humfrey, Adventurer, 645
Bateman, Robert ,, 645
Bear Island, 493 n.
Beedome, Thomas, his epigrams upon Captain James, clxxxvii
Bell Island, 191 n., 215 n.
Bell, Robert, Adventurer, 645, 649
Bennett, George ,, 646
———, Matthew, *see* Mathews, Bennett
Berley, *see* Barlow, Captain George
Best, Captain, sails under Frobisher, 58
Big Island, 209 n.
Bilson, Nathaniel, surgeon of the *Henrietta Maria*, clvi
Birds, *see* Blackbirds, Cormorants, Cranes, Crows, Ducks, Eagle, Geese, Gulls, Hawk, Jay, Mallard, Owl, Partridges, Pheasant, Plover, Ptarmigan, Ravens, Sea-mews, Stint, Swans, Teal, Thrushes.
Blackbirds, 71
Blades, Samuel, of Foxe's crew, lxxxvii, 344

Bond, Silvanus, cooper, of Hudson's ship, 630, his deposition, 630
Bonham, William, Adventurer, 645
Boorne, Richard   ,,   645
Borough, William, his *Discours of the Variation of the Cumpas*, xxxii
Bostock, Thomas, Adventurer, 645
Bowles, George   ,,   645
Bowyer, Sir Henry   ,,   645
Boyle, Hon Robert, his *New Experiments in Observations touching Cold*, clxxxviii, references to James' voyage, *ib*, notice of, *ib*, mentioned, ccvii
Brandon Hill, in Bristol, 547, hill on Charlton Island named after, clxxvi, 547, 559 *n*
Brewer, William, Adventurer, 645
Briggs, Henry —a Yorkshireman, lx, birth, lxi, first Savilian Professor, lxi, encourages Foxe, lxii, 262, death, lxiii *n*, lxxxi, 263, James visits him at Oxford, xcvii, 263, his map, 177 *n*, 179 *n*, 183 *n*, 186 *n*, 331 *n*, his warning to Foxe, 307 *n*., treatise by, 239 *seq*, a learned mathematician, 240, 262, 458 *n*, mentioned, cvi, 597 *n*, Adventurer, 646, *see also* Hubart's Hope
Briggs his Bay, named by James, clxxvi
Briggs his Mathematicks, islands named by Foxe, cix, 329, 432
Bristol, Society of Merchant Venturers of —its history, cxxxvi, one of the earliest of the incorporated Companies of Merchant Venturers, cxxxv, its commencement early in the 14th century, cxxxv, first officers of, cxxxv, incorporated by Royal Charter in 1552, cxxxv, later Charters of, cxxxv, enterprises promoted by it, cxxxvii, benefits conferred by it upon the City of Bristol, cxxxvi, its present position, cxxxv, cxxxviii, its recent efforts to promote technical education, cxxxviii, letters to Sir T. Roe from, cxlii, cli, clxvi, letters from Sir Thos. Roe to, cxxxix, cli; letter to the Earl of Danby from, cliii, clxv, letter to Lord Weston from, cxlv, clxv, letter to Mr Thos. Cary from, clxvi, promotes James's Voyage in 1631, cxxxiv, 455, 456, 594, letters from Capt James to, cl, clxvii, letters from, to Capt. James, cxliii, cxlviii, possesses a series of documents relating to the voyage of James, cxxxiv, clxv, its contract with the members of James's crew for payment of wages, clviii, petition from, presented by James to the King, cxlvii, the King's reply to the petition of, cxlix
———— the city of, Mayors of, cxxxix, cxli *n*; arms of, attached by James to his cross on Charlton Island, 571, 602, Sebastian Cabot probably born there, 31 *n*, *see* James, Capt. Thomas, of, and *Henrietta Maria* of
Bristol, John Digby, Earl of, notice of, 500 *n*., island named after him by James, clxxvi, 500, 599, an Adventurer, 645
Brooke Cobham Island, remains on, ccxv, named by Foxe, lxiii, lxiv *n*, cix, 322 *n*, 324, 427, , white cliffs of, 322 *n*., 324 *n*, mentioned, 327, 432, *see also* Marble Island.
———— Sir John, created Baron Cobham, lxiii, lxiv *n*, Briggs shows him James's letter, 263, kindness to Foxe, lxiii, 324
Brown, Tom, of the *Charles*, lxxxvii, 384 *n*
Browne, Humfrey, Adventurer, 646
———— William, poet, 274
————, or Brownel, Oliver, 113, 114 *n*, 422
Brownerigge, Mathew, Adventurer, 646
Bull, Richard   ,,   646
Bullock, Captain, his proposed expedition, ccxxvi, ccxxvii
Burlomachie, Philip, Adventurer, 642, 645, 649, 656, 659, 660, 661, 662
Burnell, John, Adventurer, 646
———— Thomas   ,,   646
Burrell, William   ,,   645, 649
Busbridge, John   ,,   645
Busby, Raphe   ,,   646
Butler, Robert, Warden of Society of Merchant Venturers of Bristol, cxxxv
Butt, Michael, of Hudson's crew, 142, 143, 145, 146, 629, his consent to the mutiny, 631
Button, Admiral Sir Thomas —mentioned, vi, his family, xxiii, place of his birth, xxiv, biographical notice of, xxii, Clark's *Life* of him, xxiii, knighted, xxii, 169 *n*, his opinion concerning a N-W Passage, xxxi, lxv, lxx, 197 *n*; his letters to Lord Dorchester concerning the search for N-W Passage, lxv, lxix, believes the passage to lie through Hubart's Hope, 331 *n*, his observations on the variation of the compass, xxxi, his voyage in 1612-13 in search of the N-W. Passage, xvii, xxix, ccxxiii, confident expectations that he would sail through the passage, xxii, xlii, Adventurers in his voyage, xx, his letter of credence from King James, xxvii, 635, instructions for his voyage summarised, xix, xxvii, instructions printed in full, 636, preparations for, xvii *n*; date of his departure, 164 *n*., names Resolution I., 165 *n*, the first to reach the western coast of Hudson's Bay, xxx, 165, explores the western coast of Hudson's Bay, 185 *n*., extent of his explorations in Hudson's Bay, xxx, 185 *n*, 341 *n*,

looks for harbour, to repair losses, 166, date of his seeking harbour, ci, 166, 169, 349, 359 n, 364, discovers and names Port Nelson, xxx, 166, 169, winters in Port Nelson, 166 n, 173 n., draws up questions for his men to answer, 170, sufferings of his crew, 167, 169, 414, loss of his ship, the *Resolution*, xxx, 167 n, nails from his ship possibly used by natives, 321 n, 333 n, returns home in the *Discovery*, xxx, explores the bay known as Ne Ultra, 179-182, his disappointment at finding no outlet on the western shore of Hudson's Bay, 185 n, 186 n, cloth brought home in his ship, ccxxiv, his willingness to return the following year, 414, Bylot with, 409, his high opinion of Gibbons, 195, 196, 201 n, his journal mentioned, 176 n, 177, 200, 413 n, no full account of his voyage ever published, xxxiii, 163 n, Foxe discovers relics of his expedition, c, ccxxx, 343, 344 n, 348, 349, 598, Foxe restores his cross, 348, Foxe brings home his inscribed board, 350, his pecuniary difficulties, lxix, prays for payment of his salary, lxix; death in 1634, xxiii, ccii n, facsimile of his autograph, lxviii; existing portraits of, xxiv

Button's Bay, identified with Hudson's Bay, 168 n, named on James's chart, clxxvi; mentioned, 426, 439

——— Isles, 157 n, 251, 282 n, 284 n, 402, 471

Button Gwinnet, signer of the Declaration of Independence, xxxiii n

Bylot, Robert, vi, sails with Baffin, xlvi, results of the voyage, xlvi, his second voyage, xlviii, 223, sails with Hudson, 128, 134, 141, 142, 629, chosen master after the mutiny, 630, 631, takes Pricket to Sir Thomas Smith, 158, his good intentions, 161, anchors off Resolution Island, 206, takes an observation, 211, 212, turns homeward, 216, names Sea Horse Point, 217, sails under Button, 218, 409, his deposition, 630, cleared of complicity in the mutiny, 631; one of the Adventurers, 646, *see also* Jones, Alderman Sir Francis, and Baffin, William.

Cabot, John, father of Sebastian, v, 31 n, 33, 34

——— Sebastian, v, account of, 31 n, sails west, 32, his voyage, 33, 35, 36

Cæsar, Sir Julius, Chancellor of the Exchequer, 644

Cater, William, Adventurer, 646

Calliver, an old kind of gun, 49, 67

Cambridge, Address to the Divinity Students in, *see* Watts, W

Canterbury, Archbishop of, one of the Adventurers, 644

Carey, Mr Allwin, ship's husband, 165 n, 230 n, an Adventurer, 646

——— Sir Robert, *see* Monmouth, Earl of

Carie, Allen, *see* Carey, Mr Allwin

——— Sir Henry, Master of the Jewels, 165 n, 644

Carleton, Browe, named by Foxe, 388 n, 394

Carleton, Sir Dudley, *see* Dorchester, Lord

Cary, Mr Thomas, Gentleman of the Bedchamber, cxliv, clxvi, 165 n, 569

Cary's Isles, named by Bylot, 230, by James, clxxvi, 491 n, 569, he anchors at, 599

Cary's Swan's Nest, whom named after, 165 n, Button at, 186 n, 187 n, mentioned, 175 n, 312, 313, 425; Foxe reaches, 315, swans chased there, 315, the tide at, 426, 428, 429

Cas[s]on, John, Adventurer, 646

Castelyne, John ,, 645

Cavendish, William, Lord, 644

——— Sir William, 644

Cecil, Sir Edward, Knight, 644

——— William, *see* Salisbury, Earl of

——— Robert, *see* Salisbury, Earl of

Challoner, Sir Thomas, Chamberlain to Henry, Prince of Wales, 645

Chamberlaine, Abraham, merchant of the city of London, 642, 645, 649, 656, 659, 660, 661, 662

——— George, Adventurer, 646

——— Peter ,, 645

——— Richard ,, 645

Chambers, John ,, 645

Champian, Richard ,, 645

Chapman, Thomas ,, 645

Charles I, lends Foxe the *Charles*, lxxii, 264, 266, goes to Woolwich to witness launching of ships, 268 n, receives Foxe's papers at Oatland Park, 416, James's audience with, cxlvii, James's address to, 453

Charles, Cape, mentioned, 254 n, 259, Foxe visits, 301, James visits, 474, 586

——— Island, situation of, 301 n.

Charles, the, Foxe's ship —Order in Council about, lxxiii, letters of marque issued for, lxxiv, previous history of, lxxxiv n, tonnage of, lxxxv, crew of, lxxxvi; cost of outfitting, cxv, is discharged from the King's service, cxvii; given to Sir John Wolstenholme, cxvii

Charles Town, named by James, clxxvi, 552, burned, 561

Charlton, Andrew, promoter of James's voyage, clviii

Charlton Island, James lands on, 507, builds house on, 509, sailors buried on, 546, 550, named on Prince Charles's birthday, 552, cairns built there, 561, 602, vetches found on, 552, account of, 566 n; contents of James's letter left at, cxxxiv, 594-603, mentioned, clxxvi, latitude of, 623, 627

Charter of the Company of Merchants of London, Discoverers of the N.-W. Passage, xx, xxxviii, contents of, xxxix, printed in full, 642

Charts, see Adams, Clement; Briggs, Henry, Foxe, Captain Luke, Hubart, Josias, Hudson, Henry, James, Captain, Thornton, John

Chase, Thomas, Adventurer, 645
Chaundler, George ,, 646
Checks, the, 166 n, 175 n, 331, see Hopes Checked
Chesterfield Inlet, 322 n
Chidley, Cape, 259, 282, 284, 402, 403
Chouart, Medart, see Groseilliers, Sieur des
Chudleigh, Mr. John, his expedition, 282 n
Church, Thomas, Adventurer, 646
Churchill Bay, 331 n, see also Hubart's Hope
Churchill, Cape, 176 n
——— River, fine harbour in, 337 n
Clements, Francis, Hudson's boatswain, 142, 145, deposed, 161, one of the mutineers, 630, depositions of, 631
——— William, lieutenant of the *Henrietta Maria*, clvi, 584
Clitherowe, Christopher, Adventurer, 646
Coats, Captain W., his description of Hudson's Bay, ccxx
Coats Island, Button near, 184 n, 185 n
Coatesworth, John, boatswain of the *Charles*, lxxxvi, 296, 382, 405
Cobham, Lord, see Brooke, Sir John
Cobreth, William (otherwise Cobreath, Colbert, Coleburne, or Coolbrand), sails under Weymouth, ccxxii, 115 n, East India Company's agreement with, ccxxii, sails with Hudson, 81 n, 115 n., dismissed by Hudson, 114, 115
Cockayne, Sir William, Alderman of London, 96 n., 645, 649
——— William, junior, 646
Cockein, William, see Cockayne
Cockin Sound, 232
Cockle (or Scurvy) grass (*Cochlearia*), 127 n, 147, 148, 150, boiled in beer, 232, 327, 564
Coke, Sir John, Secretary of State, answers to Foxe's petition, lxxi, letter from, lxxvii n, account of, 396 n
——— Mr. Walter, island named after him, 383
Colbert, William, see Cobreth
Cole, William, carpenter of the *Henrietta Maria*, clvi, death, 548

Coleburne, Master, see Cobreth
Coleridge, S. T., James's work a source of his *Ancient Mariner*, clxxxix
Comfort, Cape, named by Bylot, 216, 409, mentioned, 425
Company, East India, see East India Company
——— of Merchants of London, Discoverers of the North-West Passage mentioned, xx, xxxiv, its inception, xxxviii; Sir Thomas Smith first Governor of, xl, its membership criticised, xxxix n, 647 n, its charter summarised, xxxviii, its charter printed in full, 642, promotes Gibbons's voyage in 1614, xliv, 201 n, promotes Bylot's voyage of 1615, xlv, 203 n, promotes Bylot's voyage of 1616, xlvii, 223 n, probably promotes Hawkridge's voyage, xlix, 249 n
——— of Merchant Venturers of Bristol, see Bristol, Society of, etc.
———, Muscovy, see Muscovy Company
——— of Adventurers of England trading into Hudson's Bay, see Hudson's Bay Company
Compass, variation of the, first observed by Columbus, xxxii, Button's observations on the, xxxi, xxxii, Borough's, xxxii, Foxe's, 309, James's, 464, 607
Compton, William, Lord, Adventurer, 644
Connocke, John, the younger, Adventurer, 645
——— Richard, solicitor to the Prince of Wales, 645
Cooke, Cape, named by Foxe, cix, 396, 397
——— Isle, named by Foxe, cix, 383
——— Mr. Walter, Trinity House Assistant, see Coke, W.
Coolbrand, Master, see Cobreth
Cope, Sir Walter, Adventurer, 642, 645, 656, 659, 660, 661, 662
Cormorants, 75 n
Cornewallis, Sir Charles, Adventurer, 645
Cotton, Allen, Adventurer, 645
Couchman, John ,, 645
Covill, Thomas ,, 646
Cowles, Thomas, of Bedminster, 243
Cox, Robert, Adventurer, 645
Cranes, 104, Foxe finds, 325 n
Crispe, Ellis, Adventurer, 646
——— Nicholas ,, 646
Crowe, Sir Sackville, account of, 399 n, island named after, 399, see also Sackville Island.
Crowe Island, named by Foxe, cix, 399
Crows, 89
Cryche, Edmund, Adventurer, 645
Culpeper, Thomas ,, 645
——— William ,, 646
Cumberland, Earl of, mentioned, 283 n, 647 n.

Cumberland Isles, named, 283 n., 411, mentioned, 425
Cutts, Sir John, Adventurer, 645

Danby, Earl of, account of, 506 n; letter to Sir J. Wolstenholme, cxlvi, Bristol merchants' letter to, cliii
Danby's Island, Earl of, named by James, clxxvi, 494 n., 506, 509 n, 541, 569 n
D'Anghiera, Pietro Martire, account of, 35 n
Danvers, Sir Henry, *see* Danby, Earl of
D'Arcy, Thomas, 644, *see* Rivers, Earl
Darly-head, *see* Porpoise
Davies, Richard, Adventurer, 645
Davis, Captain John, v, his first voyage, 60, second, 65, third, 74, letter to Mr Sanderson, 78, sights entrance to Hudson's Strait in 1587, vii, mentioned, 393, *see also Motives, etc*
Dawes, Abraham, Adventurer, 646
Deane, Richard   ,,   645
De Crowe, Benjamin   ,,   645
De Lorne, or Lawne, Gideon, Adventurer, 645
Dennis, the, Frobisher's ship, 55, 57
Desire Provoked, named by Hudson, 117, 124
Desolation, Cape, 116, identification of, 122 n, Foxe reaches, 275; believed an island, 281 n, mentioned, 174, 175
Digby, John, Baron, *see* Bristol, Earl of
Digges, Sir Dudley, notice of, 118 n, author of a treatise on the N.-W. Passage, 119 n, promotes Bylot and Baffin's Voyages, 202, 223, a mathematician, 311, probably author of the *Motives*, xxxvi, one of the Adventurers, 642, 645, 649, 656, 659, 660, 661, 662
——— John, Adventurer, 645
——— Island (or Cape), named, 118, 126, 311, tide at, 151 n, number of sea-fowl there, 107, 132, 168, 220, mentioned, 132, 151, 199, 228, 425, 475, 638
——— Thomas, Adventurer, 645
Dilbridge, John   ,,   646
Disco Island, 224 n.
Discovery, the, her log-book after the mutiny, xv, abstract from, 632, commanded by Hudson, xi, xxxix, 643, commanded by Captain Ingram, xxix, 162, fifth north-west voyage, xlv, 202, 204 n, sixth, xlvi, 223
Divinity Students of Cambridge, Address to, *see* Watts, W.
Dobbs, Arthur, promotes search for N.-W. Passage, ccxvii
Dorchester, Lord, Lord of the Admiralty, lxiv, 393 n, letter to Button from, lxiv, letter from Button to, lxix, lxxi
Dorchester, Cape, named by Foxe, cix, 388 n, 389 n, 393, 394, 397

Dorset, Cape, named by Foxe, cix, 396, 397, Foxe at, 302 n
Dorset, Earl of, account of, 396 n, cape named after, 396
Drausfield, Averie, Adventurer, 645
Ducks, wild, 71, 135, 252, 350
Dunne Foxe Island, cix, 327, *see* Sentry Island.
Dye, Roger, Adventurer, 646
Dyke, Thomas   ,,   646

Eagle, 35
East India Company, promotes Knight's voyage, 106, minutes of, lxxvii, Wolstenholme's application to, lxxxii, co-operates with the Company of Discoverers of N.-W. Passage, ccxxv, 643, 656, 659, 660, 661, 662; success of, 647 n, charter of, 647 n, "Committees" of, 648 n, grants £200 towards Hawkridge's expenses, 248 n, *see* Gardiner and Gibbons
Edwards, Richard, gunner of the *Henrietta Maria*, clvi, his leg broken and amputated, 487, 602, death, 514, 602, body found and re-buried, 549; Adventurer, 646
Egg Island, identified, 333 n
Elbridge, Giles, merchant of Bristol, cxliii n, cxliv, cxlv, cxlix
Eldred, John, Adventurer, 642, 645, 649, 656, 659, 660, 661, 662
Ellesmere, Thomas, Lord Chancellor of England, 644
Ephemeris, of Origanus, 97 n, 211
——— Searle's, 211, *see also* Searle, John
Esquimaux:—brought from Newfoundland, 34, 39, shown at Westminster, 34, tents, 87, 207, 208, characteristics, 50, clothing, 50, boats, 49, 51, 87, 98, 100, 207, 208, oars, 100, burial-places of, 67, 77, 94, 319, 320, 334; manner of burial, 226, 319 n, 320 n, 321 n; barter with, 76, 77, 87, 88, 93, 136, 208, 227, 232, houses, 51, 94, good artificers, 54; marksmen, 60, native cry, 67, 87, 101, 226, images, 189, 208, weapons, 49, 67, hatchets used by, 471
Esquimaux women, faces coloured, 42, 226, two seen, 225, lick wounds like a dog, 46
Esquimaux, Cape, 173 n, 177 n, 581 n
Evans, William, the King's Porter, ccxxviii, 11, 645
Eveline, John, Adventurer, 645
Evington, Francis   ,,   645

Fabian, Robert, his Chronicle, 33; his mansion in Essex, 33 n
Fairness, Cape, named by Bylot, 210, identification of, 252 n
Falconer, Lancelot, Adventurer, 646
Ffanner, Syracke, *see* Fenner, Sydrach
Fanshawe, Sir Henry, Adventurer, 645
——— William   ,,   645

Farewell, Cape, 86 n., 204, 281
Fawcett, Thomas, printer, cxxiv
Fenner, Sydrach, of Hudson's crew, 142, 146, 629
Fenton, Thomas, Viscount, Adventurer, 644
Ferryers, William, Adventurer, 646
Ffawkener, Launcelott, *see* Falconer, Lancelot
Fisher Strait, identification of, 184 n. 376 n.
Fletcher, John, Adventurer, 645
Flyboats, 80
Foxe's Channel, named, 386 n., Foxe in, 386 n., Button in, 186 n., 197 n., tide in, 203 n., James in, 586 n., mentioned, 254 n., 395 n.
Foxe family of Hull, members of the, liv
Foxe his Farthest, named, cix, 388 n., 393
Foxe Land, not visited since Foxe's time, 386 n., incorrectly shown on modern charts, 386 n.
Foxe, Capt Luke —his ancestors, lv, little known of his personal history, liv, born at Hull, liv, his personal characteristics, cxxviii, ccviii, 360 n., admitted a burgess of Hull, lv, his wife, lvii, ccxxviii, 353 n., his intolerance of tobacco, xcv, 361, 307 n., his early life at sea, lvi, 262, his ability as a seaman, lxii n., ccix n., applies for a post as mate under Captain John Knight, lviii, 261, 262, his early interest in the search for a N.-W Passage, lvii, 261, 262, seeks acquaintance of those who had sought for a N.-W Passage, lviii, 262, 370 n., acquaintance with Henry Briggs, lx, 262, 263, 324, first encounters James, xcvii, 263, Briggs's advice to, 307 n., acquaintance with John Tapp, lviii, 262, friendship with Thos Sterne, globe-maker, lviii, lx, 262, introduced by Briggs to Sir John Brooke, lxiii, 263, 324, entertained by Sir John Brooke, 324, petitions the king for a ship, lxiv, 263, reply to his petition, lxxi, 263, the king lends him the pinnace *Charles*, lxxii, 264, 266, condition of, lxxxv, 264 n., 270 n., his expedition promoted by Sir Thos. Roe, lxxvi, lxxxi, 263, by Sir John Wolstenholme, the elder, lxxvii, lxxxi, 263, unable to sail in 1630, lxxii, 263, delayed six months, lxxi, 263, his second petition to the king, lxxii n., reply to his second petition, lxxiv, preparations for his voyage, lxxxi, 264, victualling of his ship, xcv, 264 cost of his outfit, cxv, his opinion of his outfit, lxxxviii, xcv, 264, the members of his crew, lxxxvi, 264, his pleasant relations with his crew, lxxxvii, xcv, 286 n., 342 n.; his quarrels with and contempt for the master of his ship, lxxxviii *seq.*, 300 n., 378 n., 381 n., 401 n., Wolstenholme applies to the East India Company on his behalf, lxxxii, takes out cloth to barter in Japan, lxxxiv, ccxxiv, his instructions from the king, xcvi, 266, 360, 365, 426, supplied with a map of previous discoveries, 266, his voyage in search of a N.-W Passage, iii, 261 *seq.*, his orders and articles, 266, 267, sails from Deptford, xcviii, 268, breaks his mainyard, 269, difficulty in finding a tree large enough to supply the loss, 344, 348, enters Hudson's Strait, xcviii, 282, time occupied in passing and re-passing Hudson's Strait, 398 n., makes an important geological observation, 308, his instructions for those who went ashore, 297, his ship in danger from an iceberg, 293, he discourses on ice, 288, 292, his cutwater damaged, 304, 326, repaired, 344, reaches Salisbury Island, xcviii, 302, passes Cary's Swan's Nest, xcviii, 315, passes Mansell Island, xcviii, 311, names Roe's Welcome Island, xcix, 321, reaches Cape Fullerton, xcix, 318 n., names Brooke Cobham (or Marble) Island, lxiii, xcix, 324, notes the unreliability of the compass, 309, 316, names Briggs his Mathematics, xcix, 329, enters Hubart's Hope (Churchill Bay), xcix, 331, enters Port Nelson for repairs, c, 339, reasons for putting into Port Nelson, 339, 340, finds relics of Button's expedition, c, ccxxx, 343, 344 n., 348, 349, 598, discovers an inscription left by Button, c, 344, re-erects Button's cross, 348, builds his pinnace, 342, observes the constellations, 313, abandons search on the western shore of the bay, 364, explores southern shore, ci, 341, 351 *seq.*, 426, 427, arguments for and against wintering, 365 *seq.*, 389, 413, 415, 417, some of his crew break into the hold, 406 n., finds his cock-boat useless, 295, meets and is entertained by Captain James, cii, 355, no letters from James entrusted to, 416, names Wolstenholme's Ultimum Vale (Cape Henrietta Maria), cii, 367, explores Foxe's Channel, ciii, 379 n., sickness among his crew, ciii, 374, 384, 404, 405, his return to England, civ, 407, cessation of the search for a N.-W Passage for forty years after his return, ccix, contemporary reference to his voyage, lxx, his expedition judiciously carried out, civ, cvii, 407 n., his opinion of the value of his discoveries, 429, his voyage of greater geographical importance than James's,

ccviii; his defence against James's accusations, 416, Roe's letter concerning his voyage, cv, reasons for disregarding his instructions, 364, 408, localities named by him, cviii, cix, his summary of observations, 279, his theory of the formation of icebergs, 292, 295, knew nothing of Munk's voyage in 1619, liii n, his life after his return to England, cxv, cxix, cxxii, preparation of his book, cxxii, his *North-West Fox* described, iii, cxxiii—collation of, cxxvii—literary imperfections of, cxxii, cxxv, ccix, 444—present value of, cxxvii, his book a companion to James's, iii, his chart of the Arctic Regions, cxxvii, 12, 177 n, his original MS. journal still preserved, cviii, ccxxix, 391 n, reference to his book of Courses, Latitudes, Variations, and Distances, 271, his ship, the *Charles*, granted to Sir John Wolstenholme, cxvii, petitions the Admiralty for payment of his wages, cxix, cxxi, his address to the officials of the Trinity House, 443, his death in 1635, cxv, cxxx

Foxe, Richard, father of Luke Foxe, liv, admitted a burgess of Hull, lv

Freeman, Ralphe, Adventurer, 645, 649

Fretum Hudson, 377 n, 404, 413, *see* Hudson's Strait

Frobisher, Sir Martin, v, first voyage, 37, second, 43, third voyage, 52, articles to be observed in his fleet, 52, sails up Hudson's Strait, vii, 58 n

Frobisher's Bay (or Strait), 277 n, *see also* Lumley's Inlet.

Frozen Strait, 186 n

Fullerton, Cape, identified, 177 n, 179 n, 180 n, 318 n, 426 n.

Gabriel, Frobisher's ship, 38, 43, 58, 59

Gabriel Strait, identified, 207 n, 251 n

Galfridus Monumetensis, *see* Geoffrey of Monmouth

Gardiner, Mr Christopher, offers his services to the East India Company, lxxviii

Garway, Francis, Adventurer, 646
——— Thomas ,, 645
——— William ,, 645

Gatonby, John, of Hull, his account of Hall's voyage, 96 n

Gearing, John, Adventurer, 645

Geese, wild, 160

Gellibrand, Henry, mentioned, 458 n, 606 n, account of, 612 n., his appendix touching Longitude, 612, his observation of the eclipse of the moon from Gresham College, 614, acquainted with Lansbergen, 615 n

Geoffrey of Monmouth, 15 n

Gerritzsoon, Hessel, a Dutch cartographer, viii, 121 n., 130 n, 158 n, his map, 363 n

Gibbons, Captain William —mentioned, vi, one of the Adventurers, 646, his relationship to Button, 195 n, 201 n., Button's high opinion of him, 195, 196, 201 n, his voyage in 1614 in search of the N.-W. Passage, vi, xliii, 197 n, 201, 202—mainly promoted by the Company of Merchants of London, Discoverers of the N.-W Passage, xliv, xlv, ccxxv, 201 n—partly promoted by the East India Company, ccxxv— little known about it, xliv, 201 n.— its objects, xliii, 201 n, sails in the *Discovery*, xliii, 193, 195, 201, Bylot sails with, 1614, 164 n, caught in the ice, xliv, 202, his voyage proves a total failure, xlv, 201 n., 284 n.

Gibbons Hole, *see* Saglek Bay

Gilbert, Adrian, charter granted to, xl n, 652 n.
——— Sir Humphrey, his *Discourse of a Discouerie*, 418 n, mentioned, 433

Gillam, Capt. Z., his voyage to Hudson's Bay in 1668, ccx, ccxii, ccxiii

Glanville, Edward, officer under Button, 167 n, his replies to Button's queries, 173

Goare, Robert, Adventurer, 645

God's Favour, Isle of, named by James, clxxvi, 495 n, 598

God's Mercy, Isles of, named by Hudson, 117, 124, 295 n, 308, 399, tide at, 421, 424

God's Providence, harbour named by James, clxxvi, 470

Gold, stone supposed to contain, 39, 40

Gomara, Francis Lopez de, account of, 31 n, extract from his *History*, 36

Goodlacke, Christopher, Adventurer, captain, 646

Goodlard, Captain William, whaling captain, 441 n

Gorsuche, Daniell, Adventurer, 646

Green, Henry —born in Kent, 132, sails under Hudson, 132, falls out with the surgeon, 133, quarrels with the master, 134, plans a mutiny, 139, 630(2), 631(2)—heads it, 144, causes Hudson to be abandoned, 143, called captain, 149, puts Pricket in command, 147, his confidence in the Esquimaux, 152—surprised and killed by them, xiv, 154, 155, 168, 630, his body thrown into the sea, 155, mentioned, 136, 138, 139, 140, 142, 144, 145, 153

Greene, Lawrence, Adventurer, 645
——— Reynold ,, 646

Greenewell, William ,, 642, 645, 649, 656, 659, 660, 661, 662

Greenland, 89, so called ironically, 103

Groseilliers, Sieur des, French-Canadian fur-trader, ccx, 321 n., discovers relics of Button's expedition, ccxxx, incor-

poration of the Hudson's Bay Company due to his discoveries, ccx
Guilford, Sir Henry, Adventurer, 645
Guillemot, Black, 107 *n*, 168 *n*.
Gulls, 70, 81, 89, 107, 151
Gunter, Edmund, mathematician, account of, 605 *n*, use of logarithms promoted by, 605 *n*.

Hackett, Richard, Adventurer, 646
Hakluyt, Richard, geographer, mentioned, 30, 79, 247, 444, 606, one of the Adventurers, 646
Hall, Christopher, master of the *Gabriel*, 40, pilot of Frobisher's fleet, 53, 56
——— James, of Kingston-upon-Hull, v, 86, 89, second voyage, 92, third, 95, fourth, 96, 203 *n*, death, 98, his account of Greenland, 89, 99, 279, mentioned, 421, 424, *see also* Gatonby
Hamersley, Hugh, Adventurer, 645
Hammon, David, of the *Henrietta Maria*, clvi, 551
Hanford, Humphrey, Adventurer, 645, 649
Hannah Bay, identified, 129 *n*
Hanson, Raphe, Adventurer, 646
Harbours, Button sees, 193, *see also* Aurora
Hare, Samuel, Adventurer, 646
Harrington, Sir John, Adventurer, 644
Harrison, William, Adventurer, 645, 649
Hartsfleete, Walter ,, 645
Hasilden, William ,, 645
Hatton Headland, identified, 465 *n*
Hawk, 35
Hawkins, John, Adventurer, 646
Hawkridge, Captain William —mentioned, vi, notice of him, xlix, imprisoned in Algiers, l *n*, accompanies Button, l, 167 *n*, 249 *n*, his replies to Button's queries, 170, 171, 173 *n*, his voyage in search of a N.-W Passage, xlviii, ccxxvi, 248, probable date of his voyage, 1617, ccxxvii, it is mainly promoted by the Company of Discoverers of the N.-W Passage, xlix, 249 *n*, partly promoted by the East India Company, xlix, 248 *n*, narrative of it exceedingly confused, li *n*, 249 *n*, 257 *n*, he enters Lumley Inlet, 250, makes Resolution Island, 250, sails through Hudson's Strait, 256 *n*, near Digges Iland, 256 *n*, 258, near Sea Horse Point, 254, in Davis Strait, 258, returns home, li, 256 *n*, results of his voyage valueless, l, 249 *n*, 257 *n*, does not despair of the passage, 255
Hayes, Sir Thomas, Adventurer, 645
Hayward, Sir George ,, 645
Heart Creek, valley of, 166 *n*, 342 *n*
Henbanes, 313, 317, 396, *see also* Aurora

Henrietta Maria, the, James's ship, 456 *n*., crew of, clvi; warrant for the payment of the wages of her crew, clviii; tonnage of, 456, 594, she is sunk for safety, clxiii, 519, 520, 600, damage sustained by, 592
Henrietta Maria, Cape, named by James, 367 *n*, 490, named Wolstenholme's Ultimum Vale by Foxe, 367, the limit of Hudson's discoveries westward, 131 *n*, 186 *n*
Henry, Prince of Wales, his interest in Arctic discovery, xvii *n*, 644, Point named after him, 125, 637, employs Button, 241, his orders and instructions to Button, xxviii, 636-38, mentioned, 641, 648
Hickes, Thomas, Warden of the Society of Merchant Venturers of Bristol, cxxxv
Hide, John, Adventurer, 645
Higham, Edward, Adventurer, 646
Hightlord, junior, John, Adventurer, 646
Hill, Richard, Adventurer, 646
Holdman, George ,, 645
Hollis, Sir John ,, 645
Holloway, John ,, 646
Honeywood, Robert ,, 645
Honting, John, of the *Charles*, lxxxvii
Hooke, Humphrey, merchant of Bristol, cxlix, Master of the Society of Merchant Venturers of Bristol, clviii, letter from, clxvi, letter from Captain James to, clxvii
Hopes Advance, named, 177, *see* Prince Henry's Foreland
Hope Sanderson, named, 76, Bylot touches, 225
Hopes Checked, named by Button, 165, 169, Foxe sights, 331, 336, James near, 596, latitude of, 165, 173 *n*, 177, mentioned, 170, 173, 175, 177
Hourin, mate of Foxe's ship, the *Charles*, *see* Hurin
Hourglass, sermons timed by, 52
Howard, Charles, *see* Nottingham, Earl of
Howard, Sir John, Adventurer, 645
Howe, Edmund ,, 646
Hubart, Josias, sails with Hall, 95 *n*, his replies to Button's queries, 171-173, pilot of the *Resolution*, 171 *n*, a Hull man, 171 *n*, takes an observation, 173, his chart, 163 *n*, 178 *n*, 241, sails with Bylot, 231, mentioned, 200
Hubart's Hope (Churchill Bay), xcix, cvi *n*, clx, 178 *n*, 241, 331, 333, 335, 429, 481, 597
Hubberd, Sir Henry, Attorney-General, 644, Chief Justice, 644 *n*
Hudson, Captain Henry —mentioned, vi, account of, ix, Asher's *Life* of him, ix *n*; Purchas's account of his voyages, x *n*, his first Arctic voyage in 1607, ix, his second Arctic voyage

INDEX.

in 1608, ix, his third Arctic voyage in 1609, ix, his fourth Arctic voyage in 1610, ix, xi, 114, objects of his fourth voyage, xii, promoters of it, xii, 642, encouraged by Sir John Wolstenholme, 441, victualling of his ship, 131, 138 n, 630, number of his crew, 137 n, 629, 630, enters Hudson's Strait, xii, 117, 632, enters Hudson's Bay, xiii, 120, commonly credited with first discovery of Hudson's Bay, vi, others discovered Hudson's Bay before he, vii, his knowledge of the fact, viii, extent of his discoveries in Hudson's Bay, 131 n, 341 n, 364 n, his observance of the tide at Isle of God's Mercy, 421, 424, names Nottingham Island, 310, names Digges Iland, 311, end of his own journal, 126 n, date of his seeking harbour, 359, 364, his wintering place, xiii, 130, prepares for his return home, 137, his crew mutinies, xiii, 136, causes of the mutiny, xviii, 631, is said to have distributed victuals with partiality, 138 n, 631, his arms pinioned, 143, 630, abandoned by his crew, xiii, 146, date of abandonment, 145 n, 630, his shallop never seen again, 147, possible traces of, found by James on Danby Island, 568 n, 569 n, names of those abandoned with him, 146, 629, the mutineers pillage the ship, 145, 146—they return to England, xiv, 158—bewilderment as to their course, 149 n —their ship aground, 150 n, 633—starving, 157, Hudson supposed to have discovered the N.-W. Passage, xvi, xix, 151 n; interest excited in England in his discovery, xvi, preparations for following it up, xvi, xviii, depositions of the survivors of his expedition summarised, xv—mentioned, 114 n, 118 n —printed in full, 629

Hudson, Jeffery, the Queen's dwarf, ccxxviii, 11

——— John, Hudson's son, 146, 629, sailed with his father on several voyages, 146 n.

Hudson's Bay —Hudson commonly credited with first discovery of, vi, entered by Hudson in 1610, xiii, discoverers of, before Hudson, vii, Hudson's knowledge of the fact, viii, extent of, explored by Hudson, xviii, 131 n., 341 n, Hudson's East and West Bays explained, 131 n, 365 n, 422 n, 498 n, Button's voyage to, in 1612, xvii, 162; western coast first reached by Button, xxx, 185, extent of Button's explorations in, xxx, 185 n, 341 n., Button's disappointment at finding no western outlet from, 185 n, 186 n; originally called Button's Bay, xcix, Bylot and Baffin's voyage to, in 1615, xlv, 202; Hawkridge's voyage to, xlix, 248; Munk's voyage to, liii n, Foxe's voyage to, liii, 268, Foxe's explorations in, 426, 427, Foxe's observations of the tides in, 427 seq., Foxe's chart showing, cxxvii, James's voyage to, liii, 460, James's wintering in, unwise, clxii, clxxiv, James's chart of, clxxix, James's Bay originally called, 169 n, 322 n, 533 n; southern coast of, first explored by Foxe and James, ci, 186 n., Gillam's voyage to, in 1668, ccx, ccxii, Thornton's chart of, in 1685, ccxx, first overland journey to, from Canada, ccx, 321 n., Knight's voyage to, in 1719, ccxiv, Scroggs's voyage to, in 1721, ccxvi, Middleton's voyage to, in 1741-42, ccxvii; Moor's voyage to, in 1746-47, ccxviii, Capt. W. Coats's description of, in 1751, ccxx, vegetation on the shores of, 331 n, 333 n, 335 n, 347, ridges on the west coast of, 329 n, progress of the exploration of, ccxx, latest exploration of, ccxxi, annually visited since 1670 by the ships of the Hudson's Bay Company, ccxxi, 591 n, a proposed trade route through, ccxxi, Company of Adventurers of England trading into, see Hudson's Bay Company

Hudson's Bay Company —formation of, due to explorations of Radisson and des Groseilliers, ccx, incorporation of, ccxiii, its early difficulties, ccxiii, Prince Rupert's interest in, ccxiii, Select Committee reports upon, in 1749, ccxiv n., its connection with the search for a N.-W. Passage, ccxiii, ccxxi, dispatches Knight's expedition in 1719 in search of a N.-W. Passage, ccxiv, dispatches Scroggs's expedition in 1721 in search of a N.-W. Passage, ccxvi; dispatches an expedition to the northward in 1737, ccxvi, its ships visit the Bay annually, ccxxi, 591 n

Hudson's Hold with Hope, 117, 632, 633

Hudson's Strait —reached by early Portuguese navigators, vii, entered by Frobisher in 1578, vii, 58 n.; sighted by Davis in 1587, vii, 79, entered by Weymouth in 1602, viii, 80 n, entered by Hudson, xii, 632, entered by Button in 1612, xxix, 165, 167, first carefully explored by Bylot in 1615, xlv; Bylot declares no passage through, xlvi, 220 n., named Fretum Christian by Munk, lii n, time occupied by Foxe in passing through, 398 n., ice encountered by Foxe in, 398 n, 401, by James, 587, mentioned in Button's instructions, 637

Hull, Foxe's family natives of, liv, lv

Humble, Peter, Adventurer, 646
Hume, Andrew, Foxe's quarter-master, lxxxvi, xcv, 295 n
Huntris, William, master of Hall's pinnace, 99
Hurin, master's mate of the *Charles*, lxxxvi, lxxxix, supposed author of a journal, cxii, reference to, 286 n, 391 n, Foxe names a "Throughlet" after him, cix, 381, Foxe and he make merry, 384, 385, 404 n, 405 n, mentioned, 345 n, 378 n, 381, 379 n, 405 n, 412
Hyde, Bernard, Adventurer, 646

Ice, Foxe's Dissertation on, 288, 289, the "rut" of the, 579
Icebergs, Foxe discourses on, 288
Iceland, description of, by Fitz Jonas, 17, hot springs in, 122, Piefkins visits, 102, Hudson's expedition arrives at, 121, fishery to, 436
Ingram, Captain John, master of Button's pinnace, xxix, 174, 187, 193, 646
Ironside, Richard, Adventurer, 645
Iseham, George „ 646
Isles of God's Mercy, *see* God's Mercy, Isles of

Jacob, Abraham, Adventurer, 646
James I, his letter of credence to Sir T Button, 635
James, Alderman Thomas, of Bristol, cxxxi, monument to, ccvi
James, Captain Thomas —his birth, cxxxi, ccviii, his personal history, cxxxi, cxxxii, probably a member of the Inner Temple, cxxxii, ccvii, 451, probably never married, ccvii, his personal characteristics, clxxv, ccviii, his armorial bearings, cxcv n, connection with Bristol, cxxxi, circumstances which led up to his voyage, cxxxii, 455, reported previous experience of Arctic research, cxxxiii n, his preparations for the voyage, cliv, clvii, 455, 594, buys books and manuscripts relating to Arctic exploration, 592, first encounters Foxe, xcvii, 263, rides to Oxford to see Briggs, 263, his voyage in search of a N.-W Passage, iii, xcviii, 450, his voyage promoted by Sir T Roe, cxxxix, 455, his voyage promoted by the Society of Merchant Venturers of Bristol, cxxxiv, 455, 456, 594, confidence felt in him by the Bristol merchants, clvii, tonnage of his ship, 456, selection of his crew, clv, 457, 458 n, numbers of his crew, clvi, 457 n, 594, pleasant relations with his crew, 512, 520, 524, 545, contract for payment of wages to his crew, clviii, his provisions, 457, 512, 544, 594, mathematical and other books taken by, 606, list of instruments provided by, 458, 604, observations taken by, 607, observes eclipse of the moon, 511, 614, Wolstenholme arranges for him to have an audience of the king, cxlvi, he presents to the king a petition from the Society of Merchant Venturers of Bristol, cxlvii, letters to, from the Society of Merchant Venturers of Bristol, cxliii, cxlviii, letters from him to the Society of Merchant Venturers of Bristol, cl, clxvii; goes to London to receive his instructions, 459, his instructions from the king, clvii, clix, 459 n, 596, has a service held on board, before sailing, 460, sets sail upon his voyage, clxi, 460, 594, enters Hudson's Strait, clxi, 465, lands on Resolution Island, 286, 469, 470 n, reaches Mansell Island, clxi, 475, 476, 596, grounds upon Nelson Shoal, clxii, 482, explores the southern coast-line of Hudson's Bay, clxii, 484, 485, 597, names it New South Wales, clxii, 485, 489, 597, meets and entertains Captain Foxe, clxii, 358, 489, 598, accident on board his ship, clxii, 486, reaches and names Cape Henrietta Maria, clxiii, 490, enters James's Bay, clxiii, 129, 492 n, winters on Charlton Island, clxiii, 507, 599, 600, his decision to winter in Hudson's Bay unwise, clxii, clxxiv, sinks his ship for safety, clxiii, 519, 520, 600, sickness of his men, 490, 492, 502, 545, leaves Charlton Island, clxiv, 567, finds relics of white men on Danby Island, 568—conjecture that they are traces of Hudson, 568 n, 569 n, explores Foxe's Channel, clxiv, 582 *seq*, his difficulties with the ice, clxi, clxiv, 465 *seq*, 473, 513, 514, damages sustained by his ship, 592, exaggerates the dangers met with on his voyage, clxix, 556 n, his difficulties largely due to mismanagement, clxxi, cxciv, returns to England, clxv, 592, goes with the remainder of his crew to church to return thanks for preservation, 592, his voyage of less geographical importance than Foxe's, ccix, his voyage produced no results of geographical value, clxxii, localities named by him, clxxii, cessation of the search for a N -W Passage for forty years after his return, ccix, documents relating to his voyage preserved at Bristol, cxxxiv, clxv, preparation of his book, clxxvi, his *Strange and Dangerous Voyage* described, v, clxxvii—collation of, clxxviii n—its position in English literature, clxxxvi—literary qualities of, clxxvii—later editions of, clxxxi—abridgement of, in later works, clxxxii—a chief

source of Coleridge's *Ancient Mariner*, clxxxix seq.—present value of, clxxviii, his book a companion to Foxe's, iii, his chart of Hudson's Bay and Strait, clxxix, his verses commended by Southey, clxxxix, 564 n, his observations upon temperature utilized by Boyle, clxxxviii, has an audience of the king, clxix, his life after his return to England, cxciii, appointed to the command of H M S. *Ninth Whelp*, cxciv, his naval service on the Irish coast, cxcv seq, ccii, cciii, captures a pirate, cxcvii, returns to Bristol for repairs, cxcvii, the Lord Deputy of Ireland expresses satisfaction with his services, cxcviii, cxcix, cciii, his last illness, cciii, his death in 1635, ccv, ccvi, his place of burial doubtful, ccv, his will, cciv, epigrams to his memory by Thos. Beedome, clxxxvi, his portrait, clxxix

James, Edward, Adventurer, 645
——— Mrs., widow of Edward James, ccxxxi
James's Bay, named, clxxvi, Hudson in, 129, 131 n, best account of, 494 n, originally called Hudson's Bay, xcix, 168 n, 322 n
Jay, 71
Jeffrey, Mr, courtier, see Hudson, Jeffery
Jeffereys, Thomas, Adventurer, 646
Jenkinson, Robert ,, 645
Johnson, Robert ,, 645
——— Thomas ,, 645
Jones, Alderman Sir Francis, helps to send out Bylot, 202, 223, sound named after him, 230, 230 n
——— Thomas, Adventurer, 646
Jones's Sound, see Jones, Alderman Sir F
Juet, Robert, Hudson's mate, 128, 133, 142, 143, 149, displaced, 128, proposed by the mutineers for master, 147, death of starvation, xiv, 157, 168 n, 629, mentioned, 160
Juxon, Thomas, Adventurer, 646

Kendall, Cape, identified, 183 n
King's Foreland (or Promontory), named, cix, 125, 256, 395, 425, 474 n, 637
King George Islands, situation of, 368 n
King, Henry, see King, John
King John, Hudson's quarter-master, 141, 142, 143, 161, miscalled Henry, 146 n, wrongly supposed to be the carpenter, 144 n
Kingston-upon-Hull, corporation of, 440, 443
Kirby, Jeffery, Adventurer, 645
Kirke, Jervas ,, 646
Kitchen, Robert, Admiralty agent in Bristol, cxcvi, cci, ccii
Knight, Captain James, of the Hudson's Bay Company, ccxiv, his expedition in search of a N.-W. Passage, ccxiv, his ships sunk on Marble Island, ccxv
Knight, Captain John, v, voyage, 106, he goes ashore and does not return, 109 seq, mentioned, 422
Knightly, Sir Valentine, Adventurer, 645

Ladley, Arnold, of Hudson's crew, 629, see also Ludlow
Lake, Sir Thomas, Latin secretary, 644
Lancaster Isles, 368
Lancaster, Sir James, promoter of Baffin's expedition, mentioned, 230 n, isles named after, 368, sound named after, 230, one of the Adventurers, 645, 656, 659, 660, 661, 662
Lancaster Sound, see Lancaster, Sir James
Lansbergen, Phillipus Van, Dutch mathematician, 615, 618
Leate, Nicholas, Adventurer, 642, 645, 649, 656, 659, 660, 661, 662
Leaver, Edmund, Adventurer, 646
Lee, John ,, 646
Leggatt, John, printer of James's book, clxxviii
Lennox, Ludovic, Duke of, Adventurer, 644
Le Strange, Sir Hamon, Adventurer, 645
Lever, Thomas, Adventurer, 646
Leveson, William ,, 646
Lewis, Sir Edward ,, 645
Leyson Point, identified, 191 n
Lindsey, Earl of, notice of, 373 n, Foxe names a cape after him, cix, 373, 397
Lindsey, Cape, see Lindsey, Earl of
Lisle, Robert, Viscount, Adventurer, 644
Log, use of the, 371 n, by Foxe, 371, by James, 606 n
Logarithms largely introduced by Briggs, lxi n
Lok, Michael, manuscript of, 40 n, note by, 244
Longe, Richard, merchant, of Bristol, cxliv, cxlv, cxlix, clxvi
Longitude, reckoned from London, 173, from Charlton, 618, Gellibrand on, 612
Ludlow, Lodlo, or Lullo, Arnold, 136, 142, 143, 145, 146, 161, Adventurer, 645, see also Ladley, Arnold
Lumley, John, Lord, account of, 278 n, anecdote about, 278, builds the pier at Hartlepool, 278
Lumley's Inlet, named by Davis, 277 n, mentioned, 200, 250 n, see also Frobisher's Bay
Lutterforde, Edward, Adventurer, 646
Lyon Inlet, James arrives near, 586 n

Macham, Master Samuel, letter to, 159

Magna Britannia, named by Hudson, 117
Mallard, 160
Mannering, Sir Arthur, Adventurer, 645
Mansell Island, 120 n., 256, 257 n., 311, 425, 475 n., named by Button, 188 n
Mansell, Sir Robert, Vice-Admiral, account of, 188 n., mentioned 475 n., one of the Adventurers, 645, 649, 656, 659, 660, 661, 662
Mansfield Island, *see* Mansell Island
Marble Island, *see* Brooke Cobham
Maria, Cape, *see* Henrietta Maria, Cape
Maria, the, *see Henrietta Maria*, the
Marmaduke, Captain Thomas, of Hull, 440
Marre, Master, mathematician, 605
Mary, the, *see Henrietta Maria*, the
Master's MS. Journal, the, cviii, xciv, 268
Matthews, Bennet, of Hudson's crew, 136, 142, 143, 145 n., 160, 630, his deposition, 631
Maxlisden, Richard, Adventurer, 646
Maydwell, Anthony ,, 646
Maynard, Sir William ,, 644
Merchants of London, etc., *see* Company of
Merchant Venturers of Bristol, *see* Bristol, Society of, etc.
Merricke, John, Adventurer, 642, 645, 656, 659, 660, 661, 662
Michael, the, Frobisher's ship, 38, 43
Michaelmas Bay, named by Hudson, 129, *see* Hannah Bay
Middleton, Captain Christopher —commands an expedition, ccxvii, winters at Churchill, ccxvii, explores Ut Ultra (Roe's Welcome), ccxvii, 413, returns to England, ccxvii, his statements doubted, ccxviii; proved to be true, ccxix
—— Robert, Adventurer, 645, 649
Mildmay, Robert ,, 646
Mill Isle, origin of the name, 213, 303, 379 n., Foxe sights, 380, 395, mentioned, 425
Millet, William, Adventurer, 645
Milward, John ,, 645
Molesworth, Bevell ,, 646
Monmouth, Earl of, 493 n
Monmouth, Cape, ccxxx, 493 n., 498 n
Montgomery, Philip, Earl of, Adventurer, 644
Moon, eclipses of the, 511, 614-17, 637, abnormal shape of the, 532, 537, Captain Parry's observation of the, 532 n
Moonshine (or *Moonlight*), the, Davis's ship, 65, 68, 69, 73 n
Moor, Captain Francis, his expedition, ccxviii, 413 n
Moore, Adrian (or Adam), of Hudson's crew, 142, 146, 629
—— Sir George, Adventurer, 644
Morley, Thomas ,, 646
Morris, John ,, 646

Morse, or walrus, 101, 189 n., 190 n., 327, with young, 382, seen by James, 575, morse teeth, 88, 152, 189, 190, 298
Mosquito Bay, mentioned, 149 n
Motives, the, attributed to Davis, xxxv, Sir D Digges the probable author of, xxxvi, contents of, summarized, xxxvii, printed in full, 639
Motter, Andrew (or Adrian), of Hudson's crew, 136, 140, 142, 153, 155, 161, 630, his deposition, 631
Mounteagle, William, Lord, Adventurer, 644
Mountney, Richard, Adventurer, 646
Mount Raleigh, 77, conical form of, 63 n
Mulgrave, Earl of, Edmund Sheffield, 440 n
Munk, Captain Jens —mentioned, vi, his voyage in 1619 in search of a N.-W. Passage, lii n., 583 n., names Hudson's Strait Fretum Christian, lii n., his winter haven, lii n., his voyage unknown to Foxe, lii n., English account of his voyage in preparation, liii n
Murray, Sir David, Adventurer, 645
Muscovia glass, 63, 465
Muscovy Company, 643, 656, 659, 660, 661, 662

Napper, Captain James, of the Hudson's Bay Company, his voyage northward in 1737, ccxvi, death of, ccxvi
Narwhal, 45 n., 103, 150 n., 227, 307, horn of, 88, 236, 298, darts headed with horn of, 77 n
Nash, Thomas, ccvii, 452 n., his letter to James, ccvii, 451, member of the Inner Temple, 451, 452
Nelson, Francis, master of Button's ship, death, 166, 167, Port Nelson named after, 166, Adventurer, 646 n
Nelson Shoal, situation of, 339 n., James strikes on, 482 n., 579 n
Nesfield, Peter, quarter-master of the *Charles*, lxxxvi, 343, 346
Ne Ultra (or Ut Ultra), bay known as, 179 n., 318, 319, 370 n., 413, 429, 581
Newfoundland, called Bacculaos by Cabot, 36
Newton, Adam, Adventurer, 645
New South Wales (coast of Hudson's Bay), *see* New Wales
New Wales, Button names, 170 n., 485 n., James names, clxxvi, 485, 489
New Yorkshire, named by Foxe, cix
Nicholas, Sir Edward, Secretary of State, notice of, 397 n., island named after, 302, 397
Nicholas, Isle, named by Foxe, cix, 302, 397
Norman, Robert, his *Newe Attractive*, xxxii

Northampton, Henry, Earl of, one of the Adventurers, 642; Keeper of the Privy Seal, 644

North-West Fox, Captain Luke Foxe's, described, iii, cxxvi; contains abstract of earlier voyages, iv; collation of, cxxvii

North-West Passage —long-continued search for, ii, li; Weymouth's voyage in 1602 in search of, ccxxii, 80; Hudson's voyage in 1610-11 in search of, ix, 114 *n*; Hudson thought to have discovered it, in 1610, xvi, xix, xx, xxi; Trinity House officials conjecture that it lies through Hudson's Bay, 633, 634; Sir Dudley Digges's treatise on the, xxxvi; Sir Thomas Button's voyage in 1612-13 in search of, xvii, 162; Button's letter to Lord Dorchester concerning the search for, lxv; confident expectations that Button would sail through the, xxii, xlii; Button's opinion concerning a, xxxi, lxv, 199, 197 *n*; believed by Button to lie through Hubart's Hope, 331; Hubart's opinion of the direction in which to search for the, 172; Company of Merchants of London Discoverers of the, its origin, xxxv; its charter summarized, xxxviii; Gibbons's voyage in 1614 in search of, xliii, 197 *n*, 201, 202; Bylot's voyage in 1615 in search of, xlv, 202; Bylot's voyage in 1616 in search of, xlvii, 223; Baffin's opinion concerning, xlvi, xlviii, 220 *n*; Hawkridge's voyage in search of, xlix, 248; a possible voyage by Capt. Bullock in 1618 in search of, ccxxvi; Munk's voyage in 1619 in search of, lii; Wolstenholme promotes an abortive expedition in search of, lxxvii; Briggs's treatise on the, lxi, 239 *seq*; lapse of search for a, from 1619 to 1631, liii; Foxe's voyage in 1631 in search of a, iii, liii, 261; James's voyage in 1631 in search of a, iii, liii, cxxxi, 450; James's views as to the existence of a, 589 *n*; cessation of a search for a, for forty years after the return of Foxe and James, ccix; Captain James Knight's expedition in 1719 in search of a, ccxiv; Captain John Scroggs's expedition in 1721 in search of, ccxvi; Arthur Dobbs revives the search for a, in 1740, ccxvii; Captain Christopher Middleton's expedition in 1741-42 in search of, ccxvii; reward of £20,000 offered by Parliament in 1745 for the discovery of a, ccxviii; Captain Moor's expedition in 1746-47 in search of, ccxviii; expeditions in search of, after 1747, ccxix; the Hudson's Bay Company and the search for, ccxiii; finally discovered and proved commercially valueless, ii

Nottingham, Earl of, notice of, 310 *n*.; island named after, 310, 642 *n*; admiral, 642, 644; Adventurer, 656, 659, 660, 661, 662

Nottingham Island, 197, 309, 310; tide at, 198, 374; mentioned, 425, 475

Octher, voyage of, 16
Offeley, Robert, Adventurer, 646, 649
Orpen, plant, *see* Sedum
Ortelius, Abraham, cartographer, 29; his atlas, 29 *n*
Ortell, *see* Ortelius
Owfield, Thomasine, Adventurer, 645
Owl, 107

Packington, Thomas, Adventurer, 646
Paddy, Sir William ,, 645
Palmer, John, boatswain of the *Henrietta Maria*, clvi; illness of, 492, 584
—— Rev. Thomas, a Bristol divine, 460
—— William, Adventurer, 646
Papworth, Robert ,, 646
Parham, John ,, 646
Parry, Captain, observes abnormal shapes of the moon, 532 *n*.
Partridges, 71, 89, 124, 545, *see* Ptarmigan
Passage, North-West, *see* North-West Passage.
Payne, William, Adventurer, 645
Pearepointe, *see* Pierrepoint.
Peate, Richard, Adventurer, 645
Pembroke, Cape, Button at, 191 *n*, 195 *n*; identical with Port Peregrine, 376 *n*
Penkavell, Benjamin, Adventurer, 646
—— Digorie ,, 646
—— Nicholas ,, 646
—— Peter ,, 646
—— Richard, charter granted to, 646 *n*, 652 *n*, 661 *n*
Penkavill, *see* Penkavell.
Pennington, Robert, Adventurer, 646
Peregrine, Cape, *see* Point Peregrine.
Perkins, Aden, Adventurer, 645
Pett, Phineas, shipwright to James I, xvii *n*; references to Button in his MS. autobiography, xvii *n*, 200
Pettie-dancers, 313, 317, 327, 349, 373, 374 *n*., 375, 396, *see also* Aurora.
Pheasants, 71, 89
Phettiplace, Thomas, Adventurer, 645
Phillips, Sir Edward, Master of the Rolls, 644
Philips, Cape, *see* Kendall, Cape
Pierce, Michael, of Hudson's crew, 136, 140, 142, 147, 153; wounded, 154; death, 155, 630
Pierrepoint, William, Adventurer, 646
Pigmies, 104
Plancius, Peter, geographer, of Amsterdam, viii
Plefkins, Dethmar, sent to Iceland, 102
Plover, 160

Point Barte, named by Foxe, cix, 388 n., 394
Point Carleton, named by Foxe, cix, 388 n.
Point Peregrine, named by Foxe, cix, 376, 377, 388; *see also* Pembroke, Cape
Pointell, Richard, Adventurer, 645
Polhill, Edward   „   646
Poole, Jonas, voyager, 440
Pork-fish, *see* Porpoises.
Porpoises, 345 n
Port Churchill, 178 n, 332 n, 337 n, 481, 597 n., *see also* Hubart's Hope.
Port de Boucherville, named, 218 n
Portland, Cape, *see* Portland, Earl of
Portland, Earl of, cxliv, cxlv n; notice of, 388 n; cape named after, 388, 390, 392, 397, 494 n.
Portland, Lord Weston's, *see* Weston's Portland
Port Nelson, situation of, 166 n, 169 n, 173 n; named, 166, tidal wave at, 334, 339; dangers of, 342, 350 n; mentioned, 339 n; 349; Foxe in, 426, 427, 432, 484 n, 489
Portraits, of Button, xxiv, of James, clxxix
Portuguese navigators reach Hudson's Strait, vii
Pory, John, traveller and geographer, letter from, lxx
Powlested, Henry, Adventurer, 645
Price, Arthur, master of the *Henrietta Maria*, clvi, 471, 584; cove named after him, clxxvi, 471
Prickett, Abacuk — his narrative, 120 seq, criticised, 130 n; a former servant of Sir D Digges, 121 n; sent by Hudson to look for wintering place, 130, illness, 139, his part in the mutiny, 139, 141, 143; occupies master's cabin, 147, wounded, 155; reaches Gravesend, 158, is taken by Bylot to Sir Thomas Smith, 158; doubts of his fidelity, 162, apparently substantiates his innocence, 121 n, Foxe's opinion of him, 162, a landsman, 630, one of the Adventurers, 646, his deposition, 630, his geographical statements vague, 147 n
Priestly, William, Adventurer, 645
Primum Mobile, 419 n.
Prince Charles's Cape, named by Bylot, 395, 474 n, 475 n
Prince Henry's Foreland, named, 125, 299 n
Prince's Cradle, sound named by Foxe, cix, 395
Prince's Nurse, island named by Foxe, cix, 395
Ptarmigan, Willow, 134 n, numbers killed, 134, 135, 167, 357 n., 545 n
Puckering, Sir Thomas, letter to, lxx, Adventurer, 644
Pullie, James, killed by Esquimaux, 99

Purchas, Rev Samuel, birth, ix n, preferments, x n, will, x n., his *Pilgrimage*, x n; his *Pilgrimes*, xi n.; on the search for a Passage, 239 seq, mentioned, 606
——— William, Lord Mayor of London, 34
Purser, William, master's mate of the *Ninth Whelp*, clvi, cciii

Quarles, William, Adventurer, 645
Queen Anne's Foreland, 395, 637, *see also* Queen's Cape.
Queen's Cape, cix, 383 n, 385, 392, 399

Radisson, Pierre Esprit, French-Canadian fur-trader, ccx, 321 n., Scull's *Voyages of*, ccx n
Ramsden Hall (or Hull), Alderman of Hull, 347; cape named after, cix
Ramusio, reference to, 32, 151 n
Ratier Bank, sandbank, situation of, 314 n
Ravens, 89
Ray, Robert, Adventurer, 646
Reade, Gerrard   „   646
Refraction, James's observations on, 535
Reindeer, 93, 510 n, antlers of, 51, on Brooke Cobham, 325
Resolution, the, Button's ship, xxx, 162, 164 n
Resolution Island, named by Button, 165, 283 n, Bylot and Baffin reach, 206, James lands on, 470 n, mentioned, 175, 464, 472
Reynolds, Rowland, Adventurer, 645
Ribes, species of, 63 n.
Rivers, Earl, islands named after, 283, notice of, 283 n, *see* D'Arcy, Thomas
Robins, George, Adventurer, 646
Robinson, Arthur   „   645
——— Humphrey   „   645
——— Robert   „   645
Rochester, Robert, Viscount, 644
Roe, Sir Thomas — account of, lxxv birth, lxxv, letter to Bristol merchants, civ seq, to the Mayor of Bristol, cxxxix seq; to the Earl of Danby, cxlvi, letter from, cli, letter to, clxvi, his abstract of Button's Journal supplied to Foxe, 163 n, 176 n, 177, 199, assists James, 455, 459, his embassy to Sweden, 263
Roe's Island, named by James, clxxvi, 503
Roe's Welcome, named by Foxe, cix, 179 n, 182 n, 321, explored, 182 n, burial-place at, 319, 320 n, 321 n, 370 n, 435, mentioned, 317 n, 332, 334, 335, 426, 427, 441
Rogers, Richard, Adventurer, 646
Romeny, *see* Romney
Romney, Rebecca, Lady, islands named after, 149 n., one of the Adventurers, 642, 645, 656, 659, 660, 661, 662

Romney's Island, named by Hudson, 149
Root Creek, Button's wintering-place, 166 *n.*
Ross, Sir James, reaches the North Magnetic Pole, xxxii
Rosse, Lord, Adventurer, 644
Rumney, Isaac ,, 646
Rupert, Prince, patron of an expedition to Hudson's Bay, ccxii; territory named after, ccxiii
Russell, "Exposer," one of Foxe's crew, lxxxvi, 343, 384
—— William, Adventurer, 642, 645, 649, 656, 659, 660, 661, 662

Sackville, Edward, Esq., Adventurer, 644, *see also* Dorset, Earl of
Sackville Island, named by Foxe, cix, 399
Sadler, Francis, Adventurer, 646
Saglek Bay, probably identical with Gibbons Hole, xliv, 202 *n*
St Lawrence, the river, 367 *n*
Salamander, the, Frobisher's ship, 54
Salisbury, Robert, Earl of, notice of, 304 *n*, island named after, 304, one of the Adventurers, 642 *n*, 644, 656, 659, 660, 661, 662
—— William, second Earl of, Adventurer, 304 *n*, 642
Salisbury Island, named, 175, 197, 253, 304, 307, 425, 474; Hudson makes it, on 2nd Aug., 632
Salter, Nicholas, Adventurer, 645, 649
Samoides, the, tribe, 89 *n*, 319
Sams, Sir John, Adventurer, 645
Sanderson, William, of London, 73, letter to, 78, 179, *see also* Davis, John
Sandy, Robert, Adventurer, 642, 645, 656, 659, 660, 661, 662
Savage Isles, identified, 58 *n*, 251 *n*, 402 *n*, Foxe at, 300, 398, 399, mentioned, 167, 424
Scott, Edmund, Adventurer, 645
—— George ,, 645
Scroggs, Captain John, his voyage in search of Knight's expedition, ccxvi, returns without success, ccxvi, names Whalebone Point, ccxvi
Scull, D. G., his *Voyages of Radisson*, ccx *n*
Scurvy-grass, *see* Cockle Grass.
Sea-fowl, great number of, 60, 70, breeding-places, 127, 132, *see* Birds
Sea-horse Point, named, 217, Hawk-ridge near, 254; tide at, 217, 379, Foxe reaches, 377, mentioned, 425
Seal oil, 87
Seals, 35, 89, 101, 322
Sealskin, worn by natives, 90
Sea-mews, 89
Sea-mors, *see* Morse.
Searle, John, notice of, 97 *n*; his *Ephemeris*, 211

Sea-Unicorn, *see* Narwhal.
Sedum (or Orpen), 232 *n.*, 298
Sentry Island, identified, 328 *n.*, 331 *n.*
Seracold, William, Adventurer, 645
Severn River, New, identified, 354 *n*, named by James, clxxvi, 487 *n*
Shackleton, Cape, 227 *n.*
Shark Point, 409, 410, 411
Sheffield, Edmund, *see* Mulgrave, Earl of
Shrewsbury, Gilbert, Earl of, Adventurer, 644
Simmes, Nicholas, boy in Hudson's crew, 138, 142, 630, 631 *n.*
Sleepers, the, islands in Hudson's Bay, cix, 368, 369
Sleepe, Isle, *see* Sleepers, the
Smith, Humphrey, Adventurer, 645
Smith, Cape, Hudson near, 128 *n*, 149 *n*
Smith, Captain Francis, expedition in search of N.-W. Passage, ccxviii, ccxix, 413 *n.*
Smith Island, Hudson at, 128 *n*
Smith, Sir Richard, Adventurer, 645
—— Sir Thomas, first Governor of the Company of Discoverers of N.-W Passage, xl, 649, Bylot and Prickett visit him, 158, promotes Bylot's second voyage, 223; Governor of East India Company, 643 *n.*, 649 *n*, promoter of discovery, 649; Adventurer, 645, 656, 660, 661, 662
—— Thomas, junior, Adventurer, 645
Smith's Sound, named by Baffin, 229, 230 *n.*, 237
Snaefell-Jökull, mountain in Iceland, 121 *n*
Solomon's Temples, islands, 494 *n*, 495 *n*, 498 *n*
Sorrel (*Rumex*), 127, 153, 232, 298
Southampton, Cape or Island, Button near, 184 *n*, 185 *n*, tides at, 186 *n*
—— Henry, Earl of, island named after, 642 *n*, Adventurer, 642, 644, 656, 659, 660, 661, 662
Southey, Robert, his praise of James's verses, clxxxix
Southicke, Thomas, Adventurer, 646
Southworth, Henry ,, 646
Staffe, Philip, Hudson's carpenter, 141 *n.*, 143, 144, 144 *n*, 146, 161, 629
Stapers, Hewett, Adventurer, 642, 645, 649 *n.*, 656, 659, 660, 661, 662
Steede, Sir William, Adventurer, 645
Stephens, Thomas, attorney to Henry Prince of Wales, 645, 646
Sterne, Mr Thomas, globemaker, lviii, lx, friend of Foxe, 218 *n*, 262
Stint, American, 311 *n*
Stone, Thomas, Adventurer, 645
—— William " 645, 649
Strafford, Earl of, mentioned, cxciii, 352 *n.*; his *Letters and Dispatches*, cxciii *seq.*
Strange and Dangerous Voyage, James's, described, *see* James, Captain Thomas

Strutton Island, 503 n
Styles, Oliver, Adventurer, 645
Suffolk, Thomas, Earl of, Lord Chamberlain, 642, 644, 656, 659, 660, 661, 662
Swans, wild, 135, 325
Swinhowe, George, Adventurer, 645
Syms, Nicholas, *see* Simmes.

Tappe, Mr John, bookseller, lix, his shop on Tower Hill, lix, consulted by Foxe, 262, his works, lx
Tatnam, Cape, Foxe sights, 352, James at, 484 n, 578 n
Tayler, John, merchant of Bristol, cxlv, cxlix
Teal, 160
Thomas, John, of Hudson's crew, 136, 140, 142, 143, 145, 153, wounded, 154, killed, 630
Thornton, John, his chart of Hudson's Bay, ccxx, 166, 409 n
Thrushes, 71
Tides, observations on, 379 n, 409, in James's Bay, 521, 522
Timberlake, Henry, Adventurer, 646
Tom Island, Foxe near, 318 n
Tomlinson, John, Mayor of Bristol, cxxxix, cxli n
Towerson, William, Adventurer, 645
Tradescant, John, naturalist, clxv n
Travice, Henry, Adventurer, 645
Trees, rows of, 336, number of, 355, on Charlton I, 565, birch, 71, 333 n, elder, 71, firs, 62, 346, juniper, 62, 100, spruce, 62, 346, yew, 71, willows, 100
Trinity House, the, assists Foxe, 264, Foxe's address to the, 443, depositions of the survivors of Hudson's expedition at, 629 *seq*, opinion of the Master etc. of, concerning the N.-W Passage, 633, 634, Foxe waits on the Master of the, 268 n
Trinity Isles, named by Foxe, cix, 384 n, mentioned, 398 n
Tucker, George, Adventurer, 646
Tweedy, Henry ,, 645
Twins, the, islands, 498 n, 500 n

Ugganes, George, of the *Henrietta Maria*, clvi, repairs boat, 550
Ultimum Vale (Cape Henrietta Maria), *see* Wolstenholme's Ultimum Vale.
Ungava Bay, 475 n.
Unicorn, *see* Narwhal
Upernivik, Danish settlement, 225 n
Uring, *see* Hurin.
Ut Ultra, *see* Ne Ultra.

Variation of the compass, xxxi, xxxii, 210, 271, 309, 464, 607
Vaughan, Captain David, of the Hudson's Bay Company's sloop *Discovery*, ccxiv

Venson, Master, his interest in Henry Green, 132
Vetches, 347, found on Charlton I, 552, prepared for the sick, 555

Wainusk River, identified, 362 n
Wakeley, Andrew, nautical instrument maker, 459
Walden, Theophilus, Lord, Adventurer, 642, 644, 656, 659, 660, 661, 662
Waldoe, John, Adventurer, 646
——— Robert ,, 646
Wales, New, *see* New Wales.
Warden (or Wardon), John, of the *Henrietta Maria*, clvi, death, 546, 602
Warwick, Cape (or Foreland), named 77, 282, mentioned, 433
Warwick, Earl of, notice of, 282 n.
Watkins, David, Adventurer, 646
Watson, Thomas ,, 645
Watts, Rev William, Address to the Divinity Students, 620
Weggs, Cape, mentioned, 256 n
Wentworth, Baron, *see* Strafford, Earl of
West, Francis, Adventurer, 646
Westmony Isles, 116, 121
Weston, Cape, named by Foxe, 388 n, 393 n
Weston, Richard, Lord, *see* Portland, Earl of
Weston Islands, Lord, named by James, clxxvi, 493, 599, identified, 494 n
Weston's Portland, Lord, 388, 390, 392, 393, 394, 411, 425, *see* Weston, Cape
Westwray, Thomas, Adventurer, 645
Weymouth, Captain George — sails into Hudson's Strait, viii, 123 n, Hudson sees his log, ix, account of his voyage, ccxxii, 80, mutiny of his men, 84, Cobreth sails with, in 1602, 115 n, mentioned, 422, 424
Whale-bone Point, named by Scroggs, ccxvi
Whale fishery, 441
Whales, different species of, 235 n, 274 n, 345 n
Whale Sound, 229, 235, 236, 237
Whitley, Thomas, Adventurer, 646
Whittered, John, mate of the *Henrietta Maria*, clvi, 584
Wilkinson, one of Hudson's company, 132
Willaston, William, Adventurer, 646
Willes, Richard, treatise on the N.-W Passage, 420 n, mentioned, 421, 433
Williams, John, Hudson's gunner, 132, death, 629
Willocks, 107, 168, *see also* Guillemots, Black
Willoughby d'Eresby, *see* Lindsey, Earl of
——— Sir Hugh, reference to, 517

Willoughby, Cape, named by Foxe, 388 n.

Willow Ptarmigan, see Ptarmigan.

Wilson, Edward, surgeon of Hudson's ship, 630(3), 646, sailed with Button, 646 n., not one of the mutineers, 630, his deposition, 630

——— William, boatswain with Hudson, 128, 136, 138; his part in the mutiny, 139, 141, 142, 630, 631; binds Hudson's arms behind him, 143, goes ashore with Green, 153, wounded, 154, preferred in place of Clements, 161, death, 630

Winter, Sir John, 529, account of, 529 n., Winter's Forest named after him, clxxvi, ccxxxi

Wolstenholme, Cape, 118 n., 119, 126, 425

——— Henry, Adventurer, 645, 646

——— John, father of Sir John, the elder, account of, lxxvi

——— Sir John, the elder —knighted, xlviii, equips an expedition, xlviii, 649, member of the company of Adventurers, xlix, 642, 656, 659, 660, 661, 662, account of, lxxvi, death, lxxix, buried at Stanmore, lxxix, autograph, lxxix, the *Charles* given to, cxvii, letter to, cxlvi, cape named after him, 119 n., promotes Bylot and Baffin's voyages, 202, letter from Baffin to, 233, assists Hawkridge, 248 n.

Wolstenholme, Sir John, the younger, knighted, lxxix, estate sold, lxxix, his family, lxxx, autograph, lxxx, farmer of customs, lxxix, pecuniary embarrassments, cxix; one of the Adventurers, 645, 649, 656, 659, 660, 661, 662, adventurer in eight voyages, 367, money spent on expeditions, 367

Wolstenholme Sound, 228, 237, 238

Wolstenholme's Ultimum Vale, named by Foxe, lxxviii, cii, cix, 367, 368, 388 n., 490, name cancelled, 395 n.; see Cape Henrietta Maria.

Women's Islands, 225

Woodcock, Nicholas, seaman, 440

Woodhouse, Thomas, mathematician, 135, 137 n., 142, 146, 159, 162 n., 629, note found in his desk, 142 n., 160

Woodward, Katharine, Adventurer, 646

Woolley, Mr., charges the company of the *Gabriel*, 40

Worcester, Edward, Earl of, Adventurer, 644

Wright, Edward, an eminent mathematician, xxxviii n., adviser to Henry, Prince of Wales, ccxxiii, 641, one of the Adventurers, 646

Wyche, Richard, Adventurer, 645, 649

York Factory, or Fort, post of the Hudson's Bay Company, 166 n., 357 n.

Yourin, see Hurin.

Zeni, the brothers, voyages of, ccxxii, 19, mentioned, 281

THE HAKLUYT SOCIETY
1894.

President.
CLEMENTS R. MARKHAM, Esq., C.B., F.R.S., Pres. R.G S.

Vice-Presidents.
Major-General SIR HENRY RAWLINSON, Bart., K.C.B., D.C.L., LL.D., F.R.S.
The Right Hon LORD ABERDARE, G.C.B., F.R.S.

Council

Vice-Admiral LINDESAY BRINE	A. P MAUDSLAY, Esq.
ROBERT BROWN, Esq., M A., Ph D	E. DELMAR MORGAN, Esq.
MILLER CHRISTY, Esq	Capt NATHAN, R.E.
The Hon GEORGE N. CURZON, M P.	Admiral Sir E. OMMANNEY, C.B, F R.S.
F DUCANE GODMAN, Esq., F R.S	
The Right Hon Sir MOUNTSTUART E GRANT-DUFF, G C.S I., F R.S.	E A. PETHERICK, Esq S. W SILVER, Esq
ALBERT GRAY, Esq.	COUTTS TROTTER, Esq
C. P. LUCAS, Esq.	Capt. W J L. WHARTON, R.N.

Honorary Secretary —WILLIAM FOSTER, Esq. (*India Office, S W*)

Bankers—Messrs. BARCLAY, BEVAN, TRITTON, RANSOM, BOUVERIE, & Co
1, PALL MALL EAST.

THE HAKLUYT SOCIETY, established for the purpose of printing rare or unpublished Voyages and Travels, aims at opening by this means an easier access to the sources of a branch of knowledge, which yields to none in importance, and is superior to most in agreeable variety. The narratives of travellers and navigators make us acquainted with the earth, its inhabitants and productions; they exhibit the growth of intercourse among mankind, with its effects on civilisation, and, while instructing, they at the same time awaken attention, by recounting the toils and adventures of those who first explored unknown and distant regions.

The advantage of an Association of this kind consists not merely in its system of literary co-operation, but also in its economy. The acquirements, taste, and discrimination of a number of individuals, who feel an interest in the same pursuit, are thus brought to act in voluntary combination, and the ordinary charges of publication are also avoided, so that the volumes produced are distributed among the Members at little more than the cost of printing and paper. The Society expends the whole of its funds in the preparation of works for the Members; and since the cost of each copy varies inversely as the whole number of copies printed, it is obvious that the members are gainers individually by the prosperity of the Society, and the consequent vigour of its operations.

Gentlemen desirous of becoming Members of the Hakluyt Society should intimate their intention to the Secretary, or to the Society's Agent for the delivery of its volumes, Mr CHARLES J. CLARK, 4, *Lincoln's Inn Fields*, when their names will be recorded, and on payment of their subscription of £1 1 to Mr CLARK, they will receive without further charge the volumes issued for the year.

Members and the general public are informed that the Council has approved of the following scheme for the disposal of its surplus stock.

To NEW MEMBERS —*Complete sets of back publications*, omitting Nos 1, 2, 3, 5, 6, 7, 8, 10, and 13, to be sold for £20

To MEMBERS ONLY —*A limited number of sets up to* 1883 inclusive, omitting Nos. 1—17, 19, 22, 36 and 37   48 vols. in all, to be sold for   £15 15s

To THE PUBLIC GENERALLY —*Also, a limited number of single copies* as follows —

    Nos. 23, 26, 29, 31, 34, 40, 47, 50, at   8s 6d
    Nos 18, 21, 24, 28, 30, 35, 46, 48, 51, 53, 55, 56, 58, 60 to 69, at   10s
    Nos. 16, 20, 27, 32, 33, 38, 39, 41 to 45, 49, 52, 57, at   15s
    Nos 54 and 59, at   20s

    ⁎⁎ Subject in case of Members to a discount of 15%

Members are requested to bear in mind that the power of the Council to make advantageous arrangements will depend in a great measure on the prompt payment of the subscriptions, which are payable in advance on the 1st of January, and are received by Mr. CHARLES J CLARK, 4, *Lincoln's Inn Fields*, W.C. Post Office Orders should be made payable to Mr. CHARLES J CLARK, at the *West Central Office, High Holborn*.

WORKS ALREADY ISSUED.

1—The Observations of Sir Richard Hawkins, Knt.,
In his Voyage into the South Sea in 1593. Reprinted from the edition of 1622, and edited by Capt. C. R. Drinkwater Bethune, R.N., C.B.
(First Edition out of print. See No. 57.) *Issued for* 1848.

2—Select Letters of Columbus.
With Original Documents relating to the Discovery of the New World. Translated and Edited by R. H. Major, Esq, of the British Museum.
(First Edition out of print. See No 43) (1847) *Issued for* 1849.

3—The Discoverie of the Empire of Guiana,
By Sir Walter Raleigh, Knt. Edited, with copious Explanatory Notes, and a Biographical Memoir, by Sir Robert H. Schomburgk, Phil. D, etc.
(1848.) *(Out of print.)* *Issued for* 1850.

4—Sir Francis Drake his Voyage, 1595.
By Thomas Maynarde, together with the Spanish Account of Drake's attack on Puerto Rico. Edited from the Original MSS by W. D. Cooley, Esq
(1849) *Issued for* 1850.

5—Narratives of Early Voyages
Undertaken for the Discovery of a Passage to Cathaia and India, by the Northwest, with Selections from the Records of the worshipful Fellowship of the Merchants of London, trading into the East Indies; and from MSS. in the Library of the British Museum, now first published, by Thomas Rundall, Esq.
(1849) *(Out of print)* *Issued for* 1851.

6—The Historie of Travaile into Virginia Britannia,
Expressing the Cosmographie and Commodities of the Country, together with the manners and customs of the people, gathered and observed as well by those who went first thither as collected by William Strachey, Gent., the first Secretary of the Colony, now first Edited from the original manuscript in the British Museum, by R. H. Major, Esq., of the British Museum. (1849)
(Out of print) *Issued for* 1851.

7—Divers Voyages touching the Discovery of America
And the Islands adjacent, collected and published by Richard Hakluyt. Prebendary of Bristol in the year 1582. Edited, with Notes and an introduction, by John Winter Jones, Esq, of the British Museum. (1850)
(Out of print.) *Issued for* 1852.

8—A Collection of Documents on Japan
With a Commentary by Thomas Rundall, Esq. (1850.)
(Out of print) *Issued for* 1852.

9—The Discovery and Conquest of Florida,
By Don Ferdinando de Soto. Translated out of Portuguese by Richard Hakluyt, and Edited, with notes and an introduction, by W. B. Rye, Esq, of the British Museum. (1851.)
Issued for 1853.

10—Notes upon Russia,
Being a Translation from the Earliest Account of that Country, entitled Rerum Muscoviticarum Commentarii, by the Baron Sigismund von Herberstein, Ambassador from the Court of Germany to the Grand Prince Vasiley Ivanovich, in the years 1517 and 1526. Two Volumes. Translated and Edited, with Notes and an Introduction, by R. H. Major, Esq., of the British Museum
Vol. I. (1851.) *(Out of print)* *Issued for* 1853.

11—The Geography of Hudson's Bay.

Being the Remarks of Captain W. Coats, in many Voyages to that locality, between the years 1727 and 1751. With an Appendix, containing Extracts from the Log of Captain Middleton on his Voyage for the Difcovery of the North-west Passage, in H M S "Furnace," in 1741-2. Edited by JOHN BARROW, Esq , F.R S., F S.A. (1852)

Iffued for 1854.

12—Notes upon Russia. Vol. 2. (1852.)

Iffued for 1854.

13—Three Voyages by the North-east,

Towards Cathay and China, undertaken by the Dutch in the years 1594, 1595 and 1596, with their Difcovery of Spitzbergen, their refidence of ten months in Novaya Zemlya, and their fafe return in two open boats. By Gerrit de Veer Edited by C. T. BEKE, Esq , Ph.D , F.S A. (1853)

(Firft Edition out of print See No 54) Iffued for 1855.

14-15—The History of the Great and Mighty Kingdom of China and the Situation Thereof.

Compiled by the Padre Juan Gonzalez de Mendoza. And now Reprinted from the Early Tranflation of R. Parke. Edited by SIR GEORGE T. STAUNTON, Bart. With an Introduction by R. H. MAJOR, Esq 2 vols. (1853-54)

Iffued for 1855

16—The World Encompassed by Sir Francis Drake.

Being his next Voyage to that to Nombre de Dios. Collated, with an unpublifhed Manufcript of Francis Fletcher, Chaplain to the Expedition. With Appendices illuftrative of the fame Voyage, and Introduction by W S W VAUX, Esq , M A. (1854.)

Iffued for 1856.

17—The History of the Tartar Conquerors who subdued China.

From the French of the Père D'Orleans, 1688. Tranflated and Edited by the EARL OF ELLESMERE. With an Introduction by R. H. MAJOR, Esq (1854)

Iffued for 1856.

18—A Collection of Early Documents on Spitzbergen and Greenland,

Confifting of: a Tranflation from the German of F Martin's important work on Spitzbergen, now very rare, a Tranflation from Isaac de la Peyrere's Relation de Greenland, and a rare piece entitled "God's Power and Providence fhowed in the miraculous prefervation and deliverance of eight Englifhmen left by mifchance in Greenland, anno 1630, nine months and twelve days, faithfully reported by Edward Pelham." Edited, with Notes, by ADAM WHITE, Esq , of the Britifh Mufeum. (1855)

Iffued for 1857.

19—The Voyage of Sir Henry Middleton to Bantam and the Maluco Islands.

From the rare Edition of 1606. Edited by BOLTON CORNEY, Esq (1855)

Iffued for 1857.

20—Russia at the Close of the Sixteenth Century.

Comprifing "The Ruffe Commonwealth" by Dr Giles Fletcher, and Sir Jerome Horfey's Travels, now firft printed entire from his manufcript in the Britifh Mufeum. Edited by E. A BOND, Esq , of the Britifh Mufeum. (1856.)

Iffued for 1858.

21—The Travels of Girolamo Benzoni in America, in 1542-56.

Tranflated and Edited by ADMIRAL W. H SMYTH, F R S , F S A (1857)

Iffued for 1858.

22—India in the Fifteenth Century.

Being a Collection of Narratives of Voyages to India in the century preceding the Portuguese discovery of the Cape of Good Hope; from Latin, Persian, Russian, and Italian Sources, now first translated into English. Edited, with an Introduction by R. H. MAJOR, Esq., F.S.A. (1857.)

Issued for 1859.

23—Narrative of a Voyage to the West Indies and Mexico,

In the years 1599-1602, with Maps and Illustrations. By Samuel Champlain. Translated from the original and unpublished Manuscript, with a Biographical Notice and Notes by ALICE WILMERE. (1859.)

Issued for 1859.

24—Expeditions into the Valley of the Amazons

During the Sixteenth and Seventeenth Centuries: containing the Journey of Gonzalo Pizarro, from the Royal Commentaries of Garcilasso Inca de la Vega; the Voyage of Francisco de Orellana, from the General History of Herrera, and the Voyage of Cristoval de Acuna, from an exceedingly scarce narrative written by himself in 1641. Edited and Translated by CLEMENTS R. MARKHAM, Esq. (1859.) *Issued for* 1860.

25—Early Indications of Australia.

A Collection of Documents shewing the Early Discoveries of Australia to the time of Captain Cook. Edited by R. H. MAJOR, ESQ., of the British Museum, F.S.A. (1859.) *Issued for* 1860.

26—The Embassy of Ruy Gonzalez de Clavijo to the Court of Timour, 1403-6.

Translated, for the first time, with Notes, a Preface, and an Introductory Life of Timour Beg. By CLEMENTS R. MARKHAM, Esq. (1859.)

Issued for 1861.

27—Henry Hudson the Navigator.

The Original Documents in which his career is recorded. Collected, partly Translated, and Annotated, with an Introduction by GEORGE ASHER, LL.D. (1860.) *Issued for* 1861.

28—The Expedition of Ursua and Aguirre,

In search of El Dorado and Omagua, A.D. 1560-61. Translated from the "Sexta Noticia Historiale" of Fray Pedro Simon, by W. BOLLAERT, Esq.; with an Introduction by CLEMENTS R. MARKHAM, Esq. (1861.)

Issued for 1862.

29—The Life and Acts of Don Alonzo Enriquez de Guzman.

Translated from a Manuscript in the National Library at Madrid, and edited, with Notes and an Introduction, by CLEMENTS R. MARKHAM, Esq. (1862.)

Issued for 1862.

30—Discoveries of the World by Galvano,

From their first original unto the year of our Lord 1555. Reprinted, with the original Portuguese text, and edited by VICE-ADMIRAL BETHUNE, C.B. (1862.) *Issued for* 1863.

31—Marvels described by Friar Jordanus,

Of the Order of Preachers, native of Severac, and Bishop of Columbum; from a parchment manuscript of the Fourteenth Century, in Latin, the text of which has recently been Translated and Edited by COLONEL H. YULE, C.B., F.R.G.S., late of H.M. Bengal Engineers. (1863.)

Issued for 1863.

32—The Travels of Ludovico di Varthema

In Syria, Arabia, Persia, India, etc., during the Sixteenth Century. Translated by J. WINTER JONES, Esq., F.S.A., and edited, with Notes and an Introduction, by the REV. GEORGE PERCY BADGER. (1863.)

Issued for 1864.

33—The Travels of Cieza de Leon in 1532-50

From the Gulf of Darien to the City of La Plata, contained in the firſt part of his Chronicle of Peru (Antwerp 1554). Tranſlated and edited, with Notes and an Introduction, by CLEMENTS R. MARKHAM, Esq. (1864.)
Iſſued for 1864

34—The Narrative of Pascual de Andagoya

Containing the earlieſt notice of Peru. Tranſlated and edited, with Notes and an Introduction, by CLEMENTS R. MARKHAM, Esq. (1865.)
Iſſued for 1865

35—The Coasts of East Africa and Malabar

In the beginning of the Sixteenth Century, by Duarte Barboſa. Tranſlated from an early Spaniſh manuſcript by the HON. HENRY STANLEY (1866.)
Iſſued for 1865

36—Cathay and the Way Thither.

A Collection of all minor notices of China, previous to the Sixteenth Century. Tranſlated and edited by COLONEL H. YULE, C.B. Vol 1 (1866.)
Iſſued for 1866.

37—Cathay and the Way Thither. Vol 2. (1866.)
Iſſued for 1866.

38—The Three Voyages of Sir Martin Frobisher.

With a Selection from Letters now in the State Paper Office. Edited by REAR-ADMIRAL COLLINSON, C B (1867.)
Iſſued for 1867.

39—The Philippine Islands.

Moluccas, Siam, Cambodia, Japan, and China, at the close of the 16th Century. By Antonia de Morga. Translated from the Spanish, with Notes, by LORD STANLEY of Alderley (1868.) *Iſſued for* 1868

40—The Fifth Letter of Hernan Cortes

To the Emperor Charles V, containing an Account of his Expedition to Honduras in 1525-26. Translated from the Spanish by Don Pascual de Gayangos. (1868.)
Iſſued for 1868

41—The Royal Commentaries of the Yncas.

By the Ynca Garcilasso de la Vega. Translated and Edited, with Notes and an Introduction, by CLEMENTS R. MARKHAM, Esq. Vol. I. (1869.)
Iſſued for 1869.

42—The Three Voyages of Vasco da Gama,

And his Viceroyalty, from the Lendas da India of Caspar Correa, accompanied by original documents. Translated and Edited by the LORD STANLEY of Alderley. (1869.)
Iſſued for 1869.

43—Select Letters of Christopher Columbus,

With other Original Documents, relating to his Four Voyages to the New World. Tranſlated and Edited by R. H. MAJOR, F.S.A., etc. 2nd Edit. (1870.)
Iſſued for 1870.

44—History of the Imáms and Seyyids of 'Omán,

By Salîl-Ibn-Razîk, from A.D. 661-1856. Tranſlated from the original Arabic, and edited, with Notes, Appendices, and an Introduction, continuing the Hiſtory down to 1870, by GEORGE PERCY BADGER, F.R.G.S. (1871.)
Iſſued for 1870.

45—The Royal Commentaries of the Yncas. Vol 2 (1871.) *Iſſued for* 1871.

46—The Canarian,

Or Book of the Conqueſt and Converſion of the Canarians in the year 1402, by Meſſire Jean de Bethencourt, Kt. Compoſed by Pierre Bontier and Jean le Verrier. Tranſlated and Edited, with Notes and an Introduction, by R. H. MAJOR, F.S.A. (1872.) *Iſſued for* 1871.

47—Reports on the Discovery of Peru.
Tranflated and Edited, with Notes and an Introduction, by CLEMENTS R MARKHAM, C B. (1872.) *Iffued for* 1872.

48—Narratives of the Rites and Laws of the Yncas;
Tranflated from the original Spanifh Manufcripts, and Edited, with Notes and an Introduction, by CLEMENTS R. MARKHAM, C.B., F.R S. (1873.) *Iffued for* 1872.

49—Travels to Tana and Persia,
By Jofafa Barbaro and Ambrogio Contarini; Edited by LORD STANLEY of Alderley; and Narratives of other Italian Travels in Perfia, Tranflated and Edited by CHARLES GREY, Esq. (1873.) *Iffued for* 1873.

50—Voyages of the Zeni
To the Northern Seas in the Fourteenth Century. Tranflated and Edited by R. H. MAJOR, F.S.A. (1873.) *Iffued for* 1873.

51—The Captivity of Hans Stade of Hesse in 1547-55.
Among the Wild Tribes of Eaftern Brazil; tranflated by ALBERT TOOTAL, Esq, and annotated by RICHARD F. BURTON. (1874.) *Iffued for* 1874.

52—The First Voyage Round the World by Magellan.
Tranflated from the Accounts of Pigafetta and other contemporary writers. With Notes and an Introduction by LORD STANLEY of Alderley. (1874.) *Iffued for* 1874.

53—The Commentaries of the Great Afonso Dalboquerque,
Second Viceroy of India Tranflated from the Portuguese Edition of 1774; with Notes and Introduction by WALTER DE GRAY BIRCH, Esq., F R S L Vol. 1. (1875) *Iffued for* 1875

54—Three Voyages to the North-East.
Second Edition of Gerrit de Veer's Three Voyages to the North-East by Barents. Edited, with an Introduction, by Lieut. KOOLEMANS BEYNEN, of the Royal Dutch Navy. (1876.) *Iffued for* 1876.

55—The Commentaries of the Great Afonso Dalboquerque Vol. 2. (1877.) *Iffued for* 1875.

56—The Voyages of Sir James Lancaster.
With Abstracts of Journal of Voyages preserved in the India Office, and the Voyage of Captain John Knight to seek the N.W Passage. Edited by CLEMENTS R. MARKHAM, C.B, F R S. (1877.) *Iffued for* 1877.

57—Second Edition of the Observations of Sir Richard Hawkins, Kt.,
In his Voyage into the South Sea in 1593, with the Voyages of his grandfather William, his father Sir John, and his cousin William Hawkins. Edited by CLEMENTS R. MARKHAM, C B, F R S (1878.) *Iffued for* 1877.

58—The Bondage and Travels of Johann Schiltberger,
From his capture at the battle of Nicopolis in 1396 to his escape and return to Europe in 1427: translated, from the Heidelberg MS. edited in 1859 by Profeffor Karl Freidrich Neumann, by Commander J BUCHAN TELFER, R N; with Notes by Profeffor B. BRUUN, and a Preface, Introduction, and Notes by the Translator and Editor. (1879.) *Iffued for* 1878.

59—The Voyages and Works of John Davis the Navigator.
Edited, with an Introduction and Notes, by Captain ALBERT H. MARKHAM, R.N., F.R.G S. (1880.) *Iffued for* 1878.

The Map of the World, A.D. 1600.
Called by Shakspere "The New Map, with the Augmentation of the Indies" To Illustrate the Voyages of John Davis. (1880.) *Issued for* 1878.

60—The Natural and Moral History of the Indies

By Father Joseph de Acosta. Reprinted from the English Translated Edition of Edward Grimston, 1604; and Edited, with Notes and an Introduction, by CLEMENTS R. MARKHAM, C.B., F.R.S. Vol. I, The Natural History. (1880.) *Issued for 1879.*

61—The Natural and Moral History of the Indies.

Vol. II, The Moral History. (1880.) *Issued for 1879.*

Map of Peru.

To Illustrate Nos. 33, 41, 45, 60, and 61. (1880) *Issued for 1879.*

62—The Commentaries of the Great Afonso Dalboquerque. Vol. 3. (1880.) *Issued for 1880*

63—The Voyages of William Baffin, 1612-1622.

Edited, with Notes and an Introduction, by CLEMENTS R. MARKHAM, C.B., F.R.S. (1881.) *Issued for 1880.*

64—Narrative of the Portuguese Embassy to Abyssinia.

During the years 1520 1527. By Father Francisco Alvarez. Translated from the Portuguese, and Edited, with Notes and an Introduction, by LORD STANLEY of Alderley (1881.) *Issued for 1881.*

65—The History of the Bermudas or Somer Islands.

Attributed to Captain Nathaniel Butler. Edited from a MS. in the Sloane Collection, British Museum, by General Sir J. HENRY LEFROY, R.A., K.C.M.G., C.B., F.R.S., etc. (1882.) *Issued for 1881.*

66—Diary of Richard Cocks.

Cape Merchant in the English Factory in Japan, 1615-1622, with Correspondence. Edited by EDWARD MAUNDE THOMPSON, Esq. Vol. 1. (1883.) *Issued for 1882*

67—Diary of Richard Cocks Vol. 2. (1883.) *Issued for 1882.*

68—The Second Part of the Chronicle of Peru.

By Pedro de Cieza de Leon. Translated and Edited, with Notes and an Introduction, by CLEMENTS R. MARKHAM, C.B., F.R.S. (1883.) *Issued for 1883.*

69—The Commentaries of the Great Afonso Dalboquerque. Vol. 4. (1884.) *Issued for 1883*

70-71—The Voyage of John Huyghen van Linschoten to the East Indies

From the Old English Translation of 1598. The First Book, containing his Description of the East. Edited, the First Volume by the late ARTHUR COKE BURNELL, Ph.D., C.I.E., of the Madras Civil Service; the Second Volume by Mr. P. A. TIELE, of Utrecht. (1885.) *Issued for 1884.*

72-73—Early Voyages and Travels to Russia and Persia.

By Anthony Jenkinson and other Englishmen, with some Account of the first Intercourse of the English with Russia and Central Asia by way of the Caspian Sea. Edited by E. DELMAR MORGAN, Esq., and C. H. COOTE, Esq. (1886.) *Issued for 1885.*

74—The Diary of William Hedges, Esq.,

Afterwards Sir William Hedges, during his Agency in Bengal; as well as on his Voyage out and Return Overland (1681-1687). Transcribed for the Press, with Introductory Notes, etc., by R. BARLOW, Esq., and Illustrated by copious Extracts from Unpublished Records, etc., by Col Sir H YULE, K.C.S.I., R.E., C.B., LL.D. Vol. 1, The Diary. (1887) *Issued for 1886*

75—The Diary of William Hedges, Esq. Vol 2

Sir H. Yule's Extracts from Unpublished Records, etc. (1888.)

Issued for 1886.

76—The Voyage of François Pyrard to the East Indies,

The Maldives, the Moluccas and Brazil. Translated into English from the Third French Edition of 1619, and Edited, with Notes, by ALBERT GRAY, Esq, formerly of the Ceylon Civil Service, assisted by H. C. P. BELL, Esq., of the Ceylon Civil Service. Vol. 1. (1887.) *Issued for* 1887.

7—The Voyage of François Pyrard to the East Indies, etc.

Vol. 2, Part I. (1888.) *Issued for* 1887.

78—The Diary of William Hedges, Esq. Vol. 3.

Sir H. Yule's Extracts from Unpublished Records, etc. (1889.)

Issued for 1888.

79—Tractatus de Globis, et eorum usu.

A Treatise descriptive of the Globes constructed by Emery Molyneux, and Published in 1592. By Robert Hues. Edited, with Annotated Indices and an Introduction, by CLEMENTS R. MARKHAM, C.B., F.R.S. To which is appended,

Sailing Directions for the Circumnavigation of England,

And for a Voyage to the Straits of Gibraltar. From a Fifteenth Century MS. Edited by JAMES GAIRDNER, Esq.; with a Glossary by E. DELMAR MORGAN, Esq. (1889) *Issued for* 1888.

80—The Voyage of François Pyrard to the East Indies, etc.

Vol. 2, Part II. (1890.) *Issued for* 1889.

81—The Conquest of La Plata, 1535-1555.

I.—Voyage of Ulrich Schmidt to the Rivers La Plata and Paraguai. II.—The Commentaries of Alvar Nunez Cabeza de Vaca. With Notes and Introduction by DON LUIS L. DOMINGUEZ. (1891.)

Issued for 1889.

82-83—The Voyage of François Leguat

To Rodriguez, Mauritius, Java, and the Cape of Good Hope. Transcribed from the first English Edition. Edited and Annotated by Captain PASFIELD OLIVER, late Royal Artillery. (1891) *Issued for* 1890.

84-85—The Travels of Pietro della Valle to India.

From the Old English Translation of 1664, by G. Havers. Edited, with a Life of the Author, an Introduction and Notes, by EDWARD GREY, late Bengal Civil Service. (1892) *Issued for* 1891.

86—The Journal of Christopher Columbus

During his First Voyage (1492-93), and Documents relating to the Voyages of John Cabot and Gaspar Corte Real. Translated, with Notes and an Introduction, by CLEMENTS R. MARKHAM, C.B., F.R.S. (1893.) *Issued for* 1892.

87—Early Voyages and Travels in the Levant.

I.—The Diary of Master Thomas Dallam, 1599-1600. II.—Extracts from the Diaries of Dr. John Covel, 1670-1679. With some Account of the Levant Company of Turkey Merchants. Edited by J. THEODORE BENT, Esq., F.S.A., F.R.G.S. (1893) *Issued for* 1892.

88-89—Voyages of Captain Luke Foxe and Captain Thomas James

In Search of a North-west Passage, in 1631-32; with Narratives of the Earlier N.W. Voyages of Frobisher, Davis, Weymouth, Hall, Knight, Hudson, Button, Gibbons, Bylot, Baffin, Hawkridge, and others. Edited, with Notes and an Introduction, by MILLER CHRISTY, F.L.S. (1894)

Issued for 1893

OTHER WORKS UNDERTAKEN BY EDITORS.

The Letters of Amerigo Vespucci and other Documents relating to the career of the Florentine navigator. Edited by CLEMENTS R. MARKHAM, Esq., C.B.

The True History of the Conquest of New Spain, by Bernal Diaz. Translated from the Spanish and edited by Vice-Admiral LINDESAY BRINE.

The Voyages of the Earl of Cumberland, from the Records prepared by order of the Countess of Pembroke. Edited by W. DE GRAY BIRCH, Esq., F.S.A.

Rosmital's Embassy to England, Spain, etc., in 1466. Edited by R. C. GRAVES, Esq.

A Reprint of 17th Century Books on Seamanship and Sea Matters in General, including Captain John Smith's "Seaman's Grammar", from the edition of 1692, and Sir H. Manwayring's "Seaman's Dictionary", 1644, with extracts from unpublished MSS. Edited, with Notes and an Introduction, by H. HALLIDAY SPARLING, Esq.

The Travels of Leo Africanus the Moor, from the English translation of John Pory (1600). Edited by ROBERT BROWN, Esq., M.A., Ph.D.

Histoire de la Grande Isle Madagascar, composée par le Sieur De Flacourt, 1661. Translated and edited, with Notes and an Introduction, by S. PASFIELD OLIVER, Captain late Royal Artillery, etc.

The Travels of Ibn Jobair. Edited by Professor W. ROBERTSON SMITH, Fellow of Christ's College, Cambridge.

Raleigh's Empire of Guiana. Second Edition (see No 3). Edited, with Notes, etc., by EVERARD F. IM THURN, Esq.

The Voyages of Keymis and Berrie to Guiana. Edited by JAMES RODWAY, Esq.

The Voyages of Cadamosto, the Venetian, along the West Coast of Africa, in the years 1455 and 1456. translated from the earliest Italian text of 1507, and edited by H. YULE OLDHAM, Esq., M.A., F.R.G.S.

Jens Munk's Voyage to Hudson's Bay, translated from the Danish. Edited by MILLER CHRISTY, Esq., and C. A. GOSCH, Esq.

Azurara's Chronicle of the Discovery and Conquest of Guinea. Translated and edited by C. RAYMOND BEAZLEY, Esq., M.A., Fellow of Merton, and EDGAR PRESTAGE, Esq, of Balliol College.

The Topographia Christiana of Cosmas Indicopleustes. Edited by J. W. McCRINDLE, Esq., M.A., M.R.A.S.

WORKS SUGGESTED TO THE COUNCIL FOR PUBLICATION.

Inedited Letters, etc., of Sir Thomas Roe during his Embassy to India, 1615-19.
Bernhard de Breydenbach, 1483-84, A.D. Travels in the Holy Land.
Felix Fabri, 1483. Wanderings in the Holy Land, Egypt, etc.
J. dos Santos. The History of Eastern Ethiopia. 1607.
La Argentina. An account of the Discovery of the Provinces of Rio de la Plata from 1512 to the time of Domingo Martinez de Irala, by Ruiz Diaz de Guzman.
The History of Ethiopia, by Manoel de Almeida.
Journal of the Jesuit Desideri in Tibet.
Travels of Friar Rubruquis.
Voyages of Willoughby and Chancellor.

Letters of Ortelius and Mercator
Tasman's Voyages.
Voyage of Sarmiento
Travels of the brothers Sherley in Persia
The Voyage of Ralph Fitch.
De Laet's De Imperio Magni Mogolis, 1631

LAWS OF THE HAKLUYT SOCIETY.

I. The object of this Society shall be to print, for distribution among its members, rare and valuable Voyages, Travels, Naval Expeditions, and other geographical records, from an early period to the beginning of the eighteenth century

II The Annual Subscription shall be One Guinea, payable in advance on the 1st January.

III. Each member of the Society, having paid his Subscription, shall be entitled to a copy of every work produced by the Society, and to vote at the general meetings within the period subscribed for, and if he do not signify, before the close of the year, his wish to resign, he shall be considered as a member for the succeeding year

IV. The management of the Society's affairs shall be vested in a Council consisting of twenty-one members, viz, a President, two Vice-Presidents, a Secretary, and seventeen ordinary members, to be elected annually, but vacancies occurring between the general meetings shall be filled up by the Council

V. A General Meeting of the Subscribers shall be held annually The Secretary's Report on the condition and proceedings of the Society shall be then read, and the Meeting shall proceed to elect the Council for the ensuing year.

VI. At each Annual Election, three of the old Council shall retire

VII. The Council shall meet when necessary, for the dispatch of business, three forming a quorum, including the Secretary, and the Chairman having a casting vote

VIII Gentlemen preparing and editing works for the Society, shall receive twenty-five copies of such works respectively, and an additional twenty-five copies if the work is also translated

---

*** The Society's volumes are now delivered free of charge to Subscribers, wherever resident.

LIST OF MEMBERS
OF THE
𝕳akluyt 𝕾ociety.

1894

Abercromby, Hon. John, 62, Palmerston-place, Edinburgh
Aberdare, Right Hon. Lord, F.R.S., 1, Queen's-gate, S.W., and Duffryn, Mountain Ash, Glamorganshire.
Admiralty, The (2 *copies*).
Advocates' Library, Edinburgh.
All Souls College, Oxford.
American Geographical Society, 11, West 29th Street, New York City, U.S.A.
Amherst, Lord, of Hackney, Didlington Hall, Brandon, Norfolk.
Antiquaries, the Society of, Burlington House, Piccadilly, W.
Army and Navy Club, 36, Pall-mall.
Astor Library, New York
Athenæum Club, Pall Mall

Baer, Joseph & Co., Messrs., Rossmarkt, 18, Frankfort-on-Maine.
Bain, James, Esq., 1, Haymarket
Ball, Valentine, Esq., C.B., LL.D., F.R.S., Director of the Science and Art Museum, Dublin
Bank of England Library and Literary Association.
Barlow, R. Fred., Esq., 15, Ambrose-place, Worthing, Sussex
Barrow, J., Esq., F.R.S., F.S.A., 17, Hanover-terrace, Regent's Park
Basano, Marquis de, per Messrs. Hatchard's, Piccadilly, W.
Bell and Bradfute, Messrs., 12, Bank-street, Edinburgh
Bellamy, C. H., Esq., Holyrood Villa, Brook road, Heaton Chapel, near Stockport.
Berlin Geographical Society
Berlin, the Royal Library of.
Berlin University, Geographical Institute of (Baron von Richthofen), 6, Schinkelplatz, Berlin, W.
Bethell, William, Esq., Rise, Hull
Birch, W. de G., Esq., British Museum
Birmingham Library (The)
Birmingham Central Free Library
Bodleian Library, Oxford (*copies presented*)
Bombay Asiatic Society
Boston Athenæum Library, U.S.A.
Boston Public Library.
Bouverie-Pusey, S. E. B., Esq., 21, Grosvenor-street, W
Bowdoin College, Brunswick, Maine, U.S.A.
Bremen Museum.
Brine, Vice-Admiral Lindesay, 13, Pembroke-gardens, Kensington
British Guiana Royal Agricultural and Commercial Society, Georgetown, Demerara.
British Museum (*copies presented*)
Brooke, Thos., Esq., Armitage Bridge, Huddersfield.
Brooklyn Library, Brooklyn, U.S.A.
Brooklyn Mercantile Library
Brown, Arthur W. W., Esq., 6, Sussex-square, Hyde Park, W.
Brown, J. Allen, Esq., 7, Kent-gardens, Ealing
Brown, J. Nicholas, Esq., Providence, R.I., U.S.A.
Brown, H. T., Esq., Roodeye House, Chester.
Brown, Robert, Esq., M.A., Ph.D., etc., Fersley, Rydal-road, Streatham, S.W.

Brown, General J. Marshall, 218, Middle-street, Portland, Maine, U.S.A.
Bunbury, Sir E H., Bart., 35, St James's-street, S W
Burne-Jones, E., Esq , The Grange, West Kensington, W.
Burns, J. W., Esq., Kilmahew, Dumbartonshire.

Cambridge University Library.
Canada, The Parliament Library
Carlton Club, Pall-mall.
Carlisle, The Earl of, Naworth Castle, Bampton, Cumberland.
Ceylon Branch, Royal Asiatic Society, Colombo.
Chapman, Walter, Esq , Elsenham, Westwood Park, Southampton.
Chetham's Library, Hunt's Bank, Manchester
Chicago Public Library.
Christiania University Library.
Christy, Miller, Esq., Pryors, Broomfield, near Chelmsford.
Cincinnati Public Library.
Clark, J W., Esq , Scroope House, Cambridge
Cleary, P , Esq , 200, Clarendon street, South Melbourne, Victoria, Australia.
Cohen, Herr Friedrich, Kaiserplatz, No 18, Bonn, Germany
Colonial Office (The), Downing-street, S W
Collingridge, George, Esq., Hornsby Junction, New South Wales, Australia.
Congress, Library of, Washington, United States
Constable, Archibald, Esq , 14, Parliament-street, Westminster, S.W.
Cooper, Lieut.-Col. E. H , 42, Portman-square, W.
Copenhagen Royal Library.
Cornell University
Corning, C. R., Esq , West Fort Ann, Washington County, N.Y., U S A.
Corning, H K , Esq , Villa Monnet, Morillon, Geneva.
Cotton, R. W , Esq , The Red House, Newton Abbot
Curzon, Hon George N , M P., 56, St Ermin's Mansions, Victoria-street, S.W

Dalton, Rev Canon J N , per Messrs Williams & Norgate, Henrietta street.
Danish Royal Naval Library
Davis, N. Darnell, Esq , Georgetown, Demerara, British Guiana.
Derby, The Earl of, 25, St. James's-square, S.W.
Detroit Public Library, per Mr. B. F. Stevens, 4, Trafalgar-square, W.C.
Dijon University Library, Rue Monge, Dijon
Dismorr, James Stewart, Esq , Wrotham-road, Gravesend.
Donald, C D., Esq , 172, St. Vincent-street, Glasgow.
Dorpat University, per Messrs. Sotheran and Co., 140, Strand, W.C.
Dresden Geographical Society.
Ducie, The Earl, F R.S , Tortworth Court, Falfield.
Dundas, Captain Colin M , R N , Ochtertyre, Stirling.
Dunn, John, Esq., 1, Park-row, Chicago, U S.A

Eames, Wilberforce, Esq , Lenox Library, 890, Fifth-avenue, New York, U.S A.
Edinburgh Public Library
Edwardes, T Dyer, Esq , 5, Hyde Park-gate, Kensington Gore, S W
Edwards, Mr Francis, 83, High-street, Marylebone, W.
Elton, Charles I , Esq , Q.C , F S A., 10, Cranley-place, Onslow-square, S.W.
Evans, Messrs. M , and Co., 61, Charing Cross-road, W C.

Faber, Reginald S , Esq., 10, Primrose Hill-road, N W.
Fellows Athenæum, per Messrs Kegan Paul, Trench, Trubner, & Co.
Foreign Office (The)
Foreign Office of Germany, Berlin.
Forrest, G. W., Esq , Calcutta.
Foster, William, Esq , India Office, S.W
Franks, Augustus W , Esq., F.R.S , F S A , British Museum, W C.

Gale, Henry, Esq , 45, Elvaston-place, Queen's-gate, S W
Georg, Mons. H., Lyons

George, C W., Esq., 51, Hampton road, Bristol
Gladstone Library, National Liberal Club, Whitehall place, S W.
Glasgow University Library
Godman, F. Ducane, Esq., F R S., 10, Chandos-street, Cavendish-square, W
Gore-Booth, Sir H W., Bart., Lissadell, Sligo
Gottingen University Library
Grant-Duff, Sir Mountstuart Elphinstone, G C S I., York House, Twickenham
Gray, Albert, Esq., 3, Temple Gardens, Temple, E C
Grosvenor Library, Buffalo, U S A
Guildhall Library, E C
Guillemard, F Henry H., Esq., The Old Mill House, Trumpington, Cambridge

Hamburg Commerz-Bibliothek.
Harvard College, Cambridge, Massachusetts
Hawkesbury, Lord, 2, Carlton House Terrace, S W
Heawood, Edward, Esq., B.A., F R.G S., Caius College, Cambridge
Hervey, Dudley F A., Esq., per Messrs. H S. King & Co., 45, Pall-mall
Hiersemann, Herr Karl W., 2, Königsstrasse, Leipzig
Hippisley, A E., Esq., care of J. D. Campbell, Esq., C M G., 12, Great Queen-street, Westminster. S W
Horner, J F Fortescue, Esq., Mells Park, Somersetshire
Hornick, Mrs Perry, Beau Manor Park, Loughborough
Hoskins, Admiral Sir Anthony H., K.C B., 17, Montagu-square, W
Hoyt Public Library, per Messrs Sotheran and Co., Strand
Hudson, John E., Esq., 125, Milk-street, Boston, Mass., U S A
Hull Subscription Library

India Office (21 *copies*)

Johns Hopkins University, Baltimore, U S A
Johnson, General Sir Allen B., 60, Lexham-gardens, Cromwell road, S W

Keltie, J Scott, Esq., 1, Savile-row, W
Kelvin, Lord, F R.S., LL.D., The University, Glasgow
Kensington, South, Science and Art Department
King's Inns Library, Henrietta-street, Dublin
Kimberley Public Library, per Messrs Sotheran and Co., Strand
Kleinseich, M., National Library, Paris (2 *copies*).
Koehler, Herr K F., Universitatsstrasse 26, Leipzig

Leeds Library.
Lehigh University, U S.A
Liverpool Free Public Library
Loescher, Messrs J., & Co., Via del Corso, 307, Rome
Logan, Daniel, Esq., Solicitor-General, Penang, Straits Settlements
Logan, William, Esq. (Madras Civil Service), The Priory, St Andrews, Fife
London Institution, Finsbury-circus
London Library, 12. St. James's-square
Low, Sampson, & Co (Foreign Department), St Dunstan's House, Fetter-lane, E C
Lucas, C P., Esq., Colonial Office, S.W
Luyster, S B., Esq., 10, Silver-street, W C.

Macmillan, A., Esq., 16, Bedford-street, Covent Garden, W C
Macmillan & Bowes, Messrs., Cambridge
Manchester Public Free Libraries
Manierre, George, Esq., per Mr B F. Stevens
Manila Club, The, per Mr J Bain, 1, Haymarket, S W
Mantell, Walter, Esq., Wellington, New Zealand
Markham, Rear-Admiral Albert H., F R G S., H M S Trafalgar
Markham, Clements R., Esq., C B., F R S., 21, Eccleston-square, S W
Marquand, Henry, Esq., per Mr S B. Luyster, 10, Silver-street, W C
Massachusetts Historical Society, 30, Fremont street, Boston, Mass., U S A

Massie, Admiral T L, Chester
Maudslay, A. P, Esq, 32, Montpelier-square, Knightsbridge, S W
Maund, E. A, Esq, care of Mr Kolchmann, 2, Langham-place, W
McClymont, Jas. R, Esq, Hobart, Tasmania
Melbourne, Public Library of, per Messrs E A Petherick and Co, 33, Paternoster-row, E C
Meyjes, A C, Esq, Hogarth-cottage, Harrow on-the-Hill
Michigan, University of, per Mr B. F. Stevens, 4, Trafalgar-square, W C
Mitchell Library, Ingram-street East, Glasgow
Mitchell, Wm., Esq, Union Bank of Scotland, Ltd, Aberdeen
Morgan, E. Delmar, Esq., 15, Roland-gardens, South Kensington, S W
Munich Royal Library
Murchison, Kenneth R, Esq, 116, Park-street, Park-lane, W

Nathan, Captain, R.E., 11, Pembridge-square, W
Natural History Museum, Cromwell-road, per Messrs. Dulau & Co., Soho sq
Netherlands, Geographical Society of the, per Mr Nijhoff, The Hague
Newberry Library, The, Chicago, U S.A. (W F Poole, LL.D, Librarian)
Newcastle-upon-Tyne Literary and Scientific Institute.
Newcastle-upon-Tyne Public Library.
New York State Library
Nicholson, Sir Charles, Bart, D C L, The Grange, Totteridge, Herts, N
Northbrook, The Earl of, G C S I, Stratton, Micheldever Station
North, Hon. F H, C 3, The Albany, W
Northumberland, His Grace the Duke of, Grosvenor-place, S W.
Nutt, Mr D, 270, Strand, W C

Oliver, Capt. S P, Moray House, Monckton-road, near Gosport
Oliver, Commander T W, R N, Oak Hill, Bursledon, Southampton.
Ommanney, Admiral Sir Erasmus, C B, F R S, 29, Connaught-square, Hyde Park W
Oriental Club, Hanover-square, W

Parlane, James, Esq, Rusholme, Manchester
Peabody Institute, Baltimore, U S
Peckover, Alexander, Esq, Bank House, Wisbech
Petherick, E A., Esq, 33, Paternoster row, E C
Philadelphia, Library Company of, U S A
Phillimore, Charles B, Esq, F R.G.S, Hurley Manor House, Great Marlow
Poor, Henry W, Esq, 45, Wall-street, New York
Portico Library, Manchester
Pringle, Arthur T, Esq, Madras, c.o. Messrs. G W Wheatley & Co, 10, Queen-street, Cheapside, E C.

Raffles Library, Singapore.
Ravenstein, E. G, Esq, Albion House, 91, Upper Tulse hill, S W
Rawlinson, Major-General Sir H, Bart, K.C B, 21, Charles-st., Berkeley-sq.
Reed, Mrs., Hassness, Cockermouth.
Reform Club, Pall-mall
Richards, Vice-Admiral Sir F W, K C.B., United Service Club, Pall-mall, S W.
Riggs, E F, Esq, Washington, U.S
Rittenhouse Club, Philadelphia, U.S A., per Mr. B. F Stevens, 4, Trafalgar-square, W.C
Robson, J. R., Esq, Aden, Cockington, Torquay
Rockhill, W. W, Esq, care of Fidelity Trust Company, Chestnut street, Philadelphia
Royal Colonial Institute (J S. O'Halloran, Esq, Sec.), Northumberland-avenue, W.C
Royal Engineers' Institute, Chatham
Royal Geographical Society, 1, Savile-row, W. (*copies presented*)
Royal Scottish Geographical Society, Edinburgh (John Gunn, Esq, Librarian).
Royal United Service Institution, Whitehall-yard, S W

Satow, Ernest, Esq., C M.G., 104, The Common, Upper Clapton, E
SAXE-COBURG AND GOTHA, H.R.H. the Reigning Duke of (Duke of Edinburgh), K G., K.T , etc.
Schlichter, H , Esq , 25, Alma-square, Abbey-road N.W.
Seebohm, H., Esq., F.L.S., 22, Courtfield-gardens, S.W.
Signet Library, Edinburgh (Thos. G Law, Esq., Librarian).
Silver, S W , Esq , 3, York-gate, Regent's Park, N.W.
Sinclair, W. F., Esq., Bombay C S
Société de Géographie, Paris
South African Public Library.
South Australian Legislature Library
Stanley, Lord, of Alderley, Alderley Park, Chelford, Cheshire.
St. Andrew's University
St. Louis Mercantile Library, per Mr. G. E Stechert, 30, Wellington-street, Strand, W C.
St. Martin's-in-the-Fields Free Public Library, 115, St. Martin's-lane, W.C.
St Petersburg University Library
Stevens, Messrs. H and Son, Great Russell-street.
Stockholm, Royal Library of
Strachey, Mrs Richard, 69, Lancaster-gate, Hyde-park, W.
Stride, Mrs Arthur L., Bush Hall, Hatfield, Herts
Stubbs, Captain Edward, R N , 3, Greenfield-street, Stoneycroft, Liverpool.
Surrey County School, Cranleigh.
Sydney Free Library

Temple, Major R C , Pioneer Press, Allahabad, India.
Thin, Mr. Jas , 54, 55, South Bridge, Edinburgh
Thurston, Sir John B , K.C M G , Colonial Secretary, Fiji
Toronto Public Library
Toronto University
Travellers' Club, 106, Pall-mall, S.W
Trinder, H. W , Esq , Northbrook House, Bishops Waltham, Hants
Trinder, Oliver Jones, Esq , Mount Vernon, Caterham, Surrey.
Trinity College, Cambridge
Trinity House, The Hon. Corporation of, Tower-hill, E.C
Trotter, Coutts, Esq., Athenæum Club, S W.
Trübner, Herr Karl, Strasburg.
Turnbull, Alex H , Esq , 7, St. Helen's-place, Bishopsgate-street, E.C.

Union Society, Oxford.
United States Naval Academy.
University of London, Burlington-gardens, W.
Upsala University Library.

Van Siclen, Henry K , Esq., per Mr. B F Stevens, 4, Trafalgar-square, W.C.
Vienna Imperial Library
Vignaud, Henry, Esq , U S. Legation, 59, Rue Galilee, Paris

Washington, Department of State.
Washington, Library of Navy Department.
Watkinson Library, Hartford, Connecticut, U.S.A.
Webb, Captain Sir J Sydney, The Trinity House, E C.
Webb, William Frederick, Esq., Newstead Abbey, Nottingham.
Webster, Sir Augustus, Bart., 51, Victoria-street, S.W.
Wharton, Capt. W. J. L., R.N , Florys, Princes-road, Wimbledon Park, S W.
Wilson, Edward S , Esq , Melton, Brough, East Yorkshire.
Worcester, Massachusetts, Free Library.

Yale College, U S.A
Young, Sir Allen, C B., 18, Grafton-street, W,

Zurich, Bibliothèque de la Ville.